The SQL Guide
to
®

The SQL Guide to
to
ORACLE®

Rick F. van der Lans

Translated by Andrea Gray

ADDISON-WESLEY
PUBLISHING
COMPANY

Wokingham, England · Reading, Massachusetts · Menlo Park, California · New York
Don Mills, Ontario · Amsterdam · Bonn · Sydney · Singapore
Tokyo · Madrid · San Juan · Milan · Paris · Mexico City · Seoul · Taipei

The programs in this book have been included for their instructional value. They have been tested with care but are not guaranteed for any particular purpose. The publisher does not offer any warranties or representations, nor does it accept any liabilities with respect to the programs.

Many of the designations used by manufacturers and sellers to distinguish their products are claimed as trademarks. Addison-Wesley has made every attempt to supply trademark information about manufacturers and their products mentioned in this book. A list of the trademark designations and their owners appears on p. xviii.

Cover designed by Chris Eley and printed by
The Riverside Printing Co. (Reading) Ltd.
Printed in Great Britain by T.J. Press (Padstow) Ltd, Padstow, Cornwall.

First printed 1991. Reprinted 1993, 1994 and 1995.

British Library Cataloguing in Publication Data

Lans, Rick F. van der
    The SQL guide to Oracle.
    I. Title
    005.7565

    ISBN 0–201–56545–5

Library of Congress Cataloging in Publication Data available

**Dedicated to Diane
for her continuous
support and patience**

Preface

This book contains a complete description of the database language *SQL*, as implemented in *Oracle*. It should be seen primarily as a textbook in the active sense. After reading this book you will be able to apply SQL efficiently and effectively.

Oracle is a relational database management system (RDBMS). It is a product of Oracle Corporation, whose headquarters are at Redwood Shores, California. Oracle is available on microcomputers, minicomputers and mainframes and for many operating systems, including IBM MVS, VAX VMS, MS/DOS and many UNIX systems.

Oracle Corporation supplies a whole range of other products besides their RDBMS, such as report writers, 4GLs and spreadsheets, which can speed up the development of applications.

The Oracle RDBMS knows only one database language: SQL (Structured Query Language). All operations on the database should be formulated in SQL. This means that if you are working with Oracle and want to make the most of its possibilities you will have to master SQL completely, regardless of your function: programmer, database administrator or user.

SQL, which was developed in an IBM research laboratory in the early 1970s, has grown in the 1980s to be one of the best known and accepted database languages. In the 1990s it will undoubtedly play a dominant role in the world of relational database management systems. SQL consists of a small and powerful set of statements for the manipulation, management and security of database data.

Topics

In this book we are concerned with SQL as implemented in Oracle. Every aspect of the language will be discussed in detail. The following aspects of SQL are covered:

- creating tables
- specifying primary and foreign keys
- querying data (joins, functions and subqueries)
- updating and deleting data

- using indexes
- transactions
- optimizing of statements
- view definition
- data security and auditing
- the catalog
- distributed databases
- application development with embedded SQL
- PL/SQL

Version 6 of Oracle

This book completely describes version 6 of Oracle. When this book was written, version 6 was not yet available for every operating system.

The most important improvements and changes are:

- more possibilities for specifying integrity rules
- more suitable for OLTP applications
- procedural extension of SQL, called PL/SQL
- different setup of the catalog tables

In this book the new features will be discussed in detail.

For whom is this book intended?

We recommend this book to those who want to use SQL effectively and efficiently in Oracle. It is therefore suitable for the following groups of people:

- programmers who write Oracle programs
- designers, analysts and consultants who use Oracle directly or indirectly and want to understand its possibilities and limitations
- microcomputer owners who have purchased Oracle and use it at home
- students who need to study SQL and use Oracle as the medium for this
- home students who are interested in Oracle or SQL
- users who have the authority to use SQL to query the database of the company or establishment where they work

A practical book

This book should be seen primarily as a *textbook* in the active sense, and not so much as a reference work. To this end there are many examples and exercises (with answers). Don't ignore the exercises. Experience shows that you will learn the language better and more quickly by practising often and doing many exercises.

Prerequisite knowledge

Some general knowledge of programming languages and database management systems is required.

And finally ...

I would like to use this preface to thank a number of people and companies for their contributions to this book.

First, I am grateful to Oracle Netherlands for making the software and all the necessary documentation available. I want especially to thank Peter van Langeveld, Imke Idsingh and Gordon Smith of Oracle for answering all my questions.

Secondly, I owe a great deal to Corine Cools, Andrea Gray and Frank Kornet. They all reviewed the manuscript or parts of it. Their helpful comments really improved the quality of this book.

This book would not have been published in 1991 if Diane Cools had not pushed me all the time and if she had not done so much work to complete the book. In fact, the amount of work she put in made me think for a while of putting her name on the cover as the co-author. Besides being grateful for all her effort, I am also grateful to her for having been around all these years.

My thanks also to the editors and staff of Addison-Wesley for their cooperation. I would like to thank Nicky Jaeger for her flexible and pleasant guidance.

Finally, I would like to ask readers to send comments, opinions, ideas and suggestions concerning the contents of the book to the publisher: Addison-Wesley Publishers Limited, Finchampstead Road, Wokingham, Berkshire RG11 2NZ, England, marked for the attention of Rick F. van der Lans, 'The SQL guide to Oracle'. Many thanks in anticipation of your cooperation.

Rick F. van der Lans
Sassenheim, November 1991

Contents

1

Introduction

SQL (Structured Query Language) is a database language used for formulating statements that are processed by a database management system (DBMS). In our case the DBMS is Oracle.

The paragraph above contains three important concepts: *database*, *database management system* and *database language*. In the next section we explain each of these terms.

SQL is based on the theory of the relational model. In order to use SQL some knowledge of this model is invaluable. Therefore in Section 1.2 we describe the relational model. In Section 1.3 SQL is described in brief; what can be done with the language and how it differs from other languages (such as COBOL or Pascal). Section 1.4 outlines the history of SQL. Although SQL is thought of as a very modern language, it has, in fact, a history dating back to 1972. Section 1.4 outlines the most important standards for SQL, which are topical at the moment.

Because this book deals with Oracle's implementation of SQL we describe the history and relevant aspects of Oracle in Section 1.6.

The first chapter closes with a description of the structure of the book. Each chapter is summarized in a few sentences.

1.1 Database, database management system and database language

What is a database? C.J. Date defines the concept *database* as follows (Date, 1986):

> *A database is a collection of stored operational data used by the application systems of some particular enterprise.*

Card deck files are not, then, considered to be databases. On the other hand, the large files of a bank and the state transport department *are* considered to be databases. These databases contain data about addresses and account balances or car registration plates, weights of vehicles and so on. Another example of a database would be a computer at your workplace which has information recorded about your salary.

Data in a database only becomes useful if something is done with it. According to the above definition of a database, this data is managed by special software. We generally call this software a *database management system (DBMS)*. A DBMS enables users to process database data. Without a DBMS it is impossible to look at that data, or to update or delete obsolete data in the database. It is the DBMS alone that knows where and how the data is stored. A definition of a DBMS given by R. Elmasri is as follows (Elmasri and Navathe, 1989):

> *A DBMS is a collection of programs that enables users to create and maintain a database.*

A DBMS will never change or delete the data in a database of its own accord. Someone or something has to give the command for this to happen. This could be you, as a user, but it could also be a program. In the latter case the program is the user. In other words: a user must be in a position to give a DBMS such commands as 'delete all data about the vehicle with the registration plate number DR-12-DP'.

Commands are given to a DBMS with the help of special languages. These types of languages are called *database languages*. Commands, also known as statements, that are formulated according to the rules of the database language, are entered by users and processed by the DBMS. Every DBMS, from whichever manufacturer, possesses a database language. Some DBMSs even have more than one database language. Although differences exist between all of these languages, they can be divided into groups. The *relational database languages* form one of these groups.

It is also helpful to know how a DBMS stores data in a database. A DBMS uses neither a chest of drawers nor a filing cabinet for holding information; computers work instead with storage media such as tapes, floppy disks and hard disks. The manner in which a DBMS stores information on these media is technically very complex, and will not be explained in detail in this book. In fact, it is not necessary to know this since one of the most important tasks of a DBMS is to offer *data independence*. This means that users do not need to know how or where data is stored: to them a database is a large reservoir of information. Storage methods are also completely independent from the database language being used.

Another important task of a DBMS is to maintain the *integrity* of the database data. This means, first, that the database data always satisfies the rules that apply in the real world. Take, for example, the case of an employee who may only work for one department. It should never be possible, in a database managed by a DBMS, for that particular employee to be registered as working for two departments. Second, integrity means that two different pieces of database data do not contradict one another. This is also known as *data consistency*. (As an example, in one place in a database Mr Johnson may be recorded as being born on 4 August 1964, and in another place he may be given a birth date of 14 December 1946.) These two pieces of data are obviously inconsistent. DBMSs are designed to recognize statements that can be used to specify *integrity rules*. Once these rules are entered, the DBMS will take care of their implementation.

1.2   The relational model

SQL is based on a formal mathematical theory. This theory, which consists of a set of concepts and definitions, is called the *relational model*. The relational model was defined by an Englishman called Dr Edgar F. Codd. In 1970, when Codd was still employed by IBM, he introduced the relational model in the famous article 'A Relational Model of Data for Large Shared Data Banks' (Codd, 1970). This relational model formed a theoretical basis for database languages. The model consists of a small number of simple concepts for recording data in a database, together with a number of operators to manipulate the information. These concepts and operators are borrowed principally from *set theory* and *Boolean logic*. Later, Codd presented his ideas for an improved version of the model (Codd, 1979) and (Codd, 1990).

The relational model has served as an example for the development of various database languages. These database languages are based on the concepts and ideas of that relational model. These languages, therefore, are also called *relational database languages*, and SQL is clearly an example of one. The rest of this section concentrates on the following relational model terms which will appear extensively in this book:

- table
- column
- row
- integrity rule or constraint
- primary key
- candidate key
- alternate key
- foreign key

Please note that this is not a complete list of all the terms used by the relational model. Most of these terms will be discussed in detail in Chapters 5 and 19. For more extensive descriptions refer to Codd (1990) and Date (1986).

1.2.1 Table, column and row

There is only one format in which data can be stored in a relational database: in *tables*. The official name for a table is actually *relation*. The term *relational model* stems from this name. We have chosen to use table because that is the word used in SQL. An example of a table, the PLAYERS table, is given below. This table contains data about five players, the members of a tennis club.

```
The PLAYERS table:

PLAYERNO  NAME        INITIALS  TOWN
--------  --------    --------  --------
       6  Parmenter   R         Stratford
      44  Baker       E         Inglewood
      83  Hope        PK        Stratford
     100  Parmenter   P         Stratford
      27  Collins     DD        Eltham
```

PLAYERNO, NAME, INITIALS and TOWN are the names of the *columns* in the table. The PLAYERNO column contains the values 6, 44, 83, 100 and 27. This set of values is also known as the *population* of the PLAYERNO column. The PLAYERS table has five *rows*, one for each player.

A table has two special properties:

• The intersection of a row and a column can consist of only one value, an *atomic value*. An atomic value is an indivisible unit. The database language can deal with such a unit only in its entirety.

• The rows in a table have no specific order. You don't think in terms of the first row, the last row or the following row. The contents of a table consist of a *set* of rows in the true sense of the word.

1.2.2 Integrity rule

As already described in the previous section, the contents of the tables (the rows that contain the data) have to satisfy *integrity rules*. For example, the player number of a player may not be negative, and two players may not have the same player number. Each time a table is updated the RDBMS has to check if the new data satisfies the integrity rules.

Integrity rules can have several forms. Some of them are used very frequently. That is why they have special names: primary key, candidate key, alternate key and foreign key. We will explain them in the following sections.

1.2.3 Primary key

The *primary key* of a table is a column (or a combination of a number of columns from this table) that can used for uniquely identifying rows in the table. In other words, two different rows in a table may never have the same value in their primary key, and for every row in the table the primary key must have a value. The PLAYERNO column in the PLAYERS table is the primary key for this table. Two players, therefore, may never have the same number and there may never be a player without a number.

1.2.4 Candidate key

Some tables contain more than one column (or combination of columns) that can act as a primary key. Those columns, including the primary key, that possess all the properties of a primary key are called *candidate keys*. Because a table must possess a primary key, it always has a minimum of one candidate key.

If we assume that in the PLAYERS table the NAME and INITIALS of each player are a unique combination, then these columns exist as a candidate key. This combination of two columns could also be designated as the primary key.

1.2.5 Alternate key

A candidate key which is not the primary key of a table is called an *alternate key*. One can say that zero or more alternate keys can be defined for a specific table. The term candidate key is a general term for all primary and alternate keys. The columns NAME and INITIALS from the previous example are possible alternate keys.

1.2.6 Foreign key

A *foreign key* is a column (or combination of columns) in a table in which the population is a subset of the population of a primary key of a table (this does not have to be another table). Foreign keys are sometimes called referential keys.

Suppose that next to the PLAYERS table we place a TEAMS table. The TEAMNO column is called the primary key of this table. The PLAYERNO column represents the captain of the particular team. The population of this column represents a subset of the population of the PLAYERNO column in the PLAYERS table. PLAYERNO in TEAMS is called a foreign key.

```
The TEAMS table:

TEAMNO  PLAYERNO  DIVISION
------  --------  --------
     1         6  first
     2        27  second
```

Now you can see how we are able to combine two tables. It is done by including a PLAYERNO column in the TEAMS table also, thus establishing a link with the PLAYERNO column from the PLAYERS table.

1.3   What is SQL?

SQL (Structured Query Language) is a *relational database language*. Among other things, the language consists of statements to insert, update, delete, query and protect data. We call SQL a relational database language because it is associated with data that has been defined according to the rules of the relational model. (However, we must note that on particular points the theory and SQL differ; see Codd (1990).)

There are a few things to note about SQL as a database language. Because it is a relational database language it is grouped with the non-procedural database languages. By *non-procedural* we mean that users (with the help of the various statements) have only to specify *which* data they want and not *how* this data must be found. Languages such as COBOL, Pascal or BASIC are examples of procedural languages.

SQL can be used in two ways. First, *interactively*: an SQL statement is entered on the microcomputer and processed for an immediate result. Interactive SQL is intended for application developers and end users who want to access databases themselves.

The second way is called *embedded SQL*. Here, the SQL statements are embedded in a program, written in another programming language. Results from these statements are not immediately visible to the user but are processed by the *enveloping* program. Embedded SQL appears mainly in programs developed for end users. These end users do not need to learn SQL in order to access the data, but work from simple screens and menus.

The statements and functional possibilities of interactive and embedded SQL are virtually the same. By this we mean that most statements that can be entered and processed interactively can also be included in an Oracle program as embedded SQL. To do this, embedded SQL uses a number of extra statements that enable the juxtaposition of SQL statements and non-SQL statements. In this book we are interested mainly in interactive SQL. Embedded SQL is dealt with separately in Chapter 28.

1.4   The history of SQL

The history of SQL is tightly interwoven with the history of an IBM project called *System R*. The purpose of this project was to develop an experimental relational database management system, a system which bore the same name as the project. System R was built in the IBM research laboratory in San Jose, California. The project had to demonstrate that the positive usability features of the relational model could be implemented in a system that satisfied the demands of a modern database management system.

A language called *Sequel* was chosen as the database language for System R (Astrahan, 1980). The first article about this language was written by R.F. Boyce and D.D. Chamberlin (1973). During the project the language was renamed SQL (still often pronounced 'sequel'). The system R project was implemented in three phases.

In the first phase, phase zero (from 1974 to 1975), only part of SQL was implemented. The join (for linking data from various tables) was, for example, not yet implemented and only a single-user version of the system was built. The purpose of this phase was to see whether implementation of such a system was in fact really possible. This phase was successfully concluded; see (Astrahan, 1980).

In 1976 a start was made with phase one. All the program code written for phase zero was put aside and a new start was made. Phase one comprised the total system. This meant, among other things, that the multi-user possibility and the join were incorporated. The development of phase one took place between 1976 and 1977.

In phase two, System R was evaluated. The system was installed at various places within IBM and with a large number of major IBM clients. The evaluation took place in 1978 and 1979. The results of this evaluation are described in, among other publications, Chamberlin (1980). The System R project was concluded in 1979.

The knowledge acquired and the technology developed in these three phases was used to build SQL/DS. SQL/DS was IBM's first relational database management system to become commercially available. In 1981, SQL/DS came onto the market for the operating system DOS/VSE. In 1983, the VM/CMS version arrived. In that same year, DB2 was announced. DB2 is the system for the operating systems MVS/370, MVS/XA and MVS/ESA.

IBM has published a great deal about the development of System R. This was happening at a time in which relational database management systems were being widely talked about at conferences and seminars. It was no wonder that other companies also began to build relational systems. Some of them, Oracle for example, implemented SQL as the database language. In the last few years many implementations of SQL have appeared. Existing database management systems have also been extended to include SQL support.

1.5   Standardization of SQL

There are at the moment already more than a hundred products which, in one way or another, support SQL. To avoid differences between these implementations, a number of internationally oriented groups are working on defining standards for SQL. The most important groups are: ISO, the X/Open Group and the SQL Access Group. We will describe these three standards briefly in this section.

The most important SQL-standard is without any doubt the one from *ISO* (International Standards Organization). The ISO is an internationally oriented normalization and standardization organization, and has as its objective the promotion of international, regional and national normalization. Its activities are performed by committees.

In about 1983, ANSI (the American National Standards Institute) and the ISO started on the development of an SQL standard. In 1986, the first edition of the SQL standard was completed and described in the document *ISO 9075 Database Language SQL* that was published at the beginning of 1987; see (ISO, 1987) and (van der Lans, 1989b). This report was developed under the responsibility of Technical Committee TC97. The area of activity of TC97 is described as Computing and Information Processing. It is Subcommittee SC21 which caused the standard to be developed. ANSI has completely adopted this SQL standard and published it under number X3.135-1986. This means that the standards of ISO and ANSI for SQL are identical.

The SQL standard was very weak in the area of specifying integrity rules. For this reason, it was extended in 1989 by including, amongst other things, the concepts of primary and foreign keys; see (ISO, 1989). This version of the SQL standard, which is called *SQL89* to avoid confusion, is at the time of writing still the current standard of ISO.

Immediately after the completion of the standard in 1986, a start was made on the development of a new SQL standard; see (ISO, 1991). This successor to the current standard, which is informally known as the *SQL2 standard*, will probably appear in 1992 and will replace the present standard (SQL89). The SQL2 standard is an expansion of the SQL standard. Many new statements and possibilities for existing statements have been added. For the sake of completeness we mention that the first steps towards SQL3 have been taken.

The second SQL standard we would like to discuss is the standard developed by the X/Open Group. The X/Open Group is a body that concerns itself with the specification of a supplier-independent Common Applications Environment (CAE). The CAE is directed towards *open* systems and portability. Most of the standards of the X/Open Group are based on the Unix operating system. The X/Open Group was founded in 1984 as a cooperative association among five European suppliers: Bull, Nixdorf, Olivetti, International Computers and Siemens. Later on, American suppliers joined the association, among which were: AT&T, DEC, IBM and Unisys. Oracle is currently one of the members of the X/Open Group. One of the standards, the *X/Open Portability Guide for Data Management*, is directed at SQL, see (X/Open, 1988). With its SQL standard, the X/Open Group aims at formulating SQL statements which are portable between a number of SQL products. They do however try to remain as far as possible in line with the SQL standard of ISO and ANSI. A quotation from (X/Open, 1988):

> *The X/Open definition is based closely on the ANSI standard but taking careful account of the capabilities of the leading relational database management systems . . .*

In 1989, a number of mainly American suppliers of SQL products set up a commission with the name SQL Access Group. The objective of the SQL Access Group is to define standards for the *interoperability* of SQL applications. What is meant by this is that SQL applications which have been developed with those specifications are portable between the DBMSs of the associated suppliers and that a number of different DBMSs can be simultaneously accessed by the applications. Oracle Corporation is, as one of the most important distributers of an SQL product, also a member of this group. The SQL Access Group hopes to publish a report in 1991. At the moment, however, it is not known what their SQL standard will look like and to what extent it will be in accordance with the SQL standard of ISO.

1.6   Oracle Corporation

Oracle Corporation was founded in 1977 in California. Its primary objective was to develop a relational DBMS with SQL as the database language. This goal was realized in 1979 when Oracle introduced version 2 (version 1 was never put into production). This made the product the first commercial DBMS supporting SQL. Version 2 was written in C and assembler and was available on DEC's PDP machines. Currently the product is available for many other operating systems including MS/DOS, VAX/VMS, VM/CMS, MVS, DOS/VSE, OS/2, VS and many Unix operating systems.

    In 1989 Oracle introduced version 6 of their product. The functionality of SQL in version 6 has only been slightly extended with respect to the previous version. Oracle mainly changed the internal aspects of the RDBMS. On many fronts the DBMS has been improved, which makes the DBMS suitable for a wide variety of applications.

    Version 6 is available in two forms: with or without the *Transaction Processing Option* (TPO). There are two main differences between these forms. First, the internal architecture of the TPO version is better suited for a large number of concurrent users. However, this difference has no influence on the SQL applications. An SQL application developed for a specific version will run without any problems on the other version. The second difference does have an influence on SQL. The TPO version is able to process *PL/SQL* statements. PL/SQL is a Pascal-like language, in which SQL statements can be embedded. This topic will be described in more detail in Chapter 29.

1.7   Other Oracle products

To develop a complete application you need more than just a DBMS. That's why Oracle offers a long list of other products besides a DBMS.

- *SQL*Plus:* With this product users can interactively enter and process SQL statements. SQL*Plus offers a simple built-in report writer. In Chapter 2 we describe how SQL statements can be entered with this product.

- *SQL*Graph:* This product is an extension of SQL*Plus. With SQL*Graph the result of a SELECT statement, processed with SQL*Plus, can be converted to a graph.

- *SQL*Calc:* This product is a LOTUS 1-2-3 compatible spreadsheet. With SQL*Calc users enter SQL statements to retrieve data out of the database and into the spreadsheet.

- *SQL*QMX:* With SQL*QMX SQL statements can be entered and processed just as in SQL*Plus. SQL*QMX has a simple report writer too. The main difference between SQL*QMX and SQL*Plus is that the former supports a full screen editor and SQL*Plus has a simple line editor. SQL*QMX is compatible with an IBM product called QMF (Query Management Facility).

- *Easy*SQL:* Users can use this product to query the database even if they are unfamiliar with SQL.

- *SQL*Forms:* With this product screens can be developed so that end users can easily update their data in the database without learning a complicated language. SQL*Forms is called a fourth generation language (4GL).

- *SQL*Report Writer:* The layout of reports can be defined with this product.

- *SQL*Menu:* Menus can be defined simply with SQL*Menu. Applications can be started from these menus.

- *SQL*Net:* Via SQL*Net various DBMSs can communicate with each other. This product is necessary for working with distributed databases.

- *SQL*Connect:* This product is a so-called *gateway.* It offers the facility to let Oracle communicate with the database management systems of other vendors, such as IBM's DB2.

Oracle supports a family of integrated CASE products (Computer Aided Software Engineering):

- *CASE*Dictionary:* The heart of Oracle's CASE products is formed by CASE*Dictionary. With this product all specifications are recorded unambiguously.

- *CASE*Designer:* This product is a graphical workbench for entering specifications which are developed during different phases of the system development process. Various techniques are supported.

- *CASE*Generator:* Development specifications are used by this product to generate SQL*Forms applications and databases.

For global descriptions of the application development products, we refer to Hursch (1987) and for the CASE products to Barker (1990). For more detailed descriptions of these and other products from Oracle, we refer to the various manuals that come with the products.

1.8   The structure of the book

In Chapter 2 we cover entering, correcting and processing SQL statements with SQL*Plus. You should read this chapter before you attempt the exercises and questions with Oracle.

Chapter 3 contains a detailed description of the database used by most of the examples and exercises. This database is modelled on the competition administration of a tennis club.

Chapter 4 gives a general overview of SQL. After reading this chapter you should have a global view of the possibilities of SQL and a good idea of what awaits you in this book.

Chapter 5 is the first chapter to delve more fully into particular SQL statements. It covers all statements for creating tables and we will also describe how to define synonyms.

Chapters 6 to 16 are about querying tables with the SELECT statement. Many examples are used to illustrate the techniques. We devote a great deal of space to the SELECT statement in this book because many other statements are based on it.

Chapter 17 describes how data can be updated and deleted and how new rows can be added to tables. It also describes how updates can be undone and it discusses transactions.

Chapter 18 describes how unique numbers can be generated with Oracle.

Chapter 19 describes the specifying of all types of integrity rules supported by Oracle. Primary, alternate and foreign keys are also discussed.

Chapter 20 covers how indexes can be used to improve the execution time of particular statements.

Chapter 21 describes how the execution time of SQL statements can be improved by reformulating them.

In Chapter 22 we describe views, or virtual tables. With views we define a 'layer' on the table. The user then sees the table in a form which is most appropriate to his or her needs.

Data security is the subject of Chapter 23. It describes which commands are employed to register users for use of the DBMS. At the same time it also describes how users 'known' to the system can be authorized to execute particular statements on particular data.

Chapter 24 is dedicated to auditing of database operations. In this book, by auditing we mean determining afterwards what happened to a database at a specific time. We describe the statements that can be used to do this.

Chapter 25 covers a technical subject: how and where data is stored in the database. This chapter is meant to be an introduction to this subject.

Chapter 26 discusses how data stored in another database can be accessed and data can be exchanged between two different databases; in other words, distributed databases are discussed.

Chapter 27 is a description of the catalog which fulfils a very important role within SQL. Oracle records data about databases in the catalog, such as columns in a table, names and passwords of users and indexes. This chapter primarily describes statements that query catalog tables.

We cover embedded SQL in Chapter 28. By this, we mean the development of programs, written in languages such as C, COBOL or Pascal, in which SQL statements are included.

Chapter 29 contains an introduction to the procedural extension of SQL called PL/SQL.

The book is rounded off with a number of appendices and an index. The first appendix gives the answers to the exercises from the various chapters. Appendix B contains definitions of all the SQL statements we discuss. Appendix C describes all the Oracle scalar functions. Appendix D outlines a list of differences between the SQL implementations of Oracle and DB2 of IBM. Appendix E gives the ASCII character set. Finally, Appendix F is a bibliography.

2

Starting SQL∗Plus and entering SQL statements

Before we describe the SQL statements that can be used in Oracle, and what you can do with them, we will explain how to enter interactive SQL statements.

Oracle supports two products that work with interactive SQL: *SQL∗Plus* and *SQL∗QMX*. The former comes supplied with the Oracle database management system. It is a tool with which SQL statements can be easily entered. The user also has a relatively straightforward line editor available for editing SQL statements. SQL∗QMX is bought as a separate product. Its functions are comparable to SQL∗Plus, but in contrast it has a more sophisticated full-screen editor and many reporting facilities.

In this chapter we will use SQL∗Plus to illustrate how you can enter SQL statements. We have chosen this product in favour of SQL∗QMX because it is a standard part of the Oracle DBMS. Among other topics, we will discuss:

- starting and stopping SQL∗Plus
- entering statements
- retrieving previously entered statements
- correcting statements
- parameters in SQL statements
- storing statements

If you are already familiar with these topics, or if you don't intend to execute the examples and exercises with SQL∗Plus, then you can skip this chapter and go on to Chapter 3.

2.1   Introduction to SQL∗Plus

SQL∗Plus is a tool for entering SQL statements. It is a 'normal' Oracle DBMS application issuing SQL statements for execution. Applications developed for the Oracle DBMS can be divided into two categories. In the first, programmers explicitly include the SQL statements in the application code. These are applications in which the database operations to be executed are known in advance. In the second category, users enter and process statements on the spot. SQL∗Plus (and SQL∗QMX) belongs to the second category of applications.

Each SQL statement entered by the user is passed by SQL∗Plus to the DBMS for processing. The DBMS then returns the answer to SQL∗Plus which takes care of the presentation of data on the screen. In fact, SQL∗Plus functions as a type of server. We represent the relationship between SQL∗Plus and the Oracle DBMS in Figure 2.1.

SQL∗Plus users can enter two types of statements: SQL statements and SQL∗Plus commands. The former are all referred on to the DBMS, while the latter are processed by SQL∗Plus itself without reference to the DBMS. The SQL∗Plus commands perform the following activities:

- formatting the result of a query
- storing SQL statements for repetitive use
- editing statements

Note: In this chapter we will not describe all the SQL∗Plus commands, but those which you will use more frequently. We refer to the Oracle manuals for a detailed description of all the SQL∗Plus commands.

2.2   Starting and stopping SQL∗Plus

SQL∗Plus and Oracle are applications, and therefore have to be started. Before you can start SQL∗Plus, you must first start the Oracle database management system. We are not going to describe that process in this book because it differs from one operating system to another. For this we refer you to one of the Oracle Installation Guides. In this chapter we look only at how to start SQL∗Plus. This is practically the same for any operating system environment. We will assume then that you are starting SQL∗Plus from the VAX/VMS environment.

You can start SQL∗Plus by typing in SQLPLUS. When it starts the following appears on the screen:

```
Enter user-name:
```

Here you must type in a correct user-name. What is a user-name? This requires some explanation. Every user who wants to work with Oracle must have a user-name and a password. This applies not only to SQL∗Plus or interactive SQL users, but also to those who access the database with SQL embedded in an application.

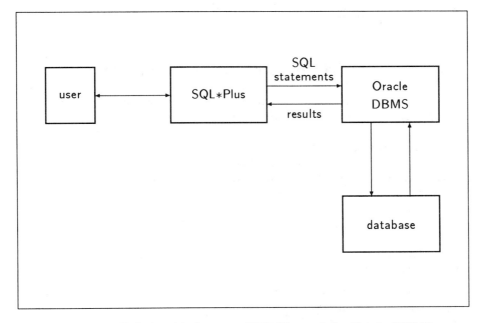

Figure 2.1: Relationship between SQL*Plus and the Oracle DBMS

During the installation of Oracle two users are registered as part of the process. One of those has the user-name SYSTEM with a password MANAGER. You will come across this name in many of the Oracle manuals. In Chapter 23 we describe how other users can be added.

In this and the following chapters we will assume that your user-name is SQLDBA and your password SQLDBAPW. (But you can also try out SYSTEM with MANAGER to see whether it works.) Let's assume, then, that you have responded to the instruction above with SQLDBA. A second instruction appears:

```
Enter password:
```

Type in the correct password, in this case SQLDBAPW. If the user-name and password you entered are recognized by Oracle you reach SQL*Plus. This is signalled by the *Oracle prompt*:

```
SQL>
```

We will refer to this throughout the book simply as the *prompt*. You can enter an SQL statement after the prompt.

In principle, you are at a point where you can interactively enter SQL statements. We will discuss what these statements are in Chapter 4. But first, we will continue on with SQL*Plus.

The EXIT and QUIT commands allow you to end SQL*Plus:

```
SQL> EXIT
```

Note: Stopping SQL∗Plus does not automatically stop the Oracle DBMS.

2.3   Entering statements and commands

SQL statements and SQL∗Plus commands are entered by typing after the prompt. Exercise: Type the following SQL∗Plus command:

```
SQL> DESCRIBE DICTIONARY
```

If you have correctly installed the sample database supplied with Oracle, then the result of that command is this:

```
Name                            Null?    Type
------------------------------  -------- ----
TABLE_NAME                               CHAR(30)
COMMENTS                                 CHAR(255)
```

The command above asks for a description of the columns from the DICTIO-NARY table. Note that below the table the prompt is there ready for the next command. Type in the following SQL statement (remember the semi-colon):

```
SQL> SELECT * FROM DICTIONARY;
```

The result is a list of all tables, including some comments.

- When we work with interactive SQL the prompt is always visible. In the following chapters we will leave the prompt out, because we want to focus on the formulation of SQL statements and not so much on the entering of them.

- SQL∗Plus demands that each SQL statement is ended with a semi-colon. We will also omit this in the following chapters. The semi-colon does not form a part of the SQL statements, but delimits them. Nevertheless, don't forget to use the semi-colon when you do the exercises if you are using SQL∗Plus.

- It is not mandatory to delimit SQL∗Plus commands with a semi-colon, but it is not wrong to do so.

- SQL statements do not have to be entered in upper case letters; lower case may also be used. There is one place where the difference is important, but we will clarify that when we come to it.

2.4   Repeated execution of statements

Oracle keeps the most recently executed SQL statement in a *command buffer*. If you want to execute the last statement again, you can type the / symbol after the prompt. The statement is re-executed without first being displayed.

If you enter the word RUN instead of the / symbol, the previous statement is displayed first and then executed.

The LIST command can be used to display the SQL statement currently held in the command buffer.

```
SQL> LIST
  1* SELECT * FROM DICTIONARY
```

SQL*Plus commands are not held in the command buffer. The LIST command and the DESCRIBE command from the previous section are therefore not placed there.

2.5   Correcting statements

Anyone can make a typing error. In such a case Oracle displays an error message. Should you type in the following incomplete SQL statement and press the return key:

```
SQL> SELECT FROM DICTIONARY;
```

Oracle will detect the error, displaying the following error message:

```
SELECT FROM DICTIONARY
       *
ERROR at line 1: ORA-0936: missing expression
```

The asterisk marks the approximate position of the error. You can now correct the statement using the CHANGE command. The following CHANGE command alters the word FROM to * FROM.

```
CHANGE /FROM/* FROM/
```

Oracle automatically displays the effect of this change:

```
  1* SELECT * FROM DICTIONARY;
```

Now you can execute the statement again using the RUN command, for example.

Sometimes statements are too long for one line. In cases like this it is possible to spread the statement over multiple lines:

```
SQL> SELECT
  2    *
  3    FROM
  4    DICTIONARY;
```

This arrangement is retained in the command buffer, so the LIST command yields the following result here:

```
1  SELECT
2  *
3  FROM
4* DICTIONARY;
```

There is an asterisk after the fourth line number. This shows the current line which is the only line that can be changed using the CHANGE command. If, for example, we want to alter the ∗ in the second line to TABLE_NAME, then we first have to make this line current. This is done simply by typing in the line number.

```
SQL> 2
```

Then SQL∗Plus displays this line:

```
2* *
```

And then it can be altered:

```
SQL> CHANGE /*/TABLE_NAME/
```

The INPUT command is used to add new lines to the statement after the current line. Conversely, the DEL command deletes the whole of the current line. Example:

```
SQL> LIST
   1  SELECT
   2  TABLE_NAME
   3  FROM
   4* DICTIONARY
SQL> 2
   2* TABLE_NAME
SQL> INPUT , REMARKS
SQL> LIST
   1  SELECT
   2  TABLE_NAME
   3  , REMARKS
   4  FROM
   5* DICTIONARY
SQL> 3
   3  , REMARKS
SQL> DEL
SQL> LIST
   1  SELECT
   2  TABLE_NAME
   3  FROM
   4* DICTIONARY
```

2.6   Commands that are too long

In the previous section we have shown that statements may be spread over multiple lines. In those examples, however, spreading was not really necessary. But statements can become quite large and thus too long to fit on one line. This does not cause problems with SQL statements; you just keep on typing on the next line. However, this does not apply to SQL*Plus commands. If an SQL*Plus command is too long for one line you have to end that line with the – symbol (this is called the *continuation symbol*); only then can you continue typing on the next line. Otherwise SQL*Plus will try to execute the first half of the command. Example:

```
SQL> DESCRIBE -
   2> DICTIONARY
```

2.7   Parameters in SQL statements

Parameters can be included in an SQL statement. Before the statement is executed, SQL*Plus asks what the value of the parameter is. A parameter begins with the & followed by an integer or word, such as &1 or &value. Example (note the semi-colon):

```
SQL> SELECT &COLUMN FROM DICTIONARY;
```

SQL*Plus comes back with the following question:

```
Enter value for COLUMN:
```

Let us assume that you type in the word TABLE_NAME. SQL*Plus then shows which substitution is to be executed in the statement.

```
Enter value for COLUMN:
old   1: SELECT &COLUMN FROM DICTIONARY;
new   1: SELECT TABLE_NAME FROM DICTIONARY;
```

An SQL statement may contain multiple parameters and a specific parameter may be used multiple times in an SQL statement.

2.8   Saving statements

We can keep SQL statements for a longer period by storing them in a separate file. The SAVE command is used to place the SQL statement in the command buffer into a file.

Suppose that you want to keep the SELECT statement from the previous section. You enter the following statement:

```
SQL> SAVE SELDICT.SQL
```

Oracle now creates a file called SELDICT.SQL and writes the SQL statement into it. In a subsequent session you can reuse this statement by first issuing a GET command:

```
SQL> GET SELDICT.SQL
```

Oracle displays the contents of the command buffer and you can execute the statement using the RUN command, say, as shown in Section 2.4. You can also fetch and process the stored SELECT statement in one step. This is done with the START command:

```
SQL> START SELDICT.SQL
```

You may replace the word START with the @ symbol.

```
SQL> @ SELDICT.SQL
```

If you issue the SAVE command and it appears that the file already exists, Oracle informs you. If you want to overwrite the contents of the file you add the word REPLACE to the SAVE command:

```
SQL> SAVE SELDICT.SQL REPLACE
```

2.9   The LOGIN.SQL file

As soon as SQL*Plus is started (and even before the SQL prompt appears) Oracle checks whether there is a file called *LOGIN.SQL* in the current directory. If it exists, it is read and all statements and commands in it executed. If it is non-existent, SQL*Plus continues on with the default start-up procedure. Both SQL*Plus commands and SQL statements can be included in the LOGIN.SQL file.

2.10   More about starting SQL*Plus

In Section 2.2 we discussed how you start SQL*Plus. Once started it asks for your user-name and password. You can also supply your user-name and password immediately. If they are correct, SQL*Plus will show the prompt at once, without asking for them. End SQL*Plus using the EXIT command and then enter the following command:

```
SQLPLUS SQLDBA/SQLDBAPW
```

In addition to this, you can specify a filename after the password. All statements in that file will be executed before the SQL prompt appears, but after the LOGIN.SQL file is executed. Example:

```
SQLPLUS SQLDBA/SQLDBAPW @SELDICT.SQL
```

Behind the scenes SQL*Plus executes a *CONNECT command* when you try to log on. This command can also be typed in directly by you, for example, if you want to work under another user-name. During a session you are allowed to switch between user-names as many times as you want. Example:

```
CONNECT SYSTEM/MANAGER
```

The counterpart of the CONNECT command is the *DISCONNECT command*. The effect of this command is that you are logged off, but are still within SQL*Plus. You are no longer able to execute SQL statements, but you can log on again with a CONNECT command. Example:

```
DISCONNECT
```

2.11   Abbreviations of SQL*Plus commands

Some commands discussed in this chapter may be abbreviated. These abbreviations are shown in the following table.

SQL*Plus command	Abbreviation
CHANGE	C
CONNECT	CONN
DESCRIBE	D
DISCONNECT	DISC
INPUT	I
LIST	L
RUN	R
SAVE	SAV
START	STA

2.12   The SET command

SQL*Plus supports the *SET command* with which the environment can be defined. In this section we give you a number of important SET commands, and we will discuss a number of other commands in other chapters.

The result of a SELECT statement can be tens or maybe hundreds of lines long. By default these lines will be presented underneath each other, so that the lines scroll off the screen. This can be prevented by using the SET PAUSE command below. SQL*Plus stops when the screen is full.

```
SET PAUSE ON
```

A blank is printed by default between the columns in the result of a SELECT statement. The number of blanks can be adjusted with the SET SPACE command. In this book we will print most examples with two blanks between the columns. We achieve this with the following command:

```
SET SPACE 2
```

2.13   The INIT.ORA file

When you start up an Oracle DBMS, a file will be read in which several parameters are specified: the *INIT.ORA file*. There are approximately 100 different parameters. These parameters affect the manner and speed with which the DBMS executes certain activities. The file can be edited using any kind of wordprocessor.

The INIT.ORA file is defined centrally and applies to all the users who log on. In this book we will not describe this file and its parameters in detail, just as we do not describe how an Oracle DBMS is started. At some points in the book we will, when necessary, indicate what the effect is of a specific parameter.

3
The tennis club
sample database

This chapter describes a database that could be used by a tennis club to administer its players' participation in a competition. Most of the examples and exercises in this book are based on this database so you should study it carefully.

3.1   Description of the tennis club

The tennis club was founded in 1980 and from the beginning some administrative data were stored in a database. The database consists of four tables:

- PLAYERS
- TEAMS
- MATCHES
- PENALTIES

The PLAYERS table contains data about members of the club. Two players cannot have the same combination of name and initials. The PLAYERS table contains no historical data. If a player gives up his or her membership, then he or she disappears from the table. In the case of moving house, the old address is overwritten with a new address. In other words, the old address is not retained anywhere.

The tennis club has two types of members: *recreational players* and *competition players*. The first group play matches only among themselves (that is, no matches against players from other clubs). The results of these friendly matches are not recorded. Competition players play in teams against other clubs and the results of these matches are recorded. Each player, regardless of whether he or she plays competitively, has a unique number assigned by the club. Each competition player must also be registered with the tennis league and this organization gives each player a unique league number. If a competition player stops playing in the competition and becomes a recreational player, then his or her league number correspondingly disappears. Therefore recreational players have no league number, but do have a player number.

The club has a number of teams taking part in competitions. The captain of each team and the division in which it is currently competing is recorded. Again, no historical data is kept in this table. If a team is promoted or relegated to another division, the record is simply overwritten with the new information. The same goes for the captain of the team; when a new captain is appointed, the number of the former captain is overwritten.

A team consists of four players. During a match each player plays against one member of the opposing team. A team does not always consist of the same people and reserves are sometimes needed when the regular players are sick or on holiday. Only players with a league number are allowed to play matches. A match is divided in three or five sets (this is pre-defined). The player who wins two sets (for a match of three sets) or three sets first (for a match of five sets) is the winner. A player either wins or loses a match; a draw is not possible. In the MATCHES table we show for each match which player was in the match and for what team he or she played. Additionally, we store with how many *sets* the player won and how many were lost. A player can play matches for several teams. Possible end results of a tennis match are 2–1 or 2–0 if one plays until one player wins two sets, or 3–2, 3–1 or 3–0 if one plays until three sets are won.

Note: For those who have read two other books of mine, *Introduction to SQL* (Van der Lans, 1989a) or *The SQL Standard* (Van der Lans, 1989b), we notice that the MATCHES table is different from the other two books in structure and contents.

If a player is badly behaved (arrives late, behaves aggressively, or does not turn up at all) then the league imposes a penalty in the form of a fine. The club pays these fines and records them in a PENALTIES table. As long as the player continues to play competitively the record of his or her penalties remains in this table.

If a player leaves the club, all his or her data from the four tables is destroyed. If the club withdraws a team, all data for that team is removed from the TEAMS and MATCHES tables. If a competition player stops playing matches and he or she will be a recreational player again, all matches and penalty data will be deleted.

Opposite is a description of the columns in each of the four tables.

PLAYERS	
PLAYERNO	Unique number of the player assigned by the club
NAME	Surname of the player
INITIALS	Initials of the player; no full stops or spaces are used after each separate letter
YEAR_OF_BIRTH	Year in which the player was born
SEX	Sex of the player: M(ale) or F(emale)
YEAR_JOINED	Year in which the player joined the club
STREET	Name of the street in which the player lives
HOUSENO	Number of the house
POSTCODE	Postcode
TOWN	Town or city in which the player lives
PHONENO	Area code followed by a hyphen and then subscriber's number
LEAGUENO	Unique league number assigned by the league or blank for recreational players

TEAMS	
TEAMNO	Unique number of the team
PLAYERNO	Player number of the player who captains the team; players may captain multiple teams
DIVISION	Division in which the league has placed the team

MATCHES	
MATCHNO	Unique number of the match
TEAMNO	Number of the team
PLAYERNO	Number of the player
WON	Number of sets that the player won in the match
LOST	Number of sets that the player lost in the match

PENALTIES	
PAYMENTNO	Unique number for each penalty the club has received and paid
PLAYERNO	Number of the player who has incurred the penalty
PEN_DATE	Date on which the penalty was paid
AMOUNT	Amount of the penalty

3.2   The contents of the tables

The contents of the tables are shown below. Except where otherwise mentioned, this data will form the basis of most examples and exercises. Some of the column names in the PLAYERS table have been shortened because of space constraints.

The PLAYERS table:

PLAYERNO	NAME	INIT	YEAR_ OF_ BIRTH	S	YEAR_ JOINED	STREET	...
6	Parmenter	R	1964	M	1977	Haseltine Lane	...
44	Baker	E	1963	M	1980	Lewis Street	...
83	Hope	PK	1956	M	1982	Magdalene Road	...
2	Everett	R	1948	M	1975	Stoney Road	...
27	Collins	DD	1964	F	1983	Long Drive	...
104	Moorman	D	1970	F	1984	Stout Street	...
7	Wise	GWS	1963	M	1981	Edgecombe Way	...
57	Brown	M	1971	M	1985	Edgecombe Way	...
39	Bishop	D	1956	M	1980	Eaton Square	...
112	Bailey	IP	1963	F	1984	Vixen Road	...
8	Newcastle	B	1962	F	1980	Station Road	...
100	Parmenter	P	1963	M	1979	Haseltine Lane	...
28	Collins	C	1963	F	1983	Old Main Road	...
95	Miller	P	1963	M	1972	High Street	...

The PLAYERS table (continued):

PLAYERNO	...	HOUSENO	POSTCODE	TOWN	PHONENO	LEAGUENO
6	...	80	1234KK	Stratford	070-476537	8467
44	...	23	4444LJ	Inglewood	070-368753	1124
83	...	16A	1812UP	Stratford	070-353548	1608
2	...	43	3575NH	Stratford	070-237893	2411
27	...	804	8457DK	Eltham	079-234857	2513
104	...	65	9437AO	Eltham	079-987571	7060
7	...	39	9758VB	Stratford	070-347689	?
57	...	16	4377CB	Stratford	070-473458	6409
39	...	78	9629CD	Stratford	070-393435	?
112	...	8	6392LK	Plymouth	010-548745	1319
8	...	4	6584RO	Inglewood	070-458458	2983
100	...	80	1234KK	Stratford	070-494593	6524
28	...	10	1294QK	Midhurst	071-659599	?
95	...	33A	57460P	Douglas	070-867564	?

The TEAMS table:

```
TEAMNO   PLAYERNO   DIVISION
------   --------   --------
     1          6   first
     2         27   second
```

The MATCHES table:

```
MATCHNO   TEAMNO   PLAYERNO   WON   LOST
-------   ------   --------   ----   ----
      1        1          6     3      1
      2        1          6     2      3
      3        1          6     3      0
      4        1         44     3      2
      5        1         83     0      3
      6        1          2     1      3
      7        1         57     3      0
      8        1          8     0      3
      9        2         27     3      2
     10        2        104     3      2
     11        2        112     2      3
     12        2        112     1      3
     13        2          8     0      3
```

The PENALTIES table:

```
PAYMENTNO   PLAYERNO   PEN_DATE    AMOUNT
---------   --------   ---------   ------
        1          6   08-DEC-80   100.00
        2         44   05-MAY-81    75.00
        3         27   10-SEP-83   100.00
        4        104   08-DEC-84    50.00
        5         44   08-DEC-80    25.00
        6          8   08-DEC-80    25.00
        7         44   30-DEC-82    30.00
        8         27   12-NOV-84    75.00
```

3.3   The structure of the database

Logical relationships exist between the tables; for example, every player number in the PENALTIES table must appear in the MATCHES table. The column of the PLAYERNO in the MATCHES table is called a *foreign key*. Figure 3.1 is a diagram of all foreign keys (not all columns are shown). An arrow under a column (or combination of columns) represents a *primary key*. An arrow from one table to another represents a foreign key.

The foreign keys are as follows:

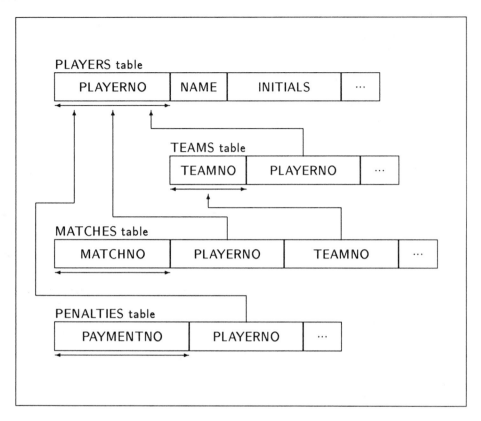

Figure 3.1: Diagram of the relationships between the tennis club database tables

- **From TEAMS to PLAYERS:** Each captain of a team is also a player. The set of player numbers from the TEAMS table is a subset of the set of player numbers from the PLAYERS table.
- **From MATCHES to PLAYERS:** Each player who competes for a particular team must appear in the PLAYERS table. The set of player numbers from the MATCHES table is a subset of the set of player numbers from the PLAYERS table.
- **From MATCHES to TEAMS:** Each team that appears in the MATCHES table must also be present in the TEAMS table, because a player can only compete for registered teams. The set of team numbers from the MATCHES table is a subset of the set of team numbers from the TEAMS table.
- **From PENALTIES to PLAYERS:** A penalty can only be imposed on players that appear in the PLAYERS table. The set of player numbers from the PENALTIES table is a subset of the set of player numbers from the PLAYERS table.

4

SQL in a nutshell

In this chapter we use examples to build up a picture of the possibilities of the database language SQL. By the time you have read it you should have an idea of what this book is going to cover. As well as this, we show how you can set up the sample database for yourself. We advise you to execute these statements if you have Oracle available.

4.1 Creating tables

The first step is to create the four tables described in the previous chapter. For this we use the *CREATE TABLE statement*. Shown below are the four CREATE TABLE statements needed.

```
CREATE     TABLE PLAYERS
           (PLAYERNO        SMALLINT      NOT NULL,
           NAME             CHAR(15)      NOT NULL,
           INITIALS         CHAR(3)       NOT NULL,
           YEAR_OF_BIRTH    SMALLINT              ,
           SEX              CHAR(1)       NOT NULL,
           YEAR_JOINED      SMALLINT      NOT NULL,
           STREET           CHAR(15)      NOT NULL,
           HOUSENO          CHAR(4)               ,
           POSTCODE         CHAR(6)               ,
           TOWN             CHAR(10)      NOT NULL,
           PHONENO          CHAR(10)              ,
           LEAGUENO         CHAR(4)               ,
           PRIMARY KEY      (PLAYERNO)            )
```

29

```
CREATE    TABLE TEAMS
          (TEAMNO          SMALLINT     NOT NULL,
          PLAYERNO         SMALLINT     NOT NULL,
          DIVISION         CHAR(6)      NOT NULL,
          PRIMARY KEY      (TEAMNO)                )

CREATE    TABLE MATCHES
          (MATCHNO         SMALLINT     NOT NULL,
          TEAMNO           SMALLINT     NOT NULL,
          PLAYERNO         SMALLINT     NOT NULL,
          WON              SMALLINT     NOT NULL,
          LOST             SMALLINT     NOT NULL,
          PRIMARY KEY      (MATCHNO)               )

CREATE    TABLE PENALTIES
          (PAYMENTNO       INTEGER      NOT NULL,
          PLAYERNO         SMALLINT     NOT NULL,
          PEN_DATE         DATE         NOT NULL,
          AMOUNT           DECIMAL(7,2) NOT NULL,
          PRIMARY KEY      (PAYMENTNO)             )
```

Explanation: In fact, Oracle does not require the statements to be entered as precisely as we have done above. In this book we have adopted this type of layout for all SQL statements in order to make them easier to read. But for Oracle it doesn't matter whether each line follows on from the last (still separated by spaces or commas of course) or as is shown above.

For each column a data type is specified (CHAR, INTEGER, SMALL-INT, DECIMAL or DATE). The data type defines which type of value may be entered into the column concerned. In the next section we will explain what the specification NOT NULL means.

Figure 3.1 shows the primary keys of the tables. A primary key of a table is a column (or combination of columns) where every value can appear only once. A primary key is a kind of integrity rule. In Oracle you specify primary keys within the CREATE TABLE statement with the words PRIMARY KEY. The names of the columns on which the primary key is built, are specified between brackets after the words PRIMARY KEY. Note that for Oracle version 6 primary keys can be defined, but Oracle will not check them. In other words, after defining a primary key multiple values can still be entered. That is why we advise you to create a unique index on each primary key. The creation of a unique index enables you to *simulate* a primary key. In Chapter 19 we discuss primary keys and other kinds of integrity rules in more detail.

```
CREATE    UNIQUE INDEX PLAYERS_PRIM ON
          PLAYERS (PLAYERNO)

CREATE    UNIQUE INDEX TEAMS_PRIM ON
          TEAMS (TEAMNO)
```

```
CREATE    UNIQUE INDEX MATCHES_PRIM ON
          MATCHES (MATCHNO)

CREATE    UNIQUE INDEX PENALTIES_PRIM ON
          PENALTIES (PAYMENTNO)
```

Users are free to choose any index names. In our four examples we use a particular model: an index name consists of the name of the table on which the index has been defined followed by the word PRIM (standing for primary key). But a name like PLYR_IX2 is also permitted.

If these four CREATE INDEX statements are executed, Oracle then checks that the primary key columns contain no duplicate values. Any attempt to update a value or add a row which will lead to duplicate values in the primary key will be rejected. In Section 4.6 we will come back to the use of indexes.

4.2   The NULL value

Columns are filled with values. A value can be, for example, a number, a word or a date. A special value is the *NULL value*. The NULL value is comparable with 'value unknown' or 'value not present'. In this book we present a NULL value by using a question mark. The PLAYERS table contains for example several NULL values (question marks) in the LEAGUENO column (see Section 3.2). This is used to denote that the particular player has no league number. NULL values must not be confused with the number zero or blank spaces. A NULL value is never equivalent to another NULL value. So, two NULL values are not equal to each other, but they are also not unequal. If we should happen to know whether two NULL values are equal or unequal, we would know 'something' about those NULL values. Then we could not say that the two values are completely unknown. Later we discuss this in more detail.

In the last section we have seen that in defining a column you are allowed to specify NOT NULL. This means that the column in every row *must* be filled. In other words, NULL values are not allowed in a NOT NULL column. For example: each player has to have a name; on the contrary a LEAGUE number is not required.

Note: In this book we assume that there is only one type of NULL value with the meaning 'value unknown'. E.F. Codd, founder of the relational model, makes a distinction between two different kinds of NULL values: 'value missing and applicable' and 'value missing and inapplicable'; see Codd (1990). Oracle does not (yet) make this distinction.

4.3   Populating tables with data

The tables are created and can now be filled with data. For this we use *INSERT statements*. For each table we give two examples. You can deduce what the other INSERT statements will be by referring to Section 3.2.

```
INSERT INTO PLAYERS VALUES
    (6, 'Parmenter', 'R', 1964, 'M', 1977,
    'Haseltine Lane', '80', '1234KK', 'Stratford',
    '070-476537', '8467')
```

```
INSERT INTO PLAYERS VALUES
    (44, 'Baker', 'E', 1963, 'M', 1980,
    'Lewis Street', '23', '4444LJ', 'Inglewood',
    '070-368753', '1124')
```

```
INSERT INTO TEAMS VALUES (1, 6, 'first')
```

```
INSERT INTO TEAMS VALUES (2, 27, 'second')
```

```
INSERT INTO MATCHES VALUES (1, 1, 6, 3, 1)
```

```
INSERT INTO MATCHES VALUES (4, 1, 44, 3, 2)
```

```
INSERT INTO PENALTIES VALUES (1, 6, '08-DEC-80', 100)
```

```
INSERT INTO PENALTIES VALUES (2, 44, '05-MAY-81, 75)
```

Explanation: The result of processing each statement is to add one new row to the table. Each alphanumeric value, such as `Parmenter` and `R`, must be enclosed in single quotation marks (see the first INSERT statement). The (column) values are separated by commas. Because Oracle still knows the sequence of the columns in the CREATE TABLE statement, it can take the values from the INSERT statement (provided they occur in the same order) and insert them into the correct columns. For the PLAYERS table, therefore, the first value is PLAYERNO, the second NAME, and so on, with the last being LEAGUENO.

4.4   Querying tables

The *SELECT statement* is used to retrieve data from tables. A number of examples will illustrate the diverse features of this statement.

Example 4.1: Get the number, name and year of birth of each player resident in Stratford; sort the result in alphabetical order of name.

```
SELECT    PLAYERNO, NAME, YEAR_OF_BIRTH
FROM      PLAYERS
WHERE     TOWN = 'Stratford'
ORDER BY NAME
```

Result:

```
PLAYERNO  NAME              YEAR_OF_BIRTH
--------  ----------------  -------------
      39  Bishop                     1956
      57  Brown                      1971
       2  Everett                    1948
      83  Hope                       1956
       6  Parmenter                  1964
     100  Parmenter                  1963
       7  Wise                       1963
```

Explanation: Get the number, name and year of birth (SELECT PLAYERNO, NAME, YEAR_OF_BIRTH) of each player (FROM PLAYERS) resident in Stratford (WHERE TOWN = 'Stratford'); sort the result in alphabetical order of name (ORDER BY NAME). After FROM we specify which table we want to query. The conditions that our requested data must satisfy come after WHERE. SELECT enables us to choose which columns we want to see. And after ORDER BY we specify the column names on which the final result should be sorted.

The table above is the result of the SELECT statement that appears on your screen including the column headings and the underlining. The layout of the table is determined by Oracle and can be altered.

A few words now about the 'default' layout created by Oracle. First, the width of a column is determined by the width of the data type of the column. Second, the name of a heading is equal to the name of the column in the SELECT statement. Third, the values in columns with an alphanumeric data type are left-justified, while those in numeric columns are right-justified. Fourth, there are two spaces between each column of the result table. In Chapter 7 we discuss how the layout of the result of a SELECT statement can be adapted.

Example 4.2: Get the number of each player born after 1960 and resident in Stratford; order the result by player number.

```
SELECT    PLAYERNO
FROM      PLAYERS
WHERE     YEAR_OF_BIRTH > 1960
AND       TOWN = 'Stratford'
ORDER BY  PLAYERNO
```

Result:

```
PLAYERNO
--------
       6
       7
      57
     100
```

Example 4.3: Get all the information about each penalty.

```
SELECT    *
FROM      PENALTIES
```

Result:

```
PAYMENTNO   PLAYERNO   PEN_DATE    AMOUNT
---------   --------   ---------   ------
        1          6   08-DEC-80   100.00
        2         44   05-MAY-81    75.00
        3         27   10-SEP-83   100.00
        4        104   08-DEC-84    50.00
        5         44   08-DEC-80    25.00
        6          8   08-DEC-80    25.00
        7         44   30-DEC-82    30.00
        8         27   12-NOV-84    75.00
```

Explanation: Get for each penalty (FROM PENALTIES) all column values (SELECT *). This statement returns the whole PENALTIES table as a result. The * character is a shorthand notation for 'all columns'. In this result you can also see how dates are printed. This can be changed.

4.5   Updating and deleting rows

In Section 4.3 we described how to add new rows to a table. This section covers the updating and deleting of existing rows.

Warning: If you execute the statements described in this section you will change the contents of the database. In the subsequent sections we assume that the original contents of the database are intact.

The *UPDATE statement* is used to change values in rows and the *DELETE statement* to remove complete rows from a table. Let us look at examples of both statements.

Example 4.4: Change the amount of each penalty incurred by player 44 to $200.

```
UPDATE    PENALTIES
SET       AMOUNT = 200
WHERE     PLAYERNO = 44
```

These changes can be seen by issuing an SELECT statement.

```
SELECT    *
FROM      PENALTIES
```

Result:

```
PAYMENTNO   PLAYERNO   PEN_DATE   AMOUNT
---------   --------   --------   ------
        1          6   08-DEC-80  100.00
        2         44   05-MAY-81  200.00
        3         27   10-SEP-83  100.00
        4        104   08-DEC-84   50.00
        5         44   08-DEC-80  200.00
        6          8   08-DEC-80   25.00
        7         44   30-DEC-82  200.00
        8         27   12-NOV-84   75.00
```

Example 4.5: Remove each penalty where the amount is greater than $30 (we assume the original contents of the PENALTIES table).

```
DELETE
FROM      PENALTIES
WHERE     AMOUNT > 30
```

Result (seen by issuing a SELECT statement):

```
PAYMENTNO   PLAYERNO   PEN_DATE   AMOUNT
---------   --------   --------   ------
        5         44   08-DEC-80   25.00
        6          8   08-DEC-80   25.00
        7         44   30-DEC-82   30.00
```

4.6   Optimizing query processing

We now look at how SELECT statements are processed, in other words how Oracle arrives at the correct answer. We will illustrate this with the following SELECT statement (again, we assume the original contents of the PENALTIES table).

```
SELECT    *
FROM      PENALTIES
WHERE     AMOUNT = 25
```

To process this statement Oracle looks row by row through the entire PENAL-TIES table. If AMOUNT equals 25, the row is included in the result table. If, like this example, the table contains few rows, Oracle can work quickly. But, if a table has thousands of rows and each must be checked, then it could take a great deal of time. In such a case the definition of an *index* can speed up the processing. You could compare an index created with Oracle with an index in a book. Later, in Chapter 20, we discuss this more fully.

An index is defined on a column or combination of columns, for example:

```
CREATE    INDEX PENALTY_INDEX ON
          PENALTIES (AMOUNT)
```

This statement defines an index called PENALTY_INDEX on the AMOUNT column in the PENALTIES table. This index ensures that in the above example Oracle only needs to look at rows in the database which satisfy the WHERE condition, and is, therefore, quicker to produce an answer. The PENALTY_INDEX index provides direct access to the rows. It is important to bear in mind the following points:

- Among other reasons, indexes are defined in order to optimize the processing of SELECT statements.

- An index is never explicitly referenced in a SELECT statement.

- During the processing of a statement Oracle itself chooses whether an existing index will be used.

- An index may be created or deleted at any time.

- When updating, inserting or deleting rows, Oracle also maintains the indexes on the tables concerned. This means that on the one hand the processing time for SELECT statements is reduced, but on the other hand, the processing time for change statements (such as INSERT, UPDATE and DELETE) is increased.

Section 4.1 dealt with a special type of index: the unique index. Oracle also uses these for optimizing processing. Unique indexes have another function as well: they guarantee that a particular column or combination of columns contains no duplicate values.

4.7 Views

A table stores rows of actual data. This means that a table occupies a particular amount of storage space; the more rows, the more storage space required. *Views* are tables that are visible to users, but which do not occupy any storage space. A view, therefore, can also be referred to as a *derived* or *virtual* table. A view behaves as though it contains actual rows of data, but in fact it contains none. Instead, the rows are derived from the base table or tables on which the view is defined.

The data in the tennis club database is divided into four tables. These tables define the structure of the database. Imagine now that you want a table for registering the player number and age of each player. This data can be retrieved from the database because the PLAYERS table contains a player number and a year of birth for each player. The age can be calculated by subtracting the year of birth from the current year.

The following statement defines a view called AGES that contains the desired data:

```
CREATE    VIEW AGES (PLAYERNO, AGE) AS
SELECT    PLAYERNO, 1990 - YEAR_OF_BIRTH
FROM      PLAYERS
```

The view AGES has two columns: PLAYERNO and AGE. It is the SELECT statement that determines the contents of the view. By using the SELECT statement shown below you can see the (virtual) contents of the view:

```
SELECT    *
FROM      AGES
```

Result:

```
PLAYERNO  AGE
--------  ---
       6   26
      44   27
      83   34
       2   42
      27   26
     104   20
       7   27
      57   19
      39   34
     112   27
       8   28
     100   27
      28   27
      95   27
```

The contents of the AGES view are *not* stored in the database, but are derived at the moment a SELECT statement (or another statement) is executed. The use of views, therefore, costs nothing extra in storage space as the contents of a view can only comprise data which is already stored.

Among other things, views can be used to:

- simplify the use of routine or repetitive statements
- restructure the way in which tables are seen
- build up SELECT statements in several steps
- protect data

Chapter 22 looks at this more closely.

4.8   User and data security

As mentioned in Chapter 2 we can start SQL*Plus by using the name SQLDBA. Other users can be added later on. Each user has to be given particular authorization or privileges. Suppose that two users, DIANE and PETE, have to work with the database of the tennis club. DIANE is only allowed to query the PLAYERS table and PETE may query and update the contents of the two tables PLAYERS and TEAMS. The passwords for DIANE and PETE are respectively J12_J and PETEPW. First we introduce both users:

```
GRANT    CONNECT
TO       DIANE, PETE
IDENTIFIED BY J12_J, PETEPW
```

After execution of this statement DIANE and PETE are allowed to login to SQL*Plus. However, they are not allowed to access tables. They have to be granted special privileges to do this. The following three statements give them the required privileges.

```
GRANT    SELECT
ON       PLAYERS
TO       DIANE

GRANT    SELECT, UPDATE
ON       PLAYERS
TO       PETE

GRANT    SELECT, UPDATE
ON       TEAMS
TO       PETE
```

When PETE has started SQL*Plus he can, for example, query the TEAMS table:

```
SELECT   *
FROM     TEAMS
```

Oracle will give an error message if DIANE enters the same SELECT statement as she has authority only to query the PLAYERS table and not the TEAMS table.

Introducing users and granting them privileges does have implications for the security of the database. Not everyone needs access to all the data in the database. GRANT statements allow users to have access only to that data which is necessary for them to carry out their work.

4.9   The catalog tables

Oracle maintains lists of user-names and passwords and the sequence in which columns in the CREATE TABLE statements have been created (see Section 4.1).

Where does Oracle record all these names, passwords, sequence numbers and so on? Oracle manages, for its own use, a number of tables in which this data is stored. These tables are called *catalog tables*. Each catalog table is an ordinary SQL table that may be queried using SELECT statements. Catalog tables, however, *cannot* be accessed using statements like UPDATE and DELETE. In any case, this is not necessary as Oracle maintains these tables itself. Among others, Oracle manages the following catalog tables:

SYS.OBJ$ This contains, for each table, data such as the name, the owner (this is the user who created the table) and the time on which the table was created.

SYS.COL$ This contains, for each column, among other things, the data type, the table to which the column belongs, whether or not the NULL value is allowed, and the sequence number of the column in the table.

SYS.IND$ This contains, for each index, the table on which the index is defined.

SYS.USER$ This contains, for each user, among other things, the name, the password and some authorities.

SYS.VIEW$ This contains, for each view, among other things, the view definition (the SELECT statement) and the number of columns.

Here are some examples of querying the catalog tables.

Example 4.6: Give the names and the times of creation of the tables which were created after 14 January 1990; sort the result in alphabetical order on name.

```
SELECT    NAME, CTIME
FROM      SYS.OBJ$
WHERE     CTIME > '14-JAN-90'
ORDER BY NAME
```

Result:

CNAME	CTIME
PLAYERS	20-FEB-90
TEAMS	20-FEB-90
PENALTIES	25-MAR-90

Explanation: Give the name and the data and time of creating (SELECT NAME, CTIME) for each table (FROM SYS.OBJ$) created after 14 January 1990 (WHERE CTIME > '14-JAN-90'); sort the result by name (ORDER BY NAME).

Example 4.7: Is there a user with the name JOHN?

```
SELECT    NAME
FROM      SYS.USER$
WHERE     NAME = 'JOHN'
```

Explanation: Give the number (SELECT NAME) of every user (FROM SYS.USER$) with the name JOHN (WHERE NAME = 'JOHN'). If this SELECT statement has a result, then there exists a user with the name JOHN. Chapter 27 is entirely devoted to the structure of catalog tables. In the other chapters the effect that particular statements can have on the contents of the catalog tables is described. In other words, when processing a particular statement leads to a change in the catalog data, this change is explained. Therefore this book discusses the catalog tables as an integral part of Oracle.

4.10   Definitions of SQL statements

In this book we use a particular formal notation method to indicate precisely the functionality of the SQL statements. Using this notation we can give a definition of an SQL statement. These definitions are clearly indicated in the text with boxes. To give you an idea of what such a definition looks like, we give a part of the definition of the CREATE INDEX statement below.

```
<create index statement> ::=
   CREATE [ UNIQUE ] INDEX <index name>
   ON <table name> ( <column list> )

<column list> ::=
   <column name> [ {,<column name>}... ]
```

If you are not familiar with this notation, we advise you to study this first before you continue with the next chapter: see Appendix B.

Because the functionality of certain SQL statements is very extensive, we do not always show the complete definition all at once, but extend it step by step. Appendix B includes the complete definitions of all SQL statements.

5
Creating tables

This chapter describes the statements for creating tables and synonyms. We take the view that the user knows which data must be stored and what the structure of the data is: that is, which tables are to be created and what the appropriate columns are. In other words, the user has, at his or her disposal, a ready-to-use database design.

If you have the Oracle software, we advise you to set up the sample database described in Chapter 3 of this book and fill the tables with the same data. Then you can recreate the examples and work through and correct the exercises yourself.

5.1 Creating new tables

The *CREATE TABLE statement* is used to set up tables in which rows of data can be stored. There are two ways to create tables. Completely new tables can be created or they can be copied from an existing table. Here, we describe the first form of this statement and in Section 5.4 we will discuss the second form.

On the next page the definition of the first form of the CREATE TABLE statement is given. Notice that this is not the complete definition. The *data type* concept is explained on the following page. *Table integrity rules* will be discussed in Chapter 19. Only two forms of the *column integrity rule* are given. This concept will also be discussed in detail in Chapter 19.

Here is an example of a CREATE TABLE statement for creating the PLAYERS table in the tennis club database.

```
<create table statement> ::=
   CREATE TABLE <table specification>
      <table schema>

<table schema> ::=
      ( <table element> [ {,<table element>}... ] )

<table element> ::=
   <column definition> |
   <table integrity rule>

<column specification> ::=
   <column name> <data type>
   [ <default expression> ]
   [ <column integrity rule>... ]

<default expression> ::=
   DEFAULT <expression>

<column integrity rule> ::=
   NULL | NOT NULL
```

```
CREATE TABLE PLAYERS (
        PLAYERNO        SMALLINT NOT NULL,
        NAME            CHAR(15) NOT NULL,
        INITIALS        CHAR(3)  NOT NULL,
        YEAR_OF_BIRTH   SMALLINT          ,
        SEX             CHAR(1)  NOT NULL,
        YEAR_JOINED     SMALLINT NOT NULL,
        STREET          CHAR(15) NOT NULL,
        HOUSENO         CHAR(4)           ,
        POSTCODE        CHAR(6)           ,
        TOWN            CHAR(10) NOT NULL,
        PHONENO         CHAR(10)          ,
        LEAGUENO        CHAR(4)          )
```

The name of the table is PLAYERS. Table names are unique within all tables belonging to the same owner. A user who enters a CREATE TABLE statement automatically becomes the *owner*. Two different users are both allowed to create a table called PLAYERS.

The *table schema* of a table contains column definitions and table integrity rules. As mentioned before, we will discuss table integrity rules in Chapter 19. In this chapter we concentrate on column definitions.

```
<data type> ::=
   <numeric data type>        |
   <alphanumeric data type>   |
   <date data type>           |
   <bytestring data type>

<numeric data type> ::=
   NUMBER [ ( {<precision>|*} [ ,<scale> ] ) ]  |
   SMALLINT                                     |
   INT                                          |
   INTEGER                                      |
   DECIMAL [ ( {<precision>|*} [ ,<scale> ] ) ] |
   DOUBLE PRECISION                             |
   REAL                                         |
   FLOAT [ ( <precision> ) ]

<alphanumeric data type> ::=
   CHAR [ ( <length> ) ]      |
   CHARACTER [ ( <length> ) ] |
   VARCHAR ( <length> )       |
   LONG VARCHAR               |
   LONG

<date data type> ::=
   DATE

<bytestring data type> ::=
   RAW [ ( <length> ) ] |
   LONG RAW

<precision> ::= <integer>

<scale> ::= [ - ] <integer>

<length> ::= <integer>
```

A column definition contains a column name, a data type, possibly a default expression and a number of column integrity rules. Each table can have up to 255 columns. Specifying a data type for a column is mandatory. Oracle supports six basic data types: NUMBER, CHAR, LONG, DATE, RAW, LONG RAW and a large set of what we could call derived data types. First we will explain the basic data types before describing the others.

For the numeric data type NUMBER you can specify how many digits you can have before and after the decimal point. For example, NUMBER(12,4) can have a maximum of eight digits before the decimal point and four after the point.

The first digit (12) represents the so-called *precision* and the second digit (4) the *scale*. The default scale is equal to zero. If an * is specified instead of the precision, then it is equal to the largest precision possible, which is equal to 38. The specified scale has to be between –38 and 38. If the scale is negative, for example –3, then the value of a recorded number is 10^3 times that same number. So, if the number 76 is recorded in a column with the data type NUMBER (7,–3) then the value is equal to 76000.

CHAR is an alphanumeric data type suitable for recording words, text and codes. The specified number gives the maximum length of the alphanumeric value that can be recorded in the particular column. The maximum length of the CHAR data type is 255. The default length is equal to 1.

The LONG data type is, like the CHAR data type, an alphanumeric data type. The only difference is that for LONG a length cannot be specified. The maximum length is fixed and is equal to 65535 characters. In other words, a column with this data type can contain a value up to 65535 characters.

Date and time indications can be recorded in a column with the DATE data type. A value with a DATE data type consists of six parts: year, month, day, hours, minutes and seconds. We will discuss the specification and the presentation of dates later. In spite of the fact that for Oracle a date also contains a time indication, we will simply talk about date values in this book.

Byte strings are recorded in a column with the RAW data type. This data type is almost never used. The maximum length of the RAW data type is 255. The default length is equal to 1.

Just as for the CHAR data type, RAW also has a LONG variant: LONG RAW. Just as for LONG a length cannot be specified; the maximum length is fixed and is equal to 65535.

Besides the data types described, Oracle also supports the following data types: SMALLINT, INT, INTEGER, DECIMAL, DOUBLE PRECISION, REAL, FLOAT, VARCHAR, CHARACTER and LONG VARCHAR, all of which are internally converted by Oracle to one of the data types above. Hence we call them *derived* data types. In fact, we do not explicitly need them; they have been added because a number of them are dictated by the ISO standard for SQL and a number are supported by IBM's SQL product DB2. The table below shows the internal conversion performed by Oracle.

derived data type	basic data type	derived data type	basic data type
SMALLINT	NUMBER(38,0)	INT	NUMBER(38,0)
INTEGER	NUMBER(38,0)	DECIMAL(p,s)	NUMBER(p,s)
DOUBLE PRECISION	NUMBER(38)	REAL	NUMBER(63)
FLOAT	NUMBER(38)	VARCHAR(l)	CHAR(l)
CHARACTER(l)	CHAR(l)	LONG VARCHAR	LONG

As we mentioned before, the user who enters the CREATE TABLE statement automatically becomes the owner of the table. A table can also be created for another user, who then becomes the owner.

Example 5.1: Create the PLAYERS table with JIM as owner.

```
CREATE TABLE JIM.PLAYERS (
        PLAYERNO      SMALLINT NOT NULL,
        NAME          CHAR(15) NOT NULL,
        :
        LEAGUENO      CHAR(4)            )
```

Explanation: By specifying the name of the user before the table name, he or she becomes the owner of that table.

5.2   Specifying NOT NULL

In Section 5.1 we showed in the definition of the CREATE TABLE statement that a column definition can include several column integrity rules. In this section we will discuss the NOT NULL integrity rule. The other types of integrity rule will be explained in Chapter 19.

Oracle supports the *NULL value* as a possible value for a column in a row. The NULL value is comparable with *value unknown* or *value not present*, and must not be confused with the number zero or a set of spaces.

In a CREATE TABLE statement you may specify NOT NULL integrity rules after the data types of the columns. The *NOT NULL integrity rule* (also called the NOT NULL *option*) can be used to point out which columns are *not* allowed to contain NULL values. In other words, every NOT NULL column must be filled with a value for every row.

Oracle allows NULL to be specified after the data type of a column. This means that a column is allowed to contain NULL values. Specifying NULL is equivalent to omitting the specification. We could have formulated the CREATE TABLE statement for the PLAYERS table in Section 4.1 as follows:

```
CREATE TABLE PLAYERS (
        PLAYERNO      SMALLINT NOT NULL,
        NAME          CHAR(15) NOT NULL,
        INITIALS      CHAR(3)  NOT NULL,
        YEAR_OF_BIRTH SMALLINT NULL    ,
        SEX           CHAR(1)  NOT NULL,
        YEAR_JOINED   SMALLINT NOT NULL,
        STREET        CHAR(15) NOT NULL,
        HOUSENO       CHAR(4)  NULL    ,
        POSTCODE      CHAR(6)  NULL    ,
        TOWN          CHAR(10) NOT NULL,
        PHONENO       CHAR(10) NULL    ,
        LEAGUENO      CHAR(4)  NULL     )
```

Exercise

5.1 Write a CREATE TABLE statement for a table called DEPARTMENTS and with the following columns: DEPTNO (code with 5 positions), BUDGET (maximum amount 999999) and LOCATION (name with a maximum of 30 positions). The DEPTNO column must always have a value provided.

5.3   The default expression

When adding new rows to a table with INSERT statements it is not necessary to specify the values for all columns of the table. If you omit values, Oracle will check whether a *default expression* has been specified for those particular columns. If so, the value of the default expression will be placed in that particular column of the new row.

Note: It is possible with Version 6 of Oracle to define default expressions, but unfortunately they are not active. According to the Oracle Corporation default expressions will be implemented in the next version. We have written this section as though default expressions work. Please do not be misled by this.

Example 5.2: Create the PENALTIES table where the default value for the AMOUNT column is $50 and the default value for the PEN_DATE column is 1 January 1990.

```
CREATE    TABLE PENALTIES
          (PAYMENTNO   INTEGER     NOT NULL,
          PLAYERNO    SMALLINT    NOT NULL,
          PEN_DATE    DATE        NOT NULL DEFAULT '01-JAN-90',
          AMOUNT      DECIMAL(7,2) NOT NULL DEFAULT 50.00)
```

Next we enter the following INSERT statement, supplying no values for the columns PEN_DATE and AMOUNT.

```
INSERT    INTO PENALTIES
          (PAYMENTNO, PLAYERNO)
VALUES    (15, 27)
```

After this statement the PENALTIES table shows this result:

```
PAYMENTNO  PLAYERNO  PEN_DATE   AMOUNT
---------  --------  ---------  ------
       15        27  01-JAN-90  50.00
```

5.4 Copying tables

In this section we describe how tables can be created by copying them from other, already existing, tables. Before we give the definition, we show you a simple example.

Example 5.3: Create a table with the same structure and contents as the TEAMS table.

```
CREATE    TABLE TEAMS_COPY AS
SELECT    *
FROM      TEAMS
```

Explanation: The first thing that Oracle does when processing the statement is to determine what the structure of the result of the SELECT statement is. This involves determining how many columns the result contains (three in this example) and what the data types of these columns are (SMALLINT for TEAMNO, SMALLINT for PLAYERNO and CHAR(6) for DIVISION respectively). Next, a CREATE TABLE statement is executed behind the scenes. The table that is created has the same table schema as the original TEAMS table. And finally, the result of the SELECT statement (the rows) will be inserted in the new table. In fact, the TEAMS table is completely copied in this example.

```
<create table statement> ::=
   CREATE TABLE <table name>
   [ ( <copy column> [ {,<copy column>}... ] ) ]
   AS <select statement>

<copy column> ::=
   <column name> [ <column integrity rule> ]
```

The column names of the new table are derived from those of the columns from the result of the SELECT statement. You may define other column names yourself.

Example 5.4: Create a table with the same contents as the TEAMS table, but with other column names.

```
CREATE    TABLE TEAMS_COPY_2
          (TNO, PNO, DIV) AS
SELECT    TEAMNO, PLAYERNO, DIVISION
FROM      TEAMS
```

Explanation: The column names of this new table are TNO, PNO and DIV. When you specify column names, you have to specify a name for each column in the SELECT statement.

Any SELECT statement may be used to define a table. Because we have not yet covered this statement in full (it is the subject of the following chapters) this form of the CREATE TABLE statement will be omitted here.

We close with an example of how a table is created, in which only the structure is copied, not the contents.

Example 5.5: Create an empty table with the same structure as the TEAMS table.

```
CREATE    TABLE TEAMS_COPY_3 AS
SELECT    TEAMNO, PLAYERNO, DIVISION
FROM      TEAMS
WHERE     1 = 2
```

Explanation: The somewhat unusual condition in the WHERE clause makes sure that the result of the SELECT statement is empty, so that no rows are inserted.

5.5   Naming tables and columns

Users are free to select almost any names for columns and tables. Oracle has only the following restrictions:

- An owner may not give two tables the same name.

- Two columns in a table may not have the same name.

- Table and column names can be up to 30 characters long.

- A name may only consist of letters, digits and the special symbols –, $ and # and must begin with a letter.

- Table and column names may not be reserved words. Appendix B includes a list of such words.

The restrictions imposed by the last two rules can be avoided by placing double quotation marks before and after the table name. The table name SELECT is incorrect, but "SELECT" is correct. This means that everywhere the table name is used, the double quotation marks must be used.

The definition of good names is extremely important. Column and table names are used in many statements and especially in SELECT statements. Awkward names, especially during interpretive use of SQL, can lead to irritating mistakes. Therefore, keep to the following guidelines for naming conventions:

- Keep the table and column names short, but not cryptic (therefore PLAYERS instead of PLYRS and STREET instead of STREETNAME).

- Use the plural form for table names (therefore PLAYERS instead of PLAYER; in this way the statement 'flows' better).

- Do not use *information bearing* names (therefore PLAYERS instead of PLAYERS_2, where the digit 2 represents the number of indexes on the table). If this information changes, it would be necessary to change the table name together with all the statements that use the table.

- Be consistent (therefore PLAYERNO and TEAMNO instead of PLAY-ERNO and TEAMNUM).

- So far as is possible, give columns with comparable populations the same name (therefore PLAYERNO in PLAYERS, PLAYERNO in TEAMS and PLAYERNO in PENALTIES).

5.6   Dropping tables

The *DROP TABLE statement* is used to delete a table from the database. Oracle removes the descriptions of the tables from all relevant catalog tables, along with all integrity rules, indexes and privileges dependent on this table. Note that views and synonyms will not be deleted.

```
<drop table statement> ::=
   DROP TABLE <table specification>

<table specification> ::= [ <user> . ] <table name>
```

Example 5.6: Drop the PLAYERS table.

```
DROP TABLE PLAYERS
```

Example 5.7: Drop the TEAMS table that has JIM as the owner.

```
DROP TABLE JIM.PLAYERS
```

5.7   Altering the table structure

The UPDATE, INSERT and DELETE statements are used to change the contents of a table. Oracle also offers the possibility of changing the structure of a table. The way to do this is with the *ALTER TABLE statement*. Different functions can be performed with this statement:

- new columns can be added to a table after it has been created and put into use

- the data types of existing columns can be changed under specific conditions
- new integrity rules can be added
- existing integrity rules can be deleted

Below we give the definition of this statement.

```
<alter table statement> ::=
   ALTER TABLE <table specification> <alter action>...

<alter action> ::=
   <alter add>                |
   <alter modify column>

<alter add> ::=
   ADD ( <column definition>
       [ {,<column definition>}... ] )

<alter modify column> ::=
   MODIFY ( <column change>
       [ {,<column change>}... ] )

<column change> ::=
   <column name> [ <data type> ] [ [ NOT ] NULL ]
```

Example 5.8: Suppose that the TEAMS table has the following structure and contents:

```
TEAMNO  PLAYERNO  DIVISION
------  --------  --------
     1         6  first
     2        27  second
```

The table must be extended to include a new column called TYPE. This column shows whether the team is a men's or women's one. The statement to do this is:

```
ALTER    TABLE TEAMS
ADD      ( TYPE CHAR(1) )
```

The TEAMS table now looks like this:

```
TEAMNO  PLAYERNO  DIVISION  TYPE
------  --------  --------  ----
     1         6  first     ?
     2        27  second    ?
```

The TYPE column is filled with a NULL value. This is also the only possible value that Oracle can use to fill the column (how would Oracle know whether, for example team 1, is a men's team?). Later on the NOT NULL integrity rule can be added to a column, but at that point the column cannot contain any NULL value or the entire table should be completely empty. In that case you may omit the data type of a column in the ALTER TABLE statement.

Example 5.9: Add a NOT NULL integrity rule for the YEAR_OF_BIRTH column.

```
ALTER   TABLE PLAYERS
MODIFY  (YEAR_OF_BIRTH NOT NULL)
```

For every existing column the NOT NULL option may be deleted.

Example 5.10: Delete the NOT NULL integrity rule that has been defined for the NAME column.

```
ALTER   TABLE PLAYERS
MODIFY  (NAME NULL)
```

The data type or the length of the data type of a column can be changed with the ALTER TABLE statement. The length of a data type may always be enlarged. Reducing the length is only permitted if the table is empty or if the column only contains NULL values. A column can only receive a new data type if every value in the column satisfies the rules of the new data type.

Example 5.11: Change the data type of the PLAYERNO column from the PLAYERS table from SMALLINT to INTEGER.

```
ALTER   TABLE PLAYERS
MODIFY  (PLAYERNO INTEGER NOT NULL)
```

Example 5.12: Increase the length of the TOWN column from 10 to 20.

```
ALTER   TABLE PLAYERS
MODIFY  (TOWN CHAR(20) NOT NULL)
```

Exercises

5.2   Find out whether Oracle can perform the following modifications:
1.   Change the data type of the LEAGUENO column to INTEGER.
2.   Change the data type of the HOUSENO column to INTEGER.
3.   Define NOT NULL for the WON column.
4.   Define NULL for the PLAYERNO columns in the PLAYERS table.
5.   Change the data type of the DATE column to CHAR(10).
6.   Reduce the length of the STREET columns to CHAR(9).

5.3   Write the ALTER TABLE statements for each of the permitted changes from the previous exercise.

5.8   The table specification

This section describes the table specification concept. A *table specification* is used in many SQL statements to identify the table that is to be accessed. For example, in the following SELECT statement we indicate which table we want to access after the keyword FROM. The word PLAYERS is here a table specification.

```
SELECT   *
FROM     PLAYERS
```

In this section we assume that the user who enters the statement is the owner of the PLAYERS table. Users are, of course, allowed to access tables owned by other users. The table specification must, in that case, be extended with the name of the owner. In the next SELECT statement we query the PLAYERS table that has user SQLDBA as the owner.

```
SELECT   *
FROM     SQLDBA.PLAYERS
```

This means that if a table is specified without the name of the owner, Oracle assumes that the user wants to use his or her own table.

In Section 4.9 we have already shown you examples of SELECT statements using table specifications consisting of two parts: SYS.OBJ$ and SYS.USER$. The user with the name SYS is, in fact, the owner of all Oracle catalog tables. In Chapter 8 we will discuss the concept of table specification again.

5.9   Tables and the catalog

Oracle uses two tables to record tables and columns in the catalog: TAB$ and COL$. Before we give you the description of these tables, we have to explain the notion of a *database object*. Examples of database objects are tables, views, and indexes. Oracle has a separate table, called the OBJ$ table, which is used to store, for each database object, some general information such as the owner, the name and the date on which the object has been created. At the time of creation a database object gets a unique number: the database object number. Oracle uses these database object numbers in other catalog tables to indicate which table or index it refers to.

Below we give a description of the OBJ$ table. The name and owner of every database object created, causes a row to be entered in the OBJ$ table. The OBJ# column is the primary key of this table. The OWNER# and NAME columns together form an alternate key.

column name	data type	description
OBJ#	NUMBER	Unique number of the database object
OWNER#	NUMBER	Number of the owner (or creator) of the database object
NAME	CHAR	Name of the database object
TYPE	NUMBER	Type of database object shown with a code: 1. index 2. table 3. cluster 4. view 5. synonym 6. sequence
CTIME	DATE	Date and time on which the database object was created
MTIME	DATE	Date and time on which the last modification of the structure on the database object was performed (for example with an ALTER TABLE statement)

Example 5.13: Show the data of the PLAYERS table.

```
SELECT   *
FROM     SYS.OBJ$
WHERE    NAME = 'PLAYERS'
```

Result:

```
OBJ#   OWNER#   NAME      TYPE   CTIME       MTIME
----   ------   -------   ----   ---------   -----
4211       50   PLAYERS      2   12-JAN-85       ?
```

Additional data about tables is registered in the TAB$ table. OBJ# is the primary key of this table. Some of these columns will be explained in other sections.

column name	data type	description
OBJ#	NUMBER	Unique number of the table
TS#	NUMBER	Number of the tablespace in which the table is recorded
FILE#	NUMBER	Number of the file in which the table is recorded
COLS	NUMBER	Number of columns in the table
AUDIT$	CHAR	Table audit specifications for the table

Specifications on columns are registered in the COL$ table. The primary key of the COL$ table is formed by the OBJ# and COL# columns.

column name	data type	description
OBJ#	NUMBER	Database object number of the table that the column belongs to
COL#	NUMBER	Database object number of the column
OFFSET	NUMBER	Offset of the column in a row of the table
NAME	CHAR	Name of the column
TYPE#	NUMBER	Data type of the column with possible data types being: 1 character 2 number 8 long 12 date 23 raw 24 long raw
LENGTH	NUMBER	Length of the column in bytes
PRECISION	NUMBER	Total number of digits of the column; only used if the data type of the column is NUMBER
SCALE	NUMBER	Number of digits after the decimal point; only used if the data type of the column is NUMBER
NULL$	NUMBER	Indication that NULL values are permitted: if zero, then NULL values are permitted; if greater than zero, NULL values are not permitted, that number is then the number of the integrity rule
DEFLENGTH	NUMBER	Length of the default value
DEFAULT$	LONG	Default value as alphanumeric literal

Example 5.14: Show data on the columns of the TEAMS table (we assume that the database object number of this table is equal to 4212).

```
SELECT   COL#, NAME, TYPE#, LENGTH, NULL$
FROM     SYS.COL$
WHERE    OBJ# = 4212
```

Result:

```
COL#  NAME        TYPE#  LENGTH  NULL$
----  ----------  -----  ------  -----
   1  TEAMNO          2      22    331
   2  PLAYERNO        2      22    332
   3  DIVISION        1      22    333
```

Note: It is very unusual (and unwise) to use database object numbers explicitly in a SELECT statement. We are using them in this chapter only because we have not yet explained all the features of the SELECT statement.

Example 5.15: Show the default values of the columns in the PENALTIES table, as defined in Section 5.3 (we assume that the database object number of this table is equal to 4213).

```
SELECT    COL#, NAME, DEFLENGTH, DEFAULT$
FROM      SYS.COL$
WHERE     OBJ# = 4213
```

Result:

COL#	NAME	DEFLENGTH	DEFAULT$
1	PAYMENTNO	?	?
2	PLAYERNO	?	?
3	PEN_DATE	7	SYSDATE
4	AMOUNT	5	50.00

Exercise

5.4   Show how the OBJ$ and the COL$ tables are filled after execution of the CREATE TABLE statement in the first exercise of this chapter.

5.10   Defining comment in the catalog

In the catalog tables there is room to store descriptions of tables and columns. These descriptions are entered using the COMMENT ON statement.

```
<comment statement> ::=
   COMMENT ON <comment specification>

<comment specification> ::=
   <documentation object> IS <alphanumeric literal>

<documentation object> ::=
   TABLE <table specification> |
   COLUMN <table specification> . <column name>
```

Example 5.16: Define comments for the PLAYERS table and the PLAYERNO column in this table.

```
COMMENT ON
TABLE   PLAYERS
IS      'Recreational and competition players'
```

and

```
COMMENT ON
COLUMN  PLAYERS.PLAYERNO
IS      'primary key'
```

You see the table name PLAYERS precedes the PLAYERNO column name, separated by a full stop. Adding a table name in the COMMENT statement is mandatory, because other tables may also have a column called PLAYERNO.

The description of a table or column is recorded in a separate catalog table, the COM$ table.

column name	data type	description
OBJ#	NUMBER	Database object number of the table or view for which the comment was created
COL#	NUMBER	Column number of the column for which the comment was specified; contains the NULL value if the comment on a table has been specified
COMMENT$	CHAR	Actual description or comment

Example 5.17: Show by executing a SELECT statement the result of the two COMMENT statements above (assume that only one user created a table with the name PLAYERS). We retrieve the database object number of the PLAYERS table with the first SELECT statement.

```
SELECT    OBJ#
FROM      SYS.OBJ$
WHERE     NAME = 'PLAYERS'
```

Assume that the answer is 4211. (In a subsequent chapter we will show you how to combine the two statements into one.)

```
SELECT    COMMENT$
FROM      SYS.COM$
WHERE     OBJ# = 4211
AND       COL# IS NULL
```

Result:

```
COMMENT$
------------------------------------
Recreational and competition players
```

Second example:

```
SELECT    COMMENT$
FROM      SYS.COM$
WHERE     OBJ# = 4211
AND       COL# = 1
```

Result:

```
TNAME     CNAME     REMARKS
-------   --------  -----------
PLAYERS   PLAYERNO  primary key
```

There is no separate statement to delete a comment; the COMMENT statement is used, but the comment provided contains no text. It looks like this:

```
COMMENT    ON
TABLE      PLAYERS
IS         ''
```

In order to change a comment you use the same statement again, providing new text. This simply overwrites the previous comment.

5.11   Synonyms for table names

You can create alternative names for a table. These names, called *synonyms*, can be used to refer to a table. The *CREATE SYNONYM statement* is used to define a synonym. You can use synonyms in other statements instead of the original name. Note, however, that the definition of a synonym does not mean that a new table has been created.

```
<create synonym statement> ::=
    CREATE [ PUBLIC ] SYNONYM <table specification>
        FOR <table specification>

<table specification> ::= [ <user> . ] <table name>
```

Example 5.18: The user KAREN wants to use MEMBERS as a synonym for the PLAYERS table. (We assume that KAREN is the owner of the PLAYERS table.)

```
CREATE SYNONYM MEMBERS FOR PLAYERS
```

When this statement has been processed the next two SELECT statements become equivalent:

```
SELECT    *
FROM      PLAYERS
```

and

```
SELECT    *
FROM      MEMBERS
```

What is the point of using synonyms? First, users can create synonyms in order to give a table or view an alternative name. They may want an alternative name if, for example, a centrally defined table name or view is not suitable for some reason.

Second, users can create synonyms for tables (or views) owned by another user. If a user accesses a table created by someone else, he or she must specify the owner in front of the table name.

Example 5.19: PETE queries the ADDRESSES table belonging to DIANE. The SELECT statement is as follows:

```
SELECT    *
FROM      DIANE.ADDRESSES
```

With the following statement a synonym is created by PETE so that he no longer has to use DIANE's name in order to access her table.

```
CREATE SYNONYM ADR FOR DIANE.ADDRESSES
```

Now the next SELECT statement suffices for PETE:

```
SELECT    *
FROM      ADR
```

A special type of synonym is the PUBLIC synonym. This type of synonym is generally created by a central function in the organization, such as a database administrator.

Example 5.20: Create a public synonym for the PLAYERS table.

```
CREATE PUBLIC SYNONYM PL
FOR     PLAYERS
```

If a user refers to the PL table after processing the statement above, then Oracle first checks to see if the user is the owner of a table or synonym named PL. If not, only then does Oracle look to see if there is a public synonym with that name.

Just as for tables, synonyms can be created for other users. Here is an example.

Example 5.21: Create the synonym PEN for the PENALTIES table with Jim as owner.

```
CREATE SYNONYM JIM.PEN FOR PENALTIES
```

Naming rules for synonyms are the same as those for tables. It follows, then, that a synonym may not be created which has the same name as an existing table or synonym.

Synonyms are recorded by Oracle in the OBJ$ table. Specific data on a synonym is recorded in the SYN$ table. The OBJ# column is the primary key of this table.

column name	data type	description
OBJ#	NUMBER	Database object number of the synonym
NODE	CHAR	Name of the database link where the table is stored on which this synonym was defined
OWNER	CHAR	Name of the owner of the table on which this synonym was defined
NAME	CHAR	Name of the table on which this synonym was defined

After all the CREATE SYNONYM statements above have been executed, the OBJ$ table looks like this:

```
OBJ#   OWNER#  NAME     TYPE  CTIME
----   ------  -------  ----  ---------
4211      50   PLAYERS     2  12-JAN-85
  :
4254      61   MEMBERS     5  30-APR-90
4255      64   ADR         5  30-APR-90
4256      50   PL          5  01-JUN-90
4257      65   PEN         5  03-JUN-90
```

and the SYN$ table:

```
OBJ#   OWNER   NAME
----   ------  ---------
4254   SQLDBA  PLAYERS
4255   DIANE   ADDRESSES
4256   SQLDBA  PLAYERS
4257   SQLDBA  PENALTIES
```

5.12   Dropping synonyms

Use the DROP SYNONYM statement to delete synonyms.

```
<drop synonym statement> ::=
    DROP [ PUBLIC ] SYNONYM <table specification>

<table specification> ::= [ <user>. ] <table name>
```

Example 5.22: Delete the synonym MEMBERS.

```
DROP SYNONYM MEMBERS
```

If a table is deleted, dependent synonyms are *not* deleted. An error message is returned when a synonym whose base table does not exist is referenced. Such a synonym becomes operative again if a new table is created with the same table name.

Exercises

5.5 Is a user allowed to create a synonym for an other user? If yes, who is the owner?

5.6 If a table is created for another user, does that user already have to exist (with GRANT CONNECT)?

5.7 The contents of which table will the user see after the following three statements?

```
CREATE SYNONYM SYN1 FOR PLAYERS

CREATE PUBLIC SYNONYM SYN1 FOR TEAMS

SELECT * FROM SYN1
```

5.13   Renaming tables

With the *RENAME statement*, the name of an existing table, view or synonym can be changed. This new name will be recorded in the catalog. All dependent objects of the table, such as indexes, privileges and views, still exist.

```
<rename statement> ::=
   RENAME <table specification> TO <table name>

<table specification> ::= [ <user> . ] <table name>
```

Example 5.23: Rename the PLAYERS table to SPORTPEOPLE.

```
RENAME PLAYERS TO SPORTPEOPLE
```

Remarks:

- Note that applications which make use of the old name of the table are not adapted by Oracle. These applications have to be corrected manually.

- All synonyms defined for a table are unusable if a table is given a new name. In fact, Oracle changes the old name of the table in the OBJ$ table, but not in the NAME column of the SYN$ table.

6
SELECT statement: common elements

The most important and most used SQL statement is the SELECT statement. This statement is used to query data in the tables, the result of this always being a table. A result table like this can be used as the basis of a report.

This book deals with the SELECT statement in eleven chapters, from Chapter 6 up to Chapter 16. This first chapter describes a number of common elements important to many SQL statements and certainly crucial to the SELECT statement. For those of you who are familiar with programming languages and other database languages, most of these concepts will be well known.

We cover the following common elements:

- literal
- system variable
- numeric expression
- alphanumeric expression
- date expression
- scalar function
- statistical function

6.1 Literals

A *literal* is a fixed or unchanging value; literals are sometimes called *constants*. Literals are used, for example, in conditions for selecting rows in SELECT statements and in INSERT statements for specifying values in a new row. Each literal has a particular data type, just like a column in a table. Oracle supports these types of literals (the names are derived from their respective data types):

```
<literal> ::=
   <numeric literal>          |
   <alphanumeric literal>     |
   <date literal>

<numeric literal>  ::=
   <integer literal>            |
   <decimal literal>            |
   <floating point literal>     |
   <alphanumeric literal>

<integer literal>  ::= [ + | - ] <integer>

<decimal literal>  ::=
   [ + | - ] <integer>   [ .<integer> ] |
   [ + | - ] <integer>.                 |
   [ + | - ] .<integer>

<floating point literal> ::=
   <mantissa> { E | e } <exponent>

<alphanumeric literal> ::= ' [ <character>... ] '

<date literal> ::= ' <day> - <month> - <year> '

<mantissa> ::= <decimal literal>

<exponent> ::= <integer literal>

<character> ::= <non quote character> | ''

<non quote character> ::=
     <digit> | <letter> | <special character>

<day> ::= <digit> [ <digit> ]

<month> ::=
   JAN | jan | FEB | feb | MAR | mar | APR | apr |
   MAY | may | JUN | jun | JUL | jul | AUG | aug |
   SEP | sep | OCT | oct | NOV | nov | DEC | dec

<year> ::= <digit> [ <digit> ]

<integer> ::= <digit>...
```

- integer literal
- decimal literal
- floating point literal
- alphanumeric literal

An *integer literal* is a whole number or integer without a decimal point, possibly preceded by a plus or minus sign. Examples are:

```
   38
  +12
-3404
  -16
```

The following examples are *not* correct integer literals:

```
342.16
 -14E5
  jim
```

A *decimal literal* is a number with or without a decimal point and possibly preceded by a plus or minus sign. Every integer literal is by definition a decimal literal. Examples are:

```
     49
  18.47
  -3400
    -16
0.83459
   -349
```

A *floating point literal* is a decimal literal followed by an exponent. Examples are:

```
Floating point literal  Value
----------------------  -----
            49             49
         18.47          18.47
         -34E2          -3400
        0.16E4           1600
          4E-3          0.004
```

An *alphanumeric literal* is a string of zero or more alphanumeric characters enclosed in quotation marks. The quotation marks are not considered to be part of the literal. Rather, they define the beginning and end of the string. The following characters are permitted in an alphanumeric literal:

```
all lower case letters   (a-z)
all upper case letters   (A-Z)
all digits               (0-9)
all remaining characters (such as ' + -  ? = and _)
```

As you will note, an alphanumeric literal can contain quotation marks. For every single quotation mark within an alphanumeric literal you must use two quotation marks instead, separate from the quotation marks already being used to enclose the literal. Some examples of correct alphanumeric literals are:

```
Alphanumeric literal  Value
--------------------  -------
'Collins'             Collins
'''tis'               'tis
'!?-@'                !?-@
''
''''                  '
'1234'                1234
```

A few incorrect examples include:

```
'Collins
''tis
'''
```

A *date literal* consists of day, month and year components enclosed between quotes and therefore represents a date. The three components are separated by colons. The month does not have to be specified in capitals. Examples include:

```
Date literal  Value
------------  ----------------
08-DEC-80     8 december 1980
19-JUN-91     19 june 1991
```

Exercise

6.1   Say which of the literals below are correct and which are incorrect; give the data type of the literal as well.

1.   41.58E-8

2.   JIM

3.   'jim'

4.   'A'14

5.   '!?'

6.   -3400

7.   '14E6'

8.   ''''''

9.   '19-JAN-1940'

6.2   System variables

A *system variable* is one which gets a value at the moment the statement using the variable is executed. System variables can have different values at different times. Every system variable has a data type: for example, integer, decimal or alphanumeric. Oracle itself gives a system variable its value.

The table below contains the list with system variables supported by Oracle. For each we give the data type and an explanation.

System variables	Data type	Description
USER	CHAR	The name of the user who is making use of SQL
SYSDATE	DATE	The actual date
ROWNUM	INTEGER	The sequence number of a row in the result of a SELECT statement
LEVEL	INTEGER	The level of a row if the CONNECT clause is used in a SELECT statement

At a certain time the system variables could have the following values:

```
System variable  Value
---------------- ----------
USER             SQLDBA
USER             DIANE
SYSDATE          08-DEC-85
SYSDATE          01-JAN-84
ROWNUM           1
LEVEL            3
```

Example 6.1: Find the numbers of the database objects owned by the user who enters the statement.

```
SELECT   OBJ#
FROM     SYS.OBJ$
WHERE    OWNER = USER
```

Example 6.2: Show the penalties that have been paid today.

```
SELECT   *
FROM     PENALTIES
WHERE    PEN_DATE = SYSDATE
```

In Chapter 12 we give examples of ROWNUM and in Chapter 13 we give examples of LEVEL.

6.3   Expressions

An *expression* is a statement consisting of a set of operands and operators that together represent one value. This value can have a alphanumeric, numeric or date data type An expression can take several shapes. We already have seen two shapes: the literal and the system variables. We use expressions for example in the SELECT and WHERE clause of a SELECT statement.

```
<expression> ::=
   <numeric expression>      |
   <alphanumeric expression> |
   <date expression>
```

6.4   Numeric expressions

A *numeric expression* is an arithmetic expression with either an integer, decimal or floating point value.

```
<numeric expression> ::=
   <numeric expression>                   |
   <column specification>                 |
   <system variable>                      |
   <scalar function>                      |
   <statistical function>                 |
   [ + | - ] <numeric expression>         |
   ( <numeric expression> )               |
   <numeric expression> <mathematical operator>
     <numeric expression>                 |
   <date expression> - <date expression>  |
   <alphanumeric expression>              |
   NULL

<column specification> ::=
   [ <table specification> . ] <column name>

<scalar function> ::=
   <function name> ( [ <parameter> [ {,<parameter>}... ] ] )

<mathematical operator> ::=
   * | / | + | -
```

Examples:

```
Numeric expression    Value
------------------    -----
14 * 8                  112
(-16 + 43) / 3            9
5 * 4 + 2 * 10           40
18E3 + 10E4           118E3
12.6 / 6.3              2.0
```

The following operators may be used in a numeric expression:

```
Operator   Meaning
--------   --------
*          multiply
/          divide
+          add
-          subtract
```

Numeric literals and columns with a numeric data type can be used alongside these operators. If required, brackets can be used in numeric expressions.

Before we give any examples, you should note the following points:

- If a column specification in a numeric expression has the value NULL, then the value of the numeric expression is by definition equal to NULL.

- The calculation of the value of a numeric expression is performed in keeping with the following priorities: (1) left to right, (2) brackets, (3) multiplication and division, (4) addition and subtraction.

- The data type of a numeric expression is taken from the most precise data type that occurs in the expression. The floating point data type is more precise than the decimal data type which is more precise than the integer data type.

- Column specifications that occur in a numeric expression must have a numeric data type.

- An alphanumeric expression can be a numeric expression. The value of the alphanumeric expression must be convertable to a numeric value.

Examples (the AMOUNT column has value 25):

```
Numeric expression   Value     Numeric expression   Value
------------------   ------    ------------------   ------
6 + 4 * 25           106       6 + 4 * AMOUNT       106
0.6E1 + 4 * AMOUNT   106.E0    (6 + 4) * 25         250
(50 / 10) * 5        25        50 / (10 * 5)        1
'25'                 25        NULL * 30            NULL
```

Incorrect numeric expressions:

```
86 + 'Jim'
((80 + 4)
4/2 (* 3)
```

Example 6.3: Give the matches where the number of sets won is at least two times higher than the number of sets lost.

To answer this we need to use an expression:

```
SELECT    *
FROM      MATCHES
WHERE     WON >= LOST * 2
```

Result:

MATCHNO	TEAMNO	PLAYERNO	WON	LOST
1	1	6	3	1
3	1	6	3	0
7	1	57	3	0

A date expression has as its value a given day. A date expression can be subtracted from another, giving a result which is the number of days between the two dates. This number is, of course, a numeric value.

Numeric expression	Value
'31-DEC-88' - '21-DEC-88'	10
'31-DEC-88' - '1-JAN-88'	365

Example 6.4: Give the numbers and dates of the penalties incurred within 200 days after 1 December 1980.

```
SELECT    PAYMENTNO, PEN_DATE
FROM      PENALTIES
WHERE     PEN_DATE - '1-DEC-80' < 200
```

Result:

PAYMENTNO	PEN_DATE
1	08-DEC-80
2	05-MAY-81
5	08-DEC-80
6	08-DEC-80

We will return to date expressions in Section 6.7, and in Section 6.8 we will cover statistical functions.

Exercise

6.2   Determine the values of the following numeric expressions:

1.   400 - (20 * 10)
2.   (400 - 20) * 10
3.   400 - 20 * 10
4.   400 / 20 * 10

6.5   Alphanumeric expressions

Just as a numeric expression has a numeric value an *alphanumeric expression* has an alphanumeric value. Alphanumeric data types, are, among others, CHAR and VARCHAR.

```
<alphanumeric expression> ::=
   <alphanumeric literal> |
   <column specification> |
   <system variable>      |
   <scalar function>      |
   <statistical function> |
   NULL                   |
   <alphanumeric expression> "||" <alphanumeric expression>

<column specification> ::=
   [ <table specification> . ] <column name>

<scalar function> ::=
   <function name> ( [ <parameter> [ {,<parameter>}... ] ] )
```

Examples:

```
Alphanumeric expression  Value
-----------------------  --------
'Jim'                    Jim
'Pete and Jim'           Pete and Jim
'1845'                   1845
TOWN                     Stratford   (for example)
USER                     PETE        (for example)
'data'||'base'           database
```

In the last example we use the || operator to concatenate the values of two alphanumeric expressions. Scalar functions are dealt with in Section 6.6.

Example 6.5: Give the player number and the address of each player resident in Stratford.

```
SELECT    PLAYERNO, STREET || ' ' || HOUSENO
FROM      PLAYERS
WHERE     TOWN = 'Stratford'
```

Result:

```
PLAYERNO  STREET || ' ' || HOUSENO
--------  ------------------------
      6   Haseltine Lane 80
     83   Magdalene Road 16A
      2   Stoney Road 43
      7   Edgecombe Way 39
     57   Edgecombe Way 39
     39   Eaton Square 78
    100   Haseltine Lane 80
```

6.6   Scalar functions

Scalar functions are used to perform calculations. A scalar function has zero, one or more *parameters*. The value of a scalar function depends on the values of the parameters. Below we give an example of the SQRT function:

```
SQRT(16)
```

Explanation: SQRT is the name of the scalar function and the number 16 is the parameter. SQRT stands for *square root*. So with SQRT(16) the square root of the number 16 is calculated.

   In Appendix C all the scalar functions are described. In this section we look at just a few examples.

Example 6.6: Give the number, name and length of the name of each player.

```
SELECT    PLAYERNO, NAME, LENGTH(NAME)
FROM      PLAYERS
```

Result:

```
PLAYERNO  NAME       LENGTH(NAME)
--------  ---------  ------------
      6   Parmenter            9
     44   Baker                5
     83   Hope                 4
      2   Everett              7
     27   Collins              7
      :   :                    :
```

Explanation: For each player in the PLAYERS table Oracle determines the value of the scalar function LENGTH(...).

Example 6.7: Get the number and name of each player whose name has exactly seven letters.

```
SELECT    PLAYERNO, NAME
FROM      PLAYERS
WHERE     LENGTH(NAME) = 7
```

Result:

```
PLAYERNO  NAME
--------  -------
       2  Everett
      27  Collins
     104  Moorman
      28  Collins
```

Explanation: From the PLAYERS table Oracle finds, using the LENGTH function, the players whose names have seven letters.

Example 6.8: Give the initials and surname of each player resident in Stratford.

```
SELECT    RTRIM(INITIALS) || '. ' || RTRIM(NAME)
FROM      PLAYERS
WHERE     TOWN = 'Stratford'
```

Result:

```
RTRIM(INITIALS) || '. ' || RTRIM(NAME)
-----------------------------------------
R. Parmenter
PK. Hope
R. Everett
GWS. Wise
M. Brown
D. Bishop
P. Parmenter
```

Explanation: First the initials are printed, followed by a full stop and a space. Finally, the surname is printed.

Example 6.9: Get the player numbers and the sex of each player, who is born after 1963. The sex must be printed with the values 'Female' or 'Male'.

```
SELECT    PLAYERNO,
          DECODE(SEX, 'F','Female', 'M','Male')
FROM      PLAYERS
WHERE     YEAR_OF_BIRTH > 1963
```

Result:

```
PLAYERNO    DECODE(SEX, 'F', 'Female', 'M','Male')
---------   ---------------------------------------
        6   Male
       27   Female
      104   Female
       57   Male
```

Explanation: The DECODE function acts as a kind of IF THEN ELSE statement, used in many programming languages, such as C and Pascal. By using this function as above, for each row that is printed the following statement is executed:

```
IF SEX = 'F' THEN
   PRINT 'Female'
ELSE IF SEX = 'M' THEN
   PRINT 'Male'
END IF
```

Example 6.10: Give the player number and the league number of each player resident in Stratford. If a player has no league number then four dashes must be printed.

```
SELECT   PLAYERNO, NVL(LEAGUENO, '----')
FROM     PLAYERS
WHERE    TOWN = 'Stratford'
```

Result:

```
PLAYERNO    NVL(LEAGUENO, '----')
---------   --------------------
        6   8467
       83   1608
        2   2411
        7   ----
       57   6409
       39   ----
      100   6524
```

Explanation: In this example the result of the NVL function is dependent on the value of the LEAGUENO column. If LEAGUENO is equal to the NULL value, four dashes will be printed; otherwise the value of the column itself is printed.

6.7   Date expressions

The value of a *date expression* identifies a day and a time in seconds precisely.

```
<date expression> ::=
   <date literal>                                         |
   <column specification>                                 |
   <system variable>                                      |
   <scalar function>                                      |
   <statistical function>                                 |
   ( <date expression> )                                  |
   <date expression> { + | - } <numeric expression> |
   <numeric expression> + <date expression>         |
   NULL

<date literal> ::=
   ' <day> - <month> - <year> '

<day> ::= <digit> [ <digit> ]

<month> ::=
   JAN | jan | FEB | feb | MAR | mar | APR | apr |
   MAY | may | JUN | jun | JUL | jul | AUG | aug |
   SEP | sep | OCT | oct | NOV | nov | DEC | dec

<year> ::= <digit> [ <digit> ]

<column specification>  ::=
   [ <table specification> . ] <column name>

<scalar function> ::=
   <function name> ( [ <parameter> [ {,<parameter>}... ] ] )
```

The following applies to the examples below:

- the PEN_DATE column has the value 30 January 1988
- the system variable SYSDATE has the system date as its value
- the scalar function TO_DATE converts an alphanumeric literal to a date

```
Date expression         Value
--------------------    ----------------
'28-AUG-88'             28 August 1988
PEN_DATE                30 January 1988
TO_DATE('25-DEC-77')    25 December 1977
SYSDATE                 5 August 1988
```

A number can be added to or subtracted from a date expression, the result being a new date as many days later (for addition) or earlier (for subtraction) than the original date expression. In doing these calculations Oracle takes into consideration the different lengths of months and leap years.

```
Date expression        Value
----------------       ----------------
'22-AUG-88' + 4        26 August 1988
4 + '22-AUG-88'        26 August 1988
'04-DEC-88' - 5        29 November 1988
'04-NOV-88' - 5        30 October 1988
'04-NOV-88' - 366      4 November 1987
'04-NOV-87' - 366      3 November 1986
```

Example 6.11: Give the number and dates of the penalties incurred in the last 1000 days.

```
SELECT    PLAYERNO, PEN_DATE
FROM      PENALTIES
WHERE     PEN_DATE > SYSDATE - 1000
```

In Chapter 5 we showed you that the value of a DATE data type is composed of six parts: years, months, days, hours, minutes and seconds. In this chapter we explained that a date literal only consists of three parts. What does that mean? Is it not possible to enter the other three parts? The answer is: Yes! We will illustrate this in this section.

In working out a date literal only years, months and days can be specified. Oracle attaches the time 00:00 in the morning (i.e. midnight) automatically. SQL*Plus prints a column with the DATE data type with only the first three parts as standard.

However, if you want to enter the time or want to see the time on a given date, you have to use the scalar functions TO_DATE and TO_CHAR respectively. We give you some examples.

Example 6.12: For each penalty incurred, give the payment number and the date on which the penalty was paid.

```
SELECT    PAYMENTNO, PEN_DATE
FROM      PENALTIES
```

Result:

```
PAYMENTNO  PEN_DATE
---------  ---------
        1  08-DEC-80
        2  05-MAY-81
        3  10-SEP-83
        4  08-DEC-84
        5  08-DEC-80
        6  08-DEC-80
        7  30-DEC-82
        8  12-NOV-84
```

Explanation: As described before, only the first three parts will be shown. If you would like to see all parts, you have to use the TO_CHAR function.

```
SELECT    PAYMENTNO, TO_CHAR(PEN_DATE, 'DD-Mon-YY HH:MI.SS')
FROM      PENALTIES
```

Result:

```
PAYMENTNO  TO_CHAR(PEN_DATE,
---------  -----------------
        1  08-DEC-80 00:00.00
        2  05-MAY-81 00:00.00
        3  10-SEP-83 00:00.00
        4  08-DEC-84 00:00.00
        5  08-DEC-80 00:00.00
        6  08-DEC-80 00:00.00
        7  30-DEC-82 00:00.00
        8  12-NOV-84 00:00.00
```

Explanation: The TO_CHAR function returns the value of a date expression as an alphanumeric value. It has two parameters. The first parameter is the date to be converted. The second parameter contains a so-called *date format* and shows how the date is to be presented. The formats that can be used are described in Appendix C. We give some more examples.

Example 6.13: For each penalty incurred, give the payment number, the date and the day on which the penalty was paid.

```
SELECT    PAYMENTNO, TO_CHAR(PEN_DATE, 'DD Month YY'),
          TO_CHAR(PEN_DATE, 'Day')
FROM      PENALTIES
```

Result:

```
PAYMENTNO  TO_CHAR(PEN_DAT  TO_CHAR(
---------  ---------------  --------
        1  8 December 80    Monday
        2  5 May 81         Tuesday
        3  10 September 83  Saturday
        4  8 December 84    Saturday
        5  8 December 80    Monday
        6  8 December 80    Monday
        7  30 December 82   Thursday
        8  12 November 84   Monday
```

The opposite function of TO_CHAR is TO_DATE. We have to use the TO_DATE function if we want to include a time in a column with the DATE data type.

Example 6.14: Enter a new penalty which has been paid at 3 o'clock in the afternoon.

```
INSERT INTO PENALTIES VALUES
(9, 44, TO_DATE('11-JAN-89 15:00','DD-Mon-YY HH24:MI'),
 75.00)
```

Explanation: The values 9, 44 and 75.00 are respectively the payment number, the player number and the penalty amount. The third value is the TO_DATE function. The TO_DATE function transforms the value of an alphanumeric expression into a date. It has two parameters. The first parameter shows which expression has to be converted. Just like the TO_CHAR function, the second parameter consists of a date format, which shows how the date is constructed. We advise you to study the functions TO_DATE and TO_CHAR carefully before working with dates.

6.8   Statistical functions

Statistical functions are used like scalar functions to perform calculations. They also have parameters. The difference between statistical and scalar functions is that all statistical functions always have one parameter and that the value of that parameter consists of a *set of elements*. Scalar functions, on the other hand, can have zero, one or more parameters whose values consist of one element only. Oracle supports the following statistical functions:

Function	Description
COUNT	Counts the number of values in a column or the number of rows in a table
MIN	Determines the smallest value in a column
MAX	Determines the largest value in a column
SUM	Calculates the sum of the values in a column
AVG	Calculates the arithmetic average of the values in a column
STDDEV	Determines the standard deviation of the values in a column
VARIANCE	Determines the variance of the values in a column

We cover statistical functions in Chapter 10.

7

Clauses of the SELECT statement

7.1 Introduction

In the preceding chapters we have already shown you several examples of SELECT statements. In this chapter these statements will be discussed in more detail. A SELECT statement is composed of a number of clauses, as the definition below shows. In Chapter 14 we extend this definition of the SELECT statement. In the following chapters all these clauses will be explained extensively.

```
<select statement> ::=
   <select clause>
   <from clause>
 [ <where clause> ]
 [ <connect by clause> ]
 [ <group by clause>
 [ <having clause> ] ]
 [ <order by clause> ]
```

The following rules are important when formulating SELECT statements:

- Each SELECT statement has a minimum of two clauses: the SELECT and the FROM clause. The other clauses, such as WHERE, GROUP BY and ORDER BY, are not mandatory.

77

• The order of the clauses is fixed: a GROUP BY clause, for example, may never come before a WHERE or FROM clause, and the ORDER BY clause (when used) is always the last.

• A HAVING clause can only be used if there is a GROUP BY clause.

Below we give a few examples of correct SELECT statements. What follows each different clause is, for the sake of clarity, represented as three dots.

```
SELECT    ...
FROM      ...
ORDER BY ...

SELECT    ...
FROM      ...
GROUP BY ...
HAVING    ...

SELECT    ...
FROM      ...
WHERE     ...
```

In the following two sections, we use two examples to illustrate how Oracle processes SELECT statements; in other words, which steps Oracle executes in order to achieve the desired result.

Exercises

7.1   What is the minimum number of clauses that must be present in a SELECT statement?

7.2   May a SELECT statement have an ORDER BY clause but no WHERE clause?

7.3   May a SELECT statement have a HAVING clause without a GROUP BY clause?

7.4   Decide what in the following SELECT statements is incorrect:

```
1.    SELECT    ...
      WHERE     ...
      ORDER BY ...

2.    SELECT    ...
      FROM      ...
      HAVING    ...
      GROUP BY ...
```

```
3.    SELECT    ...
      ORDER BY ...
      FROM      ...
      GROUP BY ...
```

7.2   Processing a SELECT statement: example 1

This section shows the steps involved when Oracle processes a SELECT statement. It takes the following statement as its starting point:

```
SELECT    PLAYERNO
FROM      PENALTIES
WHERE     AMOUNT > 25
GROUP BY PLAYERNO
HAVING    COUNT(*) > 1
ORDER BY PLAYERNO
```

This SELECT statement gives the answer to the question: find the number for each player who has incurred at least one penalty of more than $25; order the result by player number (the smallest number first).

Figure 7.1 shows the order in which Oracle processes the different clauses. What you will immediately notice is that Oracle changes the order of clauses from that in which the statement was entered. Be careful never to confuse the two.

Explanation: Processing each clause gives rise to one *intermediate result table* that consists of *zero or more rows* and *one or more columns*. This means that every clause, barring the first, has one table of zero or more rows and one or more columns as its input. The first clause, the FROM clause, picks out data from the database, and has as its input *one or more tables* from the database. Those tables that still have to be processed by a subsequent clause are called *intermediate result tables*. Oracle does not show the user any of the intermediate result tables; it is presented as a single, large process, and the only table the end user gets to see is the end result table.

The statements are not actually processed by Oracle in the way which is described here. In practice, Oracle processes as many clauses as possible simultaneously, in order to speed up the execution of the statement. Chapter 20 examines how Oracle actually processes the statements. The method of processing described above, though, is extremely well suited if you want to determine the end result of a SELECT statement 'by hand'.

We now examine the clauses one by one.

7.2.1   The FROM clause

Only the PENALTIES table is named in the FROM clause. For Oracle, this means that it will work with this table. The intermediate result from this clause is an exact copy of the PENALTIES table.

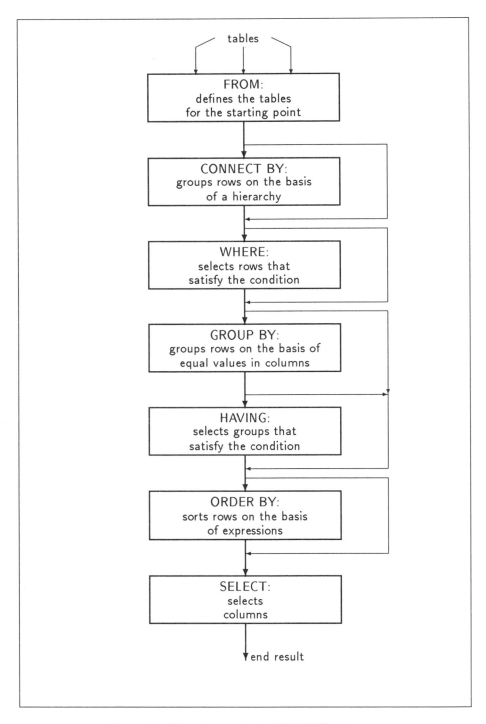

Figure 7.1: The clauses in the SELECT statement

Intermediate result:

```
PAYMENTNO  PLAYERNO  PEN_DATE   AMOUNT
---------  --------  ---------  ------
        1         6  08-DEC-80  100.00
        2        44  05-MAY-81   75.00
        3        27  10-SEP-83  100.00
        4       104  08-DEC-84   50.00
        5        44  08-DEC-80   25.00
        6         8  08-DEC-80   25.00
        7        44  30-DEC-82   30.00
        8        27  12-NOV-84   75.00
```

7.2.2   The CONNECT BY clause

There is no CONNECT BY clause, therefore the intermediate result remains unchanged and is passed to the next clause.

7.2.3   The WHERE clause

The WHERE clause specifies AMOUNT > 25 as a condition. All rows where the value in the AMOUNT column is more than 25 satisfy the condition. Therefore the rows with payment numbers of 5 and 6 are discarded, while the remaining rows form the intermediate result table from the WHERE clause:

```
PAYMENTNO  PLAYERNO  PEN_DATE   AMOUNT
---------  --------  ---------  ------
        1         6  08-DEC-80  100.00
        2        44  05-MAY-81   75.00
        3        27  10-SEP-83  100.00
        4       104  08-DEC-84   50.00
        7        44  30-DEC-82   30.00
        8        27  12-NOV-84   75.00
```

7.2.4   The GROUP BY clause

The GROUP BY clause groups the rows in the intermediate result table. Oracle divides the data into groups on the basis of the values in the PLAYERNO column (GROUP BY PLAYERNO). Rows are grouped together if, in the grouping column, they contain the same values. The rows with PAYMENTNOs of 2 and 7, for example, form one group, because the PLAYERNO column has the value of 44 in both rows.

Intermediate result:

```
PAYMENTNO   PLAYERNO   PEN_DATE                AMOUNT
---------   --------   --------------------    ------------
1                  6   08-DEC-80               100.00
2, 7              44   05-MAY-81, 30-DEC-82    75.00, 30.00
3, 8              27   10-SEP-83, 12-NOV-84    100.00, 75.00
4                104   08-DEC-84               50.00
```

Explanation: Thus, for all but the PLAYERNO column there can be more than one value in a row. The PAYMENTNO column, for example, contains two values in the second and third rows. This is not as strange as it might seem, because the data is grouped and each row is actually formed from a group of rows. It is only in the PLAYERNO column that a single value for each row of the intermediate table may be found, since this is the column by which the result is grouped.

7.2.5 The HAVING clause

In some ways you could compare the HAVING clause with the WHERE clause. The difference is that the WHERE clause acts on the intermediate table from the FROM clause and the HAVING clause on the grouped intermediate result table of the GROUP BY clause. In fact, the effect is the same; when you include a HAVING clause Oracle also selects rows by referring to a condition. In this case the condition is:

```
COUNT(*) > 1
```

This condition is satisfied in all rows (groups) where more than one penalty exists. Chapter 11 looks at this condition in detail.

Intermediate result:

```
PAYMENTNO   PLAYERNO   PEN_DATE                AMOUNT
---------   --------   --------------------    ------------
2, 7              44   05-MAY-81, 30-DEC-82    75.00, 30.00
3, 8              27   10-SEP-83, 12-NOV-84    100.00, 75.00
```

7.2.6 The ORDER BY clause

This clause has no impact on the contents of the intermediate result table, but sorts the final remaining rows. In this example the data is sorted on PLAYER-NO.

Intermediate result:

```
PAYMENTNO   PLAYERNO   PEN_DATE                AMOUNT
---------   --------   --------------------    ------------
3, 8              27   10-SEP-83, 12-NOV-84    100.00, 75.00
2, 7              44   05-MAY-81, 30-DEC-82    75.00, 30.00
```

7.2.7   The SELECT clause

The SELECT clause specifies which columns must be presented for the final result table. In other words, the SELECT clause selects columns.
The end result is:

```
PLAYERNO
--------
      27
      44
```

7.3   Processing a SELECT statement: example 2

Here is another example of SELECT statement processing.

Example 7.1: Get the player number and the league number of each player resident in Stratford; order the result by league number.

```
SELECT    PLAYERNO, LEAGUENO
FROM      PLAYERS
WHERE     TOWN = 'Stratford'
ORDER BY LEAGUENO
```

7.3.1   The FROM clause

Intermediate result:

```
PLAYERNO  NAME              ...  LEAGUENO
--------  ----------------  ---  --------
       6  Parmenter         ...  8467
      44  Baker             ...  1124
      83  Hope              ...  1608
       2  Everett           ...  2411
      27  Collins           ...  2513
     104  Moorman           ...  7060
       7  Wise              ...  ?
      57  Brown             ...  6409
      39  Bishop            ...  ?
     112  Bailey            ...  1319
       8  Newcastle         ...  2983
     100  Parmenter         ...  6524
      28  Collins           ...  ?
      95  Miller            ...  ?
```

7.3.2 The CONNECT BY clause

There is no CONNECT BY clause, therefore the intermediate result remains unchanged.

7.3.3 The WHERE clause

Intermediate result:

```
PLAYERNO    NAME              ...   LEAGUENO
--------    --------------    ---   --------
       6    Parmenter         ...   8467
      83    Hope              ...   1608
       2    Everett           ...   2411
       7    Wise              ...   ?
      57    Brown             ...   6409
      39    Bishop            ...   ?
     100    Parmenter         ...   6524
```

7.3.4 The GROUP BY clause

There is no GROUP BY clause, therefore the intermediate result remains unchanged.

7.3.5 The HAVING clause

There is no HAVING BY clause, therefore the intermediate result remains unchanged.

7.3.6 The ORDER BY clause

Intermediate result:

```
PLAYERNO  NAME              ...   LEAGUENO
--------  --------------    ---   --------
      83  Hope              ...   1608
       2  Everett           ...   2411
      57  Brown             ...   6409
     100  Parmenter         ...   6524
       6  Parmenter         ...   8467
       7  Wise              ...   ?
      39  Bishop            ...   ?
```

Note: NULL values are presented last by Oracle if the result is sorted. Chapter 12 will describe this in greater depth.

7.3.7 The SELECT clause

In the SELECT clause the PLAYERNO and LEAGUENO columns are noted and this gives the following end result:

```
PLAYERNO  LEAGUENO
--------  --------
      83  1608
       2  2411
      57  6409
     100  6524
       6  8467
       7  ?
      39  ?
```

In the following chapters the different clauses will be discussed in greater depth.

Exercise

7.5 Take the following SELECT statement and calculate the result table after each clause has been processed. Give the final result as well.

```
SELECT    PLAYERNO
FROM      PENALTIES
WHERE     PEN_DATE > '08-DEC-80'
GROUP BY  PLAYERNO
HAVING    COUNT(*) > 1
ORDER BY  PLAYERNO
```

7.4   The layout of the result

SQL*Plus creates a standard layout for the results of SELECT statements. First, the column names are printed, followed by the rows. In this way, there is a standard method of presentation for each data type. You can use SET commands of SQL*Plus (this command has already been described briefly in Section 2.12) to adapt the layout. This section shows you some features of this command.

```
<set command> ::=
   SET HEADING { ON | OFF }    |
   SET PAGESIZE <integer>      |
   SET NULL <character>...     |
   SET SPACE <integer>
```

The *SET HEADING command* enables you to suppress column headings. The default is to have them printed.

The *SET PAGESIZE command* defines how many lines fit on one page. The default is 14.

The *SET NULL command* is used to define how the NULL value has to be shown. The default is a blank. In this book a question mark is printed when a NULL value has to be shown. We have already shown this at some places in this and previous chapters.

The *SET SPACE command* defines how many blanks there are between two columns. The default is one blank. In this book usually we use two blanks.

8
SELECT statement: the FROM clause

In this chapter we describe the FROM clause, which is used to specify which table or tables are to be queried.

```
<from clause> ::=
    FROM <table reference> [ {,<table reference> }... ]

<table reference> ::=
    <table specification> [ <pseudonym> ]

<table specification> ::= [ <user> . ] <table name>
```

8.1 Tables and their owners

Two tables may have the same name if they belong to different owners. If, in a FROM clause, you refer to a table created by someone else, you *must* specify the name of the owner before the table name. This is not required if you are the owner of the table.

Example 8.1: JIM wants to see the entire contents of the ORDERS table, which has been created by WILLIAM (assume also that JIM has the authority to query this table):

```
SELECT    *
FROM      WILLIAM.ORDERS
```

Explanation: The new compound name WILLIAM.ORDERS is called a *table specification* (note the full stop between the owner's name and the table name; this full stop is mandatory). It is also known that the table name ORDERS will be *qualified* with the owner's name WILLIAM.

If the user called WILLIAM wants to see the contents of the ORDERS table, he can use the above statement, but he may also leave out his own name:

```
SELECT    *
FROM      ORDERS
```

A user is the owner of a table if he or she has entered and executed the CREATE TABLE statement which set it up, or when a CREATE TABLE statement has been entered with his or her name before the table name. A table can only ever be created by one user. The CREATE TABLE statement for the ORDERS table has, in this case, been entered by WILLIAM.

Instead of a table name you can also specify a view name or a synonym. Again, this is called a table specification.

8.2   The column specification

You may specify a table with the name of the owner. When you specify columns, you have to give an indication of which table the columns belong to. In fact, each reference to a column consists of three parts:

```
<user> . <table name> . <column name>
```

The last part is, of course, the column name itself, such as PLAYERNO or NAME. This is the only part that must always be used. The second part is the table name, for example, PLAYERS or TEAMS. Together these three parts form the *column specification*. You don't have to specify the first two parts, but it is not wrong to do so.

Example 8.2: Find the number of each team.

Here are three possible solutions. Assume that WILLIAM is the owner of the TEAMS table.

```
SELECT    TEAMNO
FROM      TEAMS

SELECT    TEAMS.TEAMNO
FROM      TEAMS

SELECT    WILLIAM.TEAMS.TEAMNO
FROM      WILLIAM.TEAMS
```

8.3 Multiple table specifications

Up until now we have used only one table specification in the FROM clause. If we want to present data in our result table from different tables, then these must all be named in the FROM clause.

Example 8.3: Find the team number and name of the captain of each team.

The TEAMS table holds information about team numbers and the player numbers of the respective captains. However, the names of the captains are not stored in the TEAMS table, but in the PLAYERS table. In other words, we need both tables. Both must be mentioned in the FROM clause.

```
SELECT   TEAMNO, NAME
FROM     TEAMS, PLAYERS
WHERE    TEAMS.PLAYERNO = PLAYERS.PLAYERNO
```

The intermediate result from the FROM clause:

TEAMNO	PLAYERNO	DIVISION	PLAYERNO	NAME	...
1	6	first	6	Parmenter	...
1	6	first	44	Baker	...
1	6	first	83	Hope	...
1	6	first	2	Everett	...
1	6	first	27	Collins	...
1	6	first	104	Moorman	...
1	6	first	7	Wise	...
1	6	first	57	Brown	...
1	6	first	39	Bishop	...
1	6	first	112	Bailey	...
1	6	first	8	Newcastle	...
1	6	first	100	Parmenter	...
1	6	first	28	Collins	...
1	6	first	95	Miller	...
2	27	second	6	Parmenter	...
2	27	second	44	Baker	...
2	27	second	83	Hope	...
2	27	second	2	Everett	...
2	27	second	27	Collins	...
2	27	second	104	Moorman	...
2	27	second	7	Wise	...
2	27	second	57	Brown	...
2	27	second	39	Bishop	...
2	27	second	112	Bailey	...
:	: :		:	:	:

```
:           :   :              :   :              :
2          27  second         8   Newcastle      ...
2          27  second        100  Parmenter      ...
2          27  second        28   Collins        ...
2          27  second        95   Miller         ...
```

Explanation: Each row from the TEAMS table is aligned beside each row from the PLAYERS table. This results in a table in which the total number of columns equals the number of columns in one table *plus* the number of columns in the other table, and in which the total number of rows equals the number of rows in one table *multiplied* by the number of rows in the other table. We call this result the *Cartesian product* of the tables concerned.

In the WHERE clause each row is now selected where the values in the TEAMS.PLAYERNO column equal those in the PLAYERS.PLAYERNO column:

```
TEAMNO  PLAYERNO  DIVISION  PLAYERNO  NAME          ...
------  --------  --------  --------  ----------    ---
     1         6  first            6  Parmenter     ...
     2        27  second          27  Collins       ...
```

End result:

```
TEAMNO  NAME
------  ----------
     1  Parmenter
     2  Collins
```

In this example, it is essential to identify the table name before the PLAYERNO column, otherwise it would be unclear to Oracle which PLAYERNO column was intended.

Conclusion: If, in the FROM clause, you use a column name that appears in more than one table, it is *mandatory* to include a table specification with the column specification.

Example 8.4: For each penalty, find the payment number, the amount of the penalty, the player number, the name and the initials of the player who incurred the penalty.

The payment numbers, amounts and player numbers are held in the PENALTIES table, while names and initials are found in the PLAYERS table. Both tables must be mentioned in the FROM clause:

```
SELECT    PAYMENTNO, AMOUNT, PENALTIES.PLAYERNO,
          NAME, INITIALS
FROM      PENALTIES, PLAYERS
WHERE     PENALTIES.PLAYERNO = PLAYERS.PLAYERNO
```

Intermediate result from the FROM clause:

PAYMENTNO	PLAYERNO	AMOUNT	...	PLAYERNO	NAME	INITIALS	...
1	6	100.00	...	6	Parmenter	R	...
1	6	100.00	...	44	Baker	E	...
1	6	100.00	...	83	Hope	PK	...
1	6	100.00	...	2	Everett	R	...
:	:	:		:	:	:	
2	44	75.00	...	6	Parmenter	R	...
2	44	75.00	...	44	Baker	E	...
2	44	75.00	...	83	Hope	PK	...
2	44	75.00	...	2	Everett	R	...
:	:	:		:	:	:	
3	27	100.00	...	6	Parmenter	R	...
3	27	100.00	...	44	Baker	E	...
3	27	100.00	...	83	Hope	PK	...
3	27	100.00	...	2	Everett	R	...
:	:	:		:	:	:	
:	:	:		:	:	:	

Intermediate result from the WHERE clause:

PAYMENTNO	PLAYERNO	AMOUNT	...	PLAYERNO	NAME	INITIALS	...
1	6	100.00	...	6	Parmenter	R	...
2	44	75.00	...	44	Baker	E	...
3	27	100.00	...	27	Collins	DD	...
4	104	50.00	...	104	Moorman	D	...
5	44	25.00	...	44	Baker	E	...
6	8	25.00	...	8	Newcastle	B	...
7	44	30.00	...	44	Baker	E	...
8	27	75.00	...	27	Collins	DD	...

End result:

PAYMENTNO	PLAYERNO	AMOUNT	NAME	INITIALS
1	6	100.00	Parmenter	R
2	44	75.00	Baker	E
3	27	100.00	Collins	DD
4	104	50.00	Moorman	D
5	44	25.00	Baker	E
6	8	25.00	Newcastle	B
7	44	30.00	Baker	E
8	27	75.00	Collins	DD

To avoid ambiguity the table name must be specified before the PLAYERNO column in the SELECT clause.

8.4   The pseudonym

In cases where multiple table specifications appear in the FROM clause, it is sometimes easier to use *pseudonyms*. Another name for a pseudonym is *alias*. Pseudonyms are temporary alternative names for table names. In the previous examples we repeated the table name in its entirety. In place of table names we can also use pseudonyms as this next example shows.

```
SELECT    PAYMENTNO, AMOUNT, PN.PLAYERNO, NAME, INITIALS
FROM      PENALTIES PN, PLAYERS P
WHERE     PN.PLAYERNO = P.PLAYERNO
```

In the FROM clause the pseudonyms are specified after the table names. In other clauses we can use these pseudonyms instead of the real table names. That the pseudonym PN is used sooner in the statement (in the SELECT clause) than that it has been declared (in the FROM clause) does not cause any problems. As you know, the FROM clause is the first clause to be processed.

In fact, in this example a pseudonym is not vital, but we will be formulating SELECT statements in this book where the table name is repeated many times, and then the value of pseudonyms becomes more obvious. Pseudonyms make for easier formulation of statements and, at the same time, give a more convenient, clearer structure to a statement.

8.5   Various examples

This section looks at a few examples illustrating various aspects of the FROM clause.

Example 8.5: Get the numbers of the captains who have incurred at least one penalty.

```
SELECT    T.PLAYERNO
FROM      TEAMS T, PENALTIES PN
WHERE     T.PLAYERNO = PN.PLAYERNO
```

Explanation: The TEAMS table includes all the players who are captains. By using the player numbers we can look up in the PENALTIES table whether a particular captain has incurred at least one penalty. For that reason, both tables are included in the FROM clause. The intermediate result from the FROM clause becomes:

```
TEAMNO  PLAYERNO  DIVISION  PAYMENTNO  PLAYERNO  ...
------  --------  --------  ---------  --------  ---
     1         6  first             1         6  ...
     1         6  first             2        44  ...
     1         6  first             3        27  ...
     1         6  first             4       104  ...
     1         6  first             5        44  ...
     1         6  first             6         8  ...
     1         6  first             7        44  ...
     1         6  first             8        27  ...
     2        27  second            1         6  ...
     2        27  second            2        44  ...
     2        27  second            3        27  ...
     2        27  second            4       104  ...
     2        27  second            5        44  ...
     2        27  second            6         8  ...
     2        27  second            7        44  ...
     2        27  second            8        27  ...
```

Intermediate result from the WHERE clause:

```
TEAMNO  PLAYERNO  DIVISION  PAYMENTNO  PLAYERNO  ...
------  --------  --------  ---------  --------  ---
     1         6  first             1         6  ...
     2        27  second            3        27  ...
     2        27  second            8        27  ...
```

End result:

```
PLAYERNO
--------
       6
      27
      27
```

Note: Oracle does not automatically remove duplicate values from the end result. In our example, then, player 27 appears twice because she incurred two penalties. If you don't want duplicate values in your result, then you need to use the word DISTINCT directly after the SELECT (we go into more detail in Chapter 10).

```
SELECT   DISTINCT T.PLAYERNO
FROM     TEAMS T, PENALTIES PN
WHERE    T.PLAYERNO = PN.PLAYERNO
```

End result:

```
PLAYERNO
--------
       6
      27
```

Example 8.6: Give the names and initials of the players who have played at least one match. Warning: a competition player does not have to appear in the MATCHES table (perhaps if he or she has been injured for the whole season).

```
SELECT   DISTINCT P.NAME, P.INITIALS
FROM     PLAYERS P, MATCHES MAT
WHERE    P.PLAYERNO = MAT.PLAYERNO
```

Result:

```
NAME        INITIALS
---------   --------
Parmenter   R
Baker       E
Hope        PK
Everett     R
Collins     DD
Moorman     D
Brown       M
Bailey      IP
Newcastle   B
```

Work out for yourself how this SELECT statement could give rise to duplicate values if DISTINCT was not used.

Example 8.7: For each match give the player number, the team number, the name of the player and the division in which the team plays.

```
SELECT   DISTINCT MAT.PLAYERNO, MAT.TEAMNO, P.NAME,
         T.DIVISION
FROM     MATCHES MAT, PLAYERS P, TEAMS T
WHERE    MAT.PLAYERNO = P.PLAYERNO
AND      MAT.TEAMNO   = T.TEAMNO
```

Result:

```
PLAYERNO   TEAMNO   NAME        DIVISION
--------   ------   ---------   --------
       2        1   Everett     first
       6        1   Parmenter   first
       8        1   Newcastle   first
       8        2   Newcastle   second
      27        2   Collins     second
      44        1   Baker       first
      57        1   Brown       first
      83        1   Hope        first
     104        2   Moorman     second
     112        2   Bailey      second
```

The order of the table specifications in a FROM clause naturally has no influence on the result the clause produces or on the end result of the statement. The SELECT clause is the only clause where you can define the order of presentation of the columns. The ORDER BY clause defines the order of the values in the rows. Therefore, the next two statements are equivalent:

```
SELECT    PLAYERS.PLAYERNO
FROM      PLAYERS, TEAMS
WHERE     PLAYERS.PLAYERNO = TEAMS.PLAYERNO
```

and

```
SELECT    PLAYERS.PLAYERNO
FROM      TEAMS, PLAYERS
WHERE     PLAYERS.PLAYERNO = TEAMS.PLAYERNO
```

8.6   Mandatory use of pseudonyms

In some SELECT statements there is no choice about whether a pseudonym is to be used or not. This situation arises when the same table is mentioned more than once in the FROM clause. Consider this example.

Example 8.8: Get the numbers of the players who are older than R. Parmenter.

```
SELECT    P.PLAYERNO
FROM      PLAYERS P, PLAYERS PAR
WHERE     PAR.NAME = 'Parmenter'
AND       PAR.INITIALS = 'R'
AND       P.YEAR_OF_BIRTH < PAR.YEAR_OF_BIRTH
```

The intermediate result from the WHERE clause is a multiplication of the PLAYERS table by itself (for simplicity we have shown only the rows from the P table in which player 6 is found: R. Parmenter):

PLAYERNO	...	YEAR_OF_B	...	PLAYERNO	...	YEAR_OF_B	...
6	...	1964	...	6	...	1964	...
44	...	1963	...	6	...	1964	...
83	...	1956	...	6	...	1964	...
2	...	1948	...	6	...	1964	...
27	...	1964	...	6	...	1964	...
104	...	1970	...	6	...	1964	...
7	...	1963	...	6	...	1964	...
57	...	1971	...	6	...	1964	...
39	...	1956	...	6	...	1964	...
:	:	:	:	:	:	:	:

```
  :   :              :   :              :   :              :   :
112   ...         1963   ...          6   ...          1964   ...
  8   ...         1962   ...          6   ...          1964   ...
100   ...         1963   ...          6   ...          1964   ...
 28   ...         1963   ...          6   ...          1964   ...
 95   ...         1934   ...          6   ...          1964   ...
  :   :              :   :              :   :              :   :
  :   :              :   :              :   :              :   :
```

The intermediate result from the WHERE clause is:

```
PLAYERNO  ...  YEAR_OF_B  ...  PLAYERNO  ...  YEAR_OF_B  ...
--------  ---  ---------  ---  --------  ---  ---------  ---
      44  ...       1963  ...         6  ...       1964  ...
      83  ...       1956  ...         6  ...       1964  ...
       2  ...       1948  ...         6  ...       1964  ...
       7  ...       1963  ...         6  ...       1964  ...
      39  ...       1956  ...         6  ...       1964  ...
     112  ...       1963  ...         6  ...       1964  ...
       8  ...       1962  ...         6  ...       1964  ...
     100  ...       1963  ...         6  ...       1964  ...
      28  ...       1963  ...         6  ...       1964  ...
      95  ...       1934  ...         6  ...       1964  ...
```

The end result is:

```
PLAYERNO
--------
      44
      83
       2
       7
      39
     112
       8
     100
      28
      95
```

In the previous examples the table name was specified before the column name in order to identify the column uniquely. In the example immediately above, this does not help because both tables have the same name. In other words, if a FROM clause refers to two tables with the same name, pseudonyms must be used.

Note: It would have been sufficient to give only one of the tables a pseudonym in that example.

```
SELECT    P.PLAYERNO
FROM      PLAYERS P, PLAYERS
WHERE     PLAYERS.NAME = 'Parmenter'
AND       PLAYERS.INITIALS = 'R'
AND       P.YEAR_OF_BIRTH < PLAYERS.YEAR_OF_BIRTH
```

Exercises

8.1 Say why the SELECT statements below are not correctly formulated.

1.  ```
    SELECT    PLAYERNO
    FROM      PLAYERS, TEAMS
    ```

2.  ```
    SELECT    PLAYERS.PLAYERNO
    FROM      TEAMS
    ```

3.  ```
    SELECT    PLAYERS.PLAYERNO
    FROM      PETE.PLAYERS, JIM.PLAYERS
    ```

8.2 For each clause of the following statement, determine the intermediate result and the end result. Also give a description of the question which underlies the statement.

```
SELECT    PLAYERS.NAME
FROM      TEAMS, PLAYERS
WHERE     PLAYERS.PLAYERNO = TEAMS.PLAYERNO
```

8.3 For each penalty, find the payment number, the amount, and the number and name of the player who incurred it.

8.4 For each penalty incurred by a team captain, find the payment number and the captain's name.

8.5 Give the numbers and names of the players who live in the same town as player 27.

8.6 Give the number and name of every competition player, as well as the number and name of the captain of each team for whom that player has competed. The result may *not* contain competition players who are themselves captains. Desired result:

PLAYERNO	NAME (PLAYERS)	PLAYERNO	NAME (CAPTAIN)
44	Baker	6	Parmenter
8	Newcastle	6	Parmenter
8	Newcastle	27	Collins
:	:	:	:
:	:	:	:
```

9
SELECT statement: the WHERE clause

In the WHERE clause, the rows which must be provided for the final result are defined by a condition or series of conditions. In this chapter we describe what kind of conditions are permitted in the WHERE clause.

9.1   Introduction

How is a WHERE clause processed? Oracle looks at all the rows individually that appear in the intermediate result table of a FROM clause. If, for a particular row, the condition is true, the row concerned is passed to the intermediate result table for the WHERE clause. This process can be formally described in the following way:

```
WHERE-RESULT := [];
FOR EACH R IN FROM-RESULT DO
   IF CONDITION = TRUE THEN
       WHERE-RESULT :+ R;
OD;
```

Explanation: The WHERE-RESULT and the FROM-RESULT represent two sets in which rows of data can be temporarily stored. R represents a row from a set. The symbol [] represents the empty set. A row is added to the set with the operator :+. This notation method is also used later in the book.

The definition of condition is shown below. In this book we consider the terms *condition* and *predicate* as equivalent and use them interchangeably.

```
<condition> ::=
    <predicate>                        |
    <predicate> OR <predicate>   |
    <predicate> AND <predicate>  |
    ( <condition> )                    |
    NOT <condition>

<predicate> ::=
    <predicate with comparison>  |
    <predicate with between>     |
    <predicate with in>          |
    <predicate with like>        |
    <predicate with null>        |
    <predicate with exists>      |
    <predicate with any all>
```

In the previous chapters you have seen many examples of possible conditions in the WHERE clause. In this chapter the following forms are described:

- the comparison operator
- conditions coupled with AND, OR and NOT
- the BETWEEN operator
- the IN operator
- the LIKE operator
- the NULL operator
- the IN operator with subquery
- the comparison operator with subquery
- · the ANY and ALL operators
- the EXISTS operator

All conditions described in this chapter are built on one or more expressions. In Chapter 6 we saw that a statistical function can be a correct expression. However, statistical functions are not permitted in the condition of a WHERE clause!

9.2   The condition with a comparison operator

The simplest form for a condition is a comparison between two expressions. Such a condition is formed by an expression (for example 83 or 15 * 100), a *comparison operator* (for example < or =) and then another expression. The value on the left of the operator is compared with the expression on the right. The condition is *true*, *false* or *unknown* depending on the operator. Oracle recognizes the following comparison operators:

Comparison operator	Meaning
=	equal to
<	less than
>	greater than
<=	less than or equal to
>=	greater than or equal to
<> or != or ∧=	not equal to

We show you the definition of this condition below. In Section 9.9 we extend this definition.

```
<predicate with comparison> ::=
   <expression> <comparison operator> <expression> |
   <row expression> { = | <> | != | ^= } ( <row expression> )

<comparison operator> ::=
   = | < | > | <= | >= | <> | != | ^=

<row expression> ::=
   ( <expression> [ {,<expression>}... ] )
```

Example 9.1: Get the number of each player resident in Stratford.

```
SELECT   PLAYERNO
FROM     PLAYERS
WHERE    TOWN = 'Stratford'
```

Result:

```
PLAYERNO
--------
       6
      83
       2
       7
      57
      39
     100
```

Explanation: Only the PLAYERNO is printed for any row where the value of the TOWN column is equal to Stratford, because then the condition TOWN = 'Stratford' is true.

Example 9.2: Give the number, the year of birth and the year of joining the club for each player who joined precisely 17 years after he or she was born.

```
SELECT    PLAYERNO, YEAR_OF_BIRTH, YEAR_JOINED
FROM      PLAYERS
WHERE     YEAR_OF_BIRTH + 17 = YEAR_JOINED
```

Result:

```
PLAYERNO  YEAR_OF_BIRTH  YEAR_JOINED
--------  -------------  -----------
      44           1963         1980
```

The condition in this statement could be expressed in other ways:

```
WHERE YEAR_OF_BIRTH = YEAR_JOINED - 17
WHERE YEAR_OF_BIRTH - YEAR_JOINED + 17 = 0
```

If the condition for rows is *unknown*, they will not be included in the result. We give you an example.

Example 9.3: Get the player numbers for those players who have a league number of 7060.

```
SELECT    PLAYERNO
FROM      PLAYERS
WHERE     LEAGUENO = '7060'
```

Result:

```
PLAYERNO
--------
     104
```

Explanation: The PLAYERNO is only printed for rows where the LEAGUENO is equal to 7060, because only then the condition is true. The rows where the LEAGUENO column has the NULL value will not be printed, because the value of such a condition is *unknown*. If the NULL value appears somewhere in a condition regardless of the type of the expression (numeric, alphanumeric or date) then it evaluates to unknown. For some statements this can lead to unexpected results. We give you an example of where the condition at first sight looks a little peculiar.

Example 9.4: Get the numbers and league numbers of the players, who have a league number.

```
SELECT    PLAYERNO, LEAGUENO
FROM      PLAYERS
WHERE     LEAGUENO = LEAGUENO
```

Result:

```
PLAYERNO   LEAGUENO
--------   --------
       6   8467
      44   1124
      83   1608
       2   2411
      27   2513
     104   7060
      57   6409
     112   1319
       8   2983
     100   6524
```

Explanation: Each row where the LEAGUENO column is filled will be printed, because here the LEAGUENO is equal to the LEAGUENO. If the LEAGUENO column is not filled, the condition evaluates to unknown. The reason is that if a NULL value appears in a condition, the value of the condition is equal to unknown. Section 9.7 describes a 'cleaner' way to answer the question above.

When comparing alphanumeric values, one expression is less than another if it comes first in alphabetical order. Examples (note that a lower case letter is not equal to its upper case equivalent):

```
Condition            Value
------------------   -----
'Jim' < 'Pete'       TRUE
'Truck' >= 'Trees'   TRUE
'Jim' = 'JIM'        FALSE
```

One date is less than another if it comes before the other in time. Examples:

```
Condition                 Value
----------------------    -----
'8-DEC-85' < '9-DEC-85'   TRUE
'2-MAY-80' > '31-DEC-79'  TRUE
```

In a comparison more values can be compared simultaneously. These combinations are called *row expressions*. A row expression consists of one or more expressions enclosed between brackets. Two row expressions R_1 and R_2 consisting of the expressions $R_1.E_1, R_1.E_2, \ldots, R_1.E_n$ and $R_2.E_1, R_2.E_2, \ldots, R_2.E_n$ are equivalent if for every E_i (where $1 <= i <= n$) $R_1.E_i = R_2.E_i$ holds. If not, then they are not equal. This means that if one of the expressions has the NULL value, the value of the condition is unknown.

Example 9.5: Give the number and name of each player who lives at Haseltine Lane in Stratford (notice the multiple brackets).

```
SELECT   PLAYERNO, NAME
FROM     PLAYERS
WHERE    (STREET, TOWN) = (('Haseltine Lane', 'Stratford'))
```

Result:

```
PLAYERNO  NAME
--------  ---------
       6  Parmenter
     100  Parmenter
```

Note: Only the operators 'equal to' and 'not equal to' can be used when row expressions are compared. The following two conditions are equivalent:

```
(E1, E2, E3) <> (E4, E5, E6)

NOT ( (E1, E2, E3) = (E4, E5, E6) )
```

Exercises

9.1 Find the number of each player born after 1960 (give at least two possible SELECT statements).

9.2 Get the number of each team whose captain is someone other than player 27.

9.3 What is the result of the following SELECT statement:

```
SELECT   PLAYERNO, LEAGUENO
FROM     PLAYERS
WHERE    LEAGUENO > LEAGUENO
```

9.4 Get the number of each player who has won one match in at least one team.

9.5 Find the number of each player who has played at least one match with five sets.

9.3   Multiple conditions with AND, OR and NOT

A WHERE clause may contain multiple conditions if the *AND*, *OR* and *NOT* operators are used.

Example 9.6: Get the number, name, sex and year of birth of each male player born after 1970.

```
SELECT   PLAYERNO, NAME, SEX, YEAR_OF_BIRTH
FROM     PLAYERS
WHERE    SEX = 'M'
AND      YEAR_OF_BIRTH > 1970
```

Result:

```
PLAYERNO   NAME   SEX   YEAR_OF_BIRTH
--------   -----  ---   -------------
      57   Brown   M             1971
```

Explanation: For every person in the PLAYERS table where the value in the SEX column equals M and the value in the YEAR_OF_BIRTH column is greater than 1970, Oracle returns four columns to the result table.

Example 9.7: Get the numbers, names and places of residence of all players who live in Plymouth or Eltham.

```
SELECT    PLAYERNO, NAME, TOWN
FROM      PLAYERS
WHERE     PLACE = 'Plymouth'
OR        PLACE = 'Eltham'
```

Result:

```
PLAYERNO   NAME      TOWN
--------   -------   --------
      27   Collins   Eltham
     104   Moorman   Eltham
     112   Bailey    Plymouth
```

Note: This SELECT statement would return an *empty result table* if OR were replaced by AND. The reason is obvious.

If a WHERE clause contains more than one AND or OR operator, all ANDs will be processed first. So in the WHERE clause (assume C1 to C3 represent conditions):

```
WHERE C1 OR C2 AND C3
```

C2 AND C3 is evaluated first. Suppose that the result of this is A1. The final result is the value of C1 OR A1. The process can also be represented in this way:

```
C2 AND C3 --> A1
C1 OR A1 --> result
```

By using brackets you can influence the order in which the conditions are evaluated. Consider the following WHERE clause:

```
WHERE (C1 OR C2) AND C3
```

The processing sequence now becomes:

```
C1 OR  C2 --> A1
A1 AND C3 --> result
```

With any given value for C1, C2 and C3 the results of the first and second examples are unlikely to be the same. Suppose, for example, that C1 is true and that C2 and C3 are false. The result of the first example is true and of the second false.

A NOT operator can be specified before each condition. The NOT operator changes the value of a condition to true if it is false and false if it is true. The NOT operator does not change the value of a condition if its value is unknown.

Example 9.8: Find the numbers, names and towns of players who *do not* live in Stratford.

```
SELECT    PLAYERNO, NAME, TOWN
FROM      PLAYERS
WHERE     TOWN <> 'Stratford'
```

Result:

```
PLAYERNO  NAME        TOWN
--------  ---------   ----------
      44  Baker       Inglewood
      27  Collins     Eltham
     104  Moorman     Eltham
     112  Bailey      Plymouth
       8  Newcastle   Inglewood
      28  Collins     Midhurst
      95  Miller      Douglas
```

This query can be formulated in another way:

```
SELECT    PLAYERNO, NAME, TOWN
FROM      PLAYERS
WHERE     NOT TOWN = 'Stratford'
```

Explanation: The rows where the condition TOWN = 'Stratford' is true are not returned. The reason is that the NOT operator has switched the truth of the condition.

Example 9.9: Give the number, town and year of birth of each player who lives in Stratford, or was born in 1963, but do not include those who were born in Stratford and born in 1963.

```
SELECT    PLAYERNO, TOWN, YEAR_OF_BIRTH
FROM      PLAYERS
WHERE     (TOWN = 'Stratford' OR  YEAR_OF_BIRTH = 1963)
AND NOT (TOWN = 'Stratford' AND YEAR_OF_BIRTH = 1963)
```

Result:

```
PLAYERNO  TOWN       YEAR_OF_BIRTH
--------  ---------  -------------
       6  Stratford           1964
      44  Inglewood           1963
      83  Stratford           1956
       2  Stratford           1948
      57  Stratford           1971
      39  Stratford           1956
     112  Plymouth            1963
      28  Midhurst            1963
```

The *truth table* below contains all possible values with AND, OR and NOT for two conditions C_1 and C_2

C_1	C_2	C_1 AND C_2	C_1 OR C_2	NOT C_1
true	true	true	true	false
true	false	false	true	false
true	unknown	unknown	true	false
false	true	false	true	true
false	false	false	false	true
false	unknown	false	unknown	true
unknown	true	unknown	true	unknown
unknown	false	false	unknown	unknown
unknown	unknown	unknown	unknown	unknown

Exercises

9.6 Give the number, the name and town of each female player who is *not* a resident of Stratford.

9.7 Find the player numbers of those who joined the club between 1970 and 1980.

9.8 Find the numbers, names and years of birth of players born in a leap year. Just in case you need a reminder, a leap year is one in which the year figure is divisible by four, except that with centuries the year figure must be divisible by 400. Therefore 1900 was not a leap year, while 2000 will be.

9.9 For each competition player born after 1965 who has won at least one match, give his or her name and initials, and the divisions of the teams in which the player has played.

9.4   The BETWEEN operator

Oracle supports a special operator which allows you to determine whether a value occurs within a given range of values.

```
<predicate with between> ::=
   <expression> [ NOT ] BETWEEN <expression>
                        AND <expresssion>
```

Example 9.10: Find the number and year of birth of each player born between 1962 and 1964.

```
SELECT   PLAYERNO, YEAR_OF_BIRTH
FROM     PLAYERS
WHERE    YEAR_OF_BIRTH >= 1962
AND      YEAR_OF_BIRTH <= 1964
```

Result:

```
PLAYERNO  YEAR_OF_BIRTH
--------  -------------
       6           1964
      44           1963
      27           1964
       7           1963
     112           1963
       8           1962
     100           1963
      28           1963
      95           1963
```

This statement can also be written using the *BETWEEN operator* and the result stays the same:

```
SELECT   PLAYERNO, YEAR_OF_BIRTH
FROM     PLAYERS
WHERE    YEAR_OF_BIRTH BETWEEN 1962 AND 1964
```

If, E1, E2 and E3 are expressions, then:

```
E1 BETWEEN E2 AND E3
```

is equivalent to:

```
(E1 >= E2) AND (E1 <= E3)
```

The consequence is that if one of the three expressions is equal to the NULL value, the entire condition is unknown.

At the same time it follows that:

```
E1 NOT BETWEEN E2 AND E3
```

is equivalent to:

```
NOT (E1 BETWEEN E2 AND E3)
```

and equivalent to:

```
(E1 < E2) OR (E1 > E3)
```

If, in this case, E1 has the NULL value, then the condition returns unknown. The condition is true if E1 is not NULL, E2 is NULL and E1 is greater than E3.

Example 9.11: Give the numbers and years of birth of the players who joined the club when they were 16, 17, 18, 19 or 20 years old.

```
SELECT    PLAYERNO, YEAR_OF_BIRTH
FROM      PLAYERS
WHERE     YEAR_JOINED - YEAR_OF_BIRTH BETWEEN 16 AND 20
```

Result:

```
PLAYERNO  YEAR_OF_BIRTH
--------  -------------
      44           1963
      27           1964
       7           1963
       8           1962
     100           1963
      28           1963
```

Exercises

9.10 Get the payment number of each penalty between $50 and $100.

9.11 Get the payment number of each penalty which is *not* between $50 and $100.

9.12 Give the numbers of the players who joined the club after they had become 16 and before their 40s.

9.5   The IN operator

Conditions can sometimes become rather cumbersome if you have to determine whether a value in a column appears in a given set of values which could be very large. Here is an illustration of this. In Section 9.8 we extend the possibilities of this condition.

```
<predicate with in> ::=
   <expression> [ NOT ] IN <row expression> |
   <row expression> [ NOT ] IN
      ( <row expression> [ {,<row expression>}... ] )

<row expression> ::=
   ( <expression> [ { ,<expression> }... ] )
```

Example 9.12: Find the number, name and town of each player who lives in Inglewood, Plymouth, Midhurst or Douglas.

```
SELECT    PLAYERNO, NAME, TOWN
FROM      PLAYERS
WHERE     TOWN = 'Inglewood'
OR        TOWN = 'Plymouth'
OR        TOWN = 'Midhurst'
OR        TOWN = 'Douglas'
```

Result:

```
PLAYERNO  NAME        TOWN
--------  ---------   ---------
      44  Baker       Inglewood
     112  Bailey      Plymouth
       8  Newcastle   Inglewood
      28  Collins     Midhurst
      95  Miller      Douglas
```

The statement and the result are correct, of course, but the statement is rather long-winded. The *IN operator* can be used to simplify the statement:

```
SELECT    PLAYERNO, NAME, TOWN
FROM      PLAYERS
WHERE     TOWN IN ('Inglewood', 'Plymouth', 'Midhurst',
          'Douglas')
```

This condition is read as follows: Each row whose TOWN value occurs in the set of four place names satisfies the condition.

Example 9.13: Get the numbers and years of birth of the players born in 1962, 1963 or 1970.

```
SELECT    PLAYERNO, YEAR_OF_BIRTH
FROM      PLAYERS
WHERE     YEAR_OF_BIRTH IN (1962, 1963, 1970)
```

Result:

```
PLAYERNO   YEAR_OF_BIRTH
--------   -------------
      44            1963
     104            1970
       7            1963
     112            1963
       8            1962
     100            1963
      28            1963
      95            1963
```

Suppose that E1, E2, E3 and E4 are expressions; then the condition:

```
E1 IN (E2, E3, E4)
```

is equivalent to the condition:

```
(E1 = E2) OR (E1 = E3) OR (E1 = E4)
```

This means that when E1 is equal to the NULL value, the condition evaluates to unknown.

At the same time it follows that the condition:

```
E1 NOT IN (E2, E3, E4)
```

is equivalent to:

```
NOT (E1 IN (E2, E3, E4))
```

and equivalent to:

```
(E1 <> E2) AND (E1 <> E3) AND (E1 <> E4)
```

In the previous examples the condition consisted of comparing one value with a list of other values. We give you some examples of the IN operator where row expressions are compared with each other.

Example 9.14: Give the numbers and names of the players who live at Haseltine Lane or Edgecombe Way in Stratford.

```
SELECT   PLAYERNO, NAME
FROM     PLAYERS
WHERE    (STREET, TOWN) IN
         (('Haseltine Lane', 'Stratford'),
          ('Edgecombe Way',  'Stratford'))
```

Result:

```
PLAYERNO  NAME
--------  ----------
       6  Parmenter
       7  Wise
      57  Brown
     100  Parmenter
```

Explanation: A row of the PLAYERS table satisfies the condition if the STREET is equivalent to Haseltine Lane *and* TOWN is equivalent to Stratford *or* STREET is equivalent to Edgecombe Way and TOWN is equivalent to Stratford.

For all row expressions in a predicate the number of expressions has to be equal. The following predicate is incorrect:

```
(TOWN) IN (('Stratford', 'Plymouth'),
           ('Midhurst','Inglewood'))
```

Exercises

9.13 Find the payment number for each penalty of $50, $75 or $100.

9.14 Give the numbers of the players who do not live in Stratford or Douglas.

9.6   The LIKE operator

The LIKE operator is used to select alphanumeric values with a particular pattern or mask.

```
<predicate with like> ::=
   <expression> [ NOT ] LIKE <expression>
```

Example 9.15: Find the name and number of each player whose name begins with a capital B.

```
SELECT   NAME, PLAYERNO
FROM     PLAYERS
WHERE    NAME LIKE 'B%'
```

Result:

```
NAME        PLAYERNO
--------    --------
Baker             44
Brown             57
Bishof            39
Bailey           112
```

After the *LIKE operator* you find an alphanumeric literal: `'B%'`. Because this literal comes after a LIKE operator and not after a comparison operator, the percent sign and the underscore, have a special meaning. Such a literal is called a *pattern* or a *mask*. In a mask, the percent sign stands for zero, one or more random characters, while the underscore stands for exactly one character.

In the SELECT statement above, then, we asked for the players whose name begins with the capital B followed by zero, one or more characters.

Example 9.16: Get the name and number of each player whose name ends with the small letter *r*.

```
SELECT    NAME, PLAYERNO
FROM      PLAYERS
WHERE     NAME LIKE '%r'
```

Result:

```
NAME        PLAYERNO
---------   --------
Parmenter          6
Baker             44
Parmenter        100
Miller            95
```

Example 9.17: Get the name and number of each player whose name has the letter *e* as the penultimate letter.

```
SELECT    NAME, PLAYERNO
FROM      PLAYERS
WHERE     NAME LIKE '%e_'
```

Result:

```
NAME        PLAYERNO
---------   --------
Parmenter          6
Baker             44
Bailey           112
Parmenter        100
Miller            95
```

If neither an underscore nor a percent sign is needed to specify the condition, you can use the = operator. The condition

```
NAME LIKE 'Baker'
```

is equivalent to

```
NAME = 'Baker'
```

Suppose that A is an alphanumeric column and M a mask, then:

```
A NOT LIKE M
```

is equivalent to:

```
NOT (A LIKE M)
```

If there is no alphanumeric expression after the LIKE operator, but for example a numeric expression, Oracle converts the data type automatically. The following statement, for example:

```
SELECT    *
FROM      MATCHES
WHERE     MATCHNO LIKE 1 || '%'
```

is equivalent to:

```
SELECT    *
FROM      MATCHES
WHERE     MATCHNO LIKE TO_CHAR(1) || '%'
```

Result:

```
MATCHNO   TEAMNO   PLAYERNO   WON   LOST
-------   ------   --------   ---   ----
      1        1          6     3      1
     10        2        104     3      2
     11        2        112     2      3
     12        2        112     1      3
     13        2          8     0      3
```

Exercises

9.15 Find the number and name of each player whose name contains the combination of letters *is*.

9.16 Find the number and name of each player whose name is six characters long.

9.17 Find the number and name of each player whose name is at least six characters long.

9.18 Find the number and name of each player whose name has an *r* as the third and penultimate letters.

9.7   The NULL operator

A NULL operator can be used to select rows who have no value in a particular column.

```
<predicate with null> ::=
   <expression> IS [ NOT ] NULL
```

One of the last examples of Section 9.2 showed how all players with a league number can be found. This statement can also be formulated in another way, a way which corresponds better to the original question (note that the word IS may *not* be replaced by the equals sign):

```
SELECT   PLAYERNO, LEAGUENO
FROM     PLAYERS
WHERE    LEAGUENO IS NOT NULL
```

If the NOT is left out, we get all the players who have *no* league number.

Example 9.18: Get the name, the number and the league number of each player whose league number is *not* equal to 8467.

```
SELECT   NAME, PLAYERNO, LEAGUENO
FROM     PLAYERS
WHERE    LEAGUENO <> '8467'
OR       LEAGUENO IS NULL
```

Result:

NAME	PLAYERNO	LEAGUENO
Baker	44	1124
Hope	83	1608
Everett	2	2411
Collins	27	2513
Moorman	104	7060
Wise	7	?
Brown	57	6409
Bishop	39	?
Bailey	112	1319
Newcastle	8	2983
Parmenter	100	6524
Collins	28	?
Miller	95	?

In the case that the condition LEAGUENO IS NULL is left out, the result table contains only rows where the LEAGUENO column is not equal to NULL and is, of course, not equal to 8467 (see table below). This is because the value of the condition LEAGUENO <> '8467' is equal to unknown if the LEAGUENO column has the value NULL.

```
NAME          PLAYERNO  LEAGUENO
----------    --------  --------
Baker               44      1124
Hope                83      1608
Everett              2      2411
Collins             27      2513
Moorman            104      7060
Brown               57      6409
Bailey             112      1319
Newcastle            8      2983
Parmenter          100      6524
```

Suppose that E1 is an expression; then:

```
E1 IS NOT NULL
```

is equivalent to:

```
NOT (E1 IS NULL)
```

Note: A condition with IS NULL or IS NOT NULL can *never* have the value unknown; work out for yourself.

Exercises

9.19   Get the number of each player who has *no* league number.

9.20   Why does the condition in the following SELECT statement make no sense?

```
SELECT    *
FROM      PLAYERS
WHERE     NAME IS NULL
```

9.8   The IN operator with subquery

Section 9.5 discussed the IN operator. If the value of a particular column occurs in a set of expressions, the row concerned satisfies the condition made using the IN operator. The expressions in such a set are written into the statement one by one by a user. The IN operator can also take another form whereby it is not necessary to list explicitly the individual expressions. Instead, Oracle determines the value of the literals at the point when the statement is processed. This process is the subject of this section.

In that same section we gave you a definition of the condition with the IN operator. The definition will be extended below.

```
<predicate with in> ::=
   <expression> [ NOT ] IN <row expression>              |
   <row expression> [ NOT ] IN
      ( <row expression> [ {,<row expression> }... ] ) |
   <expression> [ NOT ] IN <subquery>                    |
   <row expression> [ NOT ] IN <subquery>

<row expression> ::=
   ( <expression> [ {,<expression>}... ] )

<subquery> ::= ( <select statement> )
```

Example 9.19: Get the number, name and initials of each player who has played at least one match.

This question actually consists of two parts. First, we need to work out which players have played at least one match, and then we need to look for the numbers, the names and the initials of these players. The MATCHES table contains data to answer the first part, so with the following simple statement we can find out the player numbers:

```
SELECT    PLAYERNO
FROM      MATCHES
```

Result:

```
PLAYERNO
--------
       6
       6
       6
      44
      83
       2
      57
       8
      27
     104
     112
     112
       8
```

But how do we use those numbers to look up the relevant names and initials of the players from the PLAYERS table? In terms of what we have covered so far in this book, there is only one way to do it. We note down the numbers on a piece of paper and type in the next statement:

```
SELECT    PLAYERNO, NAME, INITIALS
FROM      PLAYERS
WHERE     PLAYERNO IN (6, 44, 83, 2, 57, 8, 27, 104, 112)
```

Result:

PLAYERNO	NAME	INITIALS
6	Parmenter	R
44	Baker	E
83	Hope	PK
2	Everett	R
27	Collins	DD
104	Moorman	D
57	Brown	M
112	Bailey	IP
8	Newcastle	B

This way works, of course, but it is very clumsy, and would be impractical if the MATCHES table contains many different player numbers. Because this type of statement is very common, Oracle offers the possibility of including SELECT statements *within* other statements. The statement for the example above now looks like this:

```
SELECT    PLAYERNO, NAME, INITIALS
FROM      PLAYERS
WHERE     PLAYERNO IN
          (SELECT    PLAYERNO
           FROM      MATCHES)
```

We now have no set of expressions after the IN operator as we did in the examples in Section 9.5. Instead there is another SELECT statement. This SELECT statement is called a *subquery*. A subquery has a result, of course, just like a 'normal' SELECT statement. In this example the result looks like this (remember that it is an intermediate result that is not actually seen during processing):

```
(6, 44, 83, 2, 57, 8, 27, 104, 112)
```

When Oracle processes the SELECT statement it replaces the subquery with the intermediate result of the subquery:

```
SELECT    PLAYERNO, NAME, INITIALS
FROM      PLAYERS
WHERE     PLAYERNO IN (6, 44, 83, 2, 57, 8, 27, 104, 112)
```

This now looks like a familiar statement. The result of this statement is the same as the end result that we have already shown.

The most important difference between the use of the IN operator with a set of expressions as opposed to with a subquery is that in the first instance the set of values is fixed in advance by the user, and in the second instance the values are not known until they are determined by Oracle during the processing

Example 9.20: Get the number and the name of each player who has played at least one match for the first team.

```
SELECT    PLAYERNO, NAME
FROM      PLAYERS
WHERE     PLAYERNO IN
          (SELECT    PLAYERNO
          FROM      MATCHES
          WHERE     TEAMNO = 1)
```

The intermediate result of the subquery:

```
(6, 44, 83, 2, 57, 8)
```

The result of the entire statement:

```
PLAYERNO  NAME
--------  ----------
      6   Parmenter
     44   Baker
     83   Hope
      2   Everett
     57   Brown
      8   Newcastle
```

As you can see, a subquery itself may contain conditions; even other subqueries are allowed.

Example 9.21: Give the number and name of each player who has played at least one match for the team which is *not* captained by player 6.

```
SELECT    PLAYERNO, NAME
FROM      PLAYERS
WHERE     PLAYERNO IN
          (SELECT    PLAYERNO
          FROM      MATCHES
          WHERE     TEAMNO NOT IN
                    (SELECT    TEAMNO
                    FROM      TEAMS
                    WHERE     PLAYERNO = 6))
```

The intermediate result of the *subsubquery* is:

(1)

In the subquery, now, Oracle searches for all players who do *not* appear in the set of teams captained by player 6.

Intermediate result:

```
(27, 104, 112, 8)
```

Result of the statement:

```
PLAYERNO  NAME
--------  ----------
      27  Collins
     104  Moorman
     112  Bailey
       8  Newcastle
```

Once again, users do not see any of the intermediate results.

When is a condition with an IN operator and a subquery true, when false and when is it unknown? Suppose that C is the name of a column, and that v_1, v_2, ..., v_n are values from which the intermediate result of subquery S are formed. It follows that:

```
C IN (S)
```

is equivalent to:

```
(C = v1) OR (C = v2) OR ... OR (C = vn) OR false
```

Note:

- If the subquery returns no result, it means that the entire condition evaluates to false, because at the end of this 'long-hand' condition *false* occurs.
- If C is equal to the NULL value and if the subquery retrieves at least one value, than the condition is unknown.

We can apply the same reasoning to NOT IN. The following condition:

```
C NOT IN (S)
```

is equivalent to:

```
(C <> v1) AND (C <> v2) AND ... AND (C <> vn) AND true
```

This section says that if the subquery returns no rows the condition is *true*. (Even when C has the value NULL.)

Suppose that the year of birth of player 27 is unknown. Will player 27 then appear in the end result of the following SELECT statement?

```
SELECT   *
FROM     PLAYERS
WHERE    YEAR_OF_BIRTH NOT IN
         (SELECT  YEAR_OF_BIRTH
          FROM    PLAYERS
          WHERE   TOWN = 'London')
```

The answer is: Yes. The intermediate result of the subquery is as expected empty, because no player lives in London. In other words, all players have been recorded in the result, including player 27.

In the definition of the IN operator we saw that more columns can be compared simultaneously.

Example 9.22: Give the number, the name, the street and the town of each player who lives in the same street and town as the player with number 6 or the player with number 7.

```
SELECT    PLAYERNO, NAME, STREET, TOWN
FROM      PLAYERS
WHERE     (STREET, TOWN) IN
          (SELECT   STREET, TOWN
          FROM      PLAYERS
          WHERE     PLAYERNO IN (6, 7))
```

Result:

PLAYERNO	NAME	STREET	TOWN
7	Wise	Edgecombe Way	Stratford
57	Brown	Edgecombe Way	Stratford
6	Parmenter	Haseltine Lane	Stratford
100	Parmenter	Haseltine Lane	Stratford

Example 9.23: Give the number of the player who has, just as B. Newcastle, incurred a penalty of $25 on 8 December 1980. B. Newcastle may not appear in the end result.

```
SELECT    PLAYERNO
FROM      PENALTIES
WHERE     PLAYERNO NOT IN
          (SELECT   PLAYERNO
          FROM      PLAYERS
          WHERE     (NAME, INITIALS) =
                    (('Newcastle','B')))
AND       (PEN_DATE, AMOUNT) IN
          (SELECT   PEN_DATE, AMOUNT
          FROM      PENALTIES
          WHERE     PLAYERNO =
                    (SELECT   PLAYERNO
                    FROM      PLAYERS
                    WHERE     (NAME, INITIALS) =
                              (('Newcastle', 'B'))))
```

Result:

```
PLAYERNO
--------
      44
```

In Chapter 15 we deal more extensively with the possibilities and limitations of subqueries.

Exercises

9.21 Get the number and name of each player who has incurred at least one penalty.

9.22 Get the number and name of each player who has incurred at least one penalty of more than $50.

9.23 Find the team numbers and player numbers of the team captains from the first division who live in Stratford.

9.24 Get the number and name of each player for whom at least one penalty has been received and who is not a captain of a team which plays in the first division.

9.9   The comparison operator with subquery

Subqueries can be placed not only after the IN operator, but also after the comparison, such as = or >. Here we extend the definition which we showed in Section 9.2.

```
<predicate with comparison> ::=
   <expression> <comparison operator> <expression>          |
   <expression> <comparison operator> <subquery>            |
   <row expression> { = | <> | != | ^= } (<row expression>) |
   <row expression> { = | <> | != | ^= } <subquery>

<comparison operator> ::=
   = | < | > | <= | >= | <> | != | ^=

<row expression> ::=
   ( <expression> [ {,<expression>}... ] )

<subquery> ::= ( <select statement> )
```

Example 9.24: Find the number and name of the player who captains team 1.

```
SELECT     PLAYERNO, NAME
FROM       PLAYERS
WHERE      PLAYERNO =
           (SELECT   PLAYERNO
           FROM      TEAMS
           WHERE     TEAMNO = 1)
```

The intermediate result of the subquery is player number 6. These values can now replace the subquery:

```
SELECT     PLAYERNO, NAME
FROM       PLAYERS
WHERE      PLAYERNO = 6
```

Result:

```
PLAYERNO   NAME
--------   ---------
       6   Parmenter
```

The = operator is only valid if the subquery returns one value at that precise point in time. The statement above could also have been formulated with an IN operator. There are, however, two reasons why the = operator must be chosen over the IN operator when a subquery returns one value.

- By using the = operator you signal that the subquery always has one value. If the subquery returns multiple values, then either the contents of the database are not correct or the database structure is not as you expected. In both cases the = operator is functioning as a means of control.

- By using the = operator you give Oracle information about the expected number of values to be returned by the subquery, namely one. On the basis of this information Oracle can decide on the most appropriate processing strategy.

Example 9.25: Find the number and name of each player who is older than R. Parmenter.

```
SELECT     PLAYERNO, NAME
FROM       PLAYERS
WHERE      YEAR_OF_BIRTH <
           (SELECT   YEAR_OF_BIRTH
           FROM      PLAYERS
           WHERE     NAME = 'Parmenter'
           AND       INITIALS = 'R')
```

The intermediate result of the subquery is the year 1964. The result the user sees is:

```
PLAYERNO  NAME
--------  ---------
      44  Baker
      83  Hope
       2  Everett
       7  Wise
      39  Bishop
     112  Bailey
       8  Newcastle
     100  Parmenter
      28  Collins
      95  Miller
```

As we have already mentioned, we return in more detail to subqueries in the last
section of this chapter. What we want to point out here is that a subquery in a
condition with a comparison operator should always return *only one value*. The
statement below, then, is incorrect and would not be processed by Oracle.

```
SELECT    *
FROM      PLAYERS
WHERE     YEAR_OF_BIRTH <
          (SELECT    YEAR_OF_BIRTH
          FROM       PLAYERS)
```

Exercises

9.25 Get the number and name of each player who is the same age as R. Parmenter, but R. Parmenter's number may not appear in the result.

9.26 Find the numbers of all matches played by team 2 where the number of
sets won is equal to the number of sets won in the match played by player
8 for team 2. Exclude player 8 from the result.

9.10   The ALL and ANY operators

A third way of using a subquery is with the ALL and ANY operators. These operators look rather like the IN operator with subquery.

```
<predicate with any all> ::=
   <expression> <any all operator> <row expression> |
   <expression> <any all operator> <subquery>        |
   <row expression> <any all operator> <subquery>    |
   <row expression> <any all operator>
      ( <row expression> [ {,<row expression>}... ] )

<any all operator> ::=
   <comparison operator> { ALL | ANY }

<row expression> ::=
   ( <expression> [ {,<expression>}... ] )

<subquery> ::= ( <select statement> )
```

Example 9.26: Give the numbers, names and years of birth of the oldest players. The oldest players are those whose year of birth is less than or equal to that of each other player.

```
SELECT    PLAYERNO, NAME, YEAR_OF_BIRTH
FROM      PLAYERS
WHERE     YEAR_OF_BIRTH <= ALL
          (SELECT   YEAR_OF_BIRTH
           FROM     PLAYERS)
```

Result:

```
PLAYERNO  NAME     YEAR_OF_BIRTH
--------  -------  -------------
       2  Everett          1948
```

Explanation: The intermediate result of the subquery consists of the year of birth of all players. In the SELECT statement Oracle looks to see if the year of birth of each player is less than or equal to each year of birth recorded in the intermediate result.

With the IN operator we have shown precisely when such a condition is true, false or unknown. We do the same for the ALL operator. If $y_1, y_2, \ldots, y_n$ are the years of birth of all players returned by the subquery (S), it follows that:

```
YEAR_OF_BIRTH <= ALL (S)
```

is equivalent to:

```
(YEAR_OF_BIRTH <= y1) AND
(YEAR_OF_BIRTH <= y2) AND ... AND
(YEAR_OF_BIRTH <= yn) AND true
```

This means that if the subquery returns no result the condition is *true*. If the subquery does have a result and YEAR_OF_BIRTH is equal to the NULL value, then the condition evaluates to *unknown*. The condition is also unknown when one of the YEAR_OF_BIRTH values is equal to the NULL value.

Example 9.27: Get the numbers, names and years of birth of players who are not amongst the oldest.

```
SELECT    PLAYERNO, NAME, YEAR_OF_BIRTH
FROM      PLAYERS
WHERE     YEAR_OF_BIRTH > ANY
          (SELECT    YEAR_OF_BIRTH
           FROM      PLAYERS)
```

The intermediate result of the subquery again consists of all the years of birth. But this time Oracle looks for all the players whose year of birth is greater than that of at least one other player. When such a year of birth is found Oracle knows that this player is not the oldest. The end result of this statement is the group of all players except the oldest ones. The previous example showed that Everett alone is the oldest player.

If $y_1, y_2, \ldots, y_n$ are all the years of birth returned by the subquery S, it follows that:

```
YEAR_OF_BIRTH > ANY (S)
```

is equivalent to:

```
(YEAR_OF_BIRTH > y1) OR
(YEAR_OF_BIRTH > y2) OR ... OR
(YEAR_OF_BIRTH > yn) OR false
```

From this we can deduce that if the subquery returns no values the condition is *false*.

Instead of the greater than operator and the less than or equal to operator that we used in these two examples, each comparison operator may be used.

Try to deduce for yourself that the condition C = ANY (S) is equivalent to C IN (S). And try to prove that the condition C <> ALL (S) is equivalent to C NOT IN (S) and also equivalent to NOT (C IN (S)).

The condition C = ALL (S) is, by definition, false if the subquery returns multiple values, because the value in a column can never be equal to two or more different values at the same time. We can illustrate this proposition with a simple example. Suppose that v_1 and v_2 are two different values from the intermediate result of subquery S; then it follows that C = ALL (S) is equal to (C = v1) AND (C = v2). By definition, this is false.

The converse applies for the condition: C <> ANY (S). If the subquery returns multiple values, the condition is, by definition, true. Because, again, if the result of subquery S consists of the values v_1 and v_2, then C <> ANY (S) is equivalent to (C <> v1) OR (C <> v2). And this is, by definition, true.

Example 9.28: Get the numbers of the players who have incurred at least one penalty which is higher than a penalty paid for player 27; this player may not appear in the result.

```
SELECT    DISTINCT PLAYERNO
FROM      PENALTIES
WHERE     PLAYERNO <> 27
AND       AMOUNT > ANY
          (SELECT   AMOUNT
          FROM      PENALTIES
          WHERE     PLAYERNO = 27)
```

Example 9.29: Find the numbers of the players with the lowest league number of all players living in his or her town.

```
SELECT    PLAYERNO
FROM      PLAYERS P1
WHERE     LEAGUENO <= ALL
          (SELECT   LEAGUENO
          FROM      PLAYERS P2
          WHERE     P1.TOWN = P2.TOWN)
```

Exercises

9.27 Get the player numbers of the oldest players from Stratford.

9.28 Get the player number of each player who has incurred at least one penalty (do not use the IN operator).

9.11 The EXISTS operator

In this section we discuss the last operator with which subqueries can be coupled to main queries: the *EXISTS operator*.

```
<predicate with exists> ::= EXISTS <subquery>

<subquery> ::= ( <select statement> )
```

Example 9.30: Find the names and initials of players who have incurred at least one penalty.

This question can be answered using an IN operator:

```
SELECT    NAME, INITIALS
FROM      PLAYERS
WHERE     PLAYERNO IN
          (SELECT   PLAYERNO
          FROM      PENALTIES)
```

Result:

```
NAME        INITIALS
---------   --------
Parmenter   R
Baker       E
Collins     DD
Moorman     D
Newcastle   B
```

It can also, however, be answered using the EXISTS operator.

```
SELECT    NAME, INITIALS
FROM      PLAYERS
WHERE     EXISTS
          (SELECT   *
          FROM      PENALTIES
          WHERE     PLAYERNO = PLAYERS.PLAYERNO)
```

We now come to something new in the subquery. The column specification
PLAYERS.PLAYERNO refers to a table that has been mentioned in the main
part of the statement. For this reason we call such a subquery a *correlated subquery*. By using the named column specification we establish a relationship between the subquery and the main query.

But what does this statement mean exactly? For every player in the PLAY-
ERS table separately Oracle determines whether the subquery returns a row or
not. In other words, it checks to see whether there is a result (WHERE EXISTS).
If the PENALTIES table contains at least one player number the same as that of
the player concerned, then that row satisfies the condition. We will give an example. For the first row in the PLAYERS table, player 6, Oracle executes the
following subquery (which you do not see):

```
SELECT    *
FROM      PENALTIES
WHERE     PLAYERNO = 6
```

The (intermediate) result consists of one row, so in the end result we see the
name of the player whose number is 6.

Similarly, Oracle executes the subquery for the second, third and subsequent rows of the PLAYERS table. The only thing that changes each time is
the value for PLAYERS.PLAYERNO in the condition of the WHERE clause.

Therefore the subquery can have a different intermediate result for each player in the PLAYERS table.

Example 9.31: Get the names and initials of the players who are not team captains.

```
SELECT    NAME, INITIALS
FROM      PLAYERS
WHERE     NOT EXISTS
          (SELECT    *
          FROM      TEAMS
          WHERE     PLAYERNO = PLAYERS.PLAYERNO)
```

Result:

NAME	INITIALS
Baker	E
Hope	PK
Everett	R
Moorman	D
Wise	GWS
Brown	M
Bishop	D
Bailey	IP
Newcastle	B
Parmenter	P
Collins	C
Miller	P

A condition that only contains an EXISTS operator always has the value *true* or *false* and never *unknown*. In Chapter 15 we return to the EXISTS operator and correlated subqueries.

As mentioned before, during the evaluation of a condition with the EXISTS operator, Oracle looks to see if the result of the subquery returns rows. Oracle does not look at the contents of the row. This makes it totally irrelevant what you specify in the SELECT clause. You can even specify a literal. So the statement above is equivalent to the following statement:

```
SELECT    NAME, INITIALS
FROM      PLAYERS
WHERE     NOT EXISTS
          (SELECT    'nothing'
          FROM      TEAMS
          WHERE     PLAYERNO = PLAYERS.PLAYERNO)
```

Exercises

9.29 Give the name and initial(s) of each player who is captain of at least one team.

9.30 Give the name and initial(s) of each player who is not a captain of a team in which player 112 has played.

9.12   Conditions with negation

In this section we discuss an error that is made many times with SQL. This error refers to *conditions with negation*. A condition in which we search for the rows that do not contain a specific value in a column, is (informally) called a condition with negation. A negative condition can be made by placing a NOT before a positive condition. Here are two examples to demonstrate the problem.

Example 9.32: Give the player number for every player who lives in Stratford.

```
SELECT   PLAYERNO
FROM     PLAYERS
WHERE    TOWN = 'Stratford'
```

Result:

```
PLAYERNO
--------
       6
      83
       2
       7
      57
      39
     100
```

By placing a NOT operator before the condition we get a SELECT statement with a negative condition:

```
SELECT   PLAYERNO
FROM     PLAYERS
WHERE    NOT TOWN = 'Stratford'
```

Result:

```
PLAYERNO
--------
      44
      27
```

```
104
112
  8
 28
 95
```

In this example we can also specify a negative condition using the comparison operator <> (not equal to):

```
SELECT    PLAYERNO
FROM      PLAYERS
WHERE     TOWN <> 'Stratford'
```

In the example above we find the players who do *not* live in Stratford by simply adding NOT to the condition. It went well, because the SELECT clause contains a complete candidate key of the PLAYERS table, that is the primary key PLAYERNO. Problems arise if the SELECT clause contains only a part of a candidate key or no candidate key at all. This will be illustrated with an example.

Example 9.33: Get the number of each player for whom a penalty of $25 has been received.

As far as structure goes the question and corresponding SELECT statement appear similar to those of the previous example:

```
SELECT    PLAYERNO
FROM      PENALTIES
WHERE     AMOUNT = 25
```

Lets find the players for whom not one penalty of $25 has been received. If we do it in the same way as in the last example, then the statement looks like this:

```
SELECT    PLAYERNO
FROM      PENALTIES
WHERE     NOT AMOUNT = 25
```

Result:

```
PLAYERNO
--------
       6
      44
      27
     104
      44
      27
```

If you examine the PENALTIES table, you will see that there has been a penalty of $25 for player 44. In other words, the SELECT statement does not give the required result to our original question. The reason for this is that the SELECT

clause of this statement contains not one of the candidate keys of the PENAL-
TIES table (this table only recognizes one candidate key: PAYMENTNO). The
correct answer is obtained by using a subquery along with the NOT operator:

```
SELECT    PLAYERNO
FROM      PLAYERS
WHERE     PLAYERNO NOT IN
          (SELECT   PLAYERNO
          FROM      PENALTIES
          WHERE     AMOUNT = 25)
```

The subquery determines which players have incurred a penalty of $25. In the
main query, Oracle looks to see which players do *not* appear in the result of the
subquery. But watch out: the main query does not search the PENALTIES table,
but the PLAYERS table. If the FROM clause in this statement had named the
PENALTIES table, we would have received a list of all players who had incurred
at least one penalty which was not $25, and that was not the original question.

Now that we have a negative statement defined using NOT IN, it is possible to create the positive version of the SELECT statement with a comparable
structure:

```
SELECT    PLAYERNO
FROM      PLAYERS
WHERE     PLAYERNO IN
          (SELECT   PLAYERNO
          FROM      PENALTIES
          WHERE     AMOUNT = 25)
```

Conclusion: If a SELECT clause does not contain the whole of one of the candidate keys of the table in the FROM clause, and if the WHERE clause has a
negative condition, then beware!

Exercises

9.31   Give the number of each player who has not won a single match with three
sets.

9.32   Give the team number and the division of each team for which player 6 has
not competed.

9.33   Get the number for each player who has played in teams in which player
57 has never competed.

10

SELECT statement: SELECT clause and functions

The WHERE clause is used to select rows. The intermediate result from this clause forms a *horizontal subset* of a table. In contrast, the SELECT clause selects only columns and not rows, the result forming a *vertical subset* of a table.

The possibilities, limitations and use of the SELECT clause depend on the presence or absence of a GROUP BY clause. This chapter discusses SELECT statements *without* a GROUP BY clause. In Chapter 11, which concentrates on the GROUP BY clause (among other things), we discuss the SELECT clause when the statement *does* contain a GROUP BY clause.

Much of this chapter is devoted to *statistical functions*. In Chapter 6 we referred to these functions, but did not delve into them.

```
<select clause> ::=
    SELECT [ DISTINCT | ALL ] <select element list>

<select element list> ::=
    <select element> [ {,<select element> }... ] |
    *

<select element> ::=
    <expression> [ <column heading> ] |
    <table specification>.*            |
    <correlation name>.*

<table specification> ::= [ <user> . ] <table name>
```

10.1   Selecting all columns (∗)

An asterisk (∗) is a short form notation for all columns from each table mentioned in the FROM clause. The following two SELECT statements are equivalent:

```
SELECT   *
FROM     PENALTIES
```

and

```
SELECT   PAYMENTNO, PLAYERNO, PEN_DATE, AMOUNT
FROM     PENALTIES
```

(The ∗ symbol, then, does not have the meaning of the multiplication sign in this context.) When a FROM clause refers to two or more tables, it is sometimes necessary to use a table specification in front of the asterisk in order to clarify which columns should be presented. The following three statements are equivalent, for example:

```
SELECT   PENALTIES.*
FROM     PENALTIES, PLAYERS
WHERE    PENALTIES.PLAYERNO = PLAYERS.PLAYERNO
```

and

```
SELECT   PENALTIES.PAYMENTNO, PENALTIES.PLAYERNO,
         PENALTIES.PEN_DATE, PENALTIES.AMOUNT
FROM     PENALTIES, PLAYERS
WHERE    PENALTIES.PLAYERNO = PLAYERS.PLAYERNO
```

and

```
SELECT   PEN.*
FROM     PENALTIES PEN, PLAYERS
WHERE    PEN.PLAYERNO = PLAYERS.PLAYERNO
```

10.2   Expressions in the SELECT clause

In processing the SELECT clause Oracle evaluates the intermediate result row by row. Each column expression gives rise to a value in the result row. Most of the examples of the SELECT clause that we have described so far specify only column names, but an expression may take the form of a literal, a calculation or a scalar function.

Example 10.1: Give for each match the match number, the word 'Tally', the difference between the columns WON and LOST and the value of the WON and the value of the WON columns multiplied by 10.

```
SELECT    MATCHNO, 'Tally', WON - LOST, WON * 10
FROM      MATCHES
```

Result:

```
MATCHNO             WON - LOST   WON * 10
--------   -----   -----------   --------
      1    Tally             2         30
      2    Tally            -1         20
      3    Tally             3         30
      4    Tally             1         30
      5    Tally            -3          0
      6    Tally            -2         10
      7    Tally             3         30
      8    Tally            -3          0
      9    Tally             1         30
     10    Tally             1         30
     11    Tally            -1         20
     12    Tally            -2         10
     13    Tally            -3          0
```

10.3 Removing duplicate rows with DISTINCT

A SELECT clause can be written with one or more column expressions preceded by the word DISTINCT (see the definition at the beginning of this chapter). If you specify DISTINCT, Oracle removes duplicate rows from the intermediate result.

Example 10.2: Find all the different place names from the PLAYERS table.

```
SELECT    TOWN
FROM      PLAYERS
```

Result:

```
TOWN
---------
Stratford
Inglewood
Stratford
Stratford
Eltham
Eltham
Stratford
Stratford
:
```

```
:
Stratford
Plymouth
Inglewood
Stratford
Midhurst
Douglas
```

In this result table, the towns Stratford, Inglewood and Eltham appear seven, two and two times respectively. If the statement is expanded to include DISTINCT:

```
SELECT    DISTINCT TOWN
FROM      PLAYERS
```

it produces the following result in which all but one of each group of duplicate rows is removed.

```
TOWN
----------
Stratford
Midhurst
Inglewood
Plymouth
Douglas
Eltham
```

A second example is:

```
SELECT    STREET, TOWN
FROM      PLAYERS
```

Result:

```
STREET              TOWN
----------------    ----------
Haseltine Lane      Stratford
Lewis Street        Inglewood
Magdalene Road      Stratford
Stoney Road         Stratford
Long Drive          Eltham
Stout Street        Eltham
Edgecombe Way       Stratford
Edgecombe Way       Stratford
Eaton Square        Stratford
Vixen Road          Plymouth
Station Road        Inglewood
Haseltine Lane      Stratford
Old Main Road       Midhurst
High Street         Douglas
```

This result also contains duplicate rows; for example, Edgecombe Way and Haseltine Lane in Stratford are each mentioned twice. When DISTINCT is added:

```
SELECT    DISTINCT STREET, TOWN
FROM      PLAYERS
```

the result is:

```
STREET              TOWN
---------------     ----------
Edgecombe Way       Stratford
Eaton Square        Stratford
Haseltine Lane      Stratford
High Street         Douglas
Lewis Street        Inglewood
Long Drive          Eltham
Magdalene Road      Stratford
Old Main Road       Midhurst
Station Road        Inglewood
Stoney Road         Stratford
Stout Street        Eltham
Vixen Road          Plymouth
```

DISTINCT, then, is concerned with the *whole row* and not only with the column expression that directly follows the word DISTINCT in the statement. Below we give two constructions in which the use of DISTINCT is superfluous (but not forbidden).

- When the SELECT clause includes at least one candidate key for each table specified in the FROM clause, DISTINCT is superfluous. The most important property of a candidate key is that the column that forms the candidate key never allows duplicate values. A table that has a candidate key, therefore, never has duplicate rows. The inclusion of candidate keys in the end result of a SELECT statement offers a guarantee that no duplicate rows will appear in the end result.

- When the SELECT clause results in one row with values, DISTINCT is superfluous.

Finally, the user can specify ALL in the same position in the statement as DISTINCT appears. Note that it actually has the opposite effect to DISTINCT, and does not alter the result of a 'normal' SELECT statement. In other words, these two statements are equivalent:

```
SELECT    TOWN
FROM      PLAYERS
```

and

```
SELECT    ALL TOWN
FROM      PLAYERS
```

10.4   Displaying row numbers

Oracle supports the system variable *ROWNUM*; see Chapter 6. If this variable is used in the SELECT clause, for each row in the result a row number is printed.

Example 10.3: Give for each penalty greater than $25 the payment number and the penalty amount; also add a row number to the result.

```
SELECT   ROWNUM, PAYMENTNO, AMOUNT
FROM     PENALTIES
WHERE    AMOUNT > 25
```

Result:

```
ROWNUM   PAYMENTNO   AMOUNT
------   ---------   ------
     1           1   100.00
     2           2    75.00
     3           3   100.00
     4           4    50.00
     5           7    30.00
     6           8    75.00
```

The ROWNUM variable can, just like all system variables, be used in the WHERE clause.

10.5   An introduction to statistical functions

Expressions in the SELECT clause may contain *statistical functions*. If a SELECT statement has *no* GROUP BY clause, any function in a SELECT clause operates on all rows. Oracle recognizes the following statistical functions:

Function	Meaning
COUNT	Counts the number of values in a column or the number of rows in a table
MIN	Determines the smallest value in a column
MAX	Determines the largest value in a column
SUM	Determines the sum of the values in a column
AVG	Determines the weighted arithmetic mean of the values in a column
STDDEV	Determines the standard deviation of the values in a column
VARIANCE	Determines the variance of the values in a column

If a SELECT clause contains a statistical function, then the entire SELECT statement yields only one row as an end result (reminder: we are assuming here that the SELECT statement has *no* GROUP BY clause).

```
<statistical function> ::=
   <count-function>  |
   <min-function>    |
   <max-function>    |
   <sum-function>    |
   <avg-function>    |
   <stddev-function> |
   <variance-function>
```

Example 10.4: How many players are registered in the PLAYERS table?

```
SELECT   COUNT(*)
FROM     PLAYERS
```

Result:

```
COUNT(*)
--------
      14
```

Explanation: The function COUNT(*) adds up the number of rows remaining from the FROM clause. In this case, the number equals the number of rows in the PLAYERS table.

Example 10.5: How many players live in Stratford?

```
SELECT   COUNT(*)
FROM     PLAYERS
WHERE    TOWN = 'Stratford'
```

Result:

```
COUNT(*)
--------
       7
```

Explanation: Because the SELECT clause is here processed after the WHERE clause, the number of rows where the TOWN column has the value Stratford is counted.

We look at various statistical functions in more detail in the following sections.

10.6   COUNT function

With the COUNT function an asterisk (∗) or a column name can be specified between brackets. In the second case, it is not the number of rows in a special column that will be counted, but the *not NULL values* in a table.

```
<count-function> ::=
    COUNT ( { * | [ ALL | DISTINCT ] <expression> } )
```

Example 10.6: How many league numbers are there?

```
SELECT   COUNT(LEAGUENO)
FROM     PLAYERS
```

Result:

```
COUNT(LEAGUENO)
---------------
             10
```

Explanation: The function COUNT(LEAGUENO) counts the number of values in a specific column instead of the number of rows in the intermediate result; (∗) can only be used in the COUNT function and not in the other functions.

You can also calculate the number of *different* values in a column.

Example 10.7: How many different place names are there in the TOWN column?

```
SELECT   COUNT(DISTINCT TOWN)
FROM     PLAYERS
```

Result:

```
COUNT(DISTINCT TOWN)
--------------------
                   6
```

Explanation: When DISTINCT is specified before the column name all the duplicate values are removed and then the addition is carried out.

Example 10.8: Give the number of different characters with which the names of the players start.

```
SELECT   COUNT(DISTINCT SUBSTR(NAME, 1, 1))
FROM     PLAYERS
```

Result:

```
COUNT(DISTINCT SUBSTR(NAME, 1, 1))
----------------------------------
                                 8
```

See Appendix C for a description of the SUBSTR function.

Example 10.9: Give the number of different years that appear in the PENAL-TIES table.

```
SELECT    COUNT(DISTINCT TO_CHAR(DATE, 'YYYY'))
FROM      PENALTIES
```

Result:

```
COUNT(DISTINCT TO_CHAR(DATE, 'YYYY'))
-------------------------------------
                                    5
```

In a SELECT clause we can use multiple functions at the same time.

Example 10.10: Give the number of different place names and the number of sexes represented.

```
SELECT    COUNT(DISTINCT TOWN), COUNT(DISTINCT SEX)
FROM      PLAYERS
```

Result:

```
COUNT(DISTINCT TOWN)  COUNT(DISTINCT SEX)
--------------------  --------------------
                   6                     2
```

10.7   MAX and MIN functions

With the MAX and MIN functions Oracle determines the largest and smallest values respectively in a column.

```
<max function> ::= MAX ( <function object> )

<min function> ::= MIN ( <function object> )

<function object> ::= [ ALL | DISTINCT ] <expression>
```

Example 10.11: What is the highest penalty?

```
SELECT    MAX(AMOUNT)
FROM      PENALTIES
```

Result:

```
MAX(AMOUNT)
-----------
     100.00
```

We can specify the word ALL before the column name without changing the result. By adding ALL you ensure that *all* values are considered. Duplicate values are then included twice in the calculation. In fact, in examples using the MAX and MIN functions, the addition of ALL is superfluous (as is DISTINCT), though it is not wrong. The following statement is equivalent to the one above.

```
SELECT    MAX(ALL AMOUNT)
FROM      PENALTIES
```

Example 10.12: What is the lowest penalty incurred by a player resident in Stratford?

```
SELECT    MIN(AMOUNT)
FROM      PENALTIES
WHERE     PLAYERNO IN
          (SELECT    PLAYERNO
           FROM      PLAYERS
           WHERE     TOWN = 'Stratford')
```

Result:

```
MIN(AMOUNT)
-----------
     100.00
```

Example 10.13: How many penalties are equal to the lowest one?

```
SELECT    COUNT(*)
FROM      PENALTIES
WHERE     AMOUNT =
          (SELECT    MIN(AMOUNT)
           FROM      PENALTIES)
```

Result:

```
COUNT(AMOUNT)
-------------
            2
```

Explanation: The subquery calculates the lowest penalty, which is $25. The SELECT statement calculates the number of penalties equal to this amount.

Statistical functions can occur in calculations. Here are two examples.

Example 10.14: What is the difference between the highest and lowest penalty in cents?

```
SELECT    (MAX(AMOUNT) - MIN(AMOUNT)) * 100
FROM      PENALTIES
```

Result:

```
(MAX(AMOUNT) - MIN(AMOUNT)) * 100
---------------------------------
                             7500
```

Example 10.15: Give the first letter of the name which appears last in alphabetical order in the PLAYERS table.

```
SELECT    SUBSTR(MAX(NAME), 1, 1)
FROM      PLAYERS
```

Result:

```
SUBSTR(MAX(NAME), 1, 1)
-----------------------
W
```

Explanation: First, the MAX function finds the last name in alphabetical order, and then the scalar function SUBSTR picks out the first letter from this name. See Appendix C for a description of this and other functions.

In principle, DISTINCT can be used with the MAX and MIN functions, but this, of course, doesn't change the end result (work out why not for yourself).

If a column in a special row contains only NULL values, then the value of the MIN and MAX function is also NULL.

10.8   SUM function

The SUM function calculates the sum of all values in a particular column.

```
<sum function> ::= SUM ( <function object> )

<function object> ::= [ ALL | DISTINCT ] <expression>
```

Example 10.16: What is the total amount of penalties incurred by Inglewood players?

```
SELECT    SUM(AMOUNT)
FROM      PENALTIES
WHERE     PLAYERNO IN
          (SELECT   PLAYERNO
           FROM     PLAYERS
           WHERE    TOWN = 'Inglewood')
```

Result:

```
SUM(AMOUNT)
-----------
     155.00
```

We can specify the word ALL before the column name without affecting the result. By adding ALL you explicitly demand that *all* values are considered. In contrast, the use of DISTINCT within the SUM function *can* alter the end result. If we extend the SUM function in the SELECT statement above with DISTINCT, we get the following result:

```
SELECT    SUM(DISTINCT AMOUNT)
FROM      PENALTIES
WHERE     PLAYERNO IN
          (SELECT   PLAYERNO
           FROM     PLAYERS
           WHERE    TOWN = 'Inglewood')
```

Result:

```
SUM(AMOUNT)
-----------
     130.00
```

Note: As opposed to the COUNT, MIN and MAX functions, the SUM function is only applicable to columns and expressions with a numeric data type. The other three functions can be applied to columns and expressions of both numeric and alphanumeric data types.

If a column in a special row only contains NULL values, then the value of the SUM function is also NULL.

10.9   AVG, VARIANCE and STDDEV functions

The AVG, STDDEV and VARIANCE functions calculate the arithmetic average, the standard deviation and the variance of the values in a particular column. These functions are only applicable to numeric expressions.

```
<avg function> ::= AVG ( <function object> )

<stddev function> ::= STDDEV ( <function object> )

<variance function> ::= VARIANCE ( <function object> )

<function object> ::= [ ALL | DISTINCT ] <expression>
```

Example 10.17: Give the average amount of penalties incurred by player 44.

```
SELECT   AVG(AMOUNT)
FROM     PENALTIES
WHERE    PLAYERNO = 44
```

Result:

```
AVG(AMOUNT)
-----------
      43.33
```

Explanation: $43.33 is the average of the amounts $75, $25, and $30.

Example 10.18: Which players have incurred a penalty greater than the average penalty?

```
SELECT   DISTINCT PLAYERNO
FROM     PENALTIES
WHERE    AMOUNT >
         (SELECT   AVG(AMOUNT)
          FROM     PENALTIES)
```

Result:

```
PLAYERNO
---------
       6
      27
      44
```

Explanation: The average penalty equals $60 and these players have incurred penalties higher than $60.

Adding the word ALL doesn't affect the result, as it simply reinforces the idea that *all* values are included in the calculation. On the other hand adding DISTINCT within the AVG function does influence the result.

Example 10.19: What is the *unweighted* arithmetic mean of the penalty amounts. By unweighted we mean that each different value is considered only once in the calculation.

```
SELECT    AVG(DISTINCT AMOUNT)
FROM      PENALTIES
```

Result:

```
AVG(DISTINCT AMOUNT)
--------------------
               56.00
```

Explanation: The amount $56 is equal to $100 + $75 + $50 + $30 + $25 divided by 5.

Example 10.20: Give the variance of all penalty amounts paid for player 44.

```
SELECT    VARIANCE(AMOUNT)
FROM      PENALTIES
WHERE     PLAYERNO = 44
```

Result:

```
VARIANCE(AMOUNT)
----------------
          758.33
```

Explanation: The variance is calculated according to the following steps:

1. Determine the average of the specified column.
2. Determine the absolute value for each value in the column how much it differs from the average value in that column. If the difference is negative, multiply it by –1.
3. Determine the sum of the squares of the differences.
4. Divide that sum by the number of values (in the column) minus 1.

Example 10.21: Give the standard deviation of all penalty amounts paid for player 44.

```
SELECT    STDDEV(AMOUNT)
FROM      PENALTIES
WHERE     PLAYERNO = 44
```

Result:

```
STDDEV(AMOUNT)
--------------
         27.54
```

Explanation: The standard deviation is equal to the square root of the variance. In other words, the following two expressions are equivalent: STDDEV(...) and SQRT(VARIANCE(...)).

For the three functions discussed in this section it also holds that, where a column in a given row contains only NULL values, the value of the function also equals NULL. If a column contains both NULL and 'non NULL' values then the value of the function equals the sum of all 'non NULL' values divided by the number of 'non NULL' values (and therefore not divided by the total number of values in the column). Try to find out for yourself why the following two expressions are *not* equivalent:

```
AVG(NVL(AMOUNT, 0))
```

and

```
NVL(AVG(AMOUNT), 0)
```

10.10   General rule for using statistical functions

NULL values are not included in the calculation of functions. For certain calculations this may cause very confusing results. For example, suppose the AMOUNT column allows NULL values; then the results of the following two statements are *not* necessarily the same. In the first statement Oracle divides the sum of all not NULL values by the number of rows in the PENALTIES table; in the second statement the sum of all not NULL values is divided by the number of NOT NULL values. If the AMOUNT column contains NULL values it is possible for the number of NOT NULL values in this column to be fewer than the number of rows in the PENALTIES table. However, if the AMOUNT column has been defined as NOT NULL in the CREATE TABLE statement, the results of the two SELECT statements are equal.

```
SELECT    SUM(AMOUNT) / COUNT(*)
FROM      PENALTIES

SELECT    AVG(AMOUNT)
FROM      PENALTIES
```

In this chapter we have shown that statistical functions may be used in SELECT clauses. We must, however, stress the following important rule:

If a SELECT statement has no GROUP BY clause, and if the SELECT clause has one or more statistical functions, any column name specified in that SELECT clause must occur within a statistical function.

Therefore, the statement below is not correct because the SELECT clause contains a statistical function as an expression, while the PLAYERNO column name appears outside that statistical function.

```
SELECT    COUNT(*), PLAYERNO
FROM      PLAYERS
```

The reason for this restriction is that the result of a statistical function always consists of one value, whereas the result stemming from a column specification consists of a set of values. Oracle cannot present these results together.

Note, however, that this rule is valid only for column specifications and not, for example, for literals or system variables. This next statement *is* correct:

```
SELECT    'The number of players is', COUNT(*)
FROM      PLAYERS
```

Result:

```
                                 COUNT(*)
------------------------         --------
The number of players is              14
```

In Chapter 11 we will elaborate on this rule for the SELECT clause where SE-LECT statements *do* contain a GROUP BY clause.

Exercises

10.1 Determine the value of the functions below for the following set of values in the NUM column: { 1, 2, 3, 4, 1, 4, 4, NULL, 5 }.

1.   COUNT(*)
2.   COUNT(NUM)
3.   MIN(NUM)
4.   MAX(NUM)
5.   SUM(NUM)
6.   AVG(NUM)
7.   COUNT(DISTINCT NUM)
8.   MIN(DISTINCT NUM)
9.   MAX(DISTINCT NUM)
10. SUM(DISTINCT NUM)
11. AVG(DISTINCT NUM)

10.2 What is the average penalty amount?

10.3 What is the average penalty for players who have competed for team 1?

10.4 Give the name and initials of the players, who have, for at least one team, won more sets than player 27 has won in total.

10.5 How many sets have been won in total, lost in total and what is the tally?

10.6 Give the number and year of birth of each player born in the same year as the youngest player who has played for team 1.

10.11   Specifying column headings

Behind every expression in the SELECT clause an alternative name may be specified; the *column heading*. SQL*Plus places the column heading on top of the result instead of the expression itself.

Example 10.22: Give for each penalty the payment number and the penalty amount in cents.

```
SELECT    PAYMENTNO, AMOUNT * 100 CENTS
FROM      PENALTIES
```

Result:

```
PAYMENTNO  CENTS
---------  -----
        1  10000
        2   7500
        3  10000
        4   5000
        :      :
```

When you look at the result it is clear to see that the word CENTS has been placed above the second column. It is not allowed to use a column heading in the other clauses of the SELECT statement.

11
SELECT statement: GROUP BY and the HAVING clause

The GROUP BY clause groups rows on the basis of similarities between the rows. We could, for example, group players from the PLAYERS table on the basis of the same place of residence, the result of which would be the creation of one group of players per town. From there we could then query how many players were in each group, for example. The question which could be asked is then: 'How many players are there in each town?'.

The HAVING clause has a comparable function to the WHERE clause and enables conditions to be applied to groups. Because the HAVING clause can only be used in conjunction with the GROUP BY clause, we discuss them together in this chapter.

```
<group by clause> ::=
   GROUP BY <expression> [ {,<expression>}... ]

<having clause> ::=
   HAVING <condition>
```

11.1 Grouping on one column

The simplest form of the GROUP BY clause is where only one column is grouped. Here is an example.

Example 11.1: Give all the different place names from the PLAYERS table.

```
SELECT    TOWN
FROM      PLAYERS
GROUP BY TOWN
```

You could imagine the intermediate result from the GROUP BY clause to look like this:

```
TOWN           PLAYERNO                   NAME
----------     ------------------------   --------------------
Stratford      6, 83, 2, 7, 57, 39, 100   Parmenter, Hope, ...
Midhurst       28                         Collins
Inglewood      44, 8                      Baker, Newcastle
Plymouth       112                        Bailey
Douglas        95                         Miller
Eltham         27, 104                    Collins, Moorman
```

Explanation: All rows with the same TOWN form a group. Each row in the inter-mediate result has one value in the TOWN column, while all other columns can contain multiple values. We are showing the columns in this way for illustrative purposes only; Oracle would solve this differently internally. Also, in any Ora-cle table columns *cannot* be presented as the PLAYERNO and NAME columns have been. In fact, a column which is not grouped is completely omitted from the end result, but we will return to this later in the chapter.

End result of the statement:

```
TOWN
---------
Stratford
Midhurst
Inglewood
Plymouth
Douglas
Eltham
```

We could have solved the question above in a simpler way by leaving out the GROUP BY clause and by adding DISTINCT to the SELECT clause (work this out for yourself). The use of the GROUP BY clause becomes interesting if we, for example, extend the SELECT clause with a statistical function.

Example 11.2: For each town, find the number of players.

```
SELECT    TOWN, COUNT(*)
FROM      PLAYERS
GROUP BY TOWN
```

Result:

```
TOWN        COUNT(*)
---------   --------
Stratford        7
Midhurst         1
Inglewood        2
Plymouth         1
Douglas          1
Eltham           2
```

Explanation: The COUNT(*) function is now executed against each grouped row instead of against all rows separately. In other words, the function COUNT(*) is calculated for each grouped row (for each town).

In principle, any statistical function can be used in a SELECT clause as long as that function operates on a column which is *not* grouped.

Example 11.3: For each team, give the team number, the number of matches that has been played for that team and the total number of sets won.

```
SELECT    TEAMNO, COUNT(*), SUM(WON)
FROM      MATCHES
GROUP BY TEAMNO
```

Result:

```
TEAMNO  COUNT(*)  SUM(WON)
------  --------  --------
     1         8        15
     2         5         9
```

Example 11.4: Give for each team that is captained by a player resident in Eltham, the team number and the number of matches that has been played for that team.

```
SELECT    TEAMNO, COUNT(*)
FROM      MATCHES
WHERE     TEAMNO IN
          (SELECT  TEAMNO
           FROM    TEAMS, PLAYERS
           WHERE   TEAMS.PLAYERNO = PLAYERS.PLAYERNO
           AND     TOWN = 'Eltham')
GROUP BY TEAMNO
```

Result:

```
TEAMNO  COUNT(*)
------  --------
     2         5
```

11.2   Grouping on two or more columns

A GROUP BY clause may also contain two or more columns. We illustrate this with two examples.

Example 11.5: Give for the MATCHES table all the different combinations of team numbers and player numbers.

```
SELECT    TEAMNO, PLAYERNO
FROM      MATCHES
GROUP BY TEAMNO, PLAYERNO
```

The result is not grouped by one column, but by two. All rows with the same TEAMNO and the same PLAYERNO form a group.
    The intermediate result from the GROUP BY clause:

```
TEAMNO  PLAYERNO  MATCHNO      WON       LOST
------  --------  ----------   --------  --------
     1         2  6            1         3
     1         6  1, 2, 3      3, 2, 3   1, 3, 0
     1         8  8            0         3
     1        44  4            3         2
     1        57  7            3         0
     1        83  5            0         3
     2         8  13           0         3
     2        27  9            3         2
     2       104  10           3         2
     2       112  11, 12       2, 1      3, 3
```

The end result:

```
TEAMNO  PLAYERNO
------  --------
     1         2
     1         6
     1         8
     1        44
     1        57
     1        83
     :         :
```

```
    :         :
    2         8
    2        27
    2       104
    2       112
```

The sequence of the columns in the GROUP BY clause has no effect on the end result of a statement. The following statement, therefore, is equivalent to the previous one:

```
SELECT    TEAMNO, PLAYERNO
FROM      MATCHES
GROUP BY  PLAYERNO, TEAMNO
```

As an example, let us add some functions to the SELECT statement above:

```
SELECT    TEAMNO, PLAYERNO, SUM(WON), COUNT(*), MIN(LOST)
FROM      MATCHES
GROUP BY  TEAMNO, PLAYERNO
```

Result:

TEAMNO	PLAYERNO	SUM(WON)	COUNT(*)	MIN(LOST)
1	2	1	1	3
1	6	8	3	0
1	8	0	1	3
1	44	3	1	2
1	57	3	1	0
1	83	0	1	3
2	8	0	1	3
2	27	3	1	2
2	104	3	1	2
2	112	3	2	3

Example 11.6: For each player who has incurred a penalty, give the number, the name and the total amount in penalties incurred.

```
SELECT    P.PLAYERNO, NAME, SUM(AMOUNT)
FROM      PLAYERS P, PENALTIES PEN
WHERE     P.PLAYERNO = PEN.PLAYERNO
GROUP BY  P.PLAYERNO, NAME
```

Result:

```
P.PLAYERNO   NAME        SUM(AMOUNT)
----------   ---------   -----------
         6   Parmenter        100.00
         8   Newcastle         25.00
        27   Collins          175.00
        44   Baker            130.00
       104   Moorman           50.00
```

11.3   Grouping on expressions

Until now we have only shown examples where the result was grouped on one or more columns, but you are also allowed to group on expressions. Again we give you a number of examples.

Example 11.7: Give for each year the number of penalties.

```
SELECT   TO_CHAR(PEN_DATE, 'YYYY'), COUNT(*)
FROM     PENALTIES
GROUP BY TO_CHAR(PEN_DATE, 'YYYY')
```

Result:

```
TO_CHAR   COUNT(*)
-------   --------
1980             3
1981             1
1982             1
1983             1
1984             2
```

Example 11.8: Group the players on the basis of their player numbers. Group 1 contains the players with number 1 up to and including 24. Group 2 contains the players with numbers 25 up to and including 49 etcetera. Give for each group the number of players and the highest player number.

```
SELECT   TRUNC(PLAYERNO/25), COUNT(*), MAX(PLAYERNO)
FROM     PLAYERS
GROUP BY TRUNC(PLAYERNO/25)
```

Result:

```
TRUNC(PLAYERNO/25)  COUNT(*)  MAX(PLAYERNO)
------------------  --------  -------------
                 0         4              8
                 1         4             44
                 2         1             57
                 3         2             95
                 4         3            112
```

11.4   Grouping on NULL values

If grouping is required on a column which contains NULL values, these NULL values form one group.

Example 11.9: Find the different values of LEAGUENO.

```
SELECT    LEAGUENO
FROM      PLAYERS
GROUP BY  LEAGUENO
```

Result:

```
LEAGUENO
--------
?
8467
1124
1608
2411
2513
7060
6409
1319
2983
6524
```

11.5   GROUP BY and DISTINCT

In Section 10.3 we described in which cases the use of DISTINCT in the SELECT clause is superfluous. The rules given in that section apply to SELECT statements without a GROUP BY clause. We add a rule for SELECT statements with a GROUP BY clause:

- DISTINCT (outside a statistical function) is superfluous when the SE-
  LECT clause includes all columns that are specified in the GROUP BY
  clause. The GROUP BY clause groups the rows in such a way that the col-
  umn(s) on which they are grouped no longer contain duplicate values.

11.6   General rule for using statistical functions

In the previous chapter we gave the following rule for the use of statistical functions in the SELECT clause.

*If a SELECT statement has no GROUP BY clause, and if the SELECT
clause has one or more statistical functions, any column name specified
in the SELECT clause must occur within a statistical function.*

We now add the following rule:

*If a SELECT statement does have a GROUP BY clause, any column
name specified in the SELECT clause must occur within a statistical
function or in the list of columns given in the GROUP BY clause or in
both.*

Therefore, the statement below is not correct because the TOWN column appears in the SELECT clause, but does *not* occur within a statistical function or in
the list of columns by which the result is grouped.

```
SELECT    TOWN, COUNT(*)
FROM      PLAYERS
GROUP BY PLAYERNO
```

The reason for this restriction is the same as for the first rule. The result of a
statistical function always consists of one value for each group. The result of a
column specification on which grouping is performed also always consists of one
value per group. In contrast, the result of a column specification on which *no*
grouping is performed is a set of values. As mentioned before, a result table cannot combine the two types of results arising from a grouped and an ungrouped
column specification.

Exercises

11.1   Show the different years of birth from the PLAYERS table.

11.2   For each year of birth, show the number of players born in that year.

11.3   For each player who has incurred at least one penalty, give the player number, the average penalty and the number of penalties.

11.4 For each team that has played in the first division, give the number of matches and the total number of sets won.

11.5 For each player who lives in Douglas, give the name, initials and the number of penalties incurred by him or her.

11.6 For each team, give the team number, the division and the total number of sets won.

11.7 Give for each year before 1983 (that appears in the PENALTIES table) the year and the number of penalties.

11.7 Introduction to the HAVING clause

The GROUP BY clause groups the rows of the result from the FROM clause. The HAVING clause enables you to select groups on the basis of their particular group properties. A condition in a HAVING clause looks a lot like a 'normal' condition in a WHERE clause. There is, nevertheless, one difference: expressions in a HAVING clause condition may contain statistical functions, whereas this is not possible for expressions in a WHERE clause condition (unless they appear within a subquery).

Example 11.10: Get the number of each player who has incurred more than one penalty.

```
SELECT    PLAYERNO
FROM      PENALTIES
GROUP BY  PLAYERNO
HAVING    COUNT(*) > 1
```

The intermediate result of the GROUP BY clause looks like this:

PAYMENTNO	PLAYERNO	PEN_DATE	AMOUNT
1	6	08-DEC-80	100.00
6	8	08-DEC-80	25.00
3, 8	27	10-SEP-83, 12-NOV-84	100.00, 75.00
2, 5, 7	44	05-MAY-81, 08-DEC-80, 30-DEC-82	75.00, 25.00 30.00
4	104	08-DEC-84	50.00

In the HAVING condition we specified the selection of groups where the number of rows exceeds one. The intermediate result of the HAVING clause is:

```
PAYMENTNO   PLAYERNO   PEN_DATE                  AMOUNT
---------   --------   ---------------------     -------------
3, 8              27   10-SEP-83, 12-NOV-84      100.00, 75.00
2, 5, 7           44   05-MAY-81, 08-DEC-80,     75.00, 25.00
                       30-DEC-82                 30.00
```

And finally, the end result:

```
PLAYERNO
--------
      27
      44
```

Explanation: Just as with the SELECT clause, the value of a statistical function in a HAVING clause is calculated for each group separately. In this example the number of rows for each group in the intermediate result of the GROUP BY is counted. In the next section we will discuss examples of the HAVING clause with statistical functions.

11.8   Examples of the HAVING clause

This section contains examples of applications of statistical functions in the HAVING clause.

Example 11.11: Give the number of each player whose last penalty was incurred in 1984.

```
SELECT    PLAYERNO
FROM      PENALTIES
GROUP BY  PLAYERNO
HAVING    MAX(TO_CHAR(PEN_DATE, 'YYYY')) = 1984
```

Intermediate result of the GROUP BY clause:

```
PAYMENTNO   PLAYERNO   PEN_DATE                  AMOUNT
---------   --------   ---------------------     -------------
1                  6   08-DEC-80                 100.00
6                  8   08-DEC-80                 25.00
3, 8              27   10-SEP-83, 12-NOV-84      100.00, 75.00
2, 5, 7           44   05-MAY-81, 08-DEC-80,     75.00, 25.00
                       30-DEC-82                 30.00
4                104   08-DEC-84                 50.00
```

The scalar function TO_CHAR pulls out the year figure from each date, so Oracle searches in the PEN_DATE column for the highest year figures for each row. They are respectively: 08-DEC-80, 08-DEC-80, 12-NOV-84, 30-DEC-82 and 08-DEC-84.

Result:

```
PLAYERNO
--------
      27
     104
```

Example 11.12: For each player who has incurred more than $150 worth of penalties in total, find the player number and the total amount of penalties.

```
SELECT    PLAYERNO, SUM(AMOUNT)
FROM      PENALTIES
GROUP BY PLAYERNO
HAVING    SUM(AMOUNT) > 150
```

Intermediate result from GROUP BY:

```
PAYMENTNO   PLAYERNO  PEN_DATE                    AMOUNT
---------   --------  --------------------        -------------
1                  6  08-DEC-80                   100.00
6                  8  08-DEC-80                   25.00
3, 8              27  10-SEP-83, 12-NOV-84        100.00, 75.00
2, 5, 7           44  05-MAY-81, 08-DEC-80,       75.00, 25.00
                      30-DEC-82                   30.00
4                104  08-DEC-84                   50.00
```

Result:

```
PLAYERNO  SUM(AMOUNT)
--------  -----------
      27       175.00
```

Example 11.13: For each player who is captain and who has incurred more than $80 worth of penalties in total, find the player number and the total amount of penalties.

```
SELECT    PLAYERNO, SUM(AMOUNT)
FROM      PENALTIES
WHERE     PLAYERNO IN
          (SELECT   PLAYERNO
           FROM     TEAMS)
GROUP BY PLAYERNO
HAVING    SUM(AMOUNT) > 80
```

Result:

```
PLAYERNO  SUM(AMOUNT)
--------  -----------
       6       100.00
      27       175.00
```

Example 11.14: Give the number and the total amount of penalties for each player with the highest penalty total.

```
SELECT    PLAYERNO, SUM(AMOUNT)
FROM      PENALTIES
GROUP BY  PLAYERNO
HAVING    SUM(AMOUNT) >= ALL
          (SELECT    SUM(AMOUNT)
          FROM       PENALTIES
          GROUP BY AMOUNT)
```

The intermediate result from the GROUP BY clause in the main query looks like this:

```
PAYMENTNO  PLAYERNO  PEN_DATE                 AMOUNT
---------  --------  ----------------------   -------------
1                 6  08-DEC-80                100.00
6                 8  08-DEC-80                25.00
3, 8             27  10-SEP-83, 12-NOV-84     100.00, 75.00
2, 5, 7          44  05-MAY-81, 08-DEC-80,    75.00, 25.00
                     30-DEC-82                30.00
4               104  08-DEC-84                50.00
```

The result of the subquery is:

```
AMOUNT
------
100.00
 25.00
175.00
130.00
 50.00
```

For each group (read player) Oracle determines whether the result of the function SUM(AMOUNT) is greater than or equal to all values in the result of the subquery. The final result then becomes:

```
PLAYERNO  SUM(AMOUNT)
--------  -----------
      27       175.00
```

11.9   General rule for the HAVING clause

In Section 11.6 we outlined rules for the use of columns and statistical functions in SELECT clauses. The HAVING clause requires a similar type of rule, as follows:

> *Each column specification specified in the HAVING clause must occur within a statistical function or must occur in the list of columns named in the GROUP BY clause.*

Therefore, the statement below is not correct, because the YEAR_OF_BIRTH column appears in the HAVING clause, but does *not* appear within a statistical function or in a list of columns by which grouping is performed.

```
SELECT    TOWN, COUNT(*)
FROM      PLAYERS
GROUP BY  TOWN
HAVING    YEAR_OF_BIRTH > 1970
```

The reason for this limitation is the same as that for the SELECT clause rules outlined in Section 11.6. The result of a statistical function always consists of one value for each group. The result of the column specification on which the result is grouped always consists also of only one value. On the other hand, the result of a column specification consists, where it has *not* been sorted, of a collection of values. We deal then with incompatible results, which is not allowed.

Exercises

11.8   In which towns are there more than four players?

11.9   Get the number of each player who has incurred more than $150 in penalties.

11.10 Give the name, initials and number of penalties of each player who has incurred more than one penalty.

11.11 In which years were two penalties incurred?

11.12 Give the number of the team for which the most players have played; at the same time give this number of players.

11.13 Give the team number and the division of each team for which more than four players have competed.

11.14 Give the name and initials of each player who has incurred two or more penalties of more than $40.

11.15 Give the name and initials of each player whose total penalties amount is the highest.

11.16 Get the number of each player whose total amount of penalties equals that of the player whose number is 6.

11.17 Give the numbers of the players who have incurred as many penalties as player 6.

11.18 For each team captained by a player who lives in Stratford, give the team number and the number of players who have won at least one match for that team.

11.19 In which year were the most penalties paid; include this number of penalties in the result.

12
SELECT statement: the ORDER BY clause

Just what is the sequence in which the rows of a SELECT statement are presented? If the SELECT statement has no ORDER BY clause the sequence is unpredictable. The addition of an ORDER BY clause at the end of a SELECT statement is the only guarantee that the rows in the end result will be sorted in a particular way.

```
<order by clause> ::=
   ORDER BY <sort specification>
            [ {,<sort specification>}... ]

<sort specification> ::=
   { <expression> | <sequence number> } [ ASC | DESC ]
```

12.1 Sorting on one column

The simplest manner of sorting is on one column.

Example 12.1: Find the payment number and the player number of each penalty; sort the result by player number.

```
SELECT   PAYMENTNO, PLAYERNO
FROM     PENALTIES
ORDER BY PLAYERNO
```

Result:

```
PAYMENTNO    PLAYERNO
---------    --------
        1           6
        6           8
        3          27
        8          27
        5          44
        2          44
        7          44
        4         104
```

Explanation: The eight rows are sorted on the basis of the values in the PLAY-ERNO column; the lowest value first and the highest value last.

12.2   Sorting with sequence numbers

In the ORDER BY clause we may replace expressions with *sequence numbers*. A sequence number assigns a number to each expression in the SELECT clause by which sorting must occur. This next statement is equivalent, then, to the one in the previous section:

```
SELECT    PAYMENTNO, PLAYERNO
FROM      PENALTIES
ORDER BY 2
```

The sequence number 2 stands for the second expression in the SELECT clause. In the example above sequence numbers *may* be used in place of the expression. It is essential to use sequence numbers when an expression consists of a function, a literal or a numeric expression.

Example 12.2: For each player who has incurred at least one penalty, give the total penalty amount and sort the result on this total.

```
SELECT    PLAYERNO, SUM(AMOUNT)
FROM      PENALTIES
GROUP BY PLAYERNO
ORDER BY 2
```

Result:

```
PLAYERNO  SUM(AMOUNT)
--------  -----------
       8        25.00
     104        50.00
       6       100.00
      44       130.00
      27       175.00
```

Sorting on the total is only possible if a sequence number is used, because it is not permitted to say ORDER BY SUM(AMOUNT).

12.3   Ascending and descending sorting

If you don't specify anything after an expression or sequence number, Oracle sorts the result in *ascending* order. The same result can be achieved by explicitly specifying ASC after the expression. If you specify DESC the rows are presented in *descending* order. For each data type we will clarify what ascending order entails. The sorting of values in descending order always gives the reverse presentation of the sorting in ascending order, irrespective of the data type. Ascending order for numeric values means the lowest value is presented first, and the highest last. Ascending order for alphanumeric values is the same as alphabetical order of words (such as in a dictionary): first, the words beginning with the letter A, then those with the letter B, and so on. Alphanumeric sorting is, nevertheless, not as simple as it seems. For example, does the lower case letter a come before or after the upper case A, and do digits come before or after letters? Oracle uses the internal values of the characters for its sorting. This is different for each operating system. IBM mainframes, for example, use the EBCDIC character set, while many others support the ASCII character set. In Appendix E we give the ASCII representations for each character. From this appendix you can see that upper case letters come before lower case letters and that digits come before letters.

Suppose that the following PEOPLE table is sorted by CODE.

```
The PEOPLE table:
NAME      CODE
-------   ------
Bowie     abc
Picasso   ABC
Warhol    ?abc
McLuhan   a bc
Strauss   ////
Chaplin   9abc
```

The SELECT statement:

```
SELECT   *
FROM     PEOPLE
ORDER BY CODE
```

Result:

```
NAME      CODE
-------   ----
Strauss   ////
Chaplin   9abc
Warhol    ?abc
Picasso   ABC
McLuhan   a bc
Bowie     abc
```

Ascending order of dates means that the date which comes in time before another date is presented first.

12.4   Sorting on more than one column

Multiple columns (or expressions) may be specified in an ORDER BY clause. In the first example of this chapter we ordered the result by the PLAYERNO column. Some player numbers appear more than once in the PENALTIES table though and we can't then predict how rows with the same player numbers are going to be sorted. By adding a second column specification to the ORDER BY clause we eliminate the uncertainty.

Example 12.3:   Give the payment number and the player number of each penalty; sort the result by player number and within that by payment number.

```
SELECT   PAYMENTNO, PLAYERNO
FROM     PENALTIES
ORDER BY PLAYERNO, PAYMENTNO
```

Result:

```
PAYMENTNO  PLAYERNO
---------  --------
        1         6
        6         8
        3        27
        8        27
        2        44
        5        44
        7        44
        4       104
```

Explanation: Rows with the same player number are sorted in ascending order on the PAYMENTNO column.

If we proceed from this SELECT statement:

```
SELECT    NAME, TOWN
FROM      PLAYERS
```

we can then formulate these ORDER BY clauses (work out the results for yourself):

```
ORDER BY NAME DESC
ORDER BY TOWN ASC, NAME DESC
ORDER BY NAME, TOWN
ORDER BY PLAYERS.NAME
ORDER BY PLAYERS.TOWN DESC, NAME
```

12.5   Sorting on expressions

Up till now we have only shown examples where sorting was performed on column values. Oracle also supports sorting on expressions. We give some examples.

Example 12.4: Get the numbers of all players; the result must be sorted on the value of the following calculation: divide the player number by 10 and truncate the resulting value.

```
SELECT    PLAYERNO
FROM      PLAYERS
ORDER BY TRUNC(PLAYERNO/10)
```

Result:

```
PLAYERNO
--------
       6
       7
       8
       2
      27
      28
      39
      44
      57
      83
      95
     104
     100
     112
```

Explanation: First, for each row the result of the following function is calculated: TRUNC(PLAYERNO/10). For some players this function has the same value. These results determine the order of the rows in the final result. The effect is that the player numbers are 'slightly' ordered.

Example 12.5: Give all penalties sorted on year, and within that by payment number.

```
SELECT    PEN_DATE, PAYMENTNO
FROM      PENALTIES
ORDER BY  TO_CHAR(PEN_DATE, 'YYYY'), PAYMENTNO
```

Result:

```
PEN_DATE    PAYMENTNO
---------   ---------
08-DEC-80          1
08-DEC-80          5
08-DEC-80          6
05-MAY-81          2
30-DEC-82          7
10-SEP-83          3
08-DEC-84          4
12-NOV-84          8
```

This might raise the question: isn't a sequence number a special kind of expression? The answer to this question is: No! In the ORDER BY clause a sequence number is not regarded as an expression consisting of only one numeric literal. A sequence number is seen as an exception.

12.6 Sorting and ROWNUM

In Section 10.4 we discussed the ROWNUM variable. After processing the WHERE clause the rows in the result receive their row number. If we sort the rows that form the intermediate result of the WHERE clause, the numbers are not ordered anymore. We give you two examples.

Example 12.6: Give for the first four penalties the row number, the payment number and the penalty amount.

```
SELECT    ROWNUM, PAYMENTNO, AMOUNT
FROM      PENALTIES
WHERE     ROWNUM <= 4
```

Result:

```
ROWNUM  PAYMENTNO  AMOUNT
------  ---------  ------
     1          1     100
     2          2      75
     3          3     100
     4          4      50
```

If we extend the statement with an ORDER by clause to order the result on the AMOUNT column, we will *not* have the four highest penalty amounts.

```
SELECT    ROWNUM, PAYMENTNO, AMOUNT
FROM      PENALTIES
WHERE     ROWNUM <= 4
ORDER BY  AMOUNT
```

The result is:

```
ROWNUM  PAYMENTNO  AMOUNT
------  ---------  ------
     4          4      50
     2          2      75
     1          1     100
     3          3     100
```

12.7   Sorting of NULL values

Oracle recognizes NULL values as the highest values in a column. Therefore they are always placed at the bottom of the result if the order is ascending and at the top if the order is descending. The following statement shows the result below:

```
SELECT    DISTINCT LEAGUENO
FROM      PLAYERS
ORDER BY  1 DESC
```

Result:

```
LEAGUENO
--------
?
8467
7060
6524
6409
2983
:
```

:
2513
2411
1608
1319
1124

Exercises

12.1 Give at least three different ORDER BY clauses that would sort the PLAY-ERS table in ascending order on the player number.

12.2 Say which of the following SELECT statements are incorrect:

```
1.    SELECT    *
      FROM      PLAYERS
      ORDER BY  2
```

```
2.    SELECT    *
      FROM      PLAYERS
      ORDER BY  20 DESC
```

```
3.    SELECT    PLAYERNO, NAME, INITIALS
      FROM      PLAYERS
      ORDER BY  2, INITIALS DESC, 3 ASC
```

```
4.    SELECT    *
      FROM      PLAYERS
      ORDER BY  1, PLAYERNO DESC
```

12.3 Give for each match the player number, the team number and the tally of the number of won sets minus the number of lost sets; order the result by tally in ascending order.

13
SELECT statement: the CONNECT BY clause

In this chapter we look at querying data that is *hierarchically structured*. Hierarchical structures are often to be found in practice. For example, a department could consist of a number of smaller departments, which, in turn, are divided into departments, and so on. Or, a person has two parents and these parents, themselves have two parents. This type of structure is sometimes referred to as the bills of material structure. In order to query these structures Oracle has added a *CONNECT BY clause* to the SELECT statement.

13.1　Another example

To show the features of the CONNECT BY clause, we will deviate from the standard example of the tennis club in this chapter, and use the PARTS table for all examples. This table is defined in the following way:

```
CREATE TABLE PARTS
      ( SUB    CHAR(3)      NOT NULL PRIMARY KEY,
        SUPER  CHAR(3)      NULL,
        PRICE  DECIMAL(5,2) NOT NULL )
```

The contents of the PARTS table consist of the following rows:

SUB	SUPER	PRICE
P1	?	130.00
P2	P1	15.00
P3	P1	65.00
:	:	:

```
     :      :              :
    P4     P1         20.00
    P9     P1         45.00
    P5     P2         10.00
    P6     P3         10.00
    P7     P3         20.00
    P8     P3         25.00
    P12    P7         10.00
    P10    P9         12.00
    P11    P9         21.00
```

In this table we record data about parts. Each part has a unique number (a P-number). This unique P-number is recorded in the SUB column, which forms the primary key of the table. Along with this the price of each part is also held. Next to the P-number in the SUB column, the SUPER column has data about which part belongs to which. Therefore, part P2 is a part of P1 and P5 a part of P2. Clearly, part P1 is not shown as a part of itself. In Figure 13.1 we show the hierarchical structure graphically in order to clarify it.

We already have the ability to pose certain questions about this table using the features described in previous chapters about the SELECT statement; questions such as:

- Which parts are sub-parts of P1?
- Which parts require P8?
- How many different parts are there?

But there are other questions to consider which we cannot yet answer, like:

- From which parts is P1 directly *and* indirectly built?
- How many parts are directly *and* indirectly required to build P1?

13.2   Processing the CONNECT BY clause

By using the CONNECT BY clause you can recursively read a hierarchy.

```
<connect by clause> ::=
   CONNECT BY <connect condition> [ <start with clause> ]

<connect condition> ::=
   [ PRIOR ] <expression> <comparison operator> <expression>|
   <expression> <comparison operator> [ PRIOR ] <expression>

<start with clause> ::=
   START WITH <condition>
```

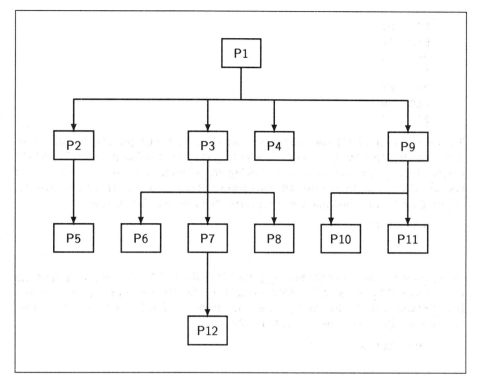

Figure 13.1: Hierarchical structure of parts

We will use two relatively simple examples to show how Oracle processes the CONNECT BY clause.

Example 13.1: Give the entire hierarchy of parts from which P1 is built.

```
SELECT    SUB, SUPER
FROM      PARTS
CONNECT   BY PRIOR SUB = SUPER
START     WITH SUB = 'P1'
```

Result:

```
SUB   SUPER
---   -----
P1    ?
P2    P1
P5    P2
P3    P1
P6    P3
 :     :
```

```
  :     :
 P7    P3
 P12   P7
 P8    P3
 P4    P1
 P9    P1
 P10   P9
 P11   P9
```

So how is this SELECT statement processed by Oracle? Or put another way, how does Oracle come by this result? Oracle begins by processing the START WITH clause. It searches for all rows satisfying the condition in the START WITH clause. These are, therefore, all rows whose value in the SUB column are P1. In our case there is just one row that forms the intermediate result:

```
 SUB   SUPER
 ---   -----
 P1    ?
```

Subsequently, Oracle reads through the SUPER-SUB hierarchy for each of the rows selected by the START WITH clause. So for P1 it determines which parts occur below it in the hierarchy. These are parts P2, P3, P4 and P9. These rows are now added to the intermediate result:

```
 SUB   SUPER
 ---   -----
 P1    ?
 P2    P1      <-- added
 P3    P1      <-- added
 P4    P1      <-- added
 P9    P1      <-- added
```

The added rows are always placed under the row to which they belong in the hierarchy. Next, Oracle searches for the sub-parts of each row just added. These rows are also appended. Intermediate result:

```
 SUB   SUPER
 ---   -----
 P1    ?
 P2    P1
 P5    P2      <-- added
 P3    P1
 P6    P3      <-- added
 P7    P3      <-- added
 P8    P3      <-- added
 P4    P1
 P9    P1
 P10   P9      <-- added
 P11   P9      <-- added
```

Note where the new rows have been added. For each of these added rows another check is done to see whether there are still more sub-parts. P7 is the only one which still has a sub-part, P12. In other words, the entire hierarchy has been processed step by step to give the end result shown above. The first step is, naturally, important. It is here that the first layer of the hierarchy is determined. This first layer is defined by the START WITH clause. If this clause were to be omitted, we would see the following end result:

```
SUB   SUPER
---   -----
P1    ?
P2    P1
P5    P2
P3    P1
P6    P3
P7    P3
P12   P7
P8    P3
P4    P1
P9    P1
P10   P9
P11   P9
P2    P1
P5    P2
P3    P1
P6    P3
P7    P3
P12   P7
P8    P3
P4    P1
P9    P1
P10   P9
P11   P9
P5    P2
P6    P3
P7    P3
P12   P7
P8    P3
P12   P7
P10   P9
P11   P9
```

This end result contains many more rows because the first step did not have one row as its beginning point, but all rows from the PARTS table. And for each row found there, the hierarchy would be read.

Example 13.2: Give the entire hierarchy of parts from which P3 is built.

```
SELECT   SUB, SUPER
FROM     PARTS
CONNECT  BY PRIOR SUB = SUPER
START    WITH SUPER = 'P3'
```

The first step is to find the rows satisfying the condition in the START WITH clause:

```
SUB  SUPER
---  -----
P6   P3
P7   P3
P8   P3
```

Then, for each of these rows, the sub-parts are sought. Only P7 has a sub-part, which is P12. This is added and the end result of the statement is shown:

```
SUB   SUPER
---   -----
P6    P3
P7    P3
P12   P7      <-- added
P8    P3
```

Note: The technique we described here to show the processing of the CONNECT BY clause if of course not the real one. Internally Oracle uses a recursive technique that is more optimized.

13.3   The LEVEL system variable

In Section 6.2 we introduced the LEVEL system variable, but did not discuss it in detail. We can use this variable to show at which level in the hierarchy a part can be found. Here is an example. Note that the START WITH clause differs from the one in the first example in this chapter.

Example 13.3: Show the entire hierarchy of parts from which P1 is built and give the level of each part.

```
SELECT   LEVEL, SUB, SUPER
FROM     PARTS
CONNECT  BY PRIOR SUB = SUPER
START    WITH SUPER = 'P1'
```

Result:

```
LEVEL   SUB   SUPER
-----   ---   -----
    1   P2    P1
    2   P5    P2
    1   P3    P1
    2   P6    P3
    2   P7    P3
    3   P12   P7
    2   P8    P3
    1   P4    P1
    1   P9    P1
    2   P10   P9
    2   P11   P9
```

By using the LPAD function in the SELECT clause (see Appendix C for a description of this function) we can represent the hierarchy more clearly in the result.

```
SELECT    LEVEL, LPAD(' ', 3*(LEVEL-1)) || SUB
FROM      PARTS
CONNECT   BY PRIOR SUB = SUPER
START     WITH SUPER = 'P1'
```

Result:

```
LEVEL   LPAD(' ', 3*(LEVEL-1)) || SUB
-----   ---------------------------
    1   P2
    2      P5
    1   P3
    2      P6
    2      P7
    3         P12
    2      P8
    1   P4
    1   P9
    2      P10
    2      P11
```

13.4   Use of PRIOR

If we study the PARTS table we have to conclude that this hierarchy of parts that we have been talking about is not explicitly shown. We know intuitively, by the use of the SUB and SUPER column names, which part consists of which. But Oracle does not know this. It must be spelled out to Oracle how the hierarchy is built. We do this in the CONNECT BY clause with the word *PRIOR*. PRIOR is placed by the column where the sub-parts are found. In other words, with PRIOR we indicate the direction in which the hierarchy should be read. To illustrate how important it is to place PRIOR correctly we will step through the following two, almost identical, statements:

```
SELECT   LPAD(' ', 3*(LEVEL-1)) || SUB
FROM     PARTS
CONNECT  BY PRIOR SUB = SUPER
START    WITH SUB = 'P3'
```

Result:

```
LPAD(' ', 3*(LEVEL-1)) || SUB
----------------------------
P3
   P6
   P7
      P12
   P8
```

and:

```
SELECT   LPAD(' ', 3*(LEVEL-1)) || SUB
FROM     PARTS
CONNECT  BY SUB = PRIOR SUPER
START    WITH SUB = 'P3'
```

Result:

```
LPAD(' ', 3*(LEVEL-1)) || SUB
----------------------------
P3
   P1
```

Explanation: In the first SELECT statement the tree is read from bottom to top. In the second situation we indicated with PRIOR that the SUPER column contained sub-parts and the SUB column super-parts. Of course, this gives an entirely different result. But the example does show that a hierarchy can be read in either direction. Here are some more examples.

Example 13.4: How many parts does P12 have 'above' itself?

```
SELECT   COUNT(SUPER)
FROM     PARTS
CONNECT  BY SUB = PRIOR SUPER
START    WITH SUB = 'P12'
```

Result:

```
COUNT(SUPER)
------------
           3
```

Example 13.5: How many parts does P1 have 'below' itself?

```
SELECT    COUNT(SUB)
FROM      PARTS
CONNECT   BY PRIOR SUB = SUPER
START     WITH SUPER = 'P1'
```

Result:

```
COUNT(SUPER)
------------
          11
```

For the sake of clarity, we mention here that the following two specifications are equivalent:

```
CONNECT BY PRIOR SUB = SUPER
```

and

```
CONNECT BY SUPER = PRIOR SUB
```

A CONNECT BY clause does not need to contain PRIOR. The following statement is syntactically correct:

```
SELECT    SUB
FROM      PARTS
CONNECT   BY SUB = SUPER
START     WITH SUPER = 'P1'
```

Result:

```
SUB
---
P2
P3
P4
P9
```

By omitting PRIOR you are indicating that the hierarchy should not be read and that only the rows satisfying the condition SUPER = 'P1' should be shown. We could have reached the same result in the following way:

```
SELECT    SUB
FROM      PARTS
WHERE     SUPER = 'P1'
```

13.5   The START WITH clause

The START WITH clause employs a condition to determine the base from which rows in the hierarchy are built. All sorts of conditions can apply here. Here are a few examples.

Example 13.6: Give the hierarchy of the parts P3 and P9.

```
SELECT    SUPER, LPAD(' ', 3*(LEVEL-1)) || SUB
FROM      PARTS
CONNECT   BY PRIOR SUB = SUPER
START     WITH SUB IN ('P3, P9')
```

Result:

```
SUPER  LPAD(' ', 3*(LEVEL-1)) || SUB
-----  ---------------------------
P3     P6
P3     P7
P7        P12
P3     P8
P9     P10
P9     P11
```

Example 13.7: Give the numbers of the parts which do not themselves have P12 as a sub-part.

```
SELECT    SUB
FROM      PARTS
WHERE     SUB NOT IN
          (SELECT   SUPER
          FROM      PARTS
          CONNECT   BY SUB = PRIOR SUPER
          START     WITH SUB = 'P12')
```

Result:

```
SUB
---
P2
P4
  :
```

```
    :
P5
P6
P8
P9
P10
P11
```

13.6   The WHERE clause

As we mentioned in Chapter 7, the WHERE clause is processed just *after* the CONNECT BY clause. This offers the possibility of selecting the LEVEL system variable in the WHERE clause.

Example 13.8: Show the hierarchy up to and including level two of parts from which P1 is built.

```
SELECT    LPAD(' ', 3*(LEVEL-1)) || SUB
FROM      PARTS
WHERE     LEVEL <= 2
CONNECT   BY PRIOR SUB = SUPER
START     WITH SUPER = 'P1'
```

Result:

```
LPAD(' ', 3*(LEVEL-1)) || SUB
-----------------------------
P2
    P5
P3
    P6
    P7
    P8
P4
P9
    P10
    P11
```

Example 13.9: Show the entire hierarchy apart from P3 and P10.

```
SELECT    LPAD(' ', 3*(LEVEL-1)) || SUB
FROM      PARTS
WHERE     SUB NOT IN ('P3', 'P10')
CONNECT   BY PRIOR SUB = SUPER
START     WITH SUPER = 'P1'
```

Result:

```
LPAD(' ', 3*(LEVEL-1)) || SUB
-----------------------------
P2
    P5
    P6
    P7
        P12
    P8
P4
P9
    P11
```

Note: You must take into consideration the fact that by removing a row with the WHERE clause an incorrect interpretation of the hierarchy could result. For example, it appears that P6, P7 and P8 fall directly under P2.

13.7   The ORDER BY clause

You may add an ORDER BY clause to a SELECT statement that contains a CONNECT BY clause. However, the hierarchy can then become cumbersome (or almost impossible) to reconstruct. Here is an example.

```
SELECT    SUB
FROM      PARTS
CONNECT   BY PRIOR SUB = SUPER
START     WITH SUB = 'P3'
ORDER BY SUB
```

Result:

```
SUB
---
P3
P6
P7
P8
P12
```

You could not infer from this list of numbers that P6, P7 and P8 are direct parts of P3 and that P12 is a part of P7.

13.8 Rules for the CONNECT BY clause

When a CONNECT BY clause occurs in a SELECT statement, the following rules apply:

- only one table may be specified in the FROM clause
- if a view is specified in the FROM clause, that view may not be a join
- the WHERE clause may not contain subqueries
- the HAVING clause may not contain subqueries

Exercises

13.1 Show the whole hierarchy of the parts from which P3 and P9 are built.

13.2 On which level of P1's hierarchy does P12 occur?

13.3 How many of the parts comprising P1 cost more than $20?

13.4 To which parts does P12 *not* belong?

14
Combining SELECT statements

Oracle supports a number of operators to combine the results of individual SELECT statements. These operators are referred to as *set operators*. Oracle recognizes the following set operators: UNION, INTERSECT and MINUS. The set operators are an extension of the functionality of the SELECT statement that we have already discussed. In Chapter 6 we gave a definition of the SELECT statement which did not include the set operators, so now we complete the definition with these operators.

```
<select statement> ::=
   <query expression> [ <order by clause> ]

<query expression> ::=
   <select block> |
   <query expression> <set operator> <query expression> |
   ( <query expression> )

<select block> ::=
     <select clause>
     <from clause>
   [ <where clause> ]
   [ <connect by clause> ]
   [ <group by clause>
   [ <having clause> ] ]

<set operator> ::= UNION | INTERSECT | MINUS
```

Explanation: Before we discuss the set operators in detail, we want you to know the differences between the first definition and this new one. A SELECT statement is built up of a *query expression*, possibly followed by an ORDER BY clause. A query expression is built with one or more *select blocks* (or *query specifications*) and may be enclosed between brackets. The following two statement are equivalent:

* ```
  SELECT    PLAYERNO
  FROM      PLAYERS
  ```

* ```
  ( SELECT    PLAYERNO
     FROM       PLAYERS )
  ```

Note that the ORDER BY clause is always specified outside the brackets.

14.1   Linking with UNION

If two select blocks are combined with the UNION operator, the end result consists of the resulting rows from either or both of the select blocks. UNION is the equivalent of the *union* operator from set theory.

Example 14.1: Give the number and place of residence of each player from Inglewood and Plymouth.

```
SELECT    PLAYERNO, TOWN
FROM      PLAYERS
WHERE     TOWN = 'Inglewood'
UNION
SELECT    PLAYERNO, TOWN
FROM      PLAYERS
WHERE     TOWN = 'Plymouth'
```

Result:

```
PLAYERNO  TOWN
--------  ---------
      44  Inglewood
       8  Inglewood
     112  Plymouth
```

Explanation: Each of the two select blocks returns a table with two columns and zero or more rows. The UNION operator places the two tables *under* one another, with the end result of the entire statement being one table.

Note: The statement above could also have been formulated using the OR operator, of course:

```
SELECT    PLAYERS, TOWN
FROM      PLAYERS
WHERE     TOWN = 'Inglewood'
OR        TOWN = 'Plymouth'
```

However, it is not always possible to substitute the OR operator for the UNION operator. Here is an example. Suppose that we have the following two tables. The RECREATION_PLAYERS table contains data about recreational players, while the COMPETITION_PLAYERS table has data about competition players.

The RECREATION_PLAYERS table:

```
PLAYERNO  NAME
--------  ------
       7  Wise
      39  Bishop
```

The COMPETITION_PLAYERS table:

```
PLAYERNO  NAME
--------  ---------
       6  Parmenter
      44  Baker
      83  Hope
```

Example 14.2: Give the numbers and names of all players.

```
SELECT    PLAYERNO, NAME
FROM      RECREATION_PLAYERS
UNION
SELECT    PLAYERNO, NAME
FROM      COMPETITION_PLAYERS
```

Result:

```
PLAYERNO  NAME
--------  ---------
       7  Wise
      39  Bishop
       6  Parmenter
      44  Baker
      83  Hope
```

When the UNION operator is used, Oracle automatically removes all duplicate rows from the end result. Therefore, specifying DISTINCT in the SELECT clause of a select block is redundant if the UNION operator is used.

Example 14.3: Give the number of each player who has incurred at least one penalty, or who is a captain or for whom both conditions apply.

```
SELECT    PLAYERNO
FROM      PENALTIES
UNION
SELECT    PLAYERNO
FROM      TEAMS
```

Result:

```
PLAYERNO
--------
       6
       8
      27
      44
     104
```

Explanation: It is clear from the result that all the duplicate rows have been deleted.

You can join more than two select blocks in a SELECT statement. Here is an example.

Example 14.4: Give the number of each player who has incurred at least one penalty, who is a captain, who lives in Stratford or for whom two or three of these conditions apply.

```
SELECT    PLAYERNO
FROM      PENALTIES
UNION
SELECT    PLAYERNO
FROM      TEAMS
UNION
SELECT    PLAYERNO
FROM      PLAYERS
WHERE     TOWN = 'Stratford'
```

Result:

```
PLAYERNO
--------
       2
       6
       7
       8
      27
      39
      44
       :
```

```
       :
      57
      83
     100
     104
```

14.2　Rules for using UNION

The following rules for using the UNION operator must be observed:

- The SELECT clauses of all relevant select blocks must have the same number of expressions.

- Expressions which will be combined (or placed under one another) in the end result must have comparable data types.

- An ORDER BY clause may only be specified after the last select block. The ordering is performed on the entire end result, only after all intermediate results have been combined.

The following SELECT statements are not written according to these rules (work through them for yourself):

- ```
  SELECT    *
  FROM      PLAYERS
  UNION
  SELECT    *
  FROM      PENALTIES
  ```

- ```
  SELECT    PLAYERNO
  FROM      PLAYERS
  WHERE     TOWN = 'Stratford'
  ORDER BY  1
  UNION
  SELECT    PLAYERNO
  FROM      TEAMS
  ORDER BY  1
  ```

Exercises

14.1　Say which of the following statements are correct and which are incorrect and give reasons:

```
1.    SELECT    ...
      FROM      ...
      GROUP BY  ...
      HAVING    ...
      UNION
      SELECT    ...
      FROM      ...
      ORDER BY  ...

2.    SELECT    PLAYERNO, NAME
      FROM      PLAYERS
      UNION
      SELECT    PLAYERNO, POSTCODE
      FROM      PLAYERS

3.    SELECT    TEAMNO
      FROM      TEAMS
      UNION
      SELECT    PLAYERNO
      FROM      PLAYERS
      ORDER BY 1

4.    SELECT    DISTINCT PLAYERNO
      FROM      PLAYERS
      UNION
      SELECT    PLAYERNO
      FROM      PENALTIES
      ORDER BY 1

5.    SELECT    ...
      FROM      ...
      GROUP BY  ...
      ORDER BY  ...
      UNION
      SELECT    ...
      FROM      ...
```

14.2 If we assume the original contents of the four tables, how many rows are there in the end results of each of the following statements?

```
1.    SELECT    TOWN
      FROM      PLAYERS
      UNION
      SELECT    TOWN
      FROM      PLAYERS
```

```
2.    SELECT    PLAYERNO
      FROM      PENALTIES
      UNION
      SELECT    PLAYERNO
      FROM      PLAYERS

3.    SELECT    YEAR_OF_BIRTH
      FROM      PLAYERS
      UNION
      SELECT    YEAR_JOINED
      FROM      PLAYERS
```

14.3   Linking with INTERSECT

If two select blocks are combined with the INTERSECT operator, the end result consists of those rows that appear in the results of both the select blocks. INTERSECT is the equivalent of the *intersection* operator from set theory.

Example 14.5: Give the number and the year of birth of each player living in Stratford and born after 1960.

```
SELECT     PLAYERNO, YEAR_OF_BIRTH
FROM       PLAYERS
WHERE      TOWN = 'Stratford'
INTERSECT
SELECT     PLAYERNO, YEAR_OF_BIRTH
FROM       PLAYERS
WHERE      YEAR_OF_BIRTH > 1960
```

Result:

```
PLAYERNO   YEAR_OF_BIRTH
--------   -------------
       6            1964
       7            1963
      57            1971
     100            1963
```

Explanation: Both select blocks produce a table with two columns and zero or more rows. The INTERSECT operator is looking for the rows appearing in both tables. The end result of the complete statement is one table.

Note: The statement above could also have been formulated using the AND operator, of course:

```
SELECT    PLAYERS, YEAR_OF_BIRTH
FROM      PLAYERS
WHERE     TOWN = 'Stratford'
AND       YEAR_OF_BIRTH > 1960
```

However, it is not always possible to substitute the INTERSECT operator for the AND operator. Here is an example.

Example 14.6: Give the number of each player who is a captain and who has incurred at least one penalty.

```
SELECT    PLAYERNO
FROM      TEAMS
INTERSECT
SELECT    PLAYERNO
FROM      PENALTIES
```

Result:

```
PLAYERNO
--------
       6
      27
```

All set operators, including the INTERSECT operator, can be used within subqueries.

Example 14.7: Give the names and the numbers of each player who is a captain and who incurred at least one penalty.

```
SELECT    PLAYERNO, NAME
FROM      PLAYERS
WHERE     PLAYERNO IN
          (SELECT    PLAYERNO
          FROM      TEAMS
          INTERSECT
          SELECT    PLAYERNO
          FROM      PENALTIES)
```

Result:

```
PLAYERNO  NAME
--------  ----------
       6  Parmentier
      27  Collins
```

14.4   Linking with MINUS

The third set operator is the MINUS operator. If two select blocks are combined with the MINUS operator, the end result consists only of the resulting rows appearing in the result of the first select block, but which do not appear in the result of the second select block. MINUS is the equivalent of the operator *difference* from set theory.

Example 14.8: Give the number and the year of birth of each player who lives in Stratford, and was *not* born after 1960.

```
SELECT    PLAYERNO, YEAR_OF_BIRTH
FROM      PLAYERS
WHERE     TOWN = 'Stratford'
MINUS
SELECT    PLAYERNO, YEAR_OF_BIRTH
FROM      PLAYERS
WHERE     YEAR_OF_BIRTH > 1960
```

Result:

PLAYERNO	YEAR_OF_BIRTH
2	1948
39	1956
83	1956

Explanation: Each of the two select blocks returns a table with two columns and zero or more rows. The MINUS operator is looking first for all rows appearing in the first select block. These are the following rows:

PLAYERNO	YEAR_OF_BIRTH
6	1964
83	1956
2	1948
7	1963
57	1971
39	1956
100	1963

Next, the operator is looking for all the rows appearing in the second select block. These are the following rows:

```
PLAYERNO  YEAR_OF_BIRTH
--------  -------------
     112           1963
       8           1962
     100           1963
      28           1963
       6           1964
      44           1963
      27           1964
     104           1970
       7           1963
      57           1971
```

Finally, all rows appearing in the first intermediate result, but not appearing in the second, will be recorded in the end result. The end result of the entire statement is, of course, one table again.

Note: The statement above could also have been formulated as follows:

```
SELECT    PLAYERS, YEAR_OF_BIRTH
FROM      PLAYERS
WHERE     TOWN = 'Stratford'
AND       NOT(YEAR_OF_BIRTH > 1960)
```

However, it is not always possible to reverse the MINUS operator the way we did above. Here is an example.

Example 14.9: Give the number of each player who incurred at least one penalty and is *not* a captain.

```
SELECT    PLAYERNO
FROM      PENALTIES
MINUS
SELECT    PLAYERNO
FROM      TEAMS
```

Result:

```
PLAYERNO
--------
       8
      44
     104
```

Example 14.10: Give the names and numbers of each player who incurred at least one penalty and is not a captain.

```
SELECT    PLAYERNO, NAME
FROM      PLAYERS
WHERE     PLAYERNO IN
          (SELECT    PLAYERNO
          FROM       PENALTIES
          MINUS
          SELECT     PLAYERNO
          FROM       TEAMS)
```

Result:

```
PLAYERNO   NAME
--------   ---------
       8   Newcastle
      44   Baker
     104   Moorman
```

The fact that Oracle supports the MINUS operator makes the INTERSECT operator superfluous. Work out for yourself that the following two statements produce the same result under all circumstances.

-
```
SELECT    PLAYERNO
FROM      TEAMS
INTERSECT
SELECT    PLAYERNO
FROM      PENALTIES
```

-
```
SELECT    PLAYERNO
FROM      TEAMS
MINUS     (SELECT    PLAYERNO
          FROM       TEAMS
          MINUS
          SELECT     PLAYERNO
          FROM       PENALTIES)
```

14.5   Set operators and the NULL value

Oracle automatically removes duplicate rows from the result if a set operator is used. That is why the following (somewhat peculiar) SELECT statement produces only one row, even if both individual select blocks have one row as intermediate results.

```
SELECT    PLAYERNO, LEAGUENO
FROM      PLAYERS
WHERE     PLAYERNO = 27
UNION
SELECT    PLAYERNO, LEAGUENO
FROM      PLAYERS
WHERE     PLAYERNO = 27
```

What will happen to NULL values? What is the result of the statement above if we substitute player number 27 by 7? Player 7 has no league number. Maybe you think that the statement will produce two rows now, due to the fact that NULL values are not considered equivalent. However, this is not true. Oracle will show in this situation only one row. Oracle considers NULL values as being equivalent when set operators are processed. This is in accordance with the theory of the relational model as defined by Codd (1990).

14.6   Combining multiple set operators

We have already seen a number of examples where multiple set operators are used within one single SELECT statement. We give you another example.

Example 14.11: Give the numbers of each player who incurred at least one penalty and who is not a captain, and add the players who live in Eltham.

```
SELECT    PLAYERNO
FROM      PENALTIES
MINUS
SELECT    PLAYERNO
FROM      TEAMS
UNION
SELECT    PLAYERNO
FROM      PLAYERS
WHERE     TOWN = 'Eltham'
```

Result:

```
PLAYERNO
--------
       8
      27
      44
     104
```

Explanation: The method of processing is as follows. First, the results of the second select block is subtracted from the first and only then will the intermediate result be coupled to the result of the third select block.

We can place brackets around select blocks to affect the sequence of processing. Below we give you the SELECT statement above, but now we have placed brackets around the last two select blocks. The result shows that the SELECT statement has been processed differently.

```
SELECT    PLAYERNO
FROM      PENALTIES
MINUS
( SELECT    PLAYERNO
  FROM      TEAMS
  UNION
  SELECT    PLAYERNO
  FROM      PLAYERS
  WHERE     TOWN = 'Eltham' )
```

Result:

```
PLAYERNO
--------
       8
      44
```

14.7   Set operators and theory

We conclude this chapter with a somewhat theoretical discussion of set operators. We give you a number of rules for working with multiple, different set operators within one SELECT statement. All the rules are based on general rules (laws) which apply to mathematical operators and set theory. We will define and explain each of these laws. We will use the following symbols and definitions:

- the symbol S_i represents the result of a random select block (i is 1, 2 or 3)
- for each S_i the SELECT clauses are union compatible
- the symbol $S\emptyset$ represents the empty result of a select block
- the symbol $\cup$ represents the UNION operator
- the symbol $\cap$ represents the INTERSECT operator
- the symbol $-$ represents the MINUS operator
- the symbol $=$ means is equal to
- the symbol $\neq$ means is not always equal to
- the symbol θ represents a random set operator

Therefore the results of two SELECT statements are equivalent if the number of rows is equivalent in the two statements and if, after the results have been ordered, rows with identical reference numbers are equivalent.

General rules:

1. $S_1 \cup S_2 = S_2 \cup S_1$
    In mathematics this law is called the *commutative law* for the UNION operator. A set operator is commutative if the order of the select blocks can be changed without affecting the final result. In other words, a set operator θ is commutative if $S_1 \ \theta \ S_2$ is equivalent to $S_2 \ \theta \ S_1$ for each pair (S_1, S_2). Notice that $S_1 - S_2 \neq S_2 - S_1$ if $S_1 \neq S_2$; so the MINUS operator is an example of a non-commutative operator.

2. $S_1 \cap S_2 = S_2 \cap S_1$
    For the INTERSECT operator the commutative law also holds.

3. $S_1 \cup S\emptyset \neq S_1$
    Adding an empty result to a non-empty result S_1 with the UNION operator does not always lead to the original result S_1. The comparison is only correct if S_1 has no duplicate rows.

4. $S_1 \cap S\emptyset = \emptyset$
    The intersection of a result with the empty set leads to an empty result regardless of whether S_1 contains or does not contain duplicate rows.

5. $S_1 - S\emptyset \neq S_1$
    The result of subtracting an empty result from a non-empty result S_1 with the MINUS operator does not always lead to S_1 itself. The comparison is only correct if S_1 contains no duplicate rows.

6. $S_1 \cup (S_2 \cup S_3) = (S_1 \cup S_2) \cup S_3$
    This law is called the *associative law* for the UNION operator. A set operator θ is associative if $(S_1 \ \theta \ S_2) \ \theta \ S_3$ is equivalent to $S_1 \ \theta \ (S_2 \ \theta \ S_3)$ for each combination of (S_1, S_2, S_3). Brackets can be left out for associative set operators, so $S_1 \cup (S_2 \cup S_3)$ is equivalent to $S_1 \cup S_2 \cup S_3$.

7. $S_1 \cap (S_2 \cap S_3) = (S_1 \cap S_2) \cap S_3$
    The same rules of the associative law apply to the INTERSECT operator.

8. $S_1 \cup (S_2 \cap S_3) = (S_1 \cup S_2) \cap (S_1 \cup S_3)$ and
    $S_1 \cap (S_2 \cup S_3) = (S_1 \cap S_2) \cup (S_1 \cap S_3)$
    These laws are called the *distributive laws*. The analogy of the properties of union and intersection with the properties of adding and multiplying numbers is noteworthy.

9. $S_1 \cup S_1 \neq S_1$
    The union of a result with itself only leads to the same result if S_1 contains no duplicate rows.

10. $S_1 \cap S_1 \neq S_1$
    The intersection of a result with itself only leads to the same result if S_1 contains no duplicate rows.

11. $S_1 - S_1 = S\emptyset$

Subtracting a result from itself leads to an empty result regardless of whether S_1 contains or does not contain duplicate rows.

12. $S_1 \cup (S_1 \cap S_2) = S_1$ and
$S_1 \cap (S_1 \cup S_2) = S_1$

These two laws are called the DeMorgan's rules and only apply if S_1 and S_2 contain no duplicate rows.

13. $S_1 - (S_1 - S_2) = S_1 \cap S_2$ and
$S_2 - (S_2 - S_1) = S_1 \cap S_2$

These rules only apply if neither S_1 nor S_2 contains duplicate rows.

14. $(S_1 \cup S_2) \cap S_1 = S_1 - S_2$

This rule always applies, even if S_1 and S_2 have duplicate rows.

15
The subquery

Before we continue with the other SQL statements, we describe in this and the following chapter two subjects that are related to the SELECT statement. The subquery will be discussed in this chapter and the join in the next chapter.

Note: There will be no introduction of new features of the SELECT statement in this chapter. So you can skip this chapter and continue with the next chapter and study this chapter later.

15.1   Rules for subqueries

A *subquery* is a SELECT statement within a condition of a SELECT statement. Other words for subquery are *subselect* or *innerselect*.

There is one difference between the definition of the subquery and the 'normal' SELECT statement, which is that an ORDER BY clause is not permitted in a subquery. However, this syntactical limitation does not lead to a limitation on functionality. The meaning of a set of values does not change if the values are arranged differently. The sets below are equal with regard to the processing of the subquery.

```
(1, 4, 8)
(8, 1, 4)
(8, 4, 1)
```

```
<subquery> ::= ( <query expression> )

<query expression> ::=
   <select block> |
   <query expression> <set operator> <query expression> |
   ( <query expression> )

<select block> ::=
   <select clause>
   <from clause>
   [ <where clause> ]
   [ <connect by clause> ]
   [ <group by clause>
   [ <having clause> ] ]

<set operator> ::= UNION | INTERSECT | MINUS
```

15.2   Range of columns

An important aspect of the subquery is the *range* of the columns. In order to explain this concept well, we use *select blocks*.

A SELECT clause marks the beginning of a select block. Thus the SELECT statement on the next page is constructed from five select blocks. A subquery belongs to the select block formed by the main statement of which it is a subquery. The columns of a table may be used in any place in the select block in which the table is specified. Therefore, in the example, columns from table A may be used in select blocks Q_1, Q_3, Q_4 and Q_5, but not in Q_2. We can say, then, that Q_1, Q_3, Q_4 and Q_5 together form the range of the columns from table A. Columns from table B may only be used in select blocks Q_3 and Q_5, making Q_3 and Q_5 the range of the table B columns.

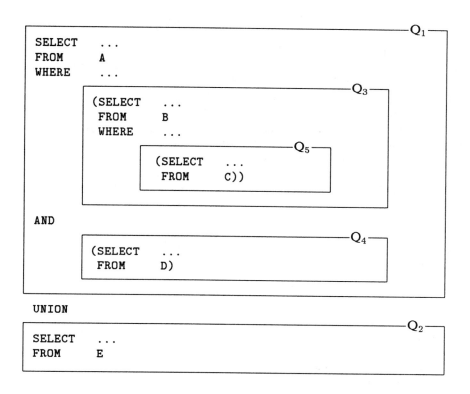

Example 15.1: Give the number and name of each player who has incurred at least one penalty.

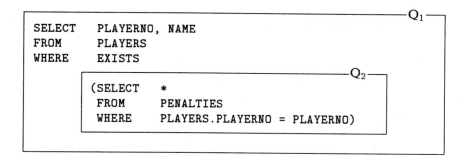

The columns from the PLAYERS table may be used in the select block Q_1 and Q_2, while columns from the PENALTIES table may only be used in select block Q_2.

In this example we take the PLAYERNO column from the PLAYERS table to use in Q_2. What would happen if, instead of PLAYERS.PLAYERNO, we specified only PLAYERNO? In this case, Oracle would interpret the column as being PLAYERNO from the PENALTIES table and this would produce a different result. To be precise, the NAME for *each* player would be presented because PLAYERNO = PLAYERNO is valid for every row in the PENALTIES table.

Select block Q_2 is called a *correlated subquery* because it contains a column belonging to a table that is specified in another select block.

If there is no table name specified before a column name in a subquery, Oracle looks first to see whether the column belongs to one of the tables named in the subquery's FROM clause. If so, then Oracle assumes that the column belongs to that table. If not, then Oracle looks to see if the the column belongs to a table named in the FROM clause of the select block of which the subquery forms a part. In fact, you will write much clearer statements by explicitly mentioning table names before the column names in these situations.

How does Oracle process the statement above? We will illustrate it by using intermediate results from the various clauses. The intermediate result of the FROM clause in select block Q_1 is a copy of the PLAYERS table:

```
PLAYERNO   NAME          ...
--------   ---------     ---
       6   Parmenter     ...
      44   Baker         ...
      83   Hope          ...
       2   Everett       ...
      27   Collins       ...
       :   :             :
       :   :             :
```

To process the WHERE clause Oracle executes the subquery against each row in the intermediate result. The intermediate result of the subquery for the first row, where the PLAYERNO equals 6, looks like this:

```
PAYMENTNO   PLAYERNO   PEN_DATE    AMOUNT
---------   --------   ---------   ------
        1          6   08-DEC-80   100.00
```

There is only one row in the PENALTIES table in which the player number equals the player number from the row in the PLAYERS table. The condition of select block Q_1 is true, since the intermediate result of the select block consists of at least one row.

The intermediate result of the subquery for the second row from select block Q_1 consists of three rows:

```
PAYMENTNO   PLAYERNO   PEN_DATE    AMOUNT
---------   --------   ---------   ------
        2         44   05-MAY-81   75.00
        5         44   08-DEC-80   25.00
        7         44   30-DEC-82   30.00
```

We see, then, that player 44 will appear in the end result. The following player, number 83, will not be included in the end result as no row in the PENALTIES table records a player number of 83.

The final result of the statement is:

```
PLAYERNO  NAME
--------  ---------
       6  Parmenter
      44  Baker
      27  Collins
     104  Moorman
       8  Newcastle
```

In processing a correlated subquery, Oracle considers a column from the outer or enveloping select block to be a literal for the subquery.

As mentioned in Chapter 6, Oracle tries, in reality, to find the most efficient processing method. Irrespective of the processing method the result is always the same.

Here are a couple of variants on the above example.

```
SELECT    PLAYERNO, NAME
FROM      PLAYERS
WHERE     EXISTS
          (SELECT   *
          FROM      PENALTIES
          WHERE     PLAYERS.PLAYERNO = PLAYERS.PLAYERNO)
```

The subquery is executed separately for each player. The WHERE clause in the subquery contains a condition which is always true, so the subquery always returns one row. Conclusion: this statement returns the names of all players.

The result would be different if the PLAYERNO column in the PLAYERS table (could) contain NULL values (work this out for yourself).

This next statement has the same effect as the first example in this section.

```
SELECT    PLAYERNO, NAME
FROM      PLAYERS P
WHERE     EXISTS
          (SELECT   *
          FROM      PENALTIES PN
          WHERE     P.PLAYERNO = PN.PLAYERNO)
```

Note: The pseudonym for the PENALTIES table can be left out without affecting the result.

Exercises

15.1 Say, for each of the columns below, in which select blocks of the SELECT statement they may be used (refer to the next figure).

1.   A.C1
2.   B.C1
3.   C.C1
4.   D.C1
5.   E.C1

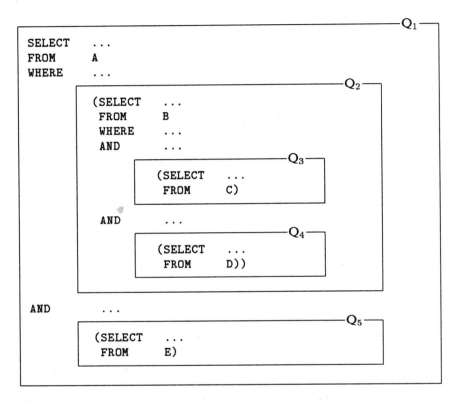

15.2 Give the name and initials of each first division competition player who has won at least one match and who has not incurred a single penalty.

15.3 Give the number and name of each player who has played for both the first and second teams.

15.3 Examples with correlated subqueries

In Chapter 9 we began to look at subqueries and correlated subqueries. A correlated subquery was defined as a subquery naming a column that belongs to a table which is specified in another select block. This section presents more complex examples of this form of the SELECT statement.

Example 15.2: Get the team number and division of each team in which player 44 has played.

```
SELECT    TEAMNO, DIVISION
FROM      TEAMS
WHERE     EXISTS
          (SELECT   *
          FROM      MATCHES
          WHERE     PLAYERNO = 44
          AND       TEAMNO = TEAMS.TEAMNO)
```

Result:

```
TEAMNO  DIVISION
------  --------
     1  first
```

Explanation: Look in the MATCHES table to check whether, for each team, there is at least one row in which the TEAMNO value equals the team number of the team concerned and the player number equals 44. We will rewrite this statement in the pseudo-language already used in other parts of this book.

```
RESULT := [];
FOR EACH T IN TEAMS DO
   RESULT_SUB := [];
   FOR EACH M IN MATCHES DO
      IF (M.PLAYERNO = 44)
      AND (T.TEAMNO = M.TEAMNO) THEN
         RESULT_SUB :+ ;
   OD;
   IF RESULT_SUB <> [] THEN
      RESULT :+ T;
OD;
```

Example 15.3: Get the number of each player who has incurred more than one penalty.

```
SELECT    DISTINCT PLAYERNO
FROM      PENALTIES PN
WHERE     PLAYERNO IN
          (SELECT   PLAYERNO
          FROM      PENALTIES
          WHERE     PAYMENTNO <> PN.PAYMENTNO)
```

Result:

```
PLAYERNO
--------
      44
      27
```

Explanation: For each row in the PENALTIES table Oracle checks whether there is another row in this table with the same player number, but a different payment number. If so, then these players have incurred at least two penalties.

Example 15.4: Give the number and the name of each player who has *not* played matches for team 1.

```
SELECT    PLAYERNO, NAME
FROM      PLAYERS
WHERE     1 <> ALL
          (SELECT   TEAMNO
          FROM      MATCHES
          WHERE     PLAYERNO = PLAYERS.PLAYERNO)
```

Result:

```
PLAYERNO  NAME
--------  ----------
      27  Collins
     104  Moorman
       7  Wise
      39  Bishop
     112  Bailey
     100  Parmenter
      28  Collins
      95  Miller
```

Explanation: The subquery produces a list of teams for whom a given player has played. The main query presents the names of those players for whom team number 1 does not appear on the list.

Example 15.5: Get the three highest league numbers.

If you simply want to find the highest league number then the following SELECT statement suffices:

```
SELECT    MAX(LEAGUENO)
FROM      PLAYERS
```

Result:

```
MAX(LEAGUENO)
-------------
8467
```

But you cannot use this statement with the MAX function to determine the *three* highest league numbers. Instead, the following statement is necessary:

```
SELECT    LEAGUENO
FROM      PLAYERS P1
WHERE     3 >
          (SELECT    COUNT(*)
          FROM      PLAYERS P2
          WHERE     P1.LEAGUENO < P2.LEAGUENO)
ORDER BY LEAGUENO DESC
```

Result:

```
LEAGUENO
--------
8467
7060
6524
```

Explanation: There is no higher league number than the highest! The second highest number has one number that is higher and the third highest has only two higher numbers. With the subquery we count, for each league number, the number of league numbers that are higher. If this shows fewer than three league numbers, then the league number concerned appears in the end result. Determining the three lowest league number is now very simple:

```
SELECT    LEAGUENO
FROM      PLAYERS P1
WHERE     3 >
          (SELECT    COUNT(*)
          FROM      PLAYERS P2
          WHERE     P1.LEAGUENO > P2.LEAGUENO)
ORDER BY LEAGUENO DESC
```

These two examples pertain to a column that contains *no* duplicate values. Neither statement is appropriate for determining the three highest (or lowest) values in a column in which duplicate values are present.

Example 15.6: Give the number of each team in which player 57 has *not* played.

```
SELECT    TEAMNO
FROM      TEAMS
WHERE     NOT EXISTS
          (SELECT    *
          FROM      MATCHES
          WHERE     PLAYERNO = 57
          AND       TEAMNO = TEAMS.TEAMNO)
```

Result:

```
TEAMNO
------
     2
```

Explanation: Give the numbers of the teams for which in the MATCHES table there is no row with that team number and the player number 57.

Example 15.7: Which players have competed for all teams named in the TEAMS table?

```
SELECT  PLAYERNO
FROM    PLAYERS P
WHERE   NOT EXISTS
        (SELECT *
         FROM   TEAMS T
         WHERE  NOT EXISTS
                (SELECT *
                 FROM   MATCHES M
                 WHERE  T.TEAMNO = M.TEAMNO
                 AND    P.PLAYERNO = M.PLAYERNO))
```

Result:

```
PLAYERNO
--------
       8
```

Explanation: We can put the original question in another way using a double negative structure: Find each player for whom no team exists in which the player concerned has never played. The two subqueries produce a list of teams for whom a given player has not played. The main query presents those players for whom the result table of the subquery is empty. Oracle determines for each player, separately, whether the subquery yields *no* result. Let us take player 27 as an example. Oracle checks whether the following statement has a result for this player.

```
SELECT  *
FROM    TEAMS T
WHERE   NOT EXISTS
        (SELECT *
         FROM   MATCHES M
         WHERE  T.TEAMNO = M.TEAMNO
         AND    M.PLAYERNO = 27)
```

This statement has a result if there is a team in which player 27 has never played. Player 27 has not played for team 1, but has for team 2. We conclude that the result of this statement consists of the data from team 1. This means that player

27 does not appear in the end result, because the WHERE clause specifies players for whom the result of the subquery is empty (NOT EXISTS).

We can do the same with player number 8. The result of the subquery, in this case, is empty, because he has played for team 1 as well as team 2. So, the condition in the main query is true and player 8 is included in the end result.

Example 15.8: Give the number of each player who has played for at least all the teams in which player 57 has ever played.

```
SELECT    PLAYERNO
FROM      PLAYERS
WHERE     NOT EXISTS
          (SELECT   *
          FROM      MATCHES M1
          WHERE     PLAYERNO = 57
          AND       NOT EXISTS
                    (SELECT   *
                    FROM      MATCHES M2
                    WHERE     M1.TEAMNO = M2.TEAMNO
                    AND       PLAYERS.PLAYERNO = M2.PLAYERNO))
```

Result:

```
PLAYERNO
--------
       6
      44
      83
       2
      57
       8
```

Explanation: This statement is similar to the previous one. But the question was not asking for players who have played for *all* teams, but for those teams in which player 57 has also played. This difference is apparent in the first subquery. Here, Oracle does not check all teams (in contrast to the subquery in the previous example), but only teams in which player 57 has played.

Example 15.9: Give the number of each player who has played for the same teams as player 57.

This question can also be put differently: Give the number of each player who, first, has played for all the teams in which player 57 has played and, second, has not played for teams in which player 57 has not played. The first part of the question is like the previous one; the second part of the question can be answered with the SELECT statement below. This statement finds all players who have competed in teams in which player 57 has not competed.

```
SELECT    PLAYERNO
FROM      MATCHES
WHERE     TEAMNO IN
          (SELECT   TEAMNO
          FROM      TEAMS
          WHERE     TEAMNO NOT IN
                    (SELECT   TEAMNO
                    FROM      MATCHES
                    WHERE     PLAYERNO = 57))
```

Combining this statement with that of the previous question supplies us with our answer:

```
SELECT    PLAYERNO
FROM      PLAYERS P
WHERE     NOT EXISTS
          (SELECT   *
          FROM      MATCHES M1
          WHERE     PLAYERNO = 57
          AND       NOT EXISTS
                    (SELECT   *
                    FROM      MATCHES M2
                    WHERE     M1.TEAMNO = M2.TEAMNO
                    AND       P.PLAYERNO = M2.PLAYERNO))
AND       PLAYERNO NOT IN
          (SELECT   PLAYERNO
          FROM      MATCHES
          WHERE     TEAMNO IN
                    (SELECT   TEAMNO
                    FROM      TEAMS
                    WHERE     TEAMNO NOT IN
                              (SELECT   TEAMNO
                              FROM      MATCHES
                              WHERE     PLAYERNO = 57)))
```

Exercises

15.4 Find the number and name of each player who has incurred at least one penalty; use a correlated subquery.

15.5 Find the number and name of each player who has won at least two matches.

15.6 Give the name and initials of each player who has incurred no penalties between 1 January 1980 and 31 December 1980.

15.7 Give the number of each player who has incurred at least one penalty that is equal to an amount which has occurred at least twice.

15.4   Transformations with subqueries

Subqueries can be related to main queries with operators, such as ANY, IN and EXISTS. Under certain conditions all the operators can be mutually transformed. This will be explained in this section. We assume the following definitions and symbols:

- T_1 and T_2 are two tables, both with columns $C_1, C_2, \ldots, C_n$
- all columns have the same data type
- C represents a random condition

All the discussed transformations only apply to subqueries in the WHERE clause and not to subqueries in the HAVING clause.

15.4.1   Transformation 1

Each formulation with the IN operator is equivalent to a formulation with the =ANY operator. So the following two SELECT statements give identical results under all conditions:

```
SELECT    *                      SELECT    *
FROM      T1                     FROM      T1
WHERE     C1 IN                  WHERE     C1 = ANY
          (SELECT    C2                    (SELECT    C2
          FROM       T2                    FROM       T2
          WHERE      C)                    WHERE      C)
```

We have already discussed this transformation in Chapter 9. We have added it here for the sake of completeness.

15.4.2   Transformation 2

Each formulation with the NOT IN operator is equivalent to a formulation with the <>ALL operator. So the following two SELECT statements give identical results under all conditions:

```
SELECT    *                      SELECT    *
FROM      T1                     FROM      T1
WHERE     C1 NOT IN              WHERE     C1 <> ALL
          (SELECT    C2                    (SELECT    C2
          FROM       T2                    FROM       T2
          WHERE      C)                    WHERE      C)
```

This transformation has also been discussed in Chapter 9.

15.4.3   Transformation 3

Certain formulations with the ANY operator are equivalent to formulations with EXISTS. So the following two SELECT statements are equivalent. The question mark represents a random comparison operator.

```
SELECT    *                    SELECT    *
FROM      T1                   FROM      T1
WHERE     C1 ? ANY             WHERE     EXISTS
          (SELECT    C2                  (SELECT    *
          FROM       T2                  FROM       T2
          WHERE      C)                  WHERE      (C)
                                         AND        T2.C2 ? T1.C1)
```

Of course this transformation is only permitted syntactically if in the place of C_2 a statistical function is not specified. In that case the word ANY can be left out entirely.

If, temporarily, we forget about the limitation specified above, can we assume that the ANY operator can be transformed into an EXISTS operator under all conditions? The answer is: No! In some situations the value of the predicate with ANY is unknown. This happens if the value of C_1 is equivalent to the NULL value *and* if the subquery is *not* empty (if the subquery is empty the ANY operator always evaluates to false). We will explain why, in this situation, the two conditions do not give the same result. Suppose that $T_1.C_1$ is equal to the NULL value and that the result of the subquery contains only one value, the number 1, for example. The ANY operator evaluates to unknown. The result of the condition with EXISTS always returns the value true or false; unknown is impossible for the EXISTS operator. In the case outlined above, the value would be false. Because the WHERE clause is made up of only one condition (accidental) the same end result is given: namely nothing. If NOT was specified before the condition, the condition of ANY would still be unknown and EXISTS would return true.

Many people initially suspect that the IN and ANY operators can always be transformed easily to an EXISTS operator. This is obviously not the case. This problem has been described by C.J. Date in an article entitled *EXISTS is not "Exists"*; see (Date, 1990).

15.4.4 Transformation 4

Certain formulations with the ALL operator are equivalent to formulations with NOT EXISTS. So the following two SELECT statements are equivalent. The question mark represents any comparison operator. (Notice that the added condition in the subquery is a negative condition.)

```
SELECT    *                    SELECT    *
FROM      T1                   FROM      T1
WHERE     C1 ? ALL             WHERE     NOT EXISTS
          (SELECT    C2                  (SELECT    *
          FROM       T2                  FROM       T2
          WHERE      C)                  WHERE      (C)
                                         AND        NOT (T2.C2 ? T1.C1))
```

This transformation is (as for the ANY operator) only permitted syntactically if in the place of C_2 a statistical function is not specified. In that case the word ALL can be left out entirely. The conditions which we described for ANY also apply to the ALL operator. The transformation is only correct if C_1 cannot contain NULL values and if the subquery is not empty.

15.4.5　Transformation 5

Each formulation with the EXISTS operator is equivalent to a formulation with a comparison operator, such as $<=$ or $>$. So the following two SELECT statements are equivalent.

```
SELECT    *                 SELECT    *
FROM      T1                FROM      T1
WHERE     EXISTS            WHERE     1 <=
          (SELECT  *                  (SELECT   COUNT(*)
          FROM     T2                 FROM      T2
          WHERE    C)                 WHERE     C)
```

15.4.6　Transformation 6

Each formulation with the NOT EXISTS operator is equivalent to a formulation with the comparison operator $>$. So, at all times, the following two SELECT statements give equal results.

```
SELECT    *                 SELECT    *
FROM      T1                FROM      T1
WHERE     NOT EXISTS        WHERE     1 >
          (SELECT  *                  (SELECT   COUNT(*)
          FROM     T2                 FROM      T2
          WHERE    C)                 WHERE     C)
```

15.4.7　General conclusion

Based on the previous rules, we can conclude that every subquery form can be transformed into the form below, where the question mark represents any comparison operator.

```
WHERE <expression> ? (SELECT COUNT(*) FROM ...)
```

The table below gives an overview of when a certain condition based on a subquery is true, false or unknown. The first column of this table contains the condition types. The other columns denote the value of such a condition based on the contents of two tables. We start from the following assumptions:

- table t1 has only one row and one column c1
- table t2 has only one column c2
- the data types of c1 and c2 are equal

Meanings of the columns in the table:

- Column 2: The value of column c1 in the only row in t1 is 1 and the value of column c2 in the only row of t2 is 1.
- Column 3: The value of column c1 in the only row in t1 is 1 and the value of column c2 in the only row of t2 is 2.
- Column 4: The value of column c1 in the only row in t1 is 1 and the value of column c2 in the only row of t2 is NULL.
- Column 5: The value of column c1 in the only row in t1 is 1 and table t2 is empty.
- Column 6: The value of column c1 in the only row in t1 is NULL and the value of column c2 in the only row of t2 is 1.
- Column 7: The value of column c1 in the only row in t1 is NULL and the value of column c2 in the only row of t2 is NULL.
- Column 8: The value of column c1 in the only row in t1 is NULL and table t2 is empty.

Condition	$c_1 = 1$ $c_2 = 1$	$c_1 = 1$ $c_2 = 2$	$c_1 = 1$ $c_2 =$ null	$c_1 = 1$ $t_2 =$ empty	$c_1 =$ null $c_2 = 1$	$c_1 =$ null $c_2 =$ null	$c_1 =$ null $t_2 =$ empty
c1 in (select c2 from t2)	true	false	unknown	false	unknown	unknown	false
c1 not in (select c2 from t2)	false	true	unknown	true	unknown	unknown	true
exists (select * from t2 where c1 = c2)	true	false	false	false	false	false	false
exists (select * from t2 where c1 <> c2)	false	true	false	false	false	false	false
not exists (select * from t2 where c1 = c2)	false	true	true	true	true	true	true
not exists (select * from t2 where c1 <> c2)	true	false	true	true	true	true	true
c1 = any (select c2 from t2)	true	false	unknown	false	unknown	unknown	false
c1 <> any (select c2 from t2)	false	true	unknown	false	unknown	unknown	false
c1 = all (select c2 from t2)	true	false	unknown	true	unknown	unknown	true
c1 <> all (select c2 from t2)	false	true	unknown	true	unknown	unknown	true

Exercise

15.8 Transform the SELECT statements below to SELECT statements of the form:

```
WHERE <expression> ? (SELECT COUNT(*) FROM ...)
```

1.  ```
    SELECT   *
    FROM     PLAYERS P
    WHERE    EXISTS
             (SELECT   *
             FROM      PENALTIES PN
             WHERE     P.PLAYERNO = PN.PLAYERNO)
    ```

2.  ```
    SELECT   *
    FROM     PLAYERS P
    WHERE    YEAR_OF_BIRTH <= ALL
             (SELECT   MAX(YEAR_OF_BIRTH)
             FROM      PLAYERS)
    ```

3.  ```
    SELECT   *
    FROM     PLAYERS P1
    WHERE    YEAR_OF_BIRTH <= ALL
             (SELECT   YEAR_OF_BIRTH
             FROM      PLAYERS P2
             WHERE     TOWN = 'Stratford')
    ```

4.  ```
    SELECT   *
    FROM     PLAYERS P1
    WHERE    PLAYERNO + 1 IN
             (SELECT   PLAYERNO
             FROM      PLAYERS P2)
    ```

16
SELECT statement: the join

You have already seen the join used in many examples in this book. In a *join* of tables, rows from these tables are combined. A SELECT statement can be called a join if, first, the FROM clause names at least two table specifications and second, if the WHERE clause has at least one condition that compares columns from the different tables.

16.1   Terminology

The columns in a SELECT statement that define the join are called, predictably, the *join columns*. In the following SELECT statement these are PLAYERS.PLAYERNO and TEAMS.PLAYERNO.

```
SELECT    PLAYERS.PLAYERNO, TEAMNO
FROM      PLAYERS, TEAMS
WHERE     PLAYERS.PLAYERNO = TEAMS.PLAYERNO
```

Between join columns there always exists a certain type of relationship. If C_1 and C_2 are two columns, then four types of relationship between C_1 and C_2 are possible:

1. The populations of C_1 and C_2 are *equal*.
2. The population of C_1 is a *subset* of that of C_2 (or C_2 of C_1).
3. The populations of C_1 and C_2 are *conjoint* (they have some values in common).
4. The populations of C_1 and C_2 are *disjoint* (they have no values in common).

If C_1 and C_2 are considered to be sets with values, the following relationships can be defined using set theory terminology.

221

1. $C_1 = C_2$
2. $C_1 \subset C_2$ (or $C_2 \subset C_1$)
3. $C_1 - C_2 \neq \emptyset$ AND $C_2 - C_1 \neq \emptyset$
4. $C_1 - C_2 = C_1$ AND $C_2 - C_1 = C_2$

This section is going to look in great detail at how the relationship between the join columns influences the result of the SELECT statement in which the join appears.

Just like 'primary key' and 'row', 'join' is a term from the relational model. The relational model differentiates between types of joins. This section will cover the following types of joins and their characteristics:

- thetajoin
- equijoin
- natural join
- outer equijoin

The general join or *thetajoin* takes this form in SQL:

```
SELECT    *
FROM      PLAYERS, TEAMS
WHERE     PLAYERS.PLAYERNO ? TEAMS.PLAYERNO
```

The question mark stands for any comparison operator. PLAYERS.PLAYERNO and TEAMS.PLAYERNO are the join columns. When the comparison operator is '=', we speak of an *equijoin*. Example:

```
SELECT    *
FROM      PLAYERS, TEAMS
WHERE     PLAYERS.PLAYERNO = TEAMS.PLAYERNO
```

The *natural join* looks like the equijoin. The difference is, however, that in the SELECT clause only one of the join columns is given in the end result. By using the asterisk (*) in the example above the user gets both join columns presented. A natural join is achieved by explicitly specifying all the required columns in the SELECT clause:

```
SELECT    PLAYERS.*, TEAMS.TEAMNO, TEAMS.DIVISION
FROM      PLAYERS, TEAMS
WHERE     PLAYERS.PLAYERNO = TEAMS.PLAYERNO
```

The join column TEAMS.PLAYERNO is not included in the SELECT clause, although the other join column PLAYERS.PLAYERNO is mentioned. An equivalent way of formulating this is:

```
SELECT    TEAMS.*, PLAYERS.NAME, PLAYERS.INITIALS, ...,
          PLAYERS.LEAGUENO
FROM      PLAYERS, TEAMS
WHERE     PLAYERS.PLAYERNO = TEAMS.PLAYERNO
```

Two forms of the equijoin exist: the *inner equijoin* and the *outer equijoin*. You will discover the difference between them by following the next example.

Example 16.1: Find, for each player, the player number, the name and the penalties incurred.

```
SELECT    PLAYERS.PLAYERNO, NAME, AMOUNT
FROM      PLAYERS, PENALTIES
WHERE     PLAYERS.PLAYERNO = PENALTIES.PLAYERNO
```

Result:

```
PLAYERNO   NAME        AMOUNT
--------   ---------   ------
       6   Parmenter   100.00
      44   Baker        75.00
      27   Collins     100.00
     104   Moorman      50.00
      44   Baker        25.00
       8   Newcastle    25.00
      44   Baker        30.00
      27   Collins      70.00
```

Indeed, this is the result of the above SELECT statement, but does it satisfy our requirements? The answer is no! This SELECT statement gives only the player number and the name of players who have incurred at least one penalty (that is, those who appear in the PENALTIES table). Because SQL is only presenting data about this subset of all players, this type of join is called an *inner* equijoin.

The result required can be achieved by extending the SELECT statement:

```
SELECT    PLAYERS.PLAYERNO, NAME, AMOUNT
FROM      PLAYERS, PENALTIES
WHERE     PLAYERS.PLAYERNO = PENALTIES.PLAYERNO
UNION
SELECT    PLAYERNO, NAME, NULL
FROM      PLAYERS
WHERE     PLAYERNO NOT IN
          (SELECT    PLAYERNO
           FROM      PENALTIES)
```

Result:

```
PLAYERNO   NAME        AMOUNT
--------   ---------   ------
       6   Parmenter   100.00
      44   Baker        75.00
      27   Collins     100.00
       :   :                :
```

```
  :    :                 :
 104   Moorman      50.00
  44   Baker        25.00
   8   Newcastle    25.00
  44   Baker        30.00
  27   Collins      70.00
  83   Hope             ?
   2   Everett          ?
   7   Wise             ?
  57   Brown            ?
  39   Bishop           ?
 112   Bailey           ?
 100   Parmenter        ?
  28   Collins          ?
  95   Miller           ?
```

This type of equijoin is called an *outer equijoin*.

A subset relationship exists between the populations of the two join columns, PENALTIES.PLAYERNO being a subset of PLAYERS.PLAYERNO.

16.2   Relationships between join columns

The influence that the relationship type has on the result of an inner equijoin and an outer equijoin will now be shown for each type of relationship between the join columns. For this, modified versions of the PLAYERS and PENALTIES tables will be used. PLAYERS.PLAYERNO and PENALTIES.PLAYERNO are the join columns.

16.2.1   The populations of the join columns are the same

Suppose that the two tables look like this:

The PLAYERS table: The PENALTIES table:

PLAYERNO	TOWN
6	Stratford
44	Inglewood
104	Eltham

PLAYERNO	AMOUNT
6	100
44	75
44	25
44	30
104	50

The inner equijoin:

```
SELECT    P.PLAYERNO, TOWN, AMOUNT
FROM      PLAYERS P, PENALTIES PN
WHERE     P.PLAYERNO = PN.PLAYERNO
```

Result:

```
PLAYERNO  TOWN        AMOUNT
--------  ---------   ------
       6  Stratford      100
      44  Inglewood       75
      44  Inglewood       25
      44  Inglewood       30
     104  Eltham          50
```

An outer equijoin returns the same result because neither of the two tables contains a row with a player number that does not appear in the other table.

16.2.2   The population of one join column is a subset

Suppose that the two tables have the following contents (the PENALTIES.PLAYERNO column is a subset of the PLAYERS.PLAYERNO column):

```
The PLAYERS table:              The PENALTIES table:

PLAYERNO  TOWN                  PLAYERNO   AMOUNT
--------  ---------             --------   ------
       6  Stratford                    6      100
      44  Inglewood                  104       50
     104  Eltham
```

The inner equijoin:

```
SELECT    P.PLAYERNO, TOWN, AMOUNT
FROM      PLAYERS P, PENALTIES PN
WHERE     P.PLAYERNO = PN.PLAYERNO
```

Result:

```
PLAYERNO  TOWN         AMOUNT
--------  ----------   ------
       6  Stratford       100
     104  Eltham           50
```

Only players who appear in both tables (and therefore in the intersection of the two populations) are included in the result. Player 44 does not occur in this intersection, so does not appear in the result.

The outer equijoin:

```
SELECT    P.PLAYERNO, TOWN, AMOUNT
FROM      PLAYERS P, PENALTIES PN
WHERE     P.PLAYERNO = PN.PLAYERNO
UNION
SELECT    PLAYERNO, TOWN, NULL
FROM      PLAYERS
WHERE     PLAYERNO NOT IN
          (SELECT   PLAYERNO
          FROM      PENALTIES)
```

Result:

```
PLAYERNO  TOWN        AMOUNT
--------  ---------   ------
       6  Stratford      100
     104  Eltham          50
      44  Inglewood        ?
```

This type of outer equijoin is sometimes referred to as a *left outer equijoin* because we do not want to lose players from our result. And if the PLAYERS table is specified first in the FROM clause, it is specified left from the PENALTIES table.

16.2.3   The populations of the join columns are conjoint

Suppose that for this example we include player 8 in the PENALTIES table. Actually, this is not really possible because player 8 does not even appear in the PLAYERS table. But we can change the rules of our database design to illustrate the point. The tables now look like this:

```
The PLAYERS table:              The PENALTIES table:

PLAYERNO  TOWN             PLAYERNO  AMOUNT
--------  ---------        --------  ------
       6  Stratford               6     100
      44  Inglewood             104      50
     104  Eltham                  8      25
```

The inner equijoin:

```
SELECT    P.PLAYERNO, TOWN, AMOUNT
FROM      PLAYERS P, PENALTIES PN
WHERE     P.PLAYERNO = PN.PLAYERNO
```

Result:

```
PLAYERNO  TOWN        AMOUNT
--------  ---------   ------
       6  Stratford      100
     104  Eltham          50
```

Only the players who appear in both tables are picked out for the result. In order to formulate an outer equijoin the SELECT statement must be extended with two subqueries.

The outer equijoin:

```
SELECT    P.PLAYERNO, TOWN, AMOUNT
FROM      PLAYERS P, PENALTIES PN
WHERE     P.PLAYERNO = PN.PLAYERNO
UNION
SELECT    PLAYERNO, TOWN, NULL
FROM      PLAYERS
WHERE     PLAYERNO NOT IN
          (SELECT   PLAYERNO
           FROM     PENALTIES)
UNION
SELECT    PLAYERNO, NULL, AMOUNT
FROM      PENALTIES
WHERE     PLAYERNO NOT IN
          (SELECT   PLAYERNO
           FROM     PLAYERS)
```

Result:

```
PLAYERNO   TOWN        AMOUNT
--------   ---------   ------
       6   Stratford      100
     104   Eltham          50
      44   Inglewood        ?
       8   ?               25
```

If we add only the last select block and not the second, we would have created a right outer equijoin.

16.2.4　The populations of the join columns are disjoint

The two tables have the following contents:

The PLAYERS table:　　　　The PENALTIES table:

```
PLAYERNO   TOWN             PLAYERNO   AMOUNT
--------   ---------        --------   ------
       6   Stratford              27      100
      44   Inglewood               8       25
     104   Eltham                 27       75
```

The inner equijoin returns absolutely no rows because the two columns have no value in common.

The outer equijoin of two columns with disjoint populations seldom occurs in practice. If it is really the intention to combine this data in one result, the join is not appropriate. It is best done with a UNION:

```
SELECT    PLAYERNO, TOWN, NULL
FROM      PLAYERS
UNION
SELECT    PLAYERNO, NULL, AMOUNT
FROM      PENALTIES
```

Result:

```
PLAYERNO  TOWN         AMOUNT
--------  ---------    ------
       6  Stratford        ?
      44  Inglewood        ?
     104  Eltham           ?
      27  ?              100
       8  ?               25
      27  ?               75
```

Conclusion: When you formulate a join you must know precisely what sort of relationship the join columns have. Do not make any assumptions about the populations of the join columns at any given point, because you may have a false impression. Determine the relationship in advance, therefore, and you can be sure of avoiding mistakes.

Exercises

16.1 Give, for *each* player, the player number and total number of sets won.

16.2 Give, for each player, the player number and the sum of all penalties incurred by him or her.

16.3 Give, for each player, the player number and a list of teams for which they have ever played.

16.3   The outer equijoin

In Section 16.1 we described the concept of *outer equijoin*. We have already seen that an outer equijoin can be formulated, but that it leads to complex SELECT statements. We will repeat an example from that section.

Example 16.2: Find, for each player, player number, the name and the penalties incurred.

```
SELECT    PLAYERS.PLAYERNO, NAME, AMOUNT
FROM      PLAYERS, PENALTIES
WHERE     PLAYERS.PLAYERNO = PENALTIES.PLAYERNO
UNION
SELECT    PLAYERNO, NAME, NULL
FROM      PLAYERS
WHERE     PLAYERNO NOT IN
          (SELECT    PLAYERNO
           FROM      PENALTIES)
```

Result:

```
PLAYERNO  NAME        AMOUNT
--------  ---------   ------
       6  Parmenter   100.00
      44  Baker        75.00
      27  Collins     100.00
     104  Moorman      50.00
      44  Baker        25.00
       8  Newcastle    25.00
      44  Baker        30.00
      27  Collins      70.00
      83  Hope             ?
       2  Everett          ?
       7  Wise             ?
      57  Brown            ?
      39  Bishop           ?
     112  Bailey           ?
     100  Parmenter        ?
      28  Collins          ?
      95  Miller           ?
```

However, Oracle supports a simpler solution to the outer equijoin with the same result:

```
SELECT    PLAYERS.PLAYERNO, NAME, AMOUNT
FROM      PLAYERS, PENALTIES
WHERE     PLAYERS.PLAYERNO = PENALTIES.PLAYERNO (+)
```

By specifying the (+) symbol after the PENALTIES.PLAYERNO column Oracle is ordered to perform an outer equijoin by itself. By placing (+) after the column of the PENALTIES table, Oracle knows that *all* rows from the other table, in this case the PLAYERS table, *must* appear in the end result. The columns in the SELECT clause which belong to the PENALTIES table, are filled automatically with NULL values for all those players for whom no penalty has been paid. We give you another example.

Example 16.3: Give for *each* player, the player number, name and the numbers and divisions of the teams (which he or she captains); order the result by player number.

```
SELECT    P.PLAYERNO, NAME, TEAMNO, DIVISION
FROM      PLAYERS P, TEAMS T
WHERE     P.PLAYERNO = T.PLAYERNO (+)
ORDER BY P.PLAYERNO
```

Result:

PLAYERNO	NAME	TEAMNO	DIVISION
2	Everett	?	?
6	Parmenter	1	first
7	Wise	?	?
8	Newcastle	?	?
27	Collins	2	second
28	Collins	?	?
39	Bishop	?	?
44	Baker	?	?
57	Brown	?	?
83	Hope	?	?
95	Miller	?	?
100	Parmenter	?	?
104	Moorman	?	?
112	Bailey	?	?

Example 16.4: Find for *each* captain, who is not a captain of a team playing in the third division, the player number and the number of penalties incurred for him or her.

```
SELECT    T.PLAYERNO, COUNT(*)
FROM      TEAMS T, PENALTIES P
WHERE     T.PLAYERNO = P.PLAYERNO (+)
AND       DIVISION <> 'third'
GROUP BY T.PLAYERNO
```

Result:

PLAYERNO	COUNT(*)
6	1
27	2

As shown in the example above, a WHERE clause can contain an outer equijoin condition besides other conditions. We have to be careful with this. Oracle considers outer equijoin conditions (conditions in which the (+) symbol appears) as a first class condition. When processing the WHERE clause, first all outer equijoin conditions are processed and then the others. In other words, Oracle performs the WHERE clause in two steps. During the first step Oracle is looking for an outer equijoin condition. This will be processed first and successively the rest of the conditions are processed with the intermediate result. We will show you that this can have consequences for certain conditions.

Example:

```
SELECT    P.PLAYERNO, TEAMNO
FROM      PLAYERS P, TEAMS T
WHERE     P.PLAYERNO = T.PLAYERNO (+)
AND       TEAMNO IS NOT NULL
```

The intermediate result after the FROM clause is of course the cartesian product of the two tables PLAYERS and TEAMS:

PLAYERNO	NAME	...	TEAMNO	PLAYERNO	DIVISION
6	Parmenter	...	1	6	first
44	Baker	...	1	6	first
83	Hope	...	1	6	first
2	Everett	...	1	6	first
27	Collins	...	1	6	first
104	Moorman	...	1	6	first
7	Wise	...	1	6	first
57	Brown	...	1	6	first
39	Bishop	...	1	6	first
112	Bailey	...	1	6	first
8	Newcastle	...	1	6	first
100	Parmenter	...	1	6	first
28	Collins	...	1	6	first
95	Miller	...	1	6	first
6	Parmenter	...	2	27	second
44	Baker	...	2	27	second
83	Hope	...	2	27	second
2	Everett	...	2	27	second
27	Collins	...	2	27	second
104	Moorman	...	2	27	second
7	Wise	...	2	27	second
57	Brown	...	2	27	second
39	Bishop	...	2	27	second
112	Bailey	...	2	27	second
8	Newcastle	...	2	27	second
100	Parmenter	...	2	27	second
28	Collins	...	2	27	second
95	Miller	...	2	27	second

Suppose that the condition TEAMNO IS NOT NULL is processed first. The result should be that not a single row is deleted from the intermediate result. Next, the first condition is processed with the following intermediate result:

PLAYERNO	NAME	...	TEAMNO	PLAYERNO	DIVISION
6	Parmenter	...	1	6	first
44	Baker	...	?	?	?
83	Hope	...	?	?	?
2	Everett	...	?	?	?
27	Collins	...	2	27	second
104	Moorman	...	?	?	?
7	Wise	...	?	?	?
57	Brown	...	?	?	?
39	Bishop	...	?	?	?
112	Bailey	...	?	?	?
8	Newcastle	...	?	?	?
100	Parmenter	...	?	?	?
28	Collins	...	?	?	?
95	Miller	...	?	?	?

End result:

PLAYERNO	TEAMNO
6	1
44	?
83	?
2	?
27	2
104	?
7	?
57	?
39	?
112	?
8	?
100	?
28	?
95	?

We could have left out the second condition, because it has, in fact, no effect at all. However, Oracle considers the outer equijoin condition as a first class condition. So this condition is processed first. Then, the intermediate result equals the last intermediate result after all conditions are processed. After that, the second condition is processed. This makes the end result equivalent to the following result:

PLAYERNO	TEAMNO
6	1
27	2

It must be clear that the second condition has had an effect now. In fact, this condition destroys the idea of the outer equijoin.

16.4   Rules for outer equijoins

For formulating SELECT statements, where the FROM clause consists of two tables (possibly the same), the following rules apply for using the (+) symbol.

- A predicate with the (+) symbol will be processed first (see the previous section).

- In a predicate of the WHERE clause the (+) symbol may only appear once. So the following condition is incorrect: C1(+) = C2(+).

- The (+) symbol only has a meaning in a predicate where two columns of different tables are compared with each other.

- The (+) symbol can only be specified after columns of one of the two tables.

16.5   Outer equijoin on more than two tables

Outer equijoins can be formulated on three or more tables. We will start with an example.

Example 16.5: Give for *each* match, the match number, the player who played the match, all payment numbers of the penalties incurred for that player and the team numbers, which he captains.

```
SELECT    M.MATCHNO, M.PLAYERNO, M.PAYMENTNO, M.TEAMNO
FROM      MATCHES M, PENALTIES PN, TEAMS T
WHERE     M.PLAYERNO = PN.PLAYERNO (+)
AND       M.PLAYERNO = T.PLAYERNO (+)
```

Result:

MATCHNO	PLAYERNO	PAYMENTNO	TEAMNO
1	6	1	1
2	6	1	1
3	6	1	1
4	44	2	1
4	44	5	1
4	44	7	1
5	83	?	1
6	2	?	1
:	:	:	:

:	:	:	:
7	57	?	1
8	8	6	1
9	27	3	2
9	27	8	2
10	104	4	2
11	112	?	2
12	112	?	2
13	8	6	2

For specifying outer equijoins on more than two tables, the same rules from the last section apply, including the following rule:

• For all tables that are involved in outer equijoin conditions, there has to be one table where the (+) symbol is not specified after one of the columns.

The WHERE clauses below are all correct with respect to the following FROM clause:

```
FROM PLAYERS P, TEAMS T, PENALTIES PN
```

The following conditions are *correct*:

• P.PLAYERNO   = PN.PLAYERNO (+) AND
  P.PLAYERNO   = T.PLAYERNO (+)

• P.PLAYERNO (+) = PN.PLAYERNO AND
  P.PLAYERNO   = T.PLAYERNO (+)

• P.PLAYERNO   = PN.PLAYERNO (+) AND
  P.PLAYERNO (+) = T.PLAYERNO

• P.PLAYERNO   = PN.PLAYERNO AND
  P.PLAYERNO (+) = T.PLAYERNO

And the following WHERE clauses are all *incorrect*:

• P.PLAYERNO (+) = PN.PLAYERNO AND
  P.PLAYERNO (+) = T.PLAYERNO

• P.PLAYERNO (+) = PN.PLAYERNO (+) AND
  P.PLAYERNO (+) = T.PLAYERNO (+)

Exercises

16.4 Determine the results of the SELECT statements below given the tables shown: T1, T2, T3 and T4. Each table has only one column.

```
T1   C          T2   C          T3   C          T4   C
-----           -----           -----           -----
         1               2               2               ?
         2               3               3               2
         3               4               5
```

1. SELECT   T1.C, T2.C
    FROM   T1, T2
    WHERE   T1.C = T2.C

2. SELECT   T1.C, T2.C
    FROM   T1, T2
    WHERE   T1.C = T2.C (+)

3. SELECT   T1.C, T2.C
    FROM   T1, T2
    WHERE   T1.C (+) = T2.C

4. SELECT   T1.C, T2.C
    FROM   T1, T2
    WHERE   T1.C (+) > T2.C

5. SELECT   T1.C, T4.C
    FROM   T1, T4
    WHERE   T1.C (+) = T4.C

6. SELECT   T1.C, T4.C
    FROM   T1, T4
    WHERE   T1.C = T4.C (+)

16.5 Determine the results of the SELECT statements below. We start with the
same four tables.

1. SELECT   T1.C, T2.C, T3.C
    FROM   T1, T2, T3
    WHERE   T1.C = T2.C AND T1.C = T3.C

2. SELECT   T1.C, T2.C, T3.C
    FROM   T1, T2, T3
    WHERE   T1.C (+) = T2.C AND T1.C = T3.C (+)

3. SELECT   T1.C, T2.C, T3.C
    FROM   T1, T2, T3
    WHERE   T1.C = T2.C (+) AND T1.C = T3.C (+)

4. SELECT   T1.C, T2.C, T3.C
    FROM   T1, T2, T3
    WHERE   T1.C = T2.C (+) AND T1.C (+) = T3.C

5. SELECT   T1.C, T2.C, T3.C
    FROM   T1, T2, T3
    WHERE   T1.C = T2.C (+) AND T1.C = T3.C

16.6   Joins without join conditions

At the beginning of this chapter we defined the concept of join as a SELECT statement, where the FROM clause contains at least two tables and where the WHERE clause contains a condition which compares the columns of different tables. This section describes a number of examples of SELECT statements which satisfy the first but not the second condition.

Example 16.6: Give for each penalty the payment number, the penalty amount and the sum of the amounts of all penalties with a lower payment number (cumulative value).

```
SELECT   P1.PAYMENTNO, P1.AMOUNT, SUM(P2.AMOUNT)
FROM     PENALTIES P1, PENALTIES P2
WHERE    P1.PAYMENTNO >= P2.PAYMENTNO
GROUP BY P1.PAYMENTNO, P1.AMOUNT
ORDER BY P1.PAYMENTNO
```

For our convenience we assume that the PENALTIES table contains the following three rows only:

PAYMENTNO	PLAYERNO	PEN_DATE	AMOUNT
1	6	08-DEC-80	100
2	44	05-MAY-81	75
3	27	10-SEP-83	100

Desired result:

PAYMENTNO	AMOUNT	SUM
1	100	100
2	75	175
3	100	275

The intermediate result of the FROM clause (we show only the columns PAYMENTNO and AMOUNT):

P1.PAYNO	P1.AMOUNT	P2.PAYNO	P2.AMOUNT
1	100	1	100
1	100	2	75
1	100	3	100
2	75	1	100
2	75	2	75
2	75	3	100
3	100	1	100
3	100	2	75
3	100	3	100

The intermediate result of the WHERE clause:

P1.PAYNO	P1.AMOUNT	P2.PAYNO	P2.AMOUNT
1	100	1	100
2	75	1	100
2	75	2	75
3	100	1	100
3	100	2	75
3	100	3	100

The intermediate result of the GROUP BY clause:

P1.PAYNO	P1.AMOUNT	P2.PAYNO	P2.AMOUNT
1	100	1	100
2	75	1, 2	100, 75
3	100	1, 2, 3	100, 75, 100

The intermediate result of the SELECT clause:

P1.PAYNO	P1.AMOUNT	SUM(P2.AMOUNT)
1	100	100
2	75	175
3	100	275

The end result is equal to the table above.

Example 16.7: Give for each penalty the payment number, the penalty amount and the percentage of the sum of all the amounts (we use the same PENALTIES table as in the previous example).

```
SELECT    P1.PAYMENTNO, P1.AMOUNT,
          (P1.AMOUNT * 100) / SUM(P2.AMOUNT)
FROM      PENALTIES P1, PENALTIES P2
GROUP BY  P1.PAYMENTNO, P1.AMOUNT
ORDER BY  P1.PAYMENTNO
```

The intermediate result of the FROM clause is equal to the result of the last example. However, the intermediate result of the GROUP BY clause is different:

P1.PAYNO	P1.AMOUNT	P2.PAYNO	P2.AMOUNT
1	100	1, 2, 3	100, 75, 100
2	75	1, 2, 3	100, 75, 100
3	100	1, 2, 3	100, 75, 100

The intermediate result of the SELECT clause:

```
P1.PAYNO  P1.AMOUNT  (P1.AMOUNT * 100) / SUM(P2.AMOUNT)
--------  ---------  -----------------------------------
       1        100                                36.36
       2         75                                27.27
       3        100                                36.36
```

Work out for yourself that this is also the final result.

16.7   Statistical functions and joins

When you use statistical functions and joins in one SELECT statement, you have to be careful. In this section we give you some examples in which the result of the statement is not what you would expect.

Example 16.8: Find, for each player, the number, name, the total amount of penalties paid and his or her total numbers of sets won.

```
SELECT    P.PLAYERNO, NAME, SUM(AMOUNT), SUM(WON)
FROM      PLAYERS P, PENALTIES PN, MATCHES M
WHERE     P.PLAYERNO = PN.PLAYERNO
AND       P.PLAYERNO = M.PLAYERNO
GROUP BY  P.PLAYERNO, NAME
```

Result:

```
PLAYERNO  NAME        SUM(AMOUNT)  SUM(WON)
--------  ---------   -----------  --------
       6  Parmenter           300         8
       8  Newcastle            50         0
      27  Collins             175         6
      44  Baker               130         9
     104  Moorman              50         3
```

From this result all players have disappeared who have played no matches and who have incurred no penalties. But are the numbers in the two columns on the right correct for the remaining players? The answer is: no! The table above shows, for example, that the total of penalties incurred for player 6 equals 300. If we look at the PENALTIES table we see that only one penalty for player 6 has been paid and that is one of $100. The reason that these two numbers do not match is that player 6 has played three matches.

Example 16.9: Find for each player who played a match, the player number and the total number of penalties.

```
SELECT    M.PLAYERNO, COUNT(*)
FROM      MATCHES M, PENALTIES PN
WHERE     M.PLAYERNO = PN.PLAYERNO
GROUP BY  M.PLAYERNO
```

Result:

```
PLAYERNO  COUNT(*)
--------  --------
       6         3
       8         2
      27         2
      44         3
     104         1
```

This answer is not correct. The number of penalties for player 6 is not three, but one and the number of penalties for player 8 is two.

Conclusion: Take good care when you use statistical functions and joins in one SELECT statement. In some situations you will not get the result you expect.

17
Updating tables

Oracle has various statements for updating the contents (rows) of tables. There are statements for inserting new rows, for changing column values and for deleting rows. This chapter describes two subjects. First, all statements for updating are described. Second, committing and undoing updates is discussed.

17.1   Inserting new rows

SQL's *INSERT statement* is used to add new rows to a table. This statement comes in two different forms: the first form of the INSERT statement allows you to add only one row, while the second allows you to populate a table with rows taken from another table. The first form is covered in this section, and the second in the following section.

```
<insert statement> ::=
   INSERT INTO <table specification>
         [ <column list> ]
   VALUES ( <expression> [ {,<expression>}... ] )

<table specification> ::= [ <user> . ] <table name>

<column list> ::=
   ( <column name> [ {,<column name>}... ] )
```

Example 17.1: A new team has enrolled in the league. This third team will be captained by player 100 and will compete in the third division.

```
INSERT INTO TEAMS
        (TEAMNO, PLAYERNO, DIVISION)
VALUES (3, 100, 'third')
```

All columns defined as NOT NULL must be inserted (work out for yourself why). The following statement is, therefore, not correct, because the PLAYERNO column has been defined as NOT NULL, and will not be specified in the statement:

```
INSERT INTO TEAMS
        (TEAMNO, DIVISION)
VALUES (3, 'third')
```

Now the statement below is correct:

```
INSERT INTO PLAYERS
        (PLAYERNO, NAME, INITIALS, SEX,
        YEAR_JOINED, STREET, TOWN)
VALUES (...)
```

Into all columns that have not been specified in an INSERT statement, NULL values will be inserted.

If NULL is specified as an expression, the specific column is filled, in that row, with the NULL value. In the following statement the LEAGUENO column is filled with NULL:

```
INSERT INTO PLAYERS
        (PLAYERNO, NAME, INITIALS, ..., LEAGUENO)
VALUES (401, 'Jones', 'OP', ..., NULL)
```

You don't have to specify the column names. If they are omitted, Oracle assumes that the order in which the values are entered is the same as the default sequence of the columns (see COL# in the SYS.COLS$ table). The following statement is, therefore, equivalent to the first INSERT statement.

```
INSERT INTO TEAMS
VALUES (3, 100, 'third')
```

You are not obliged, however, to specify columns in the default sequence. So the next statement is equivalent to the previous statement, as well as to the first.

```
INSERT INTO TEAMS (PLAYERNO, DIVISION, TEAMNO)
VALUES (100, 'third', 3)
```

If the column names had *not* been specified in this statement, the result would have been entirely different. Oracle would have considered the value 100 to be a team number, 'third' a player number and the value 3 a division. Of course, the insertion would not have been performed at all because the value 'third' is an alphanumeric literal and the PLAYERNO column has a numeric data type.

17.2 Populating one table with rows from another table

In Section 17.1 we looked at the first form of the INSERT statement, with which one row could be added to a table. The second form does not add new rows, but fills the table with rows from another table (or tables). You could say that data is *copied* from one table to another. The definition for this is:

```
<insert statement> ::=
   INSERT INTO <table specification>
   [ <column list> ]
   <select statement>

<table specification> ::= [ <user> . ] <table name>

<column list> ::=
   ( <column name> [ {,<column name>}... ] )
```

Example 17.2: Make a separate table to record the number, name, town and telephone number of each non-competition player.
    First create a table, and then define a unique index on it:

```
CREATE TABLE RECREATION_PLAYERS
        (PLAYERNO       SMALLINT NOT NULL,
         NAME           CHAR(15) NOT NULL,
         TOWN           CHAR(10) NOT NULL,
         PHONENO        CHAR(10)         ,
         PRIMARY KEY    (PLAYERNO)       )

CREATE UNIQUE INDEX REC_PLAYERS_KEY ON
        RECREATION_PLAYERS (PLAYERNO)
```

The following INSERT statement populates the RECREATION_PLAYERS table with data about recreational players registered in the PLAYERS table.

```
INSERT    INTO RECREATION_PLAYERS
          (PLAYERNO, NAME, TOWN, PHONENO)
SELECT    PLAYERNO, NAME, TOWN, PHONENO
FROM      PLAYERS
WHERE     LEAGUENO IS NULL
```

The contents of the table now look like this:

```
PLAYERNO  NAME        TOWN       PHONENO
--------  ----------  ---------  ----------
       7  Wise        Stratford  070-347689
      39  Bishop      Stratford  070-393435
      28  Collins     Midhurst   071-659599
      95  Miller      Douglas    070-867564
```

Explanation: The first part of the INSERT statement follows the pattern of the first type of INSERT statement. The second part does not consist of a row of values, but a SELECT statement. We know already that the result of a SELECT statement can be viewed as a number of rows with values. However, these rows are not displayed on the screen as the statement executes, but are stored directly in the RECREATION_PLAYERS table.

The same rules which apply to the first form of the INSERT statement apply here also. The next two statements, then, have an equivalent result to the previous one:

```
INSERT   INTO RECREATION_PLAYERS
SELECT   PLAYERNO, NAME, TOWN, PHONENO
FROM     PLAYERS
WHERE    LEAGUENO IS NULL

INSERT   INTO RECREATION_PLAYERS
         (TOWN, PHONENO, NAME, PLAYERNO)
SELECT   TOWN, PHONENO, NAME, PLAYERNO
FROM     PLAYERS
WHERE    LEAGUENO IS NULL
```

At the same time, there are several other rules:

- The SELECT statement is a fully fledged SELECT statement and therefore may include subqueries, joins, GROUP BY, set operators, functions, and so on.

- The number of columns in the INSERT INTO clause must equal the number of expressions in the SELECT clause.

- The data types of the columns in the INSERT INTO clause must conform to the data types of the expressions in the SELECT clause.

The INSERT statement can be used in many processes, principally where SQL has no other separate statement available, such as removing and renaming of columns. For all these processes, you can use much the same approach as the one we describe below.

Example 17.3: Remove the DIVISION column from the TEAMS table.

1.   Create a table with the same columns as the TEAMS table, but without the DIVISION column.

   ```
   CREATE TABLE DUMMY
        ( TEAMNO    SMALLINT NOT NULL,
          PLAYERNO  SMALLINT NOT NULL)
   ```

2.   Populate this table with all the rows from the TEAMS table.

   ```
   INSERT    INTO DUMMY
   SELECT    TEAMNO, PLAYERNO
   FROM      TEAMS
   ```

3.   Use SELECT statements against the catalog tables to determine which indexes are dependent on the TEAMS table.

4.   Drop the old TEAMS table.

   ```
   DROP TABLE TEAMS
   ```

5.   Create a new table called TEAMS which has the structure of the DUMMY table.

   ```
   CREATE TABLE TEAMS
        ( TEAMNO    SMALLINT NOT NULL PRIMARY KEY,
          PLAYERNO  SMALLINT NOT NULL)
   ```

6.   Populate the new TEAMS table with all the rows from the DUMMY table.

   ```
   INSERT    INTO TEAMS
   SELECT    *
   FROM      DUMMY
   ```

7.   Recreate indexes which Oracle automatically dropped when removing the TEAMS table. During step 3 you should have made a list of these objects and their characteristics.

8.   Drop the DUMMY table.

   ```
   DROP TABLE DUMMY
   ```

For the other processes similar steps are appropriate (work through them yourself).

17.3   Updating values in rows

The UPDATE statement is used to change values in a table. The definition of this statement reads:

```
<update statement> ::=
   UPDATE <table specification>
   SET    <update> [ {,<update>}... ]
   [ WHERE  <condition> ]

<table specification> ::= [ <user> . ] <table name>

<update> ::=
   <column name> = { <expression> | <subquery> }
```

Example 17.4: Update the league number for player 95 to 2000.

```
UPDATE PLAYERS
SET    LEAGUENO = '2000'
WHERE  PLAYERNO = 95
```

Explanation: The LEAGUENO must be changed to 2000 (SET LEAGUENO = '2000') for *every* row where the player number equals 95 (WHERE PLAYERNO = 95) in the PLAYERS table (UPDATE PLAYERS).

An UPDATE statement always refers to a table. The WHERE clause names rows which are to be updated and the SET clause attributes the new values to one or more columns.

Example 17.5: Increase all penalties by 5 per cent.

```
UPDATE    PENALTIES
SET       AMOUNT = AMOUNT * 1.05
```

Because the WHERE clause has been omitted, the update is performed on all rows in the table concerned. In this example, the AMOUNT in each row of the PENALTIES table is increased by 5 per cent.

Example 17.6: Set the number of sets won to zero for all competitors resident in Stratford.

```
UPDATE    MATCHES
SET       WON = 0
WHERE     PLAYERNO IN
          (SELECT  PLAYERNO
          FROM     PLAYERS
          WHERE    TOWN = 'Stratford')
```

Example 17.7: The Parmenter family has moved house to 83 Palmer Street in Inglewood; the post code has become 1234UU and the telephone number is unknown.

```
UPDATE   PLAYERS
SET      STREET   = 'Palmer Street',
         HOUSENO  = '83',
         TOWN     = 'Inglewood',
         POSTCODE = '1234UU',
         PHONENO  = NULL
WHERE    NAME     = 'Parmenter'
```

Explanation: An UPDATE statement can update multiple columns in a row in the same operation. In this case the PHONENO column has been filled with the NULL value. Remember the comma between each item in the SET clause.

Example 17.8: Exchange the values in the STREET and TOWN columns for player 44.

```
UPDATE   PLAYERS
SET      STREET   = TOWN,
         TOWN     = STREET
WHERE    PLAYERNO = 44
```

Explanation: The original contents of the PLAYERS table are:

```
PLAYERNO   STREET          TOWN
--------   ------------    ---------
44         Lewis Street    Inglewood
```

The UPDATE statement produces:

```
PLAYERNO   STREET          TOWN
--------   ----------      ------------
44         Inglewood       Lewis Street
```

How does Oracle process an UPDATE statement? For each row Oracle checks to see whether the condition in the WHERE clause is true. If it is, a copy of the relevant row is made. For each row which is to be altered, the expression is processed. This calculation, or process, is performed on the column values as given in the copy. The result of the process is now recorded in the original row, this being the actual update. So the copy is not altered. After the row has been processed the copy is automatically discarded.

Example 17.9: Set all penalties which are lower than the average penalty to $10.

```
UPDATE   PENALTIES
SET      AMOUNT = 10
WHERE    AMOUNT <
         (SELECT   AVG(AMOUNT)
         FROM      PENALTIES)
```

The following example will assume that the PLAYERS table has an extra column called NUMBER_OF_SETS. This column contains, for each competitor, the total number of sets played. The column is set to NULL for recreation players.

Example 17.10: Suppose some matches have been played recently. This means that new rows have been added to the MATCHES table. Write the statement that will calculate the new NUMBER_OF_SETS values and record them in the PLAYERS table.

```
UPDATE   PLAYERS
SET      NUMBER_OF_SETS =
         (SELECT   WON + LOST
          FROM     MATCHES
          WHERE    PLAYERNO = PLAYERS.PLAYERNO)
WHERE    PLAYERNO IN
         (SELECT   PLAYERNO
          FROM     MATCHES)
```

Explanation: In the WHERE clause the subquery is added to perform changes only for those players who have played matches. If we do not do this, the column NUMBER_OF_SETS will be set to zero for all players who have not played a match, while it has to be the NULL value.

In the following example we show you how we can use row expressions to update multiple columns in the same operation.

Example 17.11: The number of sets won and lost for match 2 has to equal those of match 1.

```
UPDATE   MATCHES
SET      (WON, LOST) =
         (SELECT   WON, LOST
          FROM     MATCHES
          WHERE    MATCHNO = 1)
WHERE    MATCHNO = 2
```

Exercises

17.1 Change the value F in the SEX column of the PLAYERS table to W.

17.2 Update the SEX column in the PLAYERS table as follows: where 'M' is recorded, change it to 'F',and where 'F' exists, change it to 'M'.

17.3 Increase all penalties which are higher than the average penalty by 20 per cent.

17.4 Player 95 moves house to the address of player 6.

17.4   Deleting rows from a table

The DELETE statement is used to remove rows from a table. The definition of the DELETE statement reads:

```
<delete statement> ::=
   DELETE
   FROM    <table specification>
   [ WHERE <condition> ]

<table specification> ::= [ <user> . ] <table name>
```

Example 17.12: Delete all penalties incurred by player 44.

```
DELETE
FROM    PENALTIES
WHERE   PLAYERNO = 44
```

If the WHERE clause is omitted, all rows for the specified table are deleted. This is not the same as dropping a table with the DROP statement. DELETE removes the contents, leaving the structure of the table intact, whereas the DROP statement deletes the contents and also removes the definition of the table from the catalog.

Exercises

17.5   Delete all penalties incurred by player 44 in 1980.

17.6   Delete all penalties incurred by players who have ever played for a team in the second division.

17.7   Delete all players who live in the same town as player 44, but keep the data about player 44.

17.5   Working with transactions

An update statement that has been executed succesfully can still be undone. By update, we mean every UPDATE, DELETE and INSERT statement. Oracle supports a statement which makes changes to the database permanent and another statement with which successful updates can be undone. This is the topic of this section.

A *transaction* is a set of updates to the data in the database. You end each transaction by specifying whether all updates have to be made permanent or have to be rolled back (or undone).

But how does this work? Suppose that all penalties for player 44 were removed:

```
DELETE
FROM      PENALTIES
WHERE     PLAYERNO = 44
```

The result of this statement becomes apparent when you issue the following SE-
LECT statement:

```
SELECT    *
FROM      PENALTIES
```

Result:

```
PAYMENTNO  PLAYERNO  PEN_DATE   AMOUNT
---------  --------  ---------  ------
        1         6  08-DEC-80  100.00
        3        27  10-SEP-83  100.00
        4       104  08-DEC-84   50.00
        6         8  08-DEC-80   25.00
        8        27  12-NOV-84   75.00
```

Three rows have been deleted from the table. However, the update is not yet permanent. The user (or application) has a choice now. The update can be undone
using the ROLLBACK statement or can be made permanent using the COMMIT
statement.

```
<commit statement> ::=
    COMMIT [ WORK ] [ RELEASE ]

<rollback statement> ::=
    ROLLBACK [ WORK ] [ RELEASE ]
```

Let us take the first choice. Therefore we use the following statement:

```
ROLLBACK WORK
```

Explanation: We can omit the word WORK, because it has no meaning. If we
now enter the SELECT statement used above again, it gives the following result:

```
PAYMENTNO  PLAYERNO  PEN_DATE   AMOUNT
---------  --------  ---------  ------
        1         6  08-DEC-80  100.00
        2        44  05-MAY-81   75.00
        3        27  10-SEP-83  100.00
        4       104  08-DEC-84   50.00
        5        44  08-DEC-80   25.00
        6         8  08-DEC-80   25.00
        7        44  30-DEC-82   30.00
        8        27  12-NOV-84   75.00
```

The three deleted rows appear in the result again. If we have wanted to make the update permanent, we should have used the COMMIT statement:

```
COMMIT WORK
```

After this statement the three rows would forever have been deleted from the table; the update would have been permanent.

A COMMIT or ROLLBACK statement is relevant to all the updates that are executed during the actual transaction. Now the question is: how do we mark the beginning and how do we mark the end of a transaction? We cannot mark the beginning of a transaction explicitly. The first SQL statement executed in an application, is considered the beginning of the first transaction. The end of the transaction is marked by using a COMMIT or ROLLBACK statement. From this you can conclude that an SQL statement that follows a COMMIT or ROLL-BACK statement is the first statement of the new transaction. Oracle automatically executes a ROLLBACK statement if an application stops without indicating the end of the transaction. To illustrate all this, here is a series of statements that are entered consecutively:

1. INSERT ...
2. DELETE ...
3. ROLLBACK WORK
4. UPDATE ...
5. ROLLBACK WORK
6. INSERT ...
7. DELETE ...
8. COMMIT WORK
9. UPDATE ...
10. EXIT

Explanation:

Line 1   This first SQL statement initiates the first transaction. This insert is not yet permanent.

Line 2   This delete is not yet permanent.

Line 3   A ROLLBACK statement is executed. All updates of the actual transaction are undone. These are the updates on lines 1 and 2. This ROLLBACK statement ends the transaction.

Line 4   This update is not yet permanent. Because this statement follows a ROLLBACK statement, a new transaction is started.

Line 5   A ROLLBACK statement is executed. All updates of the actual transaction are undone. This is the update on line 4.

Lines 6 – 7 These two updates are not yet permanent. Because the statement on line 6 follows a ROLLBACK statement, a new transaction is started.

Line 8   A COMMIT statement is executed. All updates of the actual transaction become permanent. These are the updates on lines 6 and 7.

Line 9   This update is not yet permanent. Because this statement follows a COMMIT statement, a new transaction is started.

Line 10   Here the application is ended with an EXIT statement. All updates of the running transaction are undone, in this case the update on line 9.

We advise you to make the last SQL statement executed by an application a COMMIT or a ROLLBACK statement. It is also best to end this statement with the RELEASE option. This option makes sure that, besides the fact that the transaction is ended, the application also logs off properly from the database.

Example 17.13: Delete all data for player 6.

```
DELETE FROM PLAYERS WHERE PLAYERNO = 6

DELETE FROM PENALTIES WHERE PLAYERNO = 6

DELETE FROM MATCHES WHERE PLAYERNO = 6

UPDATE TEAMS SET PLAYERNO = 83 WHERE PLAYERNO = 6
```

Four statements must be used to remove all the information about a particular player from the database: three DELETE statements and an UPDATE statement. In the last statement player 6 is not removed from the TEAMS table, but replaced by player 83. Player 6 can no longer be captain (because he does not exist any more), and a new captain must be registered because the PLAYERNO column in the TEAMS table is defined as NOT NULL. If you use a DELETE statement instead of an UPDATE statement, data about the team which player 6 captains will also be deleted. That is not what is intended. These four updates together form a transaction. If one of them is forgotten the database may lack integrity or consistency. Suppose that the third DELETE statement is left out. The MATCHES table then contains rows which refer to a player who does not exist. The database contains an incorrect reference and has therefore become unreliable. Therefore, between two updates in a transaction you would never issue a ROLLBACK or COMMIT. It is only justifiable after the last update has been executed.

Oracle must know at any given moment whether an update is already permanent or whether it needs to be rolled back, and this is relatively costly, both in time and computer resources. In other words, Oracle must perform extra administration to keep track of the state of each update. Along with this, it is also the case that updated data which is not permanent is locked until it is made permanent with a COMMIT or returned to its prior state with a ROLLBACK. Locked data cannot be accessed by other applications. Therefore it is always wise to keep the amount of not yet permanent data to a minimum.

Statements that modify the catalog tables, such as CREATE TABLE, DROP INDEX and COMMENT, cannot be undone. Before and after the execution of such a statement, Oracle automatically executes a COMMIT statement. So this kind of statement ends the current transaction.

Note: SQL*Plus automatically performs a COMMIT statement after each processed SQL statement. If you do not want this, you can specify this with the following SQL*Plus command:

```
SET AUTOCOMMIT OFF
```

17.6 Savepoints

In the previous section we discussed how complete transactions can be undone. It is also possible to undo only a part of a transaction by using so-called *savepoints*.

```
<savepoint statement> ::=
    SAVEPOINT <savepoint name>
```

To work with savepoints, we have to extend the definition of the ROLLBACK statement somehow:

```
<rollback statement> ::=
    ROLLBACK [ WORK ]
    [ TO [ SAVEPOINT ] <savepoint name> ]
    [ RELEASE ]
```

We give you another example to show how this works.

1.   UPDATE ...
2.   INSERT ...
3.   SAVEPOINT S1
4.   INSERT ...
5.   SAVEPOINT S2
6.   DELETE ...
7.   ROLLBACK WORK TO SAVEPOINT S2
8.   UPDATE ...
9.   ROLLBACK WORK TO SAVEPOINT S1
10. UPDATE ...
11. DELETE ...
12. COMMIT WORK RELEASE

Explanation:

Line 1   This first SQL statement initiates the first transaction. The update is not yet permanent.

Line 2   This insert is not yet permanent.

Line 3   A savepoint is defined with the name S1.

Line 4   This update is not yet permanent.

Line 5   A savepoint is defined with the name S2

Line 6   This update is not yet permanent.

Line 7   A ROLLBACK is issued. However, not all updates of the current transaction are returned to its prior state, but only the updates which are performed *after* savepoint S2. This is the update on line 6. The updates on lines 1 and 2 are not yet permanent, but are still present.

Line 8   This update is not yet permanent.

Line 9   A ROLLBACK to savepoint S1 is entered. All updates performed *after* savepoint S1 are undone. These are successively the updates on lines 4 and 8.

Lines 10 – 11   These two updates are not yet permanent.

Line 12   All non-permanent updates are made permanent. These are the updates on lines 1, 2, 10 and 11. Because of RELEASE the application is logged off from the database.

When undoing an update to a certain savepoint, only the last updates can be undone.

17.7   The LOCK TABLE statement

During a transaction all data in use is locked for others. This is done to prevent non-permanent updates by one user being overwritten by updates from another user. To keep track of which data has been locked by which application, Oracle must perform some internal administration. It is possible for a user to execute many updates on a particular table within one transaction. This means that much administration must be done internally. To avoid this, you can lock the entire table at one go at the beginning of a transaction using the *LOCK TABLE statement*.

```
<lock table statement> ::=
   LOCK TABLE <table specification>
      [ {,<table specification>}... ]
   IN <lock type> MODE [ NOWAIT ]

<lock type> ::=
   ROW SHARE              |
   ROW EXCLUSIVE          |
   SHARE UPDATE           |
   SHARE                  |
   SHARE ROW EXCLUSIVE    |
   EXCLUSIVE
```

Only base tables (tables that have been created with a CREATE TABLE statement) can be locked. A lock is released at the end of a transaction.

Example 17.14: Lock the entire PLAYERS table.

```
LOCK TABLE PLAYERS IN SHARE MODE
```

Oracle supports the following lock types:

SHARE
: This lock type ensures that the application can read the table; other applications are also allowed to read the table, but not to update it.

EXCLUSIVE
: This lock type ensures that the application can update the table; other applications are not able to gain access to the table; they can neither read it nor update it.

ROW SHARE
: This lock type ensures that the application, and other applications as well, can read and/or update the table; other applications are not, however, able to request an EXCLUSIVE lock type on the table.

ROW EXCLUSIVE
: This lock type ensures that the application, and other applications as well, are able to read and/or update the table; other applications are not, however, able to request an EXCLUSIVE or SHARE lock type on the table.

SHARE UPDATE
: This lock type is the same as the lock type ROW SHARE.

SHARE ROW EXCL.
: This lock type ensures that the application is allowed to read the whole table and that other applications are also allowed to read rows in the table, but that they are not allowed to request locks of the SHARE type on the table.

If another application holds a lock on a table, your LOCK statement on that table will be rejected. With the NOWAIT option of the LOCK statement you can indicate that if the request for a lock is not accepted, processing of the LOCK statement should be stopped. This also means that if NOWAIT is not specified, the application waits until the request for the lock is accepted.

17.8 The SET TRANSACTION statement

In Section 17.5 we said that the beginning of a transaction can not be indicated explicitly. The first SQL statement that is performed in an application or the first statement after the end of the preceding transaction is the beginning. With the *SET TRANSACTION statement* it is possible to indicate the beginning explicitly. A SET TRANSACTION statement (if it is used) has to be the first statement of a transaction.

```
<set transaction statement> ::=
   SET TRANSACTION <transaction type>

<transaction type> ::= READ ONLY
```

Currently, Oracle supports only one transaction type: READ ONLY. In a READ ONLY transaction you can only *read* data. This means that you can only perform SELECT statements. If data is read in a READ ONLY transaction it can not be updated by other applications. If the SET TRANSACTION statement is not used, only updated data is locked. This means that if the same SELECT statement is executed twice within a transaction they can give different results.

18
Generating unique numbers

Many tables have a column storing unique numbers that are used to identify the rows. Such a column is usually also the primary key of the table. We have already seen many examples of this in the book. All four sample tables have a column with unique numbers. Player numbers in the PLAYERS table, team numbers in the TEAMS table, payment numbers and match numbers are all examples of series of unique numbers. The numbers identifying the database objects in the SYS.OBJ$ catalog table are also unique. Generating new numbers is sometimes cumbersome. Oracle, however, has a simple mechanism for doing this, and that is the topic of this chapter.

18.1 Introduction

Suppose that we want to add a new team. Before we can add this team to the TEAMS table using an INSERT statement, we must determine the next team number, we could do it this way (this statement will be more complex of other concurrent applications try to do the same):

```
SELECT    NVL(MAX(TEAMNR),0) + 1
FROM      TEAMS
```

Oracle, however, supports a *sequence* concept in order to do this in a more elegant fashion. A sequence is a number generator and can be used in INSERT, UPDATE and SELECT statements. In order to illustrate the concept, assume that the TEAMS table is still empty. As soon as we create the TEAMS table we create the following sequence called TEAMNUMBERS:

```
CREATE SEQUENCE TEAMNUMBERS
```

We can subsequently raise a new set of team details with a simple INSERT statement:

```
INSERT    INTO TEAMS
          (TEAMNO, PLAYERNO, DIVISION)
VALUES    (TEAMNUMBERS.NEXTVAL, 6, 'first')
```

Explanation: NEXTVAL is a system variable standing for *next value*. The difference between this system variable and others like SYSDATE and USER is that this one cannot be specified in isolation; it must always be preceded by a sequence name. By specifying NEXTVAL with the TEAMNUMBERS sequence we generate a new number. Because this is the first time TEAMNUMBERS.NEXTVAL has been used, the number raised is 1. Each time that we use TEAMNUMBERS.NEXTVAL we get a new value that is one higher than the last.

Example 18.1: If we enter the following UPDATE statement directly after the INSERT statement above

```
UPDATE    TEAMS
SET       TEAMNO = TEAMNUMBERS.NEXTVAL
WHERE     TEAMNO = 1
```

we alter the value in the TEAMNO column to 2. The value is set to 2 because this is the second time we have invoked NEXTVAL for the TEAMNUMBERS sequence. Thus, the system variable NEXTVAL provides a value, each time it is used, that is one higher than the previous one generated.

We can apply the same techniques to player numbers, payment numbers and match numbers. Example:

```
CREATE SEQUENCE PLAYERNUMBERS
```

The use of NEXTVAL is bound by a number of rules. It can only be specified in the following places:

- In the SELECT clause in the main query of a SELECT statement (not in that of a subquery). The SELECT statement itself must satisfy the following conditions:
  - the SELECT statement may not be part of a view
  - the SELECT statement may not contain DISTINCT
  - the SELECT statement may not have an ORDER BY clause
  - the SELECT statement may not have a GROUP BY clause
  - the SELECT statement may not contain set operators such as UNION

- In the VALUES clause of an INSERT statement.

- In the SET clause of an UPDATE statement.

18.2   Supplying options

In the previous section we assumed that the first value generated is always 1, followed by 2, 3, etcetera. When you create a sequence you have a number of options available which influence the generated numbers. Here is the complete definition of the CREATE SEQUENCE statement.

```
<create sequence statement> ::=
   CREATE SEQUENCE [ <user>. ] <sequence name>
      [ <sequence option>... ]

<sequence option> ::=
   START WITH <integer>                          |
   INCREMENT BY <integer>                        |
   { MAXVALUE <integer> | NOMAXVALUE } |
   { MINVALUE <integer> | NOMINVALUE } |
   { CYCLE | NOCYCLE }                           |
   { ORDER | NOORDER }                           |
   { CACHE <integer> | NOCACHE }
```

INCREMENT BY is used to state what the next value must be, that is, the amount by which the previous value is to be increased. If this option is not specified, 1 is assumed. When the number is positive, an ascending series of numbers is generated. A negative number may be specified, in which case a descending sequence is generated.

With *MINVALUE* you specify the lowest number which may be generated. Specifying nothing for this option is equivalent to using the NOMINVALUE parameter.

MAXVALUE determines the highest possible value to be generated. Not specifying it is equivalent to using the NOMAXVALUE parameter.

START WITH indicates what the first value must be. If this option is not specified, the first value depends on whether the sequence is to be generated in ascending or descending order. For ascending order it then begins with the MINVALUE value, and if this is also not specified then it begins with 1. For a descending series it begins with the MAXVALUE value and if this is absent, with –1.

With *CYCLE* you can determine that when the highest value is reached, Oracle returns to the lowest number in the series and begins generating from there again. Not specifying an option for CYCLE has the same effect as specifying NOCYCLE. If, when NOCYCLE has been specified, the highest value has been reached, Oracle issues an error message for any subsequent request for a NEXTVAL, and does not generate a new number. If CYCLE is not specified and START WITH is, the MINVALUE option can be left out.

ORDER allows you to ensure that the numbers are generated in the correct order. This happens by default. (Notice that gaps in the numbering may still appear.) If NOORDER is specified, there is no guarantee that the numbers are generated in the proper sequence.

The *CACHE option* is not so concerned with the numbers generated but the speed with which it happens. The processing speed of applications can be increased by increasing the CACHE value. The standard size is 20. Oracle calculates 20 numbers in advance and stores them in the internal memory. You run the risk, in the event of a system failure, of the numbers that have been set aside, but not yet used, disappearing.

Example 18.2: Create a sequence called FIVES that begins with 10 and increments by five.

```
CREATE SEQUENCE FIVES
START WITH 10
INCREMENT BY 5
```

Example 18.3: Create a sequence called DESCENT that begins with 100 and *decreases* by 2 each time.

```
CREATE SEQUENCE DESCENT
START WITH 100
INCREMENT BY -2
```

Example 18.4: Create a sequence called ROUNDABOUT that begins with 100 and increments by 10. When 200 is reached, the next value must be 0.

```
CREATE SEQUENCE ROUNDABOUT
MINVALUE 0
MAXVALUE 200
START WITH 100
INCREMENT BY 10
CYCLE
```

The series of numbers generated will look like this:

```
100 110 ... 200 0 10 ... 200 0 10 ...
```

Example 18.5: Create a sequence called DEFAULT which takes the default value for each option.

```
CREATE SEQUENCE DEFAULT
MINVALUE 1       MAXVALUE 10E27-1
START WITH 1     INCREMENT BY 1
NOCYCLE          CACHE 20
ORDER
```

Exercise

18.1　Create sequences that generate the following series:

    1.　2, 4, 6, 8, 10, ...

    2.　80, 70, 60, ... , 10, 0, -10, -20, ...

    3.　1, 2, 3, 4, 1, 2, 3, 4, 1, 2, ...

    4.　0, 1, 0, 1, 0, 1, 0, ...

18.3　Querying the generated number

Sometimes you may want to find out what the last generated number was, without creating a new number. To do this you use the CURRVAL system variable (it stands for *current value*).

Example 18.6: Add a new team number and change the team number for match number 10 to this new team number.

```
INSERT   INTO TEAMS
         (TEAMNO, PLAYERNO, DIVISION)
VALUES   (TEAMNUMBERS.NEXTVAL, 6, 'first')
```

Now the update:

```
UPDATE   MATCHES
SET      TEAMNO = TEAMNUMBERS.CURRVAL
WHERE    MATCHNO = 10
```

Explanation: The CURRVAL system variable supplies the most recently generated number.

As with all system variables, when variables such as NEXTVAL and CURRVAL are used more than once in an SQL statement, they have the same respective values each time. The following (somewhat idiosyncratic) statement

```
INSERT   INTO TEAMS
         (TEAMNO, PLAYERNO, DIVISION)
VALUES   (TEAMNUMBERS.NEXTVAL, TEAMNUMBERS.NEXTVAL,
         TO_CHAR(TEAMNUMBERS.NEXTVAL))
```

inserts the following row, in which each column has the same NEXTVAL value.

```
TEAMNO  PLAYERNO  DIVISION
------  --------  --------
    4         4   4
```

CURRVAL behaves in the same way (see the previous section).

18.4   Altering and deleting sequences

You can change the options in a sequence with the ALTER SEQUENCE statement.

```
<alter sequence statement> ::=
   ALTER SEQUENCE [ . ] <sequence name>
      [ <sequence option>... ]

<sequence option> ::=
   INCREMENT BY <integer>                    |
   { MAXVALUE <integer> | NOMAXVALUE } |
   { MINVALUE <integer> | NOMINVALUE } |
   { CYCLE | NOCYCLE }                       |
   { ORDER | NOORDER }                       |
   { CACHE <integer> | NOCACHE }
```

The only option which (of course) cannot be altered is the START WITH option. If you want to begin a sequence again you must delete it all and build it afresh.

Example 18.7: Alter the FIVES sequence so that it stops when 800 is reached.

```
ALTER SEQUENCE FIVES
   MAXVALUE 800
```

The DROP SEQUENCE statement allows you to delete a sequence.

```
<drop sequence statement> ::=
   DROP SEQUENCE [ <user>. ] <sequence name>
```

Example 18.8: Delete the DESCENT sequence.

```
DROP SEQUENCE DESCENT
```

18.5   Sequences and the catalog

Sequences are registered in the SEQ$ table. The name of the sequence is recorded in the OBJ$ table. The OBJ# column is the primary key of the SEQ$ table.

column name	data type	description
OBJ#	NUMBER	Database object number of the sequence
INCREMENT$	NUMBER	Value of the INCREMENT BY option
MINVALUE	NUMBER	Value of the MINVALUE option
MAXVALUE	NUMBER	Value of the MAXVALUE option
CYCLE	NUMBER	Value of the CYCLE option; 0 if nocycle and 1 if cycle
ORDER$	NUMBER	Value of the ORDER option; 0 if no order and 1 if order
CACHE	NUMBER	Value of the CACHE option
HIGHWATER	NUMBER	Value of the last number generated
AUDIT$	CHAR	Audit specifications for the sequence

19
Specifying integrity rules

In Chapter 1 we discussed the fact that enforcement of data *integrity* in the database is one of the most important tasks undertaken by a database management system. By data integrity we mean consistency and correctness of the data. Oracle can take care of data integrity if *integrity rules* (or *constraints*) are defined. After each update, Oracle tests whether the new database contents still uphold the relevant integrity rules. In other words, it must look to see whether the state of the database is still *incorrupt*, i.e. whether it conforms to all the relevant integrity rules. A valid update transforms the incorrupt state of a database to a new incorrupt state. Therefore, by defining integrity rules constraints are placed on the possible values in tables.

> *Definition: Integrity rules are the rules with which the contents of a database must comply at all times, and they describe which updates to the database are permitted.*

Note: It is possible with Version 6 of Oracle to define all the integrity rules, but unfortunately only NOT NULL is enforced. According to the Oracle Corporation enforcement of all integrity rules will be implemented in the next version. We have written this chapter as though the integrity rules are enforced. Please do not be misled by this.

In Section 5.1 we covered only the NOT NULL integrity rule. In this chapter we look at all the types of integrity rule.

- NOT NULL integrity rule
- primary key
- alternate key
- foreign key
- row integrity rule

19.1   The CREATE TABLE statement

In Section 5.1 we said in the definition of the CREATE TABLE statement that a number of integrity rules can be defined for each table. For the sake of clarity we repeat here the relevant parts of the definition of this statement.

```
<create table statement> ::=
   CREATE TABLE <table name>
      <table schema>

<table schema> ::=
      ( <table element> [ {,<table element>}... ] )

<table element> ::=
   <column definition> |
   <table integrity rule>

<column definition> ::=
   <column name> <data type>
   [ <default expression> ]
   [ <column integrity rule>... ]
```

19.2   The NOT NULL integrity rule

The NOT NULL integrity rule is described in Chapter 5.

```
<column integrity rule> ::=
   { NULL | NOT NULL }
   [ CONSTRAINT <constraint name> ]
```

What we did not describe there was that you can give an integrity rule a name, which is recorded by Oracle in the catalog. In statements such as the ALTER TABLE statement these names can be used to delete a constraint.

Example 19.1: Define the PLAYERS table.

```
CREATE TABLE PLAYERS (
        PLAYERNO  SMALLINT
                  NOT NULL CONSTRAINT PLAYERNO_NOT_NULL,
        NAME      CHAR(15)
                  NOT NULL CONSTRAINT NAME_NOT_NULL,
        :
        :
        LEAGUENO  CHAR(4) )
```

19.3 Primary keys

A *primary key* is (informally) known as a column or group of columns in a table whose values are always unique. NULL values are not permitted in columns that form part of a primary key. Primary keys can be implemented with the CREATE TABLE and ALTER TABLE statements.

You can specify most integrity rules in two ways, as *table integrity rules* or as *column integrity rules*. In the latter case the rule becomes part of the column definition. If an integrity rule pertains to two or more columns it must be specified as a table integrity rule. In contrast, if the integrity rule pertains to only one column, then either form may be chosen.

```
<table integrity rule> ::=
   <primary key>

<primary key> ::=
   PRIMARY KEY <column list>
   [ CONSTRAINT <constraint name> ]

<column list> ::=
   ( <column name> [ {,<column name>}... ] )

<column integrity rule> ::=
   PRIMARY KEY [ CONSTRAINT <constraint name> ]
```

A primary key, then, can be defined in two ways: as a table integrity rule or as a column integrity rule.

Example 19.2: Define the TEAMS table, making the TEAMNO column the primary key called TEAMS_PRIM.

```
CREATE    TABLE TEAMS
          (TEAMNO    SMALLINT
                     NOT NULL
                     PRIMARY KEY CONSTRAINT TEAMS_PRIM,
           PLAYERNO  SMALLINT  NOT NULL,
           DIVISION  CHAR(6)   NOT NULL)
```

Explanation: The NOT NULL integrity rule is unnecessary for the TEAMNO column. By defining the column as a primary key you can be sure that Oracle will automatically check that no NULL values are entered. If you do not give a primary key a name, Oracle generates one itself. It supplies a name beginning with SYS_C followed by a six digit number. This number is an internal number used by Oracle.

In the example above the primary key is defined as a column integrity rule; it forms part of the TEAMNO column definition. We could have also built the primary key like this:

```
CREATE    TABLE TEAMS
          (TEAMNO    SMALLINT  NOT NULL,
           PLAYERNO  SMALLINT  NOT NULL,
           DIVISION  CHAR(6)   NOT NULL,
           PRIMARY KEY (TEAMNO) CONSTRAINT TEAMS_PRIM)
```

If a primary key is defined as a table integrity rule you must also specify NOT NULL for each affected column.

You can define primary keys over multiple columns in a table. They are called *composite* primary keys, and can be defined only as table integrity rules.

Example 19.3: Create a DIPLOMAS table to record, among other things, course members, courses and end dates for courses. The STUDENT, COURSE and END_DATE columns form a composite primary key.

```
CREATE    TABLE DIPLOMAS
          (STUDENT   SMALLINT  NOT NULL,
           COURSE    SMALLINT  NOT NULL,
           END_DATE  DATE      NOT NULL,
           :
           PRIMARY KEY (STUDENT, COURSE, END_DATE) )
```

By defining the primary key on three columns you can ensure that a student obtained a diploma for only one course on that particular date. Note that all columns concerned are defined as NOT NULL.

Primary keys can be added after the table has been created and even after data has been entered. The ALTER TABLE statement is used to do this.

```
<alter table statement> ::=
   ALTER TABLE <table specification> <alter action>...

<alter action> ::=
   ADD ( <primary key> )

<primary key> ::=
   PRIMARY KEY <column list>
   [ CONSTRAINT <constraint name> ]

<columns list> ::=
   ( <column name> [ {,<column name>}... ] )
```

Example 19.4: Define the PAYMENTNO column in the PENALTIES table as a primary key.

```
ALTER TABLE PENALTIES
ADD   ( PRIMARY KEY (PAYMENTNO)
         CONSTRAINT PENALTIES_PRIM )
```

If the column (or group of columns) already contains duplicate values, the statement will not be accepted.

Exercises

19.1 Is it mandatory to specify a NOT NULL integrity rule for a column defined as a primary key?

19.2 Define the primary key for the MATCHES table, as both a table and a column integrity rule.

19.4 Alternate keys

Like a primary key, an alternate key is a column or group of columns whose values are unique at all times. In Chapter 1 we suggested that an alternate key is a candidate key that is not chosen to be the primary key. An important distinction between primary and alternate keys is that the former cannot contain NULL values and the latter can (except if an explicitly defined NOT NULL integrity rule forbids it). A second difference is that a table may have many alternate keys, but only one primary key.

```
<table integrity rule> ::=
   <alternate key>

<alternate key> ::=
   UNIQUE <columns list>
   [ CONSTRAINT <constraint name> ]

<columns list> ::=
   ( <column name> [ {,<column name>}... ] )

<column integrity rule> ::=
   UNIQUE [ CONSTRAINT <constraint name> ]
```

An alternate key can also be defined in two ways: as a column or table integrity rule.

Example 19.5: Define the LEAGUENO column as an alternate key in the PLAYERS table.

```
CREATE    TABLE PLAYERS
          (PLAYERNO   SMALLINT
                      NOT NULL
                      PRIMARY KEY CONSTRAINT PLAYERS_PRIM,
               :
           PHONENO    CHAR(10)  ,
           LEAGUENO   CHAR(4)
                      UNIQUE CONSTRAINT PLAYERS_ALT )
```

The alternate key is now defined by a column integrity rule. We could also have done it this way:

```
CREATE    TABLE PLAYERS
          (PLAYERNO   SMALLINT
                      NOT NULL
                      PRIMARY KEY CONSTRAINT PLAYERS_PRIM,
               :
           PHONONO    CHAR(10)  ,
           LEAGUENO   CHAR(4)   ,
                      UNIQUE (LEAGUENO) CONSTRAINT PLAYERS_ALT)
```

Alternate keys may also be defined over multiple columns, in which case a table integrity rule is required.

Example 19.6: Define the NAME and INITIALS columns as an alternate key for the PLAYERS table.

```
CREATE    TABLE PLAYERS
          (PLAYERNO      SMALLINT  NOT NULL PRIMARY KEY,
          NAME          CHAR(15)  NOT NULL,
          INITIALS      CHAR(3)   NOT NULL,
          :
          LEAGUENO      CHAR(4)   UNIQUE  ,
          UNIQUE (NAME, INITIALS)          )
```

Once this definition is in place no two players can have the same name and initials.

19.5 Rules for candidate keys

Any arbitrary group of columns can, in principle, function as a candidate key (primary or alternate). Nevertheless, there are a number of rules which candidate key columns must follow. Some of these rules stem from the theory behind the relational model, while others are laid down by Oracle. We advise you to adhere to these rules when you define candidate keys.

Preliminary note: to illustrate some of the rules we are going to use a table called T whose columns $C_1, C_2, \ldots, C_n$ form a candidate key.

1.   A maximum of one primary key can be defined for each table.

2.   The theory requires that for each table there must be a minimum of one primary key defined. Oracle, however, does not enforce this; you can create tables without a primary key. But we strongly suggest that you do specify a primary key for each base table. Why do we make this suggestion, when updating tables with primary keys means uniqueness has to be controlled, which takes time? Because without a primary key it is possible (accidentally or deliberately) to store two identical rows in a table. The problem arising from this is that the two rows are no longer distinguishable from one another. In selection processes they satisfy the same conditions and in updating they are always updated together. And then there is a high chance of corrupting the database.

3.   Two different rows in T may not have the same values for $C_1, C_2, \ldots,$ and C_n. This is called the *uniqueness rule*. As an example, the TOWN column in the PLAYERS table should not be specified as a candidate key because many players live in the same town.

4.   None of the columns $C_1, C_2, \ldots, C_n$ can be deleted without contravening the uniqueness rule. This rule is called the *minimality rule*. In short, this means that the candidate key should not consist of an unnecessarily high number of columns. Suppose that we defined PLAYERNO and NAME as a candidate key. We already know that player numbers are unique, so in this case we would not be satisfying the minimality rule.

5.   A column name may occur only once in the candidate keys column list.

6.   A candidate key may be defined on a maximum of 16 columns.

7.   The set of columns in a candidate key may not be a subset of the set of columns in another candidate key. Oracle does not enforce this rule itself. The following two examples break this rule (work out why for yourself). Example 1:

```
CREATE    TABLE PLAYERS
          (PLAYERNO    SMALLINT  NOT NULL,
          :
          LEAGUENO    CHAR(4)    ,
          PRIMARY KEY (PLAYERNO),
          UNIQUE      (PLAYERNO, NAME) )
```

Example 2:

```
CREATE    TABLE PLAYERS
          (PLAYERNO    SMALLINT  NOT NULL,
          :
          LEAGUENO    CHAR(4)    ,
          PRIMARY KEY (PLAYERNO),
          UNIQUE      (PLAYERNO) )
```

Along with this, there is one additional rule applying to primary keys but not alternate keys.

8.   The populations of columns $C_1, C_2, \ldots, C_n$ may not contain NULL values. This rule is known either as the *first integrity rule* or the *entity integrity rule*. What would happen if we allowed NULL values in a primary key? It would then be possible to insert two rows with NULL values as the primary key value and other columns with identical data. These two rows would then not be uniquely identifiable; they would always satisfy the same conditions for selection or updating. In fact, you cannot infringe this rule, as Oracle requires that the columns concerned be defined as NOT NULL.

19.6   Candidate keys and indexes

As we mentioned at the beginning of the chapter candidate keys are not regulated by Version 6 of Oracle. Therefore, you can, for example, define the PLAYERNO column in the PLAYERS table as a primary key, but Oracle will not control continued uniqueness of the player numbers. You can force the uniqueness through the definition of a unique index.

Example 19.7: Define a unique index on the PLAYERNO column of the PLAY-ERS table.

```
CREATE    UNIQUE INDEX PLAYERS_PRIM
ON        PLAYERS (PLAYERNO)
```

Example 19.8: Define an index on the NAME and INITIALS columns in the
PLAYERS table.

```
CREATE    UNIQUE INDEX PLAYERS_ALT
ON        PLAYERS (NAME, INITIALS)
```

After these CREATE INDEX statements Oracle ensures that the primary keys
do not contain duplicate values. Oracle prevents any attempt to update or insert
rows which will lead to duplicate values in a primary key. In Chapter 20 we return
in more detail to the use of indexes.

19.7 Foreign keys

In the sample database there are a number of rules concerned with the relationships between the tables (see Chapter 3). For example, all player numbers
recorded in the TEAMS table must occur in the PLAYERNO column of the
PLAYERS table. Also, all team numbers in the MATCHES table must appear
in the TEAMNO column of the TEAMS table. These sorts of relationships are
called referential integrity rules. Referential integrity rules are a special type
of integrity rule. They can be implemented as foreign keys with the CREATE
TABLE or ALTER TABLE statements. We give a definition first and then a number of examples.

```
<table integrity rule> ::=
   <foreign key>

<foreign key> ::=
   FOREIGN KEY <column list>
      <referential specification>

<column integrity rule> ::=
   <referential specification>

<referential specification> ::=
   REFERENCES <table specification> [ <column list> ]
   [ CONSTRAINT <constraint name> ]

<column list> ::=
   ( <column name> [ {,<column name>}... ] )
```

Example 19.9: Create the TEAMS table so that all player numbers (captains) must appear in the PLAYERS table. We assume that the PLAYERS table has already been created with the PLAYERNO column as the primary key.

```
CREATE    TABLE TEAMS
          (TEAMNO    SMALLINT  NOT NULL PRIMARY KEY,
          PLAYERNO   SMALLINT  NOT NULL,
          DIVISION   CHAR(6)   NOT NULL,
          FOREIGN KEY (PLAYERNO)
             REFERENCES PLAYERS
             CONSTRAINT TEAMS_FOR_PNO )
```

Before we give an explanation of this statement we will introduce two new terms. A table in which a foreign key is defined is called a *referencing table* and a table to which a foreign key points is called a *referenced table*. (This terminology conforms to that used in Date, 1990.) So in the example above TEAMS is the referencing table and PLAYERS the referenced table.

What is the actual effect of defining a foreign key? After the statement above has been executed, Oracle will guarantee that each non-NULL value inserted in the foreign key already occurs in the primary key of the referenced table. In the example above, this means that for each new player number in the TEAMS table a check is carried out as to whether that number already occurs in the PLAYERNO column (primary key) of the PLAYERS table. If this is not the case the user or application receives an error message and the update is rejected. This applies also to updating the PLAYERNO column in the TEAMS table with the UPDATE statement. We could also say that Oracle guarantees that the population of the PLAYERNO column in the TEAMS table is always a subset of the PLAYERNO column in the PLAYERS table. This means, for example, that the following SELECT statement never returns any rows:

```
SELECT  *
FROM    TEAMS
WHERE   PLAYERNO NOT IN
        (SELECT  PLAYERNO
        FROM     PLAYERS)
```

Naturally, the definition of a foreign key has a huge influence on the updating of the tables involved. We will illustrate this with a number of examples. We are assuming here that the PLAYERS and TEAM tables have the same data as the tables described in Chapter 3.

- The deletion of a player from the PLAYERS table is now only permitted if that player is not a captain.

- The updating of a player number in the PLAYERS table is only possible if that player is not a captain.

- For inserting new players into the PLAYERS table there are no restrictions laid down by the foreign key.

- For deleting existing teams from the TEAMS table there are no restrictions laid down by the foreign key.

- The updating of a player number (captain) in the TEAMS table is only permitted if the new player number already occurs in the PLAYERS table.

- The insertion of new teams into the TEAMS table is only permitted if the new player number already occurs in the PLAYERS table.

For clarity as far as the terminology is concerned, we refer to the PLAYERNO column in the TEAMS table as the foreign key and the referential integrity rule is the form of control, in this case that each player number added to the TEAMS table must occur in the PLAYERS table.

A foreign key can consist of one or more columns. If it has only one column it can be defined in two different ways, as a table or column integrity rule. In the example above it is defined as a table integrity rule, but we could have formulated it as a column integrity rule in the following way:

```
CREATE    TABLE TEAMS
          (TEAMNO    SMALLINT  NOT NULL PRIMARY KEY,
          PLAYERNO   SMALLINT  NOT NULL
                     REFERENCES PLAYERS
                     CONSTRAINT TEAMS_FOR_PNO,
          DIVISION   CHAR(6)   NOT NULL)
```

The following rules apply when a foreign key is specified:

- The referenced table must already exist, having been created by a CREATE TABLE statement, or must be the table which is currently being created. The referencing table is then the same as the reference table. The referenced table may not be a view.

- A primary key must be defined for the referenced table.

- The number of columns in the foreign key must be the same as the number of columns in the primary key of the referenced table.

- The data types of the columns in the foreign key must match those of the columns in the primary key of the referenced table.

- A column name (or combination of column names) may be specified after the referenced table name. If this is done, this column (combination) must be the table's primary key. When no column name is specified the referenced table must have a primary key.

- A NULL value is permitted in a foreign key, though a primary key can never contain NULL values. This means that the contents of a foreign key are correct if each non-NULL value occurs in a specific primary key.

Below we give the definitions of three tables from the sample database, including all primary and foreign keys.

```
CREATE    TABLE TEAMS
          (TEAMNO           SMALLINT      NOT NULL,
          PLAYERNO          SMALLINT      NOT NULL,
          DIVISION          CHAR(6)       NOT NULL,
          PRIMARY KEY (TEAMNO)
             CONSTRAINT TEAMS_PRIM                   ,
          FOREIGN KEY (PLAYERNO)
             REFERENCES PLAYERS
             CONSTRAINT TEAMS_FOR_PNO )
```

Explanation: Team captains must be players who occur in the PLAYERS table. Players who are captains cannot be deleted.

```
CREATE    TABLE MATCHES
          (MATCHNO          SMALLINT      NOT NULL,
          TEAMNO            SMALLINT      NOT NULL,
          PLAYERNO          SMALLINT      NOT NULL,
          WON               SMALLINT      NOT NULL,
          LOST              SMALLINT      NOT NULL,
          PRIMARY KEY (MATCHNO)
             CONSTRAINT MATCHES_PRIM               ,
          FOREIGN KEY (TEAMNO)
             REFERENCES TEAMS
             CONSTRAINT MATCHES_FOR_TNO    ,
          FOREIGN KEY (PLAYERNO)
             REFERENCES PLAYERS
             CONSTRAINT MATCHES_FOR_PNO     )
```

Explanation: A match may only be played by someone who appears in the PLAYERS table and may only be played for a team that is recorded in the TEAMS table. Players and teams may be deleted only if their numbers do not occur in the MATCHES table.

```
CREATE    TABLE PENALTIES
          (PAYMENTNO        INTEGER       NOT NULL,
          PLAYERNO          SMALLINT      NOT NULL,
          PEN_DATE          DATE          NOT NULL,
          AMOUNT            DECIMAL(7,2)  NOT NULL,
          PRIMARY KEY (PAYMENTNO)
             CONSTRAINT PENALTIES_PRIM                  ,
          FOREIGN KEY (PLAYERNO)
             REFERENCES PLAYERS
             CONSTRAINT PENALTIES_FOR_PNO          )
```

Explanation: A penalty can only be inserted for someone who is recorded in the PLAYERS table. If a player is deleted from the PLAYERS table, his or her penalties are removed from the PENALTIES table.

For clarity we note that the following constructions *are* permitted:

- A column may be part of multiple foreign keys.

- A subset of columns in a primary key, or the entire set of columns in a primary key, may form a foreign key.

- The referenced and referencing table associated with a foreign key may be the same. Such a table is called a *self referencing table* and the construction *self referential integrity*.

- For two foreign keys F_1 and F_2 it is possible for the referencing table of F_1 and the referenced table for F_2 to be the same, and for the referencing table of F_2 to be the same as the referenced table for F_1. This is called *cross referential integrity*.

  Cross referential integrity can give rise to problems. If F_1 is defined and F_2 does not yet exist, the foreign key cannot be defined. The solution to this is to define the foreign key later using the ALTER TABLE statement. This is our next topic.

Foreign keys can be added separately after a table has been created and populated with data.

```
<alter table statement> ::=
   ALTER TABLE <table specification> <alter action>...

<alter action> ::=
   ADD <foreign key>

<foreign key> ::=
   FOREIGN KEY [ <constraint name> ] <column list>
      <referential specification>

<referential specification> ::=
   REFERENCES <table specification>

<column list> ::=
   ( <column name> [ {,<column name>}... ] )
```

Example 19.10: Add a foreign key to the PENALTIES table.

```
ALTER TABLE PENALTIES
ADD  (FOREIGN KEY (PLAYERNO)
         REFERENCES PLAYERS
         CONSTRAINT PENALTIES_FOR_PNO )
```

Exercises

19.3 Can a self-referencing table be created with a CREATE TABLE statement?

19.4 Which updates are no longer permitted after the following definition:

```
CREATE    TABLE MATCHES
          (MATCHNO    SMALLINT NOT NULL,
                      PRIMARY KEY,
           TEAMNO     SMALLINT NOT NULL
                      REFERENCES TEAMS,
           PLAYERNO   SMALLINT NOT NULL
                      REFERENCES PLAYERS,
           WON        SMALLINT NOT NULL,
           LOST       SMALLINT NOT NULL)
```

19.8   Row integrity rules

Primary, alternate and foreign keys are special types of integrity rules that occur frequently in practice. Alongside these, each database also recognizes a number of other special integrity rules. For example, the SEX column in the PLAYERS table may contain only two different values: M or F. We can specify a number of rules of this type and we refer to them as *row integrity rules*.

```
<table integrity rule> ::=
   <row integrity rule>

<column integrity rule> ::=
   <row integrity rule>

<row integrity rule> ::=
   CHECK ( <condition> )
```

Example 19.11: Create the PLAYERS table and ensure that the SEX column contains only the values M or F.

```
CREATE    TABLE PLAYERS
          (PLAYERNO   SMALLINT
                      NOT NULL
                      PRIMARY KEY CONSTRAINT PLAYERS_PRIM,
           :
```

```
             :
          SEX          CHAR(1)
                       NOT NULL
                       CHECK(SEX IN ('M', 'F'))
                          CONSTRAINT SEX_MF,
             :
```

Example 19.12: Create the PLAYERS table and ensure that all values in the YEAR_OF_BIRTH column are greater than 1920.

```
       CREATE    TABLE PLAYERS
                 (PLAYERNO        SMALLINT
                                  NOT NULL
                                  PRIMARY KEY CONSTRAINT PLAYERS_PRIM,
                    :
                 YEAR_OF_BIRTH    SMALLINT
                                  CHECK(YEAR_OF_BIRTH > 1920)
                                  CONSTRAINT YEAR_OF_BIRTH_1920,
                    :
```

If you specify an integrity rule which compares two or more columns from a table, you must define the row integrity rule as a table integrity rule.

Example 19.13: Create the PLAYERS table and include a rule to ensure that all values in the YEAR_OF_BIRTH column are smaller than their corresponding value in the YEAR_JOINED column. In other words, take care that a player can join the club only after he or she has been born.

```
       CREATE    TABLE PLAYERS
                 (PLAYERNO        SMALLINT
                                  NOT NULL
                                  PRIMARY KEY CONSTRAINT PLAYERS_PRIM,
                    :
                 YEAR_OF_BIRTH    SMALLINT,
                 YEAR_JOINED      SMALLINT NOT NULL,
                    :
                 CHECK(YEAR_OF_BIRTH < YEAR_JOINED)
                    CONSTRAINT YEAR_OF_BIRTH_GT_YEAR_JOINED
                    :
```

In fact, the NOT NULL option is a special variant on the row integrity rule. Instead of NOT NULL we can specify the following column integrity rule for appropriate columns:

```
       CHECK( COLUMN IS NOT NULL )
```

We advise you, nevertheless, to use the NOT NULL option in preference because Oracle can control this more efficiently.

You should note that a combination of row integrity rules can lead to a situation in which a table can no longer be populated. Oracle does not check this itself. After the following statement no more rows can be inserted into the PLAYERS table:

```
CREATE    TABLE PLAYERS
          (PLAYERNO        SMALLINT
          :
          YEAR_OF_BIRTH  SMALLINT NOT NULL,
          YEAR_JOINED    SMALLINT NOT NULL,
          :
          CHECK(YEAR_OF_BIRTH < YEAR_JOINED),
          CHECK(YEAR_OF_BIRTH > 1900),
          CHECK(YEAR_JOINED  < 1880),
          :
```

Row integrity rules can be added after the table has been created using the ALTER TABLE statement.

```
<alter table statement> ::=
   ALTER TABLE <table specification> <alter action>...

<alter action> ::=
   ADD <row integrity rule>

<row integrity rule> ::=
   CHECK ( <condition> )
   [ CONSTRAINT <constraint name> ]
```

Example 19.14: Define an integrity rule that guarantees that each payment number in the PENALTIES table is greater than zero.

```
ALTER TABLE PENALTIES
ADD   ( CHECK (PAYMENTNO > 0)
            CONSTRAINT PAY_NO_POSITIVE )
```

Exercises

19.5 Define an integrity rule that ensures that each penalty amount in the PENALTIES table is greater than zero.

19.6 Define an integrity rule that guarantees that the total number of sets in a match in the MATCHES table is always less than six.

19.9   Deleting integrity rules

In Chapter 5 we have already discussed the features of the ALTER TABLE statement. Here we illustrate its features for deleting integrity rules.

```
<alter table statement> ::=
   ALTER TABLE <table specification> <alter action>...

<alter action> ::=
   DROP CONSTRAINT <constraint name>
```

Example 19.15: Delete the NOT NULL integrity rule defined on the NAME column in the PLAYERS table.

```
ALTER TABLE PLAYERS
DROP  CONSTRAINT NAME_NOT_NULL
```

The effect of this statement is equivalent to:

```
ALTER TABLE PLAYERS
MODIFY (NAME NULL)
```

If you have created an integrity rule and not given it a name you need first to look in the catalog to determine the name assigned to it. See Section 19.10 for more detail.

Example 19.16: Delete the primary key from the PENALTIES table.

```
ALTER TABLE PENALTIES
DROP  CONSTRAINT PENALTIES_PRIM
```

When a primary key is deleted all foreign keys referring to it are also deleted.

Example 19.17: Delete the foreign key called TEAMS_FOR_PNO defined for the TEAMS table.

```
ALTER TABLE TEAMS
DROP  CONSTRAINT TEAMS_FOR_PNO
```

19.10   Integrity rules and the catalog

Oracle uses three catalog tables for recording all data about integrity rules: CON$, CDEF$ and CCOL$. The CON$ table contains, for each integrity rule, the unique integrity rule number, the name and the owner. The CON# column forms the primary key. NAME and OWNER together form an alternate key.

When no name is specified at the time an integrity rule is created, Oracle generates a name itself. The name begins with SYS_C followed by a six digit number. This number is the same as the integrity rule number of the rule itself, padded with zeros.

column name	data type	description
OWNER	NUMBER	Number of the user who created the integrity rule
NAME	CHAR(30)	Unique name of the integrity rule
CON#	NUMBER	Unique number of the integrity rule

The CDEF$ table records the type of integrity rule and other details. Below the columns of this table are shown. The CON# column is the primary key here as well.

column name	data type	description
CON#	NUMBER	Unique number of the integrity rule
OBJ#	NUMBER	Database object number of the table on which the integrity rule is defined
COLS	NUMBER	Number of columns on which the integrity rule is defined (for a column integrity rule this number equals 1)
TYPE	NUMBER	Type of integrity rule: 1. row integrity rule (CHECK) 2. primary key 3. alternate key (UNIQUE) 4. foreign key 5. view integrity rule (WITH CHECK OPTION)
ROBJ#	NUMBER	Database object number of the table to which the foreign key points (this column is used only for foreign keys)
RCON#	NUMBER	Number of the primary key to which the foreign key points (this column is used only for foreign keys)
CONDLENGTH	NUMBER	Length of the condition of the row integrity rule (this column is used only for row integrity rules)
CONDITION	LONG	Condition of the row integrity rule (this column is used only for row integrity rules)

The third table that records data about integrity rules is the CCOL$ table. This table is used to identify the columns on which an integrity rule is defined. The primary key is formed by the CON#, OBJ# and COL# columns.

column name	data type	description
CON#	NUMBER	Unique number of the integrity rule
OBJ#	NUMBER	Database object number of the table on which the integrity rule is defined
COL#	NUMBER	Sequence number of the column in the table on which the integrity rule is defined
POS#	NUMBER	Sequence number of the column in the integrity rule

Below we show how defining an integrity rule affects the contents of the catalog tables.

Example 19.18: Define the PLAYERS table.

```
CREATE TABLE PLAYERS (
        PLAYERNO        SMALLINT
                        NOT NULL
                        PRIMARY KEY CONSTRAINT PLAYERS_PRIM,
        NAME            CHAR(15)
                        NOT NULL
                        CONSTRAINT NAME_NOT_NULL,
        YEAR_OF_BIRTH   SMALLINT
                        CHECK(YEAR_OF_BIRTH > 1920),
        :
        :
        LEAGUENO        CHAR(4),
        UNIQUE          (NAME, INITIALS),
        CHECK           (YEAR_OF_BIRTH < YEAR_JOINED) )
```

and define the TEAMS table:

```
CREATE TABLE TEAMS (
        TEAMNO    SMALLINT  NOT NULL
                  PRIMARY KEY CONSTRAINT TEAMS_PRIM,
        PLAYERNO  SMALLINT  NOT NULL,
        DIVISION  CHAR(6)   NOT NULL,
        FOREIGN KEY (PLAYERNO)
            REFERENCES PLAYERS
            CONSTRAINT TEAMS_FOR_PNO )
```

The CON$ table:

```
CON#  NAME
----  -------------
2302  PLAYERS_PRIM
2303  SYS_C002303
2304  NAME_NOT_NULL
2305  SYS_C002305
2306  SYS_C002306
 :    :
2312  TEAMS_FOR_PNO
```

The CDEF$ table (the PLAYERS table has object number 4211 and TEAMS number 4212):

CON#	OBJ#	COLS	TYPE	ROBJ#	RCON#	CONDLENGTH	CONDITION
2302	4211	1	2	?	?	?	?
2303	4211	1	1	?	?	21	PLAYERNO IS NOT NULL
2304	4211	1	1	?	?	16	NAME IS NOT NULL
2305	4211	1	1	?	?	13	YEAR_OF_BIRTH >1920
2306	4211	2	3	?	?	?	?
2307	4211	2	1	?	?	16	YEAR_OF_BIRTH < YEAR_JOINED
:	:	:	:	:	:	: :	
2312	4212	1	4	4211	2302	? ?	

The CCOL$ table:

CON#	OBJ#	COL#	POS#
2302	4211		
2303	4211		
2304	4211		
2305	4211		
2306	4211		
2306	4211	3	2
2306	4211	7	2
2307	4211		
:	:		
2312	4212		

20
Using indexes

Some SQL statements have a reasonably constant or predictable execution time. Examples include the CREATE TABLE and GRANT statements. Users have no way of influencing their execution time; there is no way of reducing their execution time. However, this is not the case for all statements. The time required to process SELECT, UPDATE and DELETE statements varies from one statement to the next. One SELECT statement may be processed in two seconds, while another could take minutes. You can influence the time Oracle needs to execute these types of statements. There are many techniques available for decreasing the execution time of SELECT, UPDATE and DELETE statements (known as *optimization*). We describe the following techniques:

- creating indexes
- alternative ways of formulating statements
- tuning the physical storage structure
- including statements in a program (embedded SQL)

This chapter discusses creating indexes and how they work. In the following chapter we discuss the second technique and Chapter 25 describes the third technique. The last technique will be covered in Chapter 28.

20.1 How an index works

Preliminary remark: This section does not so much cover an SQL statement, but provides insight into how Oracle uses indexes. You should view this section as background information.

Oracle has two methods of accessing rows in a table: the *sequential access* method and the *direct access* method

Sequential access is best described as 'browsing through a table row by row'. Oracle reads each row in the table. If only one row is sought, and if the table has many rows, this method is, of course, very time-consuming and inefficient. It is comparable to going through a telephone book page by page. If you are looking for the number of someone whose name begins with an L, you certainly don't want to start looking in the As.

When Oracle uses the direct access method, it reads only the rows that exhibit the required characteristics. To do this, however, an *index* is necessary. An index is a type of alternative access to a table and can be compared with an index in a book.

An index in Oracle is built like a *tree*, consisting of a number of *nodes*. Figure 20.1 is a pictorial representation of an index. On the left of the figure is the index structure itself, and on the right, two columns from the PLAYERS table. The nodes of the index are represented by the rectangles. The node on the far left forms the beginning point of the index and is known as the *root*. Each node contains a maximum of three ordered values from the PLAYERNO column. Each value in a node points to another node or to a row in the PLAYERS table (Figure 20.1 does not include every 'pointer') and each row in the table is referenced through at least one node. A node that points to a row is called a *leaf page*. The values in a node are ordered. For each node, apart from the root, the values are always less than or equal to the value that pointed to that node. Leaf pages are themselves linked to one another; a leaf page has a pointer to the leaf page with the next set of values. In Figure 20.1 we represent these pointers with the thick vertical arrows.

Broadly speaking, Oracle has two algorithms available for use with indexes. One of the algorithms is for searching for rows in which a particular value occurs, and the other is for browsing through a whole table or a part of a table via an ordered column. We will illustrate these two algorithms with two examples. First, here is an example of how Oracle uses the index to select a particular row.

Example 20.1: Suppose that all rows with player number 44 must be found.

Step 1   Search the root of the index. This root becomes the active node.

Step 2   Is the active node a leaf page? If so, continue with step 4; if not, continue with step 3.

Step 3   Does the active node contain the value 44? If so, the node to which this value points becomes the active node; go back to step 2. If not, choose the lowest value that is higher than 44 in the active node. The node to which this value points becomes the active node; go back to step 2.

Step 4   Search for the value 44 in the active node. This value now points to all the rows in the PLAYERS table where the PLAYERNO column equals 44. Retrieve all these rows from the database for further processing.

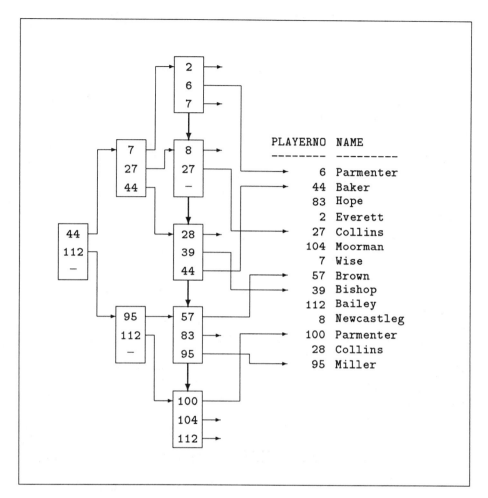

Figure 20.1: Pictorial representation of an index tree

Without browsing through all the rows, Oracle has found the desired row(s). In most cases, the time spent searching for rows can be reduced considerably if Oracle can use an index.

In this next example Oracle uses the index to retrieve ordered rows from a table.

Example 20.2: Give all players ordered by the player number.

Step 1   Search the leaf page with the lowest value. This leaf page becomes the active node.

Step 2   Retrieve all rows to which the values in the active node are pointing for further processing.

Step 3   If there is a subsequent leaf page, make this the active node and continue with step 2.

Updating values in rows, or adding or deleting rows, means that Oracle must
automatically alter the index. So the index tree is always consistent with the
contents of the table.

You can define an index on a non-unique column like the NAME column.
The result of this is that values in a leaf page point to multiple rows; there is one
pointer for each row in which the value occurs.

Indexes can also be defined on combinations of values. Each value in a
node is then, in fact, a concatenation of the individual values. The leaf pages
point to rows in which that combination of values appears.

There are two other important observations to note about the use of indexes:

•   Index rows are just like rows in tables and are stored in files. So, an index
takes up physical storage space (just like an index in a book).

•   Updates to tables can lead to updates to indexes. When an index must be
updated, Oracle tries, where it can, to fill the gaps in the nodes in order to
complete the process as quickly as possible. But an index can become so
'full' that a new index must be created and this can necessitate a total *reorganization* of the index. Such a reorganization can be very time-consuming.

This section presents a very simplified picture of the workings of an index. In
practice, for example, a node in an index tree can accommodate not just three,
but many values. For a more detailed description we refer you to Date (1986).

20.2   Processing a SELECT statement: the steps

Chapter 6 described the clauses of a SELECT statement and how they are processed one after another. These clauses provide the 'structure' around which
Oracle builds a *basic strategy* for processing a statement. By basic strategy we
are assuming sequential access of the data. This section discusses how the use of
an index can change the basic strategy to an *optimized strategy*.

Oracle tries to choose the most efficient strategy for processing each statement. This analysis is performed by a Oracle module called the *optimizer*. (The
analysis of statements is also referred to as *query optimization*.) The optimizer
defines a number of alternative strategies for each statement. It estimates which
strategy is likely to be the most efficient, on the basis of such factors as the expected execution time and the presence of indexes (in the absence of indexes,
this can be the basic strategy). Oracle then executes the statement according to
its chosen strategy.

Here are some illustrations of optimized processing strategies. We leave
the CONNECT BY clause out of consideration.

Example 20.3: Get all information about player 44. (We assume that there is an index defined on the PLAYERNO column.)

```
SELECT   *
FROM     PLAYERS
WHERE    PLAYERNO = 44
```

The FROM clause: Normally, Oracle would retrieve all rows from the PLAYERS table. Speeding up the processing by using an index means that only the rows where the value in the PLAYERNO column equals 44 are fetched.
Intermediate result:

```
PLAYERNO  NAME   ...
--------  -----  ---
      44  Baker  ...
```

The WHERE clause: In this example, this clause was processed at the same time as the FROM clause.
The SELECT clause: All columns are presented.
The difference between the basic strategy and this optimized strategy can be represented in another way.
Basic strategy:

```
RESULT := [];
FOR EACH P IN PLAYERS DO
    IF P.PLAYERNO = 44 THEN
        RESULT :+ P;
OD;
```

Optimized strategy:

```
RESULT := [];
FOR EACH P IN PLAYERS WHERE PLAYERNO = 44 DO
    RESULT :+ P;
OD;
```

With the first strategy all rows are fetched by the FOR EACH statement. The second strategy works much more selectively. When an index is used, only those rows where the player number equals 44 are retrieved.

Example 20.4: Give the number and town of each player whose number is lower than 10 and who lives in Stratford; order the result by number.

```
SELECT   PLAYERNO, TOWN
FROM     PLAYERS
WHERE    PLAYERNO < 10
AND      TOWN = 'Stratford'
ORDER BY PLAYERNO
```

The FROM clause: Fetch all rows where the player number is smaller than 10. Again, use the index on the PLAYERNO column. Fetch the rows in ascending order, thus accounting for the ORDER BY clause. This is simple, because the values in an index are always ordered.

Intermediate result:

```
PLAYERNO   ...   TOWN          ...
--------   ---   ---------     ---
       2   ...   Stratford     ...
       6   ...   Stratford     ...
       7   ...   Stratford     ...
       8   ...   Inglewood     ...
```

The WHERE clause: The WHERE clause specifies two conditions. Each row in the intermediate result satisfies the first condition that has already been evaluated in the FROM clause. Now, only the second condition must be evaluated.

Intermediate result:

```
PLAYERNO   ...   TOWN          ...
--------   ---   ---------     ---
       2   ...   Stratford     ...
       6   ...   Stratford     ...
       7   ...   Stratford     ...
```

The ORDER BY clause: Thanks to the use of an index during the processing of the FROM clause, no extra sorting needs to be done. The intermediate result, then, is the same as the table shown above.

The SELECT clause: Two columns are selected.

Intermediate result:

```
PLAYERNO  TOWN
--------  ---------
       2  Stratford
       6  Stratford
       7  Stratford
```

Here are the basic strategy and the optimized strategy for this example:

Basic strategy:

```
RESULT := [];
FOR EACH P IN PLAYERS DO
    IF (P.PLAYERNO < 10)
    AND (P.TOWN = 'Stratford') THEN
        RESULT :+ P;
OD;
```

Optimized strategy:

```
RESULT := [];
FOR EACH P IN PLAYERS WHERE PLAYERNO < 10 DO
   IF P.TOWN = 'Stratford' THEN
      RESULT :+ P;
OD;
```

Example 20.5: Give the name and initials of each player who lives in the same place as player 44.

```
SELECT    NAME, INITIALS
FROM      PLAYERS
WHERE     TOWN =
          (SELECT    TOWN
           FROM      PLAYERS
           WHERE     PLAYERNO = 44)
```

Here are the two strategies.
    Basic strategy:

```
RESULT := [];
FOR EACH P IN PLAYERS DO
   HELP := FALSE;
   FOR EACH P44 IN PLAYERS DO
      IF (P44.TOWN = P.TOWN)
      AND (P44.PLAYERNO = 44) THEN
         HELP := TRUE;
   OD;
   IF HELP = TRUE THEN
      RESULT :+ P;
OD;
```

Optimized strategy:

```
RESULT := [];
FIND P44 IN PLAYERS WHERE PLAYERNO = 44;
FOR EACH P IN PLAYERS WHERE TOWN = P44.TOWN
   RESULT := P;
OD;
```

These were relatively simple examples. As the statements become more complex, so too is it more difficult for Oracle to determine the optimal strategy, and this adds to processing time as well, of course.

If you want to know more about the optimization of SELECT statements, refer to Kim *et al.* (1985). You don't, however, need this knowledge to understand SQL statements. That is why we have only given a summary of the topic.

Exercise

20.1 Write, for the following two statements, the basic strategy and an optimized
strategy; assume that there is an index defined on each column mentioned
in the query.

```
1.        SELECT    *
          FROM      TEAMS
          WHERE     TEAMNO > 1
          AND       DIVISION = 'second'

2.        SELECT    P.PLAYERNO
          FROM      PLAYERS P, MATCHES M1
          WHERE     P.PLAYERNO = M1.PLAYERNO
          AND       YEAR_OF_BIRTH > 1963
```

20.3 Creating and dropping indexes

The definition of the CREATE INDEX statement is as follows:

```
<create index statement> ::=
   CREATE [ UNIQUE ] INDEX [ <user> . ] <index name>
   ON     <table specification>
   ( <column in index> [ {,<column in index>}... ] )
   [ COMPRESS | NOCOMPRESS ]

<table specification> ::= [ <user> . ] <table name>

<column in index> ::=
   <column name> [ ASC | DESC ]
```

Two examples of non-UNIQUE INDEXes:

```
CREATE    INDEX PLAY_PC
ON        PLAYERS (POSTCODE)

CREATE    INDEX MAT_WL
ON        MATCHES (WON, LOST)
```

Chapter 5 looked at some examples defining UNIQUE INDEXes. Here is another:

```
CREATE    UNIQUE INDEX PL_NAME_INIT
ON        PLAYERS (NAME, INITIALS)
```

Once this statement has been processed, Oracle prevents any two identical combinations of name and initials from being inserted into the PLAYERS table.

Note: A column on which a UNIQUE index has been defined can contain only one NULL value, whereas a column with a non-UNIQUE index can contain multiple NULL values.

Including the options ASC (ASCending), DESC (DESCending), COMPRESS and NOCOMPRESS serves no purpose. The only reason that they have been added is to be compatible with previous versions of Oracle and with other SQL products on the market. You will see that nowhere in any of the catalog tables is this specification stored.

Indexes can be created for other users. We give you an example. After execution of the following statement, JOHN is the owner of the table.

```
CREATE    INDEX JOHN.HIS_INDEX
ON        PENALTIES (AMOUNT)
```

Indexes can be created at any time. You don't have to create all the indexes for a table as soon as the CREATE TABLE statement has finished executing. You can also create indexes on tables that already have data in them. But creating a unique index on a table where the column concerned already contains duplicate values can be problematic. Oracle notes this and does not create the index. The duplicate values have to be removed by the user first before the index can be created. The following SELECT statement will help locate the duplicate values (where C is the column on which the index must be defined):

```
SELECT    C
FROM      T
GROUP BY C
HAVING    COUNT(*) > 1
```

The following restrictions apply when you create an index:

- Because indexes are, just like tables, database objects, a user cannot assign a name to an index which he or she already used for a table, view or synonym.
- An index can be defined on a maximum of 16 columns.
- An index cannot be defined on a column whose data type is LONG.

The DROP INDEX statement is used to remove indexes.

```
<drop index statement> ::=
   DROP INDEX [ <user> . ] <index name>
```

Examples:

```
DROP INDEX PLAY_PC
```

and:

```
DROP INDEX MAT_WL
```

When you drop a UNIQUE index you do not need to specify the word UNIQUE.

Certain circumstances can lead to an index that is not correct any more. This can be determined with the *VALIDATE INDEX statement*. This statement checks if the pointers from the index tree to the rows in the table are still correct. However, the statement does not repair the index. If the statement shows that there is something incorrect, you are supposed to drop the index and recreate it yourself.

```
<validate index statement> ::=
    VALIDATE INDEX [ <user> . ] <index name>
```

Example 20.6: Determine if the PLAY_PC index is correct.

```
VALIDATE INDEX PLAY_PC
```

20.4   Indexes and the catalog

Just as with tables and views, certain data about indexes is also recorded in the OBJ$ catalog table. Special index data are recorded in the IND$ table. Below we give the descriptions of the columns of the IND$ table. The OBJ# column is the primary key of this table.

column name	data type	description
OBJ#	NUMBER	Database object number of the index
BO#	NUMBER	Database object number of the table on which the index is defined
COLS	NUMBER	Number of columns in the index
UNIQUE$	NUMBER	Whether the index in UNIQUE (1) or non UNIQUE (0)

The columns on which the index is defined are stored in a separate table, the ICOL$ table. The primary key of the ICOL$ table is formed by the OBJ# and COL# columns.

column name	data type	description
OBJ#	NUMBER	Database object number of the index
BO#	NUMBER	Database object number of the table on which the index is defined
COL#	NUMBER	Column number of the column on which the index is defined
POS#	NUMBER	Sequence number of the column in the index

The examples of indexes from this section would be recorded in the OBJ$, IND$ and the ICOL$ table as follows (we only show you the important columns).

The OBJ$ table:

OBJ#	NAME	TYPE#
5001	PLAY_PC	1
5002	MAT_WL	1
5003	PL_NAME_INIT	1

The IND$ table:

OBJ#	BO#	COLS	UNIQUE$
5001	4211	1	0
5002	4214	2	0
5003	4211	2	1

The ICOL$ table:

OBJ#	BO#	COL#	POS#
5001	4211	10	1
5002	4214	3	1
5002	4214	4	2
5003	4211	2	1
5003	4211	3	2

20.5   Choosing columns for indexes

In order to be absolutely sure that inefficient processing of SELECT statements is not due to the absence of an index, you could create an index on every column and combination of columns. And if you were going to be entering only SELECT statements against the data, this could well be a good approach. But such a solution does raise a number of problems, not the least of them being the cost of index storage space. Another important disadvantage is that each data update (via an INSERT, UPDATE or DELETE statement) requires a corresponding index update. The update will take significantly longer if many indexes also need to be updated. So, a choice has to be made. Here are some guidelines.

20.5.1   A UNIQUE index on primary keys

It is important for the primary key and all alternate keys not to contain duplicate values. Many statements and programs depend on this. The only way in which Oracle can guarantee uniqueness of values in columns is to use a unique index.

Therefore, you should always create a unique index on each primary and candidate key. Also, specify all columns which are a part of a primary key as NOT NULL (see Section 5.2).

20.5.2   An index on foreign keys

Joins can take a long time to execute if there are no indexes defined on the join columns. For a large percentage of joins, the join columns are also, in fact, keys of the tables concerned. They can be primary and alternate keys, but also foreign keys. According to the first rule of thumb, you should already have an index on the primary and candidate key columns. What remains now is to define indexes on the foreign keys. In the sample database, then, you would define the following indexes for the TEAMS and MATCHES tables:

```
CREATE    INDEX T_PLAYERNO
ON        TEAMS (PLAYERNO)

CREATE    INDEX M_PLAYERNO
ON        MATCHES (PLAYERNO)

CREATE    INDEX M_TEAMNO
ON        MATCHES (TEAMNO)
```

20.5.3   An index on columns included in selection criteria

SELECT, UPDATE, and DELETE statements execute faster if there is an index defined on the columns named in the WHERE clause.
Example:

```
SELECT    *
FROM      PLAYERS
WHERE     TOWN = 'Stratford'
```

Oracle selects rows on the basis of the value in the TOWN column and processing this statement is more efficient if there is an index on this column. This was discussed extensively in the earlier sections of this chapter.

Nevertheless, you should only place an index on a column which has many different values, and not on one like SEX in the PLAYERS table which has only two different values, F and M. If, via a SELECT statement, we search for all players of a particular sex, we will probably find a distribution of half men and half women in the rows. If Oracle uses an index in this case, the processing time will probably be longer than if the rows are read sequentially.

An index is not just worthwhile when the = operator is used, but also for <, <=, > and >=. (Note that the <> operator does not appear in this list.) But this is only true when the number of rows selected is much smaller than the number of rows not selected.

If a WHERE clause contains an AND operator, an index should be defined on the two columns to ensure more efficient execution.

Example:

```
SELECT   *
FROM     PLAYERS
WHERE    NAME = 'Collins'
AND      INITIALS = 'DD'
```

Associated index:

```
CREATE   INDEX NAME_INIT
ON       PLAYERS (NAME, INITIALS)
```

In some cases, when you are executing such a query, it can suffice to have an index on only one of the columns. Suppose that duplicate names occur seldom in the NAME column and suppose that this is the only column with an index. Oracle will find all the rows that satisfy the condition NAME = 'Collins' by using this index. Only infrequently will it retrieve a few too many rows. In this case, an index on the combination of columns will take up more storage space than necessary, and will not significantly improve the processing of the SELECT statement.

Indexes defined on combinations of columns are also used for selections in which only the first column (or columns) of the index are specified. Therefore, the NAME_INIT index above is used by Oracle to process the condition, NAME = 'Collins', but not for INITIALS = 'DD'. The INITIALS column is not the first one in the NAME_INIT index.

20.5.4   An index on columns used for ordering

If Oracle needs to order the result of a SELECT statement by a column that has no index, a separate (time-consuming) sort process must be performed. This extra sorting can be avoided if you define an index on the relevant column. When Oracle fetches the rows from the database (with the FROM clause) this index can then be used. The intermediate result from the FROM clause is already ordered by the correct column. After that, no extra sorting is necessary. This rule is only valid if the column does not contain many NULL values (because NULL values are not stored in an index) and if the SELECT statement does not have a WHERE clause with a selection criteria that can be optimized.

20.5.5   No index on ...

Finally, we give you a number of guidelines for when an index should *not* be defined.

- Create no index on a column with very few different values, for example a column such as SEX.

- Create no index on a very small table.

- Create no index on a column which consists of many NULL values, because NULL values are not stored in the leaves of indexes.

Closing remark: Naturally, it makes little sense to define two indexes on the same column or combination of columns. Consult the ICOL$ table to check whether by creating a new index you are simply replicating an existing one.

20.6   TRACE and EXPLAIN

This chapter describes how the execution time of a statement can be improved. But imagine that a statement is fully optimized and that the execution time is too long. Then Oracle offers two ways of finding out why it takes so long. You can switch on the *trace* or query the processing strategy with the EXPLAIN statement. Both subjects are quite complex, and we refer you to the Oracle manual called *Performance Tuning Guide*.

21
Optimization of statements

In the last chapter we showed that the presence of an index can improve the execution time of particular statements. The question remains, though, as to whether the Oracle optimizer can, in fact, develop the best processing strategy for all statements. Unfortunately, the answer is 'No'! Some statements are written in such a way that the optimizer is in no position to develop the fastest processing strategy. This occurs principally when WHERE clause conditions are too complex or when the optimizer is taken up a 'false trail'. In addition, even when indexes are available, Oracle sometimes chooses a sequential processing strategy.

In practice, it appears that certain forms of SQL statements are not easily optimized and give rise to longer processing times. By reformulating such statements you give Oracle a better chance of developing an optimal processing strategy. In this section we give you a number of guidelines for formulating statements with faster execution in mind. In other words, we are giving the optimizer a 'helping hand'.

Note: In new versions of Oracle the optimizer will improve, of course, and will be able to develop good processing strategies for still more statements. Therefore the following guidelines will have to be tested for validity against each new version of the product.

21.1 Avoid the OR operator

In some cases Oracle will not use an index if the condition in the WHERE clause contains the OR operator. These statements can be rewritten in two ways. In certain circumstances we can replace the condition with one containing an IN operator, or replace the whole statement with two SELECT statements linked with UNION.

Example 21.1: Give the names and initials of players 6, 83 and 44.

```
SELECT   NAME, INITIALS
FROM     PLAYERS
WHERE    PLAYERNO = 6
OR       PLAYERNO = 83
OR       PLAYERNO = 44
```

If there is an index on the PLAYERNO column, Oracle will use it. But Oracle can create a more efficient strategy if the condition in the SELECT statement is simply replaced by the IN operator:

```
SELECT   NAME, INITIALS
FROM     PLAYERS
WHERE    PLAYERNO IN (6, 83, 44)
```

For UPDATE and DELETE statements the same applies.

Example 21.2: Get the players who were born in 1963 plus the players who live in Stratford.

```
SELECT   *
FROM     PLAYERS
WHERE    YEAR_OF_BIRTH = 1963
OR       TOWN = 'Stratford'
```

Oracle will develop a partially sequential processing strategy irrespective of the presence of indexes on the TOWN and YEAR_OF_BIRTH columns. But in this example we cannot replace the OR operator with an IN operator. What we can do is replace the whole statement with two SELECT statements linked with UNION.

```
SELECT   *
FROM     PLAYERS
WHERE    YEAR_OF_BIRTH = 1963
UNION
SELECT   *
FROM     PLAYERS
WHERE    TOWN = 'Stratford'
```

UPDATE and DELETE statements like this *cannot* be adapted using the UNION operator. In such a case, two separate statements are necessary:

Example 21.3: Update penalties of $100 or those incurred on 1 December 1980 to $150.

```
UPDATE   PENALTIES
SET      AMOUNT = 150
WHERE    AMOUNT = 100
OR       PEN_DATE = '01-DEC-80'
```

Another formulation:

```
UPDATE    PENALTIES
SET       AMOUNT = 150
WHERE     AMOUNT = 100
```

and

```
UPDATE    PENALTIES
SET       AMOUNT = 150
WHERE     PEN_DATE = '01-DEC-80'
```

Let us return to the example with the SELECT statement. With UNION, Oracle automatically removes duplicate rows (that is, DISTINCT is assumed). In fact, in this case there are no duplicate rows because the SELECT clause names the primary key of the PLAYERS table.

If the original SELECT statement had looked like the next one shown (no primary key columns in the SELECT clause), the alternative construction with UNION would not have been possible. Why? Because this statement could produce duplicate rows that would, with the UNION operator, be deleted (and that is not the intention). The two versions would give different results.

```
SELECT    NAME
FROM      PLAYERS
WHERE     YEAR_OF_BIRTH = 1963
OR        TOWN = 'Stratford'
```

By adding DISTINCT the duplicate rows are legitimately removed and the use of UNION becomes possible.

21.2   Isolate columns in conditions

When an index is defined on a column that occurs in a calculation or scalar function, that index is not used.

Example 21.4: Find the players who were born ten years before 1979.

```
SELECT    *
FROM      PLAYERS
WHERE     YEAR_OF_BIRTH + 10 = 1979
```

On the left of the = comparison operator you see an expression that contains both a column name and a literal. To the right of the same operator there is another literal. The index on the YEAR_OF_BIRTH column will not be used. You could expect, however, a faster execution with the next statement, which reformulates the previous one:

```
SELECT    *
FROM      PLAYERS
WHERE     YEAR_OF_BIRTH = 1969
```

Now the expression to the left of the comparison operator contains only a column name. In other words, the column has been isolated.

21.3   Use the BETWEEN operator

If a WHERE clause specifies values in a particular range using the AND operator, Oracle will generally not use an index efficiently. In such cases, we can replace the AND operator with the BETWEEN operator.

Example 21.5: Find the numbers of the players born in the period 1962 – 1965.

```
SELECT    PLAYERNO
FROM      PLAYERS
WHERE     YEAR_OF_BIRTH >= 1962
AND       YEAR_OF_BIRTH <= 1965
```

An index on the YEAR_OF_BIRTH column will not be used here, whereas in the next example with the condition adapted it will be considered:

```
SELECT    PLAYERNO
FROM      PLAYERS
WHERE     YEAR_OF_BIRTH BETWEEN 1962 AND 1965
```

21.4   Avoid particular forms of the LIKE operator

In some cases, when an index is defined on a column used with the LIKE operator in a WHERE clause condition, the index will not be considered. If the mask in the LIKE operator begins with a percent sign or an underscore character, the index cannot be used.

Example 21.6: Find the players whose name ends with the letter *n*.

```
SELECT    *
FROM      PLAYERS
WHERE     NAME LIKE '%n'
```

The index will not be used, but unfortunately there is no alternative solution for this example.

21.5   Add redundant conditions to joins

Sometimes joins can be accelerated easily by adding an extra condition to the WHERE clause, which does not change the end result.

Example 21.7: Give the payment number, the name of the player for all penalties incurred for player 44.

```
SELECT    PAYMENTNO, NAME
FROM      PENALTIES PN, PLAYERS P
WHERE     PN.PLAYERNO = P.PLAYERNO
AND       PN.PLAYERNO = 44
```

In some situations Oracle can develop a more efficient processing strategy if the condition is extended with a redundant condition; see below. Naturally, the result of the statement does not change.

```
SELECT    PAYMENTNO, NAME
FROM      PENALTIES PN, PLAYERS P
WHERE     PN.PLAYERNO = P.PLAYERNO
AND       PN.PLAYERNO = 44
AND       P.PLAYERNO = 44
```

21.6   Avoid the HAVING clause

You can specify conditions in two places in a SELECT statement, in the WHERE and in the HAVING clause. You must always try to place as many conditions in the WHERE clause as possible and as few as possible in the HAVING clause. The main reason is that indexes are not used for conditions specified in HAVING clauses.

Example 21.8: Find, for each player with a number higher than 40, the player number and the number of penalties incurred.

```
SELECT    PLAYERNO, COUNT(*)
FROM      PENALTIES
GROUP BY  PLAYERNO
HAVING    PLAYERNO >= 40
```

The condition stated in the HAVING clause can also be specified in the WHERE clause. This makes the HAVING clause completely superfluous:

```
SELECT    PLAYERNO, COUNT(*)
FROM      PENALTIES
WHERE     PLAYERNO >= 40
GROUP BY  PLAYERNO
```

21.7 Using the INTERSECT and MINUS operator

Oracle's optimizer processes the set operators INTERSECT and MINUS efficiently. So try to use these operators if possible and required.

Example 21.9: Give the numbers of the captains for whom at least one penalty has been paid.

We can formulate this with a subquery:

```
SELECT    DISTINCT PLAYERNO
FROM      TEAMS
WHERE     PLAYERNO IN
          (SELECT    PLAYERNO
           FROM      PENALTIES)
```

We advise you to formulate this statement with an INTERSECT operator:

```
SELECT    PLAYERNO
FROM      TEAMS
INTERSECT
SELECT    PLAYERNO
FROM      PENALTIES
```

Notice that we can apply this transformation because we *only* have to find the numbers of the captains.

We should remark that, if you use set operators, you should avoid using them needlessly. Section 14.6 describes how certain SELECT statements with set operators can be converted to equivalent statements.

21.8 Make the SELECT clause as small as possible

The SELECT clause of a main query is used for formulating the data that has to be presented. Avoid the use of unnecessary columns. This may have a negative effect on processing speed.

You are allowed to specify multiple expressions in the SELECT clause of a subquery if that subquery is coupled to the main query with the EXISTS operator. However, the end result of the SELECT statement is not affected by the expressions specified. Therefore, the advice is to formulate only one expression consisting of one literal in the SELECT clause.

Example 21.10: Give the numbers and names of the players for whom at least one penalty has been paid.

```
SELECT    PLAYERNO, NAME
FROM      PLAYERS
WHERE     EXISTS
          (SELECT    '1'
           FROM      PENALTIES
           WHERE     PENALTIES.PLAYERNO = PLAYERS.PLAYERNO)
```

21.9 Avoid DISTINCT

Specifying DISTINCT in the SELECT clause leads to the removal of duplicate rows from a result. This may have a negative effect on processing time. Therefore, avoid the use of DISTINCT when it is not required or even superfluous. In Section 10.3 we described when DISTINCT is not needed. DISTINCT is not necessary in subqueries.

Example 21.11: Find, for each match, the match number and the name of the player.

```
SELECT    DISTINCT MATCHNO, NAME
FROM      MATCHES, PLAYERS
WHERE     MATCHES.PLAYERNO = PLAYERS.PLAYERNO
```

DISTINCT is unnecessary here, because the SELECT clause contains the primary key of the MATCHES table as well as a condition on the primary key of the PLAYERS table.

21.10 Avoid data type conversions

Oracle automatically performs data type conversions. The following condition is, for example correct, even if the numeric PLAYERNO column is compared with an alphanumeric literal:

```
WHERE PLAYERNO = '44'
```

Converting data types adversely affects the processing speed. If this type of conversion is not really required, then try to avoid it.

21.11 The smallest table as last

When you formulate joins it is possible for the sequence of tables in the FROM clause to affect the processing speed adversely. The rule is: specify the table with the smallest number of qualifying rows last in the FROM clause. So the FROM clause in the following SELECT statement

```
SELECT    TEAMS.TEAMNO, PLAYERS.NAME, PLAYERS.INITIALS
FROM      TEAMS, PLAYERS
WHERE     PLAYERS.PLAYERNO = TEAMS.PLAYERNO
```

can better be replaced by the following, because the TEAMS table has less rows:

```
FROM      PLAYERS, TEAMS
```

If, on the other hand, the SELECT statement includes a condition that restricts the number of rows from the PLAYERS table, you should first specify the TEAMS table (as below). Because then PLAYERS is the smallest table, it is the table with the smallest number of qualifying rows.

```
SELECT    TEAMS.TEAMNO, PLAYERS.NAME, PLAYERS.INITIALS
FROM      TEAMS, PLAYERS
WHERE     PLAYERS.PLAYERNO = TEAMS.PLAYERNO
AND       PLAYERS.PLAYERNO = 27
```

21.12   The ROWID

The fastest SELECT statements are those where the WHERE clause contains a condition based on the so-called *ROWID*. ROWIDs are described in Chapter 25 where we will return to this subject.

Exercise

21.1   Give other formulations for the following statements:

```
1.   SELECT    *
     FROM      PLAYERS
     WHERE     (TOWN = 'Stratford'
     AND       STREET = 'Edgecombe Way')
     OR        (NOT (YEAR_OF_BIRTH >= 1960))

2.   SELECT    *
     FROM      TEAMS
     WHERE     TEAMNO IN
               (SELECT    TEAMNO
                FROM      MATCHES
                WHERE     WON * LOST = WON * 4)

3.   SELECT    DISTINCT TEAMNO
     FROM      MATCHES
     WHERE     TEAMNO IN
               (SELECT    TEAMNO
                FROM      TEAMS
                WHERE     NOT (DIVISION <> 'second'))
```

```
4.   SELECT    DISTINCT P.PLAYERNO
     FROM      PLAYERS P, MATCHES M
     WHERE     P.PLAYERNO <> M.PLAYERNO
```

22

Views

Oracle recognizes two types of tables: real tables, generally known as *base tables*, and derived tables, also called *views*. Base tables are created with CREATE TABLE statements, and of the two table types, are the only ones in which data can be stored. Familiar examples are the PLAYERS and TEAMS tables from the tennis club database.

A derived table, or view, stores *no* rows itself. Rather, it exists, and can be seen, as a prescription or formula for combining data from base tables to make a 'virtual' table. The word virtual is used because a view only exists when it is named in an SQL statement. At that moment, Oracle takes the prescription that makes up the *view formula*, executes it and presents the user with what seems to be a real table.

This chapter describes how views are created and how they can be used. Some useful applications include the simplification of routine statements and the reorganization of data structures in and between tables. The last section looks at restrictions on querying and updating views.

22.1 Creating views

Views are created with the *CREATE VIEW statement.*

```
<create view statement> ::=
   CREATE VIEW <view name>
      [ <column list> ] AS
      <select statement>
      [ <with check option> ]

<with check option> ::=
   WITH CHECK OPTION [ CONSTRAINT <constraint name> ]

<column list> ::=
   ( <column name> [ {,<column name>}... ] )
```

Example 22.1: Create a view with all town names from the PLAYERS table.

```
CREATE    VIEW TOWNS AS
SELECT    DISTINCT TOWN
FROM      PLAYERS
```

Example 22.2: Create a view with the player numbers and league numbers of all players with a league number.

```
CREATE    VIEW C_PLAYERS AS
SELECT    PLAYERNO, LEAGUENO
FROM      PLAYERS
WHERE     LEAGUENO IS NOT NULL
```

These two CREATE VIEW statements, then, create two views: TOWNS and C_PLAYERS. The contents of each view are defined by a SELECT statement. So the view formula comprises a normal SELECT statement. These two views now exist to be queried as though they were base tables. The C_PLAYERS view can even be updated (we will return to this subject in Section 22.5).

Example 22.3: Get all information about competition players whose numbers run from 6 to 44 inclusive.

```
SELECT    *
FROM      C_PLAYERS
WHERE     PLAYERNO BETWEEN 6 AND 44
```

Result:

```
PLAYERNO  LEAGUENO
--------  --------
       6  8467
      44  1124
      27  2513
       8  2983
```

Without the C_PLAYERS view you would need a longer SELECT statement to retrieve the same information.

```
SELECT    PLAYERNO, LEAGUENO
FROM      PLAYERS
WHERE     LEAGUENO IS NOT NULL
AND       PLAYERNO BETWEEN 6 AND 44
```

Example 22.4: Remove the competition player whose league number is 7060.

```
DELETE
FROM      C_PLAYERS
WHERE     LEAGUENO = '7060'
```

When this statement is executed, the row in the base table, the PLAYERS table, is deleted where the LEAGUENO column equals 7060.

The contents of a view are not stored, but derived the moment the view is referenced. This means that the view contents, by definition, always concur with the contents of the base table. Every change made to the data in a base table is immediately visible in a view that accesses that data. Users need never be concerned about the integrity of view data, as long as the integrity of the base tables is maintained.

A view formula may specify another view.

Example 22.5: Create a view with all competition players whose numbers run from 6 to 44 inclusive.

```
CREATE    VIEW SEVERAL AS
SELECT    *
FROM      C_PLAYERS
WHERE     PLAYERNO BETWEEN 6 AND 44

SELECT    *
FROM      SEVERAL
```

Result:

```
PLAYERNO  LEAGUENO
--------  --------
       6  8467
      44  1124
      27  2513
       8  2983
```

Note: There is one restriction when you define a view: an ORDER BY clause is not allowed.

With the CREATE SYNONYM statement synonyms can be defined for views. You can also use the COMMENT ON statement to enter a comment for a view. Here, views and tables can be regarded as equivalent.

Just like a basic table, a view can be created for another user. Then the other user will be the owner.

Example 22.6: Create again the SEVERAL view, but now with JIM as the owner.

```
CREATE    VIEW JIM.SEVERAL AS
SELECT    *
FROM      C_PLAYERS
WHERE     PLAYERNO BETWEEN 6 AND 44
```

The *DROP VIEW statement* is used to delete a view.

```
<drop view statement> ::=
   DROP VIEW <table specification>

<table specification> ::= [ <user> . ] <table name>
```

22.2   The column names of views

The column names in a view are the same as the column names in the SELECT clause. The two columns in the SEVERAL view are called PLAYERNO and LEAGUENO. A view, therefore, inherits the column names. You can also explicitly define column names for views.

Example 22.7: Create a view with the player number, the name, the initials and the year of birth of each player who lives in Stratford.

```
CREATE    VIEW SFD_FOLK (PNO, NAME, INIT, BORN) AS
SELECT    PLAYERNO, NAME, INITIALS, YEAR_OF_BIRTH
FROM      PLAYERS
WHERE     TOWN = 'Stratford'

SELECT    *
FROM      SFD_FOLK
WHERE     PNO > 90
```

Result (note the column names):

```
PNO   NAME        INIT  BORN
---   ---------   ----  ----
100   Parmenter   P     1963
```

These new column names are permanent. You can no longer refer to the columns PLAYERNO or YEAR_OF_BIRTH in the SFD_FOLK view.

If an expression in the SELECT clause of a view formula does *not* consist of a column identifier, but is a function or calculation, then it is mandatory to provide names for the columns. In the following view definition, then, you may not leave out the column names TOWN and NUMBER.

```
CREATE    VIEW RESIDENT (TOWN, NUMBER) AS
SELECT    TOWN, COUNT(*)
FROM      PLAYERS
GROUP BY TOWN
```

Exercises

22.1 Create a view called NUMBER_PLAYERS that contains all the team numbers and the total number of players who have played for that team. (Assume that at least one player has competed for each team.)

22.2 Create a view called WINNERS that contains the number and name of each player who, for at least one team, has won one match.

22.3 Create a view called TOTAL_PENALTIES that records the total amount of penalties for each player who has incurred at least one penalty.

22.3   Updating views: the WITH CHECK OPTION

We have already looked at a number of examples of views being updated. In fact, what is happening is that the underlying tables are being updated. Nevertheless, updating views can have unexpected results. Let us illustrate this with a few examples.

Example 22.8: Create a view of all players born before 1950.

```
CREATE    VIEW VETERAN AS
SELECT    *
FROM      PLAYERS
WHERE     YEAR_OF_BIRTH < 1950
```

Now we would like to alter the year of birth of the veteran whose player number is 2 from 1948 to 1960. The update statement reads:

```
UPDATE    VETERAN
SET       YEAR_OF_BIRTH = 1960
WHERE     PLAYERNO = 2
```

This is a correct update. The year of birth of player number 2 in the PLAYERS table is altered. The unexpected or undesired effect of this update, though, is that if we look at the *view* using a SELECT statement, player 2 no longer appears. This is because when the update occurred the player ceased to satisfy the condition specified in the view formula.

If you extend the view definition with the so-called *WITH CHECK OPTION*, Oracle will ensure that such an unexpected effect does not arise.

The view definition then becomes:

```
CREATE    VIEW VETERAN AS
SELECT    *
FROM      PLAYERS
WHERE     YEAR_OF_BIRTH < 1950
WITH      CHECK OPTION
```

If a view includes the 'WITH CHECK OPTION' clause all changes via UPDATE and INSERT statements are controlled for validity:

- An UPDATE statement is correct if the rows that are updated still belong to the (virtual) contents of the view after the update.

- An INSERT statement is correct if the new rows belong to the (virtual) contents of the view.

The WITH CHECK OPTION clause can only be used in conjunction with views updatable according to the rules mentioned in Section 22.5.

22.4   Views and the catalog

Information about views is recorded in various tables. In the OBJ$ the name and owner of views are stored. The descriptions of the columns of a view are registered in the COLS$ table. For each view that contains a WITH CHECK OPTION, one row is added to the tables CON$ and CDEF$; these tables have been discussed in Section 19.10. The view formula is stored in a separate table, the VIEW$ catalog table (see below). The OBJ# column is the primary key of this table.

column name	data type	description
OBJ#	NUMBER	Database object number of the view
COLS	NUMBER	Number of columns in the view
TEXTLENGTH	NUMBER	The length of the view formula
TEXT	LONG	The view formula (SELECT statement)

The columns of the views inherit the data type of the column expression from the SELECT clause of the view formula. Just as for the columns of a base table, the definitions of the columns of a view are recorded in the COL$ table.

The XREF$ table records which base tables appear in the view formula. The columns OWNER and NAME together form the primary key of this table. The XREF$ table has the following structure:

column name	data type	description
OWNER	CHAR	Name of the owner of the view
NAME	CHAR	Name of the view
ROWNER	CHAR	Name of the owner of the base table on which the view is defined
RNAME	CHAR	Name of the base table on which the view is defined

For each base table on which a view is definied one row is added to the XREF$ table. This means that if the formula of a view contains three different tables, three rows are inserted. If a specific table appears twice or more in a view formula, this fact is only registred once. A special situation is when a view is defined on other views. What is than stored in the XREF$ table? The answer is clear: the underlying base table(s) are stored and not the underlying view.

As an example we show how the XREF$ table is filled after the creation of the following three views (we assume that the YOUTH and PENALTIES_X views are created by SQLDBA and the PENALTIES_Y view by DIANE):

Example 1:

```
CREATE    VIEW YOUTH AS
SELECT    P2.PLAYERNO
FROM      PLAYERS P1, PLAYERS P2
WHERE     P1.YEAR_OF_BIRTH > P2.YEAR_OF_BIRTH
AND       P1.PLAYERNO = 6
```

Example 2:

```
CREATE    VIEW PENALTIES_X AS
SELECT    PN.PAYMENTNO, P.NAME, PN.AMOUNT
FROM      PENALTIES PN, PLAYERS P
WHERE     PN.PLAYERNO = P.PLAYERNO
```

Example 3:

```
CREATE    VIEW PENALTIES_Y AS
SELECT    PAYMENTNO, NAME
FROM      PENALTIES_X
WHERE     AMOUNT > 25
```

Contents of the XREF$ table:

```
OWNER     NAME          ROWNER   ROWNER
------    -----------   ------   ----------
SQLDBA    YOUTH         SQLDBA   PLAYERS
SQLDBA    PENALTIES_X   SQLDBA   PENALTIES
SQLDBA    PENALTIES_X   SQLDBA   PLAYERS
DIANE     PENALTIES_Y   SQLDBA   PENALTIES
DIANE     PENALTIES_Y   SQLDBA   PLAYERS
```

22.5   Limitations on updating

As we mentioned, there are also restrictions placed on updating views (that is, updating tables through views). A view can only be updated if the view formula satisfies the following conditions. The first seven conditions apply to all update statements.

1.   The SELECT clause may not contain DISTINCT
2.   The SELECT clause may not contain statistical functions
3.   The FROM clause may specify only one table
4.   The SELECT statement may not contain a GROUP BY clause (and therefore also no HAVING clause)
5.   The SELECT statement may not contain set operators

In addition, the following restriction holds for the UPDATE statement:

6.   A virtual column may not be updated

The BEGIN_AGE column in the following view may not be updated (though the PLAYERNO column may be updated):

```
CREATE    VIEW AGES
          (PLAYERNO, BEGIN_AGES) AS
SELECT    PLAYERNO, YEAR_JOINED - YEAR_OF_BIRTH
FROM      PLAYERS
```

The following restriction holds for the INSERT statement:

7.   The SELECT clause must contain all NOT NULL columns from the table which are specified in the FROM clause

That is why INSERT statements may not be executed on the following view, because the view does not contain all NOT NULL columns, such as SEX and TOWN:

```
CREATE    VIEW PLAYERS_NAMES AS
SELECT    PLAYERNO, NAME, INITIALS
FROM      PLAYERS
```

Exercise

22.4   This chapter has shown many examples of views. For each of these views say whether an UPDATE, INSERT or DELETE statement may be performed on it:

1.   TOWNS
2.   C_PLAYERS
3.   SEVERAL
4.   SFD_FOLK

5.   RESIDENT
6.   VETERAN
7.   YOUTH
8.   AGES
9.   PLAYERS_NAMES

22.6   Processing view statements

How does Oracle process statements which refer to views? The processing steps
(see Chapter 6) cannot be executed one by one as happens for tables. As soon as
Oracle reaches the FROM clause and attempts to fetch rows from the database,
it stumbles on a problem, as a view contains no stored rows. So which rows must
be retrieved when a statement refers to a view? Oracle knows that it is dealing
with a view (thanks to a routine look in the catalog). Therefore, in order to make
processing possible, it executes an extra step before moving on to the other steps.
In this first step, the view formula is included in the statement.

Suppose that you create the following view:

```
CREATE    VIEW EXPENSIVE_PLAYERS AS
SELECT    *
FROM      PLAYERS
WHERE     PLAYERNO IN
          (SELECT   PLAYERNO
           FROM     PENALTIES)
```

Example 22.9: Get the number of each player who has incurred at least one
penalty and lives in Stratford.

```
SELECT    PLAYERNO
FROM      EXPENSIVE_PLAYERS
WHERE     TOWN = 'Stratford'
```

The first step comprises the merging of the view formula into the SELECT statement. This step produces the following statement:

```
SELECT    PLAYERNO
FROM      PLAYERS
WHERE     TOWN = 'Stratford'
AND       PLAYERNO IN
          (SELECT   PLAYERNO
           FROM     PENALTIES)
```

Now Oracle can process this statement moving through the steps. In short, there
emerges an additional step which is executed before the other steps.

Final result:

```
PLAYERNO
--------
       6
```

Here is another example, using the SFD_FOLK view from Section 22.2.

Example 22.10: Delete all Stratford people born after 1965.

```
DELETE
FROM      SFD_FOLK
WHERE     BORN > 1965
```

After the inclusion of the view formula the statement reads:

```
DELETE
FROM      PLAYERS
WHERE     YEAR_OF_BIRTH > 1965
AND       TOWN = 'Stratford'
```

Exercise

22.5 What will the following statements look like after the respective view formulae have been merged?

```
1.    SELECT    BORN - 1900, COUNT(*)
      FROM      SFD_FOLK
      GROUP BY 1

2.    SELECT    PNO
      FROM      EXPENSIVE_PLAYERS, SFD_FOLK
      WHERE     EXPENSIVE_PLAYERS.PLAYERNO = SFD_FOLK.PNO

3.    UPDATE    SFD_FOLK
      SET       BORN = 1950
      WHERE     PNO = 7
```

22.7   Useful applications of views

Views can be used in a great variety of ways and in this section we look at some of them. There is no special significance in the order in which they are discussed.

22.7.1   Simplification of routine statements

Statements that are executed frequently, or are structurally similar, can be simplified through the use of views.

Example 22.11: Suppose that these two statements are frequently entered:

```
SELECT    *
FROM      PLAYERS
WHERE     PLAYERNO IN
          (SELECT    PLAYERNO
           FROM      PENALTIES)
AND       TOWN = 'Stratford'
```

and

```
SELECT    TOWN, COUNT(*)
FROM      PLAYERS
WHERE     PLAYERNO IN
          (SELECT    PLAYERNO
           FROM      PENALTIES)
GROUP BY TOWN
```

Both statements are concerned only with the players who have incurred a penalty, so this subset of players can be accessed via a view:

```
CREATE    VIEW PEN_PLAYERS AS
SELECT    *
FROM      PLAYERS
WHERE     PLAYERNO IN
          (SELECT    PLAYERNO
           FROM      PENALTIES)
```

Now these two SELECT statements can be greatly simplified by using instead the PEN_PLAYERS view:

```
SELECT    *
FROM      PEN_PLAYERS
WHERE     TOWN = 'Stratford'
```

and

```
SELECT    TOWN, COUNT(*)
FROM      PEN_PLAYERS
GROUP BY TOWN
```

Example 22.12: Suppose that the PLAYERS table is often joined with the MATCHES table:

```
SELECT    ...
FROM      PLAYERS, MATCHES
WHERE     PLAYERS.PLAYERNO = MATCHES.PLAYERNO
AND       ...
```

In this case the SELECT statement becomes simpler if the join is defined as a view:

```
CREATE    VIEW PLAY_MAT AS
SELECT    ...
FROM      PLAYERS, MATCHES
WHERE     PLAYERS.PLAYERNO = MATCHES.PLAYERNO
```

What was a join statement now takes this simplified form:

```
SELECT    ...
FROM      PLAY_MAT
WHERE     ...
```

22.7.2 Reorganizing tables

The structure of a database is designed and implemented on the basis of a particular situation. This situation can change from time to time, which means that the structure may also have to change. For example, a new column is added to a table, or two tables are joined to make a single table. In most cases, the reorganization of a database requires the alteration of already developed and operational statements. Such alterations can be time-consuming and expensive. Appropriate use of views can keep this time and cost to a minimum. Let us see how.

Example 22.13: Give the name and initials of each competition player and also the divisions in which he or she has played.

```
SELECT    DISTINCT NAME, INITIALS, DIVISION
FROM      PLAYERS P, MATCHES M1, TEAMS T
WHERE     P.PLAYERNO = M1.PLAYERNO
AND       M1.TEAMNR = T.TEAMNR
```

Result:

```
NAME         INITIALS  DIVISION
---------    --------  --------
Parmenter    R         first
Baker        E         first
Hope         PK        first
Everett      R         first
Collins      DD        second
Moorman      D         second
Brown        M         first
Bailey       IP        second
Newcastle    B         first
Newcastle    B         second
```

Assume that the database structure has to be reorganized: the TEAMS and MATCHES tables have been combined to form the RESULTS table shown below:

TEAMNO	PLAYERNO	WON	LOST	CAPTAIN	DIVISION
1	6	3	1	6	first
1	6	2	3	6	first
1	6	3	0	6	first
1	44	3	2	6	first
1	83	0	3	6	first
1	2	1	3	6	first
1	57	3	0	6	first
1	8	0	3	6	first
2	27	3	2	27	second
2	104	3	2	27	second
2	112	2	3	27	second
2	112	1	3	27	second
2	8	0	3	27	second

The CAPTAIN column in the RESULTS table is the former PLAYERNO column from the TEAMS table. This column has been given another name, otherwise there would have been two columns called PLAYERNO. All statements that refer to the two tables now have to be rewritten, including the SELECT statement above. One solution, which renders a total rewrite unnecessary, is to define two views on the results table. These two views represent the former TEAMS and MATCHES tables respectively:

```
CREATE    VIEW TEAMS (TEAMNO, PLAYERNO, DIVISION) AS
SELECT    DISTINCT TEAMNO, CAPTAIN, DIVISION
FROM      RESULTS
```

and

```
CREATE    VIEW MATCHES AS
SELECT    TEAMNO, PLAYERNO, WON, LOST
FROM      RESULTS
```

The virtual contents of each of these two views are the same as the contents of the two original tables. Not one statement has to be rewritten, including the SELECT statement from the beginning of this section.

Of course, you cannot manage every reorganization of the database structure with views. It might be decided, for example, to store data about male and female players in separate tables. Each new table acquires the same columns as the PLAYERS table, but omits the SEX column. It is no longer possible to construct the original PLAYERS table with a view, because the UNION operator is necessary, and this operator cannot be specified in a view formula.

22.7.3 Stepwise building of SELECT statements

Suppose you have to answer the following question: Give the name and initials of each Stratford player who has incurred a penalty which is higher than the average penalty for players from the second team, and who played for at least one first division team. You could write a huge SELECT statement to answer this, but you could also build a query in a stepwise fashion.

First of all, create a view of all the players who have incurred a penalty which is greater than the average penalty for players from the second team:

```
CREATE    VIEW GREATER AS
SELECT    DISTINCT PLAYERNO
FROM      PENALTIES
WHERE     AMOUNT >
          (SELECT   AVG(AMOUNT)
          FROM      PENALTIES
          WHERE     PLAYERNO IN
                    (SELECT   PLAYERNO
                    FROM      MATCHES
                    WHERE     TEAMNO = 2))
```

Then create a view of all players who have competed for a team in the first division:

```
CREATE    VIEW FIRST AS
SELECT    DISTINCT PLAYERNO
FROM      MATCHES
WHERE     TEAMNO IN
          (SELECT   TEAMNO
          FROM      TEAMS
          WHERE     DIVISION = 'first')
```

Using these two views, answering the original question is quite simple:

```
SELECT    NAME, INITIALS
FROM      PLAYERS
WHERE     TOWN = 'Stratford'
AND       PLAYERNO IN
          (SELECT   PLAYERNO
          FROM      GREATER)
AND       PLAYERNO IN
          (SELECT   PLAYERNO
          FROM      FIRST)
```

The problem is, so to speak, split into 'mini-problems' and executed in steps. In this way, you can, if you want to, avoid writing a complex and long SELECT statement.

22.7.4 Specifying integrity rules

By using the WITH CHECK OPTION clause, it is possible to lay down rules for determining which values may be entered into columns.

Example 22.14: The SEX column in the PLAYERS table may contain either the value M or the value F, and nothing else. You can use the WITH CHECK OPTION clause to provide an automatic control for this. The following view should be defined:

```
CREATE    VIEW PLAYERS_SEX AS
SELECT    *
FROM      PLAYERS
WHERE     SEX IN ('M', 'F')
WITH      CHECK OPTION
```

To follow this up we give nobody the possibility of updating the PLAYERS table directly; instead they have to do so via the PLAYERS_SEX view. The WITH CHECK OPTION clause tests every update (that is, every UPDATE and INSERT statement) to see whether the new value falls into the permitted range.

22.7.5 Data security

Views can also be used to protect or screen parts of tables. Chapter 23 deals with this topic in detail.

Exercise

22.6 Decide whether or not the following reorganizations of the database structure are possible through the use of views.

1. The LEAGUENO column is removed from the PLAYERS table and placed in a separate table with a PLAYERNO column. If a player has no league number he or she does not appear in this new table.

2. The NAME column is added to the PENALTIES table but also remains in the PLAYERS TABLE.

3. The TOWN column is removed from the PLAYERS table and placed together with the PLAYERNO column in a separate table.

23
User and data security

Data stored in a database is a valuable asset to the owner (usually a company). Data has to be made secure in at least two ways. First, care must be taken that incorrect data cannot be entered. We can do this by specifying integrity rules such as primary and foreign keys. Integrity rules are described in depth in Chapter 19. Second, it must be guaranteed that only authorized users can access data. This is done to prevent unauthorized users from deleting, mutilating or copying illegally data, intentionally or unintentionally. This form of security is the subject of this chapter.

23.1 Introduction

An Oracle database is protected in two ways against unauthorized use. Each user who accesses (or logs on to) a database has an identification obligation. He or she must identify him or herself with a *user-name* and a *password*. We have already seen an example of this in Chapter 2. To start SQL*PLUS the user has to enter his name and password as follows:

```
SQLPLUS SQLDBA/SQLDBAPW
```

In this example, SQLDBA is the name of the user and SQLDBAPW the password. A user must at all times provide a name and a password regardless of the application that is used to access an Oracle database. Do not forget that SQL*Plus is just an ordinary application which uses a database.

Besides the identification obligation to log on, Oracle supports a second form of protection. A user who can log on is not necessarily capable of accessing the tables. First we must give privileges to the users explicitly. Examples of privileges are the right to query the PLAYERS table and the right to change the LEAGUENO column. For granting (and withdrawing) of specific privileges Oracle supports two statements: GRANT and REVOKE.

Names, passwords and privileges of users are registered in specific catalog tables. Oracle constantly queries these tables to check if the user, for example, has the specific privileges.

This chapter describes how new user-names and privileges can be entered into the catalog, how privileges can be withdrawn, and how users can be removed from the catalog. We also describe the structure of the catalog tables.

23.2   The users SYS and SYSTEM

You may wonder how (after the installation of Oracle) you can access an Oracle database for the first time with, for example, SQL*Plus, when there is an identification obligation. The answer to this question is simple. During the installation of Oracle, Oracle automatically enters two users, called *SYS* and *SYSTEM*. Both users have the so-called DBA authority. This means that both users can do everything that Oracle allows. SYS is the user from where Oracle creates all the catalog tables. That is why we have to specify SYS as owner when we query a catalog table. SYSTEM is used during installation to create a number of other tables and views. We advise you never to remove these users.

After installation the password of SYSTEM is MANAGER. This password is used everywhere in the Oracle manuals (and also in this book). With the statement below you can change this password to, for example, ASIMOV. (In one of the following sections we will describe the other features of this statement.)

```
GRANT        CONNECT
TO           SYSTEM
IDENTIFIED BY ASIMOV
```

We also advise you never to use the users SYS and SYSTEM for your daily activities. Instead, define a third user who also owns all privileges. You can use the following statement to accomplish this:

```
GRANT        DBA
TO           SQLDBA
IDENTIFIED SQLDBAPW
```

The user who is entered with this statement has the name SQLDBA and password SQLDBAPW. In this chapter we assume that you have created this user.

23.3   Introducing new users

In the previous section we gave an example to show you how a new user can be entered. We extend this subject in this section. To introduce new users in the catalog and to grant specific privileges, Oracle supports only one statement, the *GRANT statement*. This statement has several forms. This section looks at the introduction of new users with the GRANT statement. For the granting of specific privileges to users see the following sections. In Chapter 25 we discuss the last form of the GRANT statement.

```
<grant statement> ::=
   GRANT CONNECT
   TO      <user> [ {,<user>}... ]
   IDENTIFIED BY <password> [ {,<password>}... ]
```

Example 23.1: Introduce two new users: JIM with the password JIM_GOT and PETE with the password ETEP.

```
GRANT      CONNECT
TO         JIM, PETE
IDENTIFIED BY JIM_GOT, ETEP
```

Every user who has been CONNECTed may log on to Oracle and is allowed to perform all operations that require no privileges. He or she may, for example, use the HELP function of SQL*Plus or enter a COMMIT statement.

In many operating systems, such as VAX/VMS, UNIX and MPE/XL, a user has to enter a name and password when he or she tries to log on. The process of logging on to, for instance, SQL*Plus, can be simplified by setting the name of the Oracle user equal to his or her operating system name. We illustrate this with an example.

Assume that the operating system name of a user is VA3161. With the following GRANT statement we introduce this new user to Oracle:

```
GRANT      CONNECT
TO         OPS$VA3161
IDENTIFIED BY PASS1
```

What is new here is the addition OPS$ to the name of the user. The user can now log on to SQL*Plus as follows:

```
SQLPLUS /
```

Only the slash has to be entered now. Oracle checks if a user exists with a name equal to OPS$ followed by his or her operating system name. In the manuals this way of logging on is called *automatic log on*.

User-names and passwords are stored in the USER$ table. The structure of this table is presented below. The USER# column forms the primary key of the USER$ table and NAME forms an alternate key. This means that two different users may not have the same name.

column name	data type	description
USER#	NUMBER	Unique number of the user. Three numbers are reserved: 0 for SYS, 1 for PUBLIC and 2 for SYSTEM
NAME	CHAR	Name of the user
PASSWORD	CHAR	Password of the user. Passwords are recorded encrypted and are only readable by Oracle
CTIME	DATE	Date and time on which the user was entered
PTIME	DATE	Date and time on which the password was cancelled. If this is not known, then this column is filled with the NULL value
CONNECT$	NUMBER	1 if the user has CONNECT authority; otherwise a 0
DBA$	NUMBER	1 if the user has DBA authority; otherwise a 0
RESOURCE$	NUMBER	1 if the user has RESOURCE authority; otherwise a 0

If we suppose that only the users SQLDBA, JIM and PETE are recorded in the catalog, the USER$ table looks like this:

```
USER#   NAME    CTIME       CONNECT$  DBA$  RESOURCE$
-----   ------  ---------   --------  ----  ---------
    0   SYS     08-FEB-88          1     1          1
    1   PUBLIC  08-FEB-88          1     0          0
    2   SYSTEM  08-FEB-88          1     1          1
   50   SQLDBA  20-JAN-89          1     1          1
   61   JIM     31-APR-90          1     0          0
   62   PETE    01-JAN-90          1     0          0
```

In this table you see the three users created by us (SQLDBA, JIM and PETE), the users discussed in the last section (SYS and SYSTEM) and finally, a (still) unknown user called PUBLIC. We will explain PUBLIC in Section 23.5. We have left out the PASSWORD column, because the contents of this column are not readable. This has been done for security reasons.

Each user is allowed to change his or her own password using the GRANT CONNECT statement.

Example 23.2: Change the password of JIM into JIM1.

```
GRANT       CONNECT
TO          JIM
IDENTIFIED BY JIM1
```

Oracle knows from the USER$ table that the user JIM already exists. The statement is therefore interpreted to mean change the password, and not introduce a new user.

Changing the password can also be performed with a special statement, the *ALTER USER statement.* However, this statement can only be used by users with DBA authority such as SYSTEM and SQLDBA.

Example 23.3: Change the password of JIM into JIM1.

```
ALTER USER JIM IDENTIFIED BY JIM1
```

23.4   Granting database privileges

JIM and PETE, who were introduced to Oracle in the previous section, do not yet have any authority to work with the data. Nearly every statement they enter will be rejected at the moment. Oracle would execute only such trivial statements as GRANT CONNECT or the EXIT command. The GRANT statement must be used explicitly to give additional privileges to JIM and PETE.

Oracle supports two types of privilege: *database privileges* and *table privileges*. This section describes the granting of the first type, the database privileges.

We have already mentioned DBA authority. We call this type of privilege a database privilege, because it concerns the entire database, or in other words, all tables. Oracle knows two database privileges: *DBA* and *RESOURCE*. A user with the DBA authority is allowed to execute, without any restriction, all SQL statements on all tables, indexes, views etc. You must have, for example, DBA authority to perform such tasks as introducing new users and to grant DBA authority. The DBA authority is the most powerful authority that a user can receive.

```
<grant statement> ::=
   GRANT   DBA
   TO      <user> [ {,<user>}... ]
   [ IDENTIFIED BY <password> [ {,<password>}... ] ]
```

Example 23.4: Give user KATE DBA authority; her password is CACTUS.

```
GRANT      DBA
TO         KATE
IDENTIFIED BY CACTUS
```

Explanation: If this user already exists, then his or her existing password will be overwritten. IDENTIFIED BY is required if the user does not yet exist.

The second database authority is RESOURCE. This authority gives somebody the possibility to create tables by himself and he is allowed to do anything with those tables. So this user may query and update his or her own tables and may remove the entire table with the DROP TABLE statement.

```
<grant statement> ::=
   GRANT   RESOURCE
   TO      <user> [ {,<user>}... ]
```

Example 23.5: Give RESOURCE authority to LUKE (we assume that LUKE already exists as a user).

```
GRANT   RESOURCE
TO      LUKE
```

Explanation: As can be seen in the definition above, you cannot use IDENTI-FIED BY when granting the RESOURCE privilege. This means that such a user always has to be entered first with a GRANT CONNECT statement.

DBA and RESOURCE authorities are maintained in the USER$ table. The entries for KATE and LUKE, after the execution of the above statements, look like this:

```
USER#  NAME   CTIME       CONNECT$  DBA$  RESOURCE$
-----  -----  ---------   --------  ----  ---------
   75  KATE   30-AUG-90          1     1          1
   76  LUKE   30-AUG-90          1     0          1
```

23.5   Granting table privileges

Note: In this section we are assuming, unless otherwise mentioned, that the user called SQLDBA enters the statements.

Table privileges are privileges applicable to only one specific table. A table privilege may only be granted by the owner of the table or by a user with DBA authority. Oracle supports the following table privileges:

- *SELECT:* This privilege gives a user the right to access the table concerned with the SELECT statement. (S)he can also include the table in a view formula. In fact, a user must have the SELECT privilege for every table (or view) specified in a view formula.

- *INSERT:* This privilege gives a user the right to add rows to the table concerned with the INSERT statement.

- *DELETE:* This privilege gives a user the right to remove rows from the table concerned with the DELETE statement.

- *UPDATE:* This privilege gives a user the right to change values in the table concerned with the UPDATE statement.

- *INDEX:* This privilege gives a user the right to create and drop indexes on the table concerned.

- *ALTER:* This privilege gives a user the right to add new columns to the table concerned and to change data types.

- *REFERENCES:* This privilege gives a user the right to define foreign keys on the table concerned.

- *ALL* or *ALL PRIVILEGES:* This privilege is a shortened form for all the privileges named above.

```
<grant statement> ::=
   GRANT <table privileges>
   ON    { <table specification> | <sequence name> }
   TO    <grantees>
   [ WITH GRANT OPTION ]

<table privileges> ::=
   ALL [ PRIVILEGES ] |
   <table privilege> [ {,<table privilege>}... ]

<table privilege> ::=
   ALTER      |
   DELETE     |
   INDEX      |
   INSERT     |
   REFERENCES |
   SELECT     |
   UPDATE [ <column list> ]

<column list> ::= ( <column name> [ {,<column name>}... ]

<table specification> ::= [ <user>. ] <table name>

<grantees> ::=
   PUBLIC |
   <user> [ {,<user>}... ]
```

Here are a few examples of how table privileges may be granted.

Example 23.6: Give JIM the SELECT privilege on the PLAYERS table.

```
GRANT    SELECT
ON       PLAYERS
TO       JIM
```

Explanation: After this GRANT statement has been processed JIM may use any acceptable SELECT statement to query the PLAYERS table, irrespective of who has created the table.

Example 23.7: Give JIM the INSERT and UPDATE privileges for all columns in the TEAMS table:

```
GRANT    INSERT, UPDATE
ON       TEAMS
TO       JIM
```

With the UPDATE privilege you can state which columns may be updated. Specifying no columns implies that the privilege extends to *all* columns in the table.

Example 23.8: Give PETE the UPDATE privilege for the PLAYERNO and DIVISION columns of the TEAMS table:

```
GRANT   UPDATE (PLAYERNO, DIVISION)
ON      TEAMS
TO      PETE
```

A privilege can be granted to one user, a number of users or to PUBLIC. If a privilege is granted to PUBLIC, each user who has been introduced now has that privilege. It also applies to all users introduced after the granting of the privilege and means that once a user is entered into the system, (s)he automatically receives all the privileges granted to PUBLIC.

Example 23.9: Give all users the SELECT and INDEX privileges on the PENALTIES table:

```
GRANT   SELECT, INDEX
ON      PENALTIES
TO      PUBLIC
```

The table privileges SELECT and ALTER can also be granted to sequences (see Chapter 18). A user needs SELECT authority for a sequence if he or she wants to use the sequence with the NEXTVAL and CURRVAL system variables, when he or she is not the owner. ALTER authority is required for changing specifications of the sequence with the ALTER SEQUENCE statement.

Example 23.10: Give JIM the authority to use the DESCENT sequence.

```
GRANT   SELECT
ON      DESCENT
TO      JIM
```

23.6   Passing on privileges: WITH GRANT OPTION

A GRANT statement can be concluded with the WITH GRANT OPTION clause. This means that all users named in the TO clause can *themselves* pass on the privilege or (part of the privilege) to other users.

Example 23.11: Give JIM the INDEX privilege on the TEAMS table, and allow him to pass it on to other users:

```
GRANT   INDEX
ON      TEAMS
TO      JIM
WITH    GRANT OPTION
```

Because of the WITH GRANT OPTION clause, JIM can pass this privilege on to PETE, say:

```
GRANT   INDEX
ON      TEAMS
TO      PETE
```

JIM can himself extend the statement with WITH GRANT OPTION, so that PETE, in turn, can pass on the privilege.

If a user is given a table privilege via the WITH GRANT OPTION clause, (s)he can grant that privilege on the table without being the owner of it.

23.7 Table privileges and the catalog

All table privileges are stored in the catalog table called TABAUTH$. The primary key of this table is the SEQUENCE# column. The table has the following structure:

column name	data type	description
OBJ#	NUMBER	Database object number of the table, view or sequence on which the privilege was granted
GRANTOR#	NUMBER	Number of the user who granted the privilege
GRANTEE#	NUMBER	Number of the user who has received the privilege
TIME	DATE	Date and time on which the privilege was granted
SEQUENCE#	NUMBER	Unique sequence number of the privilege
ALTER$	NUMBER	2 if the user holds the ALTER privilege; 3 if the user holds the ALTER privilege with the GRANT OPTION; 1 if the user holds the privilege just for some columns and 0 if the user does not hold the ALTER privilege
DELETE$	NUMBER	See the ALTER$ column
INDEX$	NUMBER	See the ALTER$ column
INSERT$	NUMBER	See the ALTER$ column
SELECT$	NUMBER	See the ALTER$ column
UPDATE$	NUMBER	See the ALTER$ column
REFERENCES$	NUMBER	See the ALTER$ column

The columns on which UPDATE privileges are held are recorded in a separate catalog table, the COLAUTH$ table. This table has the following structure:

column name	data type	description
OBJ#	NUMBER	Database object number of the table on which the privilege was granted
GRANTOR#	NUMBER	Number of the user who has granted the privilege
GRANTEE#	NUMBER	Number of the user who has received the privilege
TIME	DATE	Date and time on which the privilege was granted
SEQUENCE#	NUMBER	Unique number of the GRANT statement
NAME	CHAR	Name of the column on which the privilege was granted
UPDATE$	NUMBER	2 if the user holds UPDATE privilege; 3 if the user holds the UPDATE privilege with the GRANT OPTION and 0 if the user does not hold the UPDATE privilege
REFERENCES$	NUMBER	See the UPDATE$ column
SELECT$	NUMBER	See the UPDATE$ column
INSERT$	NUMBER	See the UPDATE$ column

The GRANT statements that we entered as examples in the previous two sections result in the following updates to the TABAUTH$ and COLAUTH$ table. (The names of the last columns are shortened; A = ALTER$, D = DELETE$, X = INDEX$, I = INSERT$, S = SELECT$, U = UPDATE$ and R = REFERENCES$.) You can also see that if a privilege is granted to PUBLIC, this is recorded with the user number 1. This is the number with which PUBLIC is registered in the USER$ table.

The TABAUTH$ table:

OBJ#	GRANTOR#	GRANTEE#	SEQUENCE#	A	D	X	I	S	U	R
4211	50	61	11	0	0	0	0	2	0	0
4212	50	61	12	0	0	0	2	0	2	0
4212	50	62	13	0	0	0	0	0	2	0
4214	50	1	14	0	0	2	0	2	0	0
4212	50	61	15	0	0	3	0	0	0	0
4212	61	62	16	0	0	2	0	0	0	0

The COLAUTH$ table:

OBJ#	GRANTOR#	GRANTEE	SEQUENCE#	NAME	UPDATE$
4212	50	61	1	PLAYERNO	2
4212	50	61	1	DIVISION	2

Exercise

23.1 What do the USER$ and TABAUTH$ tables look like after the following GRANT statements have been issued? The first three statements have been entered by SQLDBA.

```
GRANT    CONNECT
TO       REGINA, OLGA, SUSAN
IDENTIFIED BY RP, MAC, SUE
```

```
GRANT     SELECT
ON        PLAYERS
TO        PUBLIC

GRANT     INSERT
ON        PLAYERS
TO        OLGA
WITH      GRANT OPTION
```

OLGA enters these statements:

```
GRANT     INSERT
ON        PLAYERS
TO        REGINA

GRANT     INSERT
ON        PLAYERS
TO        SUSAN
WITH      GRANT OPTION
```

SUSAN enters these statements:

```
GRANT     INSERT
ON        PLAYERS
TO        REGINA
```

23.8   Revoking privileges

The opposite of the GRANT statement is the *REVOKE statement*. This statement
has different forms too. In this section we describe how you use the REVOKE
statement to remove connect and database privileges.

```
<revoke statement> ::=
   REVOKE { CONNECT | DBA | RESOURCE }
   FROM   <user> [ {,<user>}... ]
```

Example 23.12: Remove JIM's connect privilege.

```
REVOKE    CONNECT
FROM      JIM
```

After this statement JIM is no longer in a position to start up SQL∗Plus. Only
users with DBA authority can issue the REVOKE CONNECT statement.

In revoking the connect privilege from a user, Oracle does *not* drop the tables, indexes and so on which have been created by this user. If this also needs to be done the DROP statement should be used. The catalog tables show which tables, views and indexes the user created.

Users cannot be deleted from the catalog. Do not try to remove users with DELETE statements on the catalog tables. This could damage the database.

Example 23.13: LUKE's RESOURCE privilege is withdrawn.

```
REVOKE    RESOURCE
FROM      LUKE
```

23.9   Revoking table privileges

You use the *REVOKE statement* to withdraw specific privileges on tables and sequences from users. This statement has the opposite effect to the GRANT statement.

```
<revoke statement> ::=
    REVOKE <table privileges>
    ON     { <table specification> | <sequence name> }
    FROM   <grantees>

<table privileges> ::=
    ALL [ PRIVILEGES ] |
    <table privilege> [ {,<table privilege>}... ]

<table privilige> ::=
    ALTER      |
    DELETE     |
    INDEX      |
    INSERT     |
    REFERENCES |
    SELECT     |
    UPDATE

<table specification> ::= [ <user>.] <table name>

<grantees> ::=
    PUBLIC |
    <user> [ {,<user>}... ]
```

Example 23.14: JIM's SELECT privilege on the PLAYERS table is to be withdrawn (we assume that the situation is as it was at the end of Section 23.7):

```
REVOKE    SELECT
ON        PLAYERS
FROM      JIM
```

Oracle now deletes from the TABAUTH$ table the relevant entry for that authority.

Example 23.15: Take the INDEX authority on the TEAMS table from JIM.

```
REVOKE    INDEX
ON        TEAMS
FROM      JIM
```

This form of the REVOKE statement does not lead to the removal of users.

23.10 Security of and through views

GRANT statements can refer to tables, but also to views (see the definition of the GRANT statement). Let us look at this more closely.

Because privileges can also be granted for views, it is possible to provide users with access to only a part of a table, or only to derived or summarized information. Here are examples of both features.

Example 23.16: Give DIANE the privilege to read only the names and addresses of non-competitive players.

First, DIANE must be introduced to the system.

```
GRANT        CONNECT
TO           DIANE
IDENTIFIED BY SLOPE
```

Second, a view is created specifying which data she may see:

```
CREATE    VIEW NAR AS
SELECT    NAME, INITIALS, STREET, HOUSENO, TOWN
FROM      PLAYERS
WHERE     LEAGUENO IS NULL
```

The last step is to grant DIANE the SELECT privilege on the NAR view:

```
GRANT    SELECT
ON       NAR
TO       DIANE
```

With this statement DIANE has access to only that part of the PLAYERS table defined in the view formula.

Example 23.17: Ensure that GERARD can look only at the number of players in each town. First, we introduce GERARD.

```
GRANT     CONNECT
TO        GERARD
IDENTIFIED BY PI_314
```

The view that we use looks like this:

```
CREATE    VIEW PLAYERS_PER_TOWN (TOWN, NUMBER) AS
SELECT    TOWN, COUNT(*)
FROM      PLAYERS
GROUP BY TOWN
```

Now we give GERARD authority for the above view:

```
GRANT     SELECT
ON        PLAYERS_PER_TOWN
TO        GERARD
```

Four types of privilege can be applied to views: INSERT, UPDATE, DELETE and SELECT. The INDEX, ALTER and REFERENCE privileges are not permissible because the INDEX and ALTER statements cannot refer to a view.

23.11   Overview of required privileges

We end this chapter with an overview of the privileges which are required for using certain SQL statements. First a few notes:

- We have restricted ourself to only those SQL statements which have been described in this book (some of them will be described in the next chapters).

- A user with DBA privilege may execute all SQL statements without restrictions. This is why we have not specified this privilege explicitly in the tables.

- In some statements *owner* is mentioned as part of the privilege. This means that if a user is the owner of the object (table, view, etc.) he or she may execute that statement. A user is the owner of an object if he or she created the object or if it was created for that user.

- Some objects, such as tables, synonyms and indexes, can be created for another user. In this case the creator is not the owner. DBA authority is necessary for this.

SQL statement	required privileges
ALTER CLUSTER	Owner of cluster
ALTER INDEX	Owner of index
ALTER SEQUENCE	Owner of sequence
ALTER TABLE	Owner of table; ALTER privilege for table
ALTER TABLESPACE	
ALTER USER	
AUDIT system audit spec	
AUDIT ... ON table	Owner of table
AUDIT ... ON DEFAULT	
COMMENT	Owner of table; ALTER privilege for table
COMMIT	None
CONNECT	CONNECT privilege
CREATE CLUSTER	RESOURCE privilege
CREATE DATABASE	
CREATE DATABASE LINK	CONNECT privilege for remote database
CREATE PUBLIC DATABASE LINK	
CREATE INDEX	Owner of table; INDEX privilege for table
CREATE SEQUENCE	RESOURCE privilege
CREATE SYNONYM	Owner of table (or view); SELECT privilege for table (or view)
CREATE PUBLIC SYNONYM	
CREATE TABLE	RESOURCE privilege
CREATE TABLESPACE	
CREATE VIEW	SELECT privilege for table(s)
DELETE	Owner of table; DELETE privilege for table
DROP CLUSTER	Owner of cluster
DROP DATABASE LINK	Owner of database link
DROP PUBLIC DATABASE LINK	
DROP INDEX	Owner of index
DROP SEQUENCE	Owner of sequence
DROP SYNONYM	Owner of synonym
DROP PUBLIC SYNONYM	
DROP TABLE	Owner of table
DROP TABLESPACE	
DROP VIEW	Owner of view
GRANT CONNECT (to change password)	Every user
GRANT system privilege	
GRANT table privilege	Owner of table; privilege received via WITH GRANT OPTION
GRANT RESOURCE ON tablespace	

SQL statement	required privileges
INSERT	Owner of table; INSERT privilege for table
LOCK TABLE	Owner of table; ALTER, DELETE, INSERT, SELECT or UPDATE privilege on table
NOAUDIT system audit spec	
NOAUDIT ... ON table	Owner of table
NOAUDIT ... ON DEFAULT	
RENAME	Owner of table, view or synonym
REVOKE	See GRANT
ROLLBACK	None
SELECT	Owner of table(s); SELECT privilege for table
SELECT INTO	Owner of table(s); SELECT privilege for table
UPDATE	Owner of table; UPDATE privilege for table
VALIDATE INDEX	Owner of index

24
Auditing SQL statements

Sometimes you need to be able to determine what happened in the database at a given point. You may want to know, for example, who deleted a table on a particular day or when the most recent update of the PLAYERS table occurred. Oracle offers a facility to discover this type of thing after the event. Oracle is able to document the fact that particular SQL statements have been processed. Note that the SQL statement itself is not recorded, only that such a statement has been executed. This recording process is called *auditing*.

The result of auditing, the record of certain SQL statements having been executed, is stored in a catalog table. In the literature we also see the contents of this catalog table referred to as the *audit trail*. Like the other catalog tables, this one can also be queried with SELECT statements. Among others, the following questions can be answered by querying this table:

- Who has logged on when?
- When was the most recent update on the PLAYERS table performed?
- How often has the user JIM updated the MATCHES table?
- Who has given the PLAYERS table a new name?

In this chapter, we describe which SQL statements are supported when it comes to auditing. Along with this, we cover in detail the catalog tables recording the audit specifications and the audit trail. We close the chapter with two pieces of advice concerning use of auditing.

24.1   The AUDIT_TRAIL parameter

Oracle's default position is *not* to audit. The INIT.ORA file has a parameter
called *AUDIT_TRAIL* that can have either TRUE or FALSE as a value. If the
parameter is set to FALSE auditing is switched off and AUDIT statements have
no effect. The statements are effective, however, if the parameter is set to TRUE
when Oracle starts up. We assume that it is set to TRUE throughout this chapter.

24.2   System audit specifications

You use the *AUDIT statement* to specify which SQL statements you want to track.
Those which are to be audited are referred to in this book as the *audit specification*. Audit specifications are recorded in catalog tables.

Oracle supports two types of audit specification: *system* and *table* audit
specifications. We look at the former in this section and the latter in the next.

```
<audit statement> ::=
    AUDIT <system audit specifications>
    [ WHENEVER [ NOT ] SUCCESSFUL ]

<system audit specifications> ::=
    ALL |
    <system audit specification>
       [ {,system audit specification>}... ]

<system audit specification> ::=
    CONNECT | RESOURCE | DBA | NOT EXISTS
```

The four system audit specifications have the following meaning:

CONNECT   Each time an Oracle user logs on or off with the CONNECT
               statement, a record is placed in the catalog.

RESOURCE   Each time a user executes an SQL statement requiring a RE-
               SOURCE privilege, such as CREATE TABLE, a record is
               placed in the catalog.

DBA   Each time a user executes an SQL statement requiring the DBA
               privilege, such as GRANT DBA and AUDIT RESOURCE, this
               is recorded in the catalog.

NOT EXISTS   Each time a user executes an SQL statement that returns the
               Oracle –942 error message, this is recorded in the catalog. Ex-
               amples of when this error message appears include when a user

tries to query a non-existent table or when access to it is forbidden.

ALL   The specification of ALL is equivalent to specifying all four system audit specifications above.

Example 24.1: Audit all SQL statements for which the DBA privilege is necessary.

```
AUDIT DBA
```

Explanation: Once this statement has been issued, Oracle tracks all statements requiring the DBA privilege to execute, irrespective of who enters the statements.

Note: Should the AUDIT_TRAIL parameter equal FALSE, the audit specifications are still recorded but the actual auditing is not activated. Auditing only occurs if the parameter is set to TRUE.

We did not specify the WHENEVER option in the statement above. In this case all relevant statements are recorded, whether they executed successfully or not. When WHENEVER SUCCESSFUL is specified, only correctly executed statements are recorded in the catalog. Oracle can reject statements containing syntax errors or incorrect privileges. Such statements are not recorded then. The opposite of WHENEVER SUCCESSFUL is, of course, WHENEVER NOT SUCCESSFUL. These statements are registered which could not be executed.

Example 24.2: Track the correctly executed CONNECT statements.

```
AUDIT CONNECT
WHENEVER SUCCESSFUL
```

Example 24.3: Track only the incorrectly executed statements.

```
AUDIT ALL
WHENEVER NOT SUCCESSFUL
```

Note: Entering a second AUDIT statement (and this applies to all AUDIT statements covered in this chapter) does not cancel out the effect of the previous AUDIT statement.

Specifying multiple audit specifications in one statement has the same effect as specifying them in separate statements. The following statement:

```
AUDIT DBA, CONNECT
WHENEVER SUCCESSFUL
```

has the same effect as these two:

```
AUDIT DBA
WHENEVER SUCCESSFUL
```

and

```
AUDIT CONNECT
WHENEVER SUCCESSFUL
```

Exercises

24.1   What is the effect of an AUDIT statement if the AUDIT_TRAIL parameter is set to FALSE?

24.2   Formulate the AUDIT statement that tracks all correctly executed statements requiring the RESOURCE privilege.

24.3   Formulate the AUDIT statement that tracks all correctly and incorrectly executed system audits.

24.4   Formulate the AUDIT statement that tracks all statements where users try to access a non-existent table or index.

24.3   Table audit specifications

Table audit specifications are defined using the second form of the AUDIT statement. A table audit specification is defined for one specific table or sequence. This facility enables you to track precisely which SQL statements are issued against a given table or sequence.

```
<audit statement> ::=
   AUDIT <table audit specifications>
   ON <audit object>
   [ BY { SESSION | ACCESS } ]
   [ WHENEVER [ NOT ] SUCCESSFUL ]

<audit object> ::=
   <tabel specification> |
   <sequence name> |
   DEFAULT

<table audit specifications> ::=
   ALL |
   <table audit specification>
      [ {,table audit specification>}... ]

<table audit specification> ::=
   ALTER | AUDIT | COMMENT | DELETE | GRANT | INDEX |
   INSERT | LOCK | RENAME | SELECT | UPDATE

<table identifier> ::= [ <user> . ] <table name>
```

Each table audit specification is related to one or two SQL statements:

ALTER   ALTER TABLE statement
AUDIT   AUDIT statement
COMMENT   COMMENT ON statement
DELETE   DELETE statement
GRANT   GRANT and REVOKE statement
INDEX   CREATE INDEX and DROP INDEX statement
INSERT   INSERT statement
LOCK   LOCK statement
RENAME   RENAME statement
SELECT   SELECT and CREATE TABLE ... AS SELECT statement
UPDATE   UPDATE statement

Example 24.4: Track each UPDATE, INSERT and DELETE statement against
the PLAYERS table, but record them only if the update executes succesfully.

```
AUDIT UPDATE, INSERT, DELETE
ON    PLAYERS
BY    ACCESS
WHENEVER SUCCESSFUL
```

Explanation: By specifying BY ACCESS, every update is recorded. Therefore,
if an application updates the PLAYERS table twenty times with an UPDATE
statement, that is also recorded twenty times. The WHENEVER SUCCESSFUL
option, as with system audit specifications, instructs Oracle to track only successful operations. There are a number of reasons why an update can fail, among
them being that the statement is syntactically incorrect, the table to be accessed
is being used at that point by another user, or the update attempts to insert an
already existing value into a primary key.

In contrast to auditing each SQL statement, an audit can be maintained on
a per session basis. A *session* is the period between logging on and off to Oracle.
(You can start a new session in SQL*Plus by executing a DISCONNECT and
a CONNECT command successively.) The individual SQL statements are not
audited; rather, the fact that a particular type of SQL statement has been executed (against the table noted) during the session is recorded.

Example 24.5: For each session, audit the UPDATE, INSERT and DELETE
statement against the PLAYERS table, irrespective of whether the update is successful or not.

```
AUDIT UPDATE, INSERT, DELETE
ON    PLAYERS
BY    SESSION
```

Specifying neither BY ACCESS nor BY SESSION has the same effect as specifying BY SESSION. Therefore the following statement is equivalent to the previous
one:

```
AUDIT UPDATE, INSERT, DELETE
ON   PLAYERS
```

The table audit specifications formulated thus far are only concerned with the table noted in the ON clause. It is also possible to initiate a table audit specification for all tables created after the AUDIT statement. Here is an example.

Example 24.6: Every SELECT statement accessing tables created from now on must be audited.

```
AUDIT SELECT
ON   DEFAULT
BY   ACCESS
```

Explanation: If we now create a REFEREES table, for example, once the CREATE TABLE statement has executed, the following statement is processed in the background:

```
AUDIT SELECT
ON   REFEREES
BY   ACCESS
```

All table audit specifications, apart from ALTER and INDEX, can also be applied to views. For sequences, only ALTER, AUDIT, GRANT and SELECT can be specified.

Exercises

24.5 Write an AUDIT statement to track COMMENT ON, RENAME and GRANT statements against the PLAYERS table on a sessional basis.

24.6 Write an AUDIT statement to track all statements executed directly against the MATCHES table. Track the individual statements.

24.4   Audit specifications and the catalog

No separate catalog table exists for recording audit specifications. Table audit trails are recorded in the TAB$ table (see Section 5.9), the VIEW$ table (see Section 22.4) and the SEQ$ table (see Section 18.5). The system audit specifications are stored in TAB$. We will first describe the recording of the table audit specifications.

The table audit specifications are stored in the AUDIT$ columns of the TAB$, VIEW$ and SEQ$ tables. These columns have a data type of CHAR(24). Two positions are reserved for each type of table audit specification (there are eleven of them) and the two final positions are not used. The first character in each pair represents what is to be tracked in the event of a successful execution of an SQL statement; the second in each pair indicates what is to be tracked when the SQL statement is unsuccessful. A position can be filled with one of the following values:

−   not to be audited
A   should be audited after each SQL statement (BY ACCESS)
S   should be audited only at the end of a session (BY SESSION)

The following SELECT statement can be used to find out what the current table audit specifications are. From this statement we can also show the meaning of each position (we have incorporated a $ sign into words such as ALTER as they are reserved words):

```
SELECT    O.NAME,
    SUBSTR(AUDIT$,1,1)  || '/' || SUBSTR(AUDIT$,2,1)   ALTER$,
    SUBSTR(AUDIT$,3,1)  || '/' || SUBSTR(AUDIT$,4,1)   AUDIT$,
    SUBSTR(AUDIT$,5,1)  || '/' || SUBSTR(AUDIT$,6,1)   COMMENT$,
    SUBSTR(AUDIT$,7,1)  || '/' || SUBSTR(AUDIT$,8,1)   DELETE$,
    SUBSTR(AUDIT$,9,1)  || '/' || SUBSTR(AUDIT$,10,1)  GRANT$,
    SUBSTR(AUDIT$,11,1) || '/' || SUBSTR(AUDIT$,12,1)  INDEX$,
    SUBSTR(AUDIT$,13,1) || '/' || SUBSTR(AUDIT$,14,1)  INSERT$,
    SUBSTR(AUDIT$,15,1) || '/' || SUBSTR(AUDIT$,16,1)  LOCK$,
    SUBSTR(AUDIT$,17,1) || '/' || SUBSTR(AUDIT$,18,1)  RENAME$,
    SUBSTR(AUDIT$,19,1) || '/' || SUBSTR(AUDIT$,20,1)  SELECT$,
    SUBSTR(AUDIT$,21,1) || '/' || SUBSTR(AUDIT$,22,1)  UPDATE$
FROM      SYS.TAB$ T, SYS.OBJ$ O, SYS.USER$ U
WHERE     T.OBJ# = O.OBJ#
AND       O.OWNER# = U.USER#
AND       U.NAME = 'SQLDBA'
```

The following AUDIT statements result in the AUDIT$ column being filled:

```
AUDIT SELECT, UPDATE
ON    PLAYERS
BY    ACCESS
WHENEVER SUCCESSFUL

AUDIT INSERT
ON    PLAYERS
BY    SESSION
```

Contents of the AUDIT$ column:

```
AUDIT$
----------------------
------------SS----A-A-
```

The system audit specifications are recorded in the catalog in a different manner. During the installation of Oracle a table called _system_auditing_options_ (note the underscores) is created. This table is never populated or queried. Because it does exist, though, it appears in the TAB$ table. Just like table audit specifications, the system audit specifications are stored in the AUDIT$ column in the TAB$ table, in the row for the _system_auditing_options_ table. In this case only the first eight positions are used. Positions 1 and 2 are used for CONNECT, 3 and 4 for DBA, 5 and 6 for NOT EXISTS and 7 and 8 for RESOURCE. Only the – and S codes are used in conjunction with this table. The A code is not relevant because a system audit specification, by definition, pertains to the whole session.

The following SELECT statement is used to query the actual system audit specifications. Again, we show what each pair of character position means.

```
SELECT
    SUBSTR(AUDIT$,1,1) || '/' || SUBSTR(AUDIT$,2,1) CONNECT$,
    SUBSTR(AUDIT$,3,1) || '/' || SUBSTR(AUDIT$,4,1) DBA$,
    SUBSTR(AUDIT$,5,1) || '/' || SUBSTR(AUDIT$,6,1) NOTEXISTS$,
    SUBSTR(AUDIT$,7,1) || '/' || SUBSTR(AUDIT$,8,1) RESOURCE$
FROM     SYS.TAB$ T, SYS.OBJ$ O
WHERE    T.OBJ# = O.OBJ#
AND      O.NAME = '_system_auditing_options_'
```

Possible result from this statement:

```
CONNECT$  DBA$  NOTEXISTS$  RESOURCE$
--------  ----  ----------  ---------
-/S       S/S   -/S         S/S
```

The table audit specifications defined for DEFAULT are, like the system audit specifications, stored in the AUDIT$ column of the TAB$ table. To do this, Oracle uses a table called _default_auditing_options_ Filling the AUDIT$ column is the same process as for the normal table audit specifications, while the default specifications can be queried using the same SELECT statement as that for normal table audit specifications, with the addition of the following condition:

```
O.NAME = '_default_auditing_options_'
```

24.5   Use of the audit trail

As we mentioned earlier, the audit trail is logged in a catalog table called AUD$. The SESSIONID, ENTRYID and STATEMENT columns form the table's primary key. Particular database operations can result in the addition of one or more rows to the AUD$ table. A database operation can include an SQL statement or, for example, logging on to or off from the database. Some SQL statements cause multiple rows to be inserted. One example would be a SELECT statement joining two tables, both of which were to be audited, resulting in two new rows in the

AUD$ table. Let us look at the structure of this table (not all the columns are shown):

column name	data type	description
SESSIONID	NUMBER	Number of the Oracle session, determined by the USERENV('SESSIONID') function
ENTRYID	NUMBER	Unique number of the actual audit, determined by the USERENV('ENTRYID') function
STATEMENT	NUMBER	Sequence number of the SQL statement within the session; not all SQL statements are audited, therefore not all numbers are present
TIMESTAMP	DATE	Date and time at which the row in the audit trail was entered
USERID	CHAR	Name of the user who performed the database operation
USERHOST	CHAR	Identification of the machine on which the database operation was performed
TERMINAL	CHAR	Identification of the terminal from where the database operation was performed, the same as determined by the USERENV('TERMINAL') function
ACTION	NUMBER	Code representing the type of database operation performed and audited; see the description below
RETURNCODE	NUMBER	Number of the Oracle error message generated after the database operation; a successful operation is indicated by a zero
OBJ$CREATOR	CHAR	Name of the owner of the database object accessed
OBJ$NAME	CHAR	Name of the database object accessed, such as a table name or index name
AUTH$PRIVILE-GES	CHAR	Privileges granted or revoked as a result of the GRANT or REVOKE database operation; see description below
AUTH$GRANTEE	CHAR	Name of the user receiving the privilege
NEW$NAME	CHAR	New name of the table as a result of the RENAME database operation on a table
SES$ACTIONS	CHAR	Code representing the types of SQL statements executed during the session: see description below
LOGOFF$LREAD	NUMBER	Total number of logical reads executed by the DBMS, the column being filled only if the value in the ACTION column is 61 (LOGOFF)
LOGOFF$PREAD	NUMBER	Total number of physical reads executed by the DBMS, the column being filled only if the value in the ACTION column is 61 (LOGOFF)
LOGOFF$LWRITE	NUMBER	Total number of logical writes executed by the DBMS, the column being filled only if the value in the ACTION column is 61 (LOGOFF)
LOGOFF$DEAD	NUMBER	Total number of deadlocks during the session, the column being filled only if the value in the ACTION column is 61 (LOGOFF)

The ACTION column contains a code that indicates which type of database operation has occurred. Most codes have to do with particular SQL statements, others with specific actions like logging off from Oracle. The table below shows each code's meaning. The ACTION column is 63 (SESSION) if an audit has to be performed at the end of a session.

code	description	code	description
0	UNKNOWN	1	CREATE TABLE
2	INSERT	3	SELECT
4	CREATE CLUSTER	5	ALTER CLUSTER
6	UPDATE	7	DELETE
8	DROP CLUSTER	9	CREATE INDEX
10	DROP INDEX	11	ALTER INDEX
12	DROP TABLE	13	CREATE SEQUENCE
14	ALTER SEQUENCE	15	ALTER TABLE
16	DROP SEQUENCE	17	GRANT OBJECT
18	REVOKE OBJECT	19	CREATE SYNONYM
20	DROP SYNONYM	21	CREATE VIEW
22	DROP VIEW	23	VALIDATE INDEX
26	LOCK	27	UNDEFINED
28	RENAME	29	COMMENT
30	AUDIT OBJECT	31	NOAUDIT OBJECT
32	CREATE DATABASE LINK	33	DROP DATABASE LINK
34	CREATE DATABASE	35	ALTER DATABASE
36	CREATE ROLLBACK SEGMENT	37	ALTER ROLLBACK SEGMENT
38	DROP ROLLBACK SEGMENT	39	CREATE TABLESPACE
40	ALTER TABLESPACE	41	DROP TABLESPACE
42	ALTER SESSION	43	ALTER USER
49	ALTER SYSTEM	60	LOGON
61	LOGOFF	62	CLEANUP
63	SESSION	64	AUDIT SYSTEM
65	NOAUDIT SYSTEM	66	AUDIT DEFAULT
67	NOAUDIT DEFAULT	68	GRANT SYSTEM
69	REVOKE SYSTEM	70	CREATE PUBLIC SYNONYM
71	DROP PUBLIC SYNONYM	72	CREATE PUBLIC DB. LINK
73	DROP PUBLIC DB. LINK	80	USER COMMENT

The SES$ACTIONS column is used only if a session has been audited, that is, if the ACTION column has 63 (SESSION) as its value. In this column, for each separate type of SQL statement a code is used to show whether a statement of that type has been executed within the session. The meanings of these codes are:

–	statements of this type have not been executed
S	all statements of this type have been executed with success
F	execution of all statements of this type have failed
B	some statements of this type have failed and some were executed with success (both)

You can use the following SELECT statement to analyse the contents of the column and work out the meaning of each position in it:

```
SELECT    SUBSTR(SES$ACTIONS,1,1)    ALTER$,
          SUBSTR(SES$ACTIONS,2,1)    AUDIT$,
          SUBSTR(SES$ACTIONS,3,1)    COMMENT$,
          SUBSTR(SES$ACTIONS,4,1)    DELETE$,
          SUBSTR(SES$ACTIONS,5,1)    GRANT$,
          SUBSTR(SES$ACTIONS,6,1)    INDEX$,
          SUBSTR(SES$ACTIONS,7,1)    INSERT$,
          SUBSTR(SES$ACTIONS,8,1)    LOCK$,
          SUBSTR(SES$ACTIONS,9,1)    RENAME$,
          SUBSTR(SES$ACTIONS,10,1)   SELECT$,
          SUBSTR(SES$ACTIONS,11,1)   UPDATE$
FROM      AUD$
```

Oracle fills the AUTH$PRIVILEGES column when the database operation was a GRANT statement on a table. The data type in this column is CHAR(6), so one position is reserved for each of the six table privileges supported by Oracle. The first position is for the ALTER privilege and the other positions are reserved for DELETE, INDEX, INSERT, SELECT and UPDATE respectively. Each position can have one of the following values: – (no privilege), Y (privilege granted) or G (privilege granted with the WITH GRANT OPTION). If the ALL privilege has be granted, all positions are filled with Y (or G).

Here are a few examples of SELECT statements on the audit table.

Example 24.7: Name the users who have succeeded in logging on to Oracle since 1 January 1990.

```
SELECT    USERID
FROM      SYS.AUD$
WHERE     TIMESTAMP > '01-JAN-90'
```

Example 24.8: How many users have not logged on successfully?

```
SELECT    COUNT(*)
FROM      SYS.AUD$
WHERE     ACTION = 60
AND       RETURNCODE <> 0
```

Example 24.9: When was the PLAYERS table owned by SQLDBA last updated, and by whom?

```
SELECT    TIMESTAMP, USERID
FROM      SYS.AUD$
WHERE     OBJ$NAME = 'PLAYERS'
AND       OBJ$CREATOR = 'SQLDBA'
AND       ACTION IN (2, 6, 7)
AND       TIMESTAMP >= ALL
          (SELECT    TIMESTAMP
           FROM      SYS.AUD$
           WHERE     OBJ$NAME = 'PLAYERS'
           AND       OBJ$CREATOR = 'SQLDBA'
           AND       ACTION IN (2, 6, 7))
```

Example 24.10: How often has the user JIM updated the MATCHES table?

```
SELECT    COUNT(*)
FROM      SYS.AUD$
WHERE     OBJ$NAME = 'MATCHES'
AND       OBJ$CREATOR = 'SQLDBA'
AND       ACTION IN (2, 6, 7)
AND       USERID = 'JIM'
```

Example 24.11: Who has renamed the PLAYERS table?

```
SELECT    USERID
FROM      SYS.AUD$
WHERE     OBJ$NAME = 'PLAYERS'
AND       OBJ$CREATOR = 'SQLDBA'
AND       ACTION = 28
```

Example 24.12: Who gave JIM the SELECT privilege on the PLAYERS table?

```
SELECT    USERID
FROM      SYS.AUD$
WHERE     OBJ$NAME = 'PLAYERS'
AND       OBJ$CREATOR = 'SQLDBA'
AND       ACTION = 17
AND       SUBSTR(AUTH$PRIVILEGES,5,1) IN ('Y', 'G')
AND       AUTH$GRANTEE = 'JIM'
```

Exercise

24.7 Write SELECT statements to answer the following questions:

1.   From which terminal was the MATCHES table most recently up-
      dated?

2.   How often was the PLAYERS table accessed with a SELECT state-
      ment in the period 1 January 1990 to 31 March 1990 inclusive?

3.   Which table has been structurally changed with an ALTER or RE-
        NAME statement by someone other than its owner?

24.6   Deleting audit specifications

You can delete audit specifications again using the *NOAUDIT statement*. The definition of this statement is very similar to that of the AUDIT statement. The only
difference is that the NOAUDIT statement does not support the BY SESSION
and BY ACCESS options. Like AUDIT, NOAUDIT takes two forms: one for
deleting system audit specifications and one for table audit specifications. We
show both forms simultaneously.

```
<noaudit statement> ::=
   <noaudit system statement> |
   <noaudit table statement>

<noaudit system statement> ::=
   NOAUDIT <system audit specifications>
   [ WHENEVER [ NOT ] SUCCESSFUL ]

<system audit specifications> ::=
   ALL | <system audit specification>
         [ {,system audit specification>}... ]

<system audit specification> ::=
   CONNECT | RESOURCE | DBA | NOT EXISTS

<noaudit table statement> ::=
   NOAUDIT <table audit specifications>
   ON { <table identifier> | DEFAULT }
   [ WHENEVER [ NOT ] SUCCESSFUL ]

<table audit specifications> ::=
   ALL | <table audit specification>
         [ {,table audit specification>}... ]

<table audit specification> ::=
   ALTER | AUDIT | COMMENT | DELETE | GRANT | INDEX |
   INSERT | LOCK | RENAME | SELECT | UPDATE

<table specification> ::= [ <user> . ] <table name>
```

Example 24.13: Stop auditing correctly processed statements requiring the DBA privilege.

```
NOAUDIT  DBA
WHENEVER SUCCESSFULL
```

Example 24.14: Stop auditing all CONNECT statements.

```
NOAUDIT  CONNECT
```

Example 24.15: Stop auditing both successful and unsuccessful executions of the UPDATE statement against the TEAMS table.

```
NOAUDIT UPDATE
ON      TEAMS
```

24.7   General advice

We close this chapter with two pieces of advice. First, auditing slows down the execution of statements. There are two good reasons for this. The first is that Oracle must do an INSERT or UPDATE in the AUD$ table after every statement and this takes time. Another reason is that all audit information is written to the same catalog table, which means that if too many SQL statements are tracked a system-wide bottleneck can develop. Our advice is, therefore, to audit only when necessary.

Second, auditing populates the AUD$ table. We advise you, then, to clear this table periodically. If you use this table extensively it can quickly become large. If you want to keep the data for later use, it can be copied to a separate table. The following statement shows a simple way to set up a copy table:

```
CREATE   TABLE AUDIT_COPY_1 AS
SELECT   *
FROM     SYS.AUD$
```

25
Physical storage structure

As a user of an Oracle database you only see and access tables. How and where the rows of the tables are really stored is not relevant for you. Oracle makes this entirely transparent. Even in the chapters on creating tables and indexes (Chapters 5 and 20 respectively) we did not discuss this. In other words, we have not yet explained the *physical storage structure*. In fact, an understanding of this topic is not mandatory, because if nothing is specified in a CREATE statement, Oracle determines this itself. In this chapter we describe the set of concepts and SQL statements which you should be familiar with and use when you create a physical storage structure. The following concepts will be discussed:

* databases
* tablespaces
* segments
* extents
* clusters
* rowid

Explanation: This chapter contains a general description of the physical storage structure of Oracle databases. You should see this chapter as an introduction to this topic. Not all the concepts will be described, but only the most important ones and not all the details will be discussed. If you are going to develop operational applications, we advise you to study this topic thoroughly (for this we refer to the *Database Administrator's Guide*). The way in which the storage structure is set up has a significant influence on the performance of the entire database.

25.1   Creating databases

Throughout the book we have assumed that you log on to Oracle and can then create and manipulate tables and indexes. However, you do not log on to Oracle, but to a specific *database*. A database is, put simply, a set of tables with related catalog tables. On a computer system multiple, mutually independent databases can be installed. This means that during logging on you have to indicate in some way which database you are going to work with. The way in which this happens, differs for each operating system. Usually this means that certain parameters of the operating system point to specific databases. For each separate user those parameters can be defined. We refer to the installation manuals of Oracle for details about this.

During the installation of Oracle a database can be installed. Later, new databases can be created with the CREATE DATABASE statement. This SQL statement cannot, however, be entered with SQL*Plus. We have to use a product called *SQL*DBA* to do this. SQL*DBA is similar to SQL*Plus and is also supplied with the Oracle DBMS. The method of logging on and entering statements is identical. There are, however, two essential differences:

- A number of SQL*Plus commands do not work under SQL*DBA.

- SQL*DBA supports some very powerful non-SQL commands, which cannot be processed by SQL*Plus.

Example 25.1: Create a new database called SPORTDB.

```
CREATE DATABASE SPORTDB
```

Explanation: With this statement a new database called SPORTDB is created. Each database has a unique name. The statement above has the following effects:

- One *file* is created (all data belonging to a database are stored in operating system files, or in short files; possible data that is stored, are rows of a table, leaves of an index tree and catalog data)

- All catalog tables are created

- The specifications of the catalog tables are stored in the catalog tables themselves

- Two users are entered: SYS and SYSTEM (see Chapter 23)

The name of the first database is requested during the installation of Oracle. After this name has been entered, Oracle executes a CREATE DATABASE statement to create that first database.

Note: Normally a user or application only works with tables from the same database. The distributed facilities of Oracle allow you to access and combine multiple databases at the same time. We will return to this subject in Chapter 26.

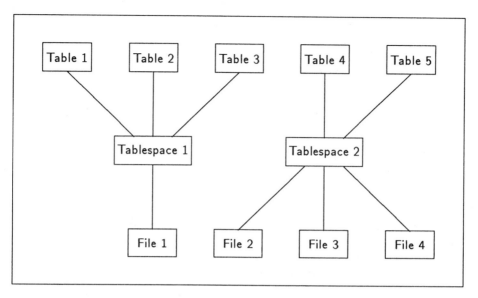

Figure 25.1: Relationships between tables, tablespaces and files

25.2   Tablespaces

In the previous section we mentioned that a database consists of a set of tables. This is correct from the point of view of the user. On the physical level a database looks completely different. From this point of view each database consists of one or more so-called *tablespaces*. A tablespace is a set of interrelated files. In fact, tablespaces are used to group files in logical units. So, a tablespace is an Oracle concept, like a table, whereas a file is a concept of the operating system. When you create a database, a tablespace, called *SYSTEM*, is created automatically.

When you create a table or index you can indicate in which tablespace the data (rows or leaves) should be stored. A table or index is always stored in one tablespace. If a tablespace consists of multiple files, Oracle determines in which file the rows are really stored. As mentioned above, multiple tables can be stored in a tablespace. You could, for example, store all four tables from the example database in one specific tablespace. All the catalog tables are registered together in the SYSTEM tablespace during the creation of a database. A file can only belong to one tablespace at any time. In Figure 25.1 the relationships between tables, tablespaces and files are shown graphically.

Below we give a definition of the statement for creating tablespaces. We will extend this definition later.

```
<create tablespace statement> ::=
   CREATE TABLESPACE <tablespace name>
   DATAFILE <file specification>
     [ {,<file specification>}... ]

<file specification> ::=
   '<file name>' [ SIZE <size-specification> ] [ REUSE ]

<size-specification> ::=
   <integer> [ K | M ]
```

Here are some examples.

Example 25.2: Create a tablespace called TS_TEAMS for storing the TEAMS table.

```
CREATE TABLESPACE TS_TEAMS
DATAFILE 'TEAMS.DAT' SIZE 10K
```

Explanation: This tablespace is (for the present) built on only one file. The SIZE option indicates the actual size of the file in bytes. To avoid long numbers, a K or M may be specified. A capital K (Kilo) means that the value has to be multiplied by 1024 and a capital M (Mega) means that the value has to be multiplied by 1024^2. In the example the file will be 10K bytes in size. This space is directly taken up on disk. Therefore, in spite of the fact that there is no data stored yet, on disk the space is already taken.

After creating the TS_TEAMS tablespace we can store the TEAMS table in it:

```
CREATE    TABLE TEAMS
            (TEAMNO    SMALLINT  NOT NULL,
             PLAYERNO  SMALLINT  NOT NULL,
             DIVISION  CHAR(6)   NOT NULL)
   TABLESPACE TS_TEAMS
```

Explanation: The name of the tablespace in which the data should be stored can be specified after the table schema.

Example 25.3: Create a tablespace called HUGE.

```
CREATE TABLESPACE HUGE
DATAFILE 'PART1.DAT' SIZE 2M    REUSE,
          'PART2.DAT' SIZE 3M    REUSE,
          'PART3.DAT' SIZE 450K REUSE
```

Explanation: This tablespace consists of three files with a total size of 5570K bytes. The effect of specifying REUSE is that if the file concerned already exists (or is in use) it will be overwritten. If REUSE has not been specified and the file already exists, the statement is rejected.

With the ALTER TABLESPACE statement files can be added later on.

```
<alter tablespace statement> ::=
   ALTER TABLESPACE <tablespace name>
   ADD DATAFILE <file specification>
                  [ {,<file specification>}... ]
```

Example 25.4: Add a fourth file to the HUGE tablespace.

```
ALTER TABLESPACE HUGE
ADD DATAFILE 'PART4.DAT' SIZE 2M
```

Explanation: After this statement was executed the total size of the tablespace has increased to 7418K bytes (work this out for yourself).

We mentioned above that each table is stored in a tablespace. What happens if you do not specify a tablespace when you create a table? The answer to this question depends on the user who creates the table. A *default tablespace* can be defined for each user. If this is not done, the table is stored automatically in the tablespace called SYSTEM. With the *ALTER USER statement* we can define a default tablespace for each user (we went through an example of this statement in Chapter 23 for changing a user's password). Below we show you the definition of this statement.

```
<alter user statement> ::=
   ALTER USER <user>
      [ IDENTIFIED BY <password> ]
      [ DEFAULT TABLESPACE <tablespace name> ]
```

Example 25.5: Define TS_TEAMS as the default tablespace for JOHN.

```
ALTER   USER JOHN
DEFAULT TABLESPACE TS_TEAMS
```

A tablespace can be deleted with the DROP TABLESPACE statement.

```
<drop tablespace statement> ::=
   DROP TABLESPACE <tablespace name>
   [ INCLUDING CONTENTS ]
```

If the INCLUDING CONTENTS option is not specified and if the deleted tablespace still contains data, then the statement is rejected. But if it is specified, the tablespace will be deleted, including all tables, indexes and other database objects dependent to the tablespace.

25.3   Segments and extents

The internal structure of a tablespace is built up from segments and extents. A *segment* contains data from a table, for example. Oracle supports five types of segments, of which we will discuss only the table and index segments in this book. A segment consists of *extents* which are contiguous pieces of storage space in a specific file. In practice, the size of an extent ranges between 4000 and 16000 bytes. Each segment has an *initial* extent and zero, one or more additional extents.

If an (empty) table or index is stored in a tablespace, a new segment is created consisting of one initial extent. If new rows are added to a table with IN-SERT statements and the size of the initial extent is not sufficient, then additional extents are automatically added.

In the CREATE statements for tables and indexes, specifications on extents can be indicated. Below follows a part of the definition of the CREATE TABLE statement. We refer to Chapter 5 for a description of the table schema concept.

```
<create table statement> ::=
    CREATE TABLE <table name>
        <table schema>
        [ TABLESPACE <tablespace name> ]
        [ <storage specification> ]

<storage specification> ::=
    STORAGE ( <storage parameter>... )

<storage parameter> ::=
    INITIAL <size specification> |
    NEXT <size specification>    |
    MINEXTENTS <integer>         |
    MAXEXTENTS <integer>         |
    PCTINCREASE <integer>
```

The meaning of these parameters is shown below:

INITIAL   This parameter indicates the size in bytes of the initial ex-
                     tent that is allocated during the creation of a table. The de-
                     fault size of the initial extent is 10240 bytes. The minimum
                     size of an initial extent is 4096 bytes and the maximum size
                     is 4095 megabytes. Each number is rounded to the nearest
                     1024 bytes.

NEXT   This parameter indicates the size in bytes of each additional
                     extent that is allocated. The default size of an additional ex-
                     tent is 10240 bytes. The minimum size of an additional extent

is 2048 bytes and the maximum size is 4095 megabytes. Each number is rounded to the nearest 1024 bytes.

MINEXTENTS   This parameter indicates how many extents are actually allocated when the table is created. If the value is equal to one, then only the initial extent is created.

MAXEXTENTS   This parameter indicates the maximum number of extents which can ever be allocated to the segment. If this parameter is not specified, then its value is set to 9999.

PCTINCREASE   This parameter indicates how much larger an additional extent must be with respect to the previous one. If this percentage is equal to zero, all additional extents will have the same size. If this percentage is greater than zero, then the extents will become larger each time. The default value of the percentage is 50.

Example 25.6: Create the PENALTIES table.

```
CREATE    TABLE PENALTIES
          (PAYMENTNO    INTEGER      NOT NULL PRIMARY KEY,
           PLAYERNO     SMALLINT     NOT NULL,
           PEN_DATE     DATE         NOT NULL
                        DEFAULT '01-JAN-90'  ,
           AMOUNT       DECIMAL(7,2) NOT NULL,
                        DEFAULT 50.00         )
TABLESPACE HUGE
STORAGE (INITIAL       100K
         NEXT          20K
         MINEXTENTS    1
         MAXEXTENTS    1000
         PCTINCREASE   10 )
```

These parameters can also be specified for indexes. Here is an example.

Example 25.7: Define an index on the PLAYERS table.

```
CREATE    UNIQUE INDEX PL_NAME_INIT
ON        PLAYERS (NAME, INITIALS)
TABLESPACE HUGE
STORAGE   (INITIAL     50K
           NEXT        50K
           PCTINCREASE 0 )
```

When you create a table or an index, you can specify a tablespace and a storage specification. If only a tablespace has been indicated and not a storage specification, then Oracle uses the default values for the five storage parameters.

However, you can indicate for each separate tablespace what the default storage parameters are. Here is an extension to the definition of the CREATE TABLESPACE statement to cover this:

```
<create tablespace statement> ::=
    CREATE TABLESPACE <tablespace name>
    DATAFILE <file specification>
            [ {,<file specification>}... ]
    [ DEFAULT <storage specification> ]
```

Example 25.8: Create a tablespace called TS_PLAYERS for storing the PLAYERS table.

```
CREATE    TABLESPACE TS_PLAYERS
DATAFILE  'PLAYERS.DAT' SIZE 10M
DEFAULT   STORAGE (INITIAL     20K
                   NEXT        20K
                   MINEXTENTS  2
                   MAXEXTENTS  100
                   PCTINCREASE 0 )
```

The default storage specification does not have to be specified directly with the creating of a tablespace, but can be specified with the ALTER TABLESPACE statement afterwards. Here is an example.

Example 25.9: Define default storage parameters for the TS_TEAMS tablespace.

```
ALTER TABLESPACE TS_TEAMS
DEFAULT  STORAGE (INITIAL     10K
                  NEXT        10K
                  PCTINCREASE 0 )
```

New parameters will only become effective for new tables created in the TS_TEAMS tablespace; they have no effect on those tables already contained in the tablespace.

25.4   Privileges and tablespaces

In Chapter 23 we discussed two forms of the GRANT statement. In this section we describe the third and last form. With the GRANT statement you can specify which tablespaces a particular user may use and also how much physical storage space of the tablespace the user may occupy.

```
<grant statement> ::=
   GRANT   RESOURCE [ ( <size specification> ) ]
   ON      <tablespace name>
   TO      <users>

<size-specification> ::=
   <integer> [ K | M ]

<users> ::=
   PUBLIC | <user> [ {,<user>}... ]
```

Example 25.10: Give John the privilege to create tables in the HUGE tablespace.

```
GRANT   RESOURCE
ON      HUGE
TO      JOHN
```

Example 25.11: Give everyone the privilege to create tables and indexes in the GENERAL tablespace.

```
GRANT   RESOURCE
ON      GENERAL
TO      PUBLIC
```

Example 25.12: Give Kate the privilege to create tables and indexes in the HUGE tablespace. However, the space that the tables and indexes may occupy should not exceed 200 kilobytes.

```
GRANT   RESOURCE (200K)
ON      HUGE
TO      KATE
```

25.5 Clusters

This section deals with *clusters*. Clusters are defined to decrease the execution time of certain SELECT statements, particularly the joins. In a cluster rows of different tables with equal column values, can be stored together. Suppose that we frequently perform joins between the TEAMNO column in the TEAMS table and the TEAMNO column in the MATCHES table. By storing these two tables in a cluster, all rows from the MATCHES table with a particular team number are physically stored close to the row of the TEAMS table with the same team

number. Because rows are physically stored close to each other based on team
numbers, we call TEAMNO the *cluster key*. To make this possible a cluster has to
be created before the two tables are created.

```
<create cluster statement> ::=
    CREATE CLUSTER [ .] <cluster name>
    ( <cluster column> [ {,<cluster column>}... ] )
    [ TABLESPACE <tablespace name> ]
    [ <storage specification> ]

<cluster column> ::=
    <column name> <data type>
```

Example 25.13: Store the TEAMS and MATCHES table in one cluster.

```
CREATE CLUSTER TEAMNRS
        (TEAMNO SMALLINT)
```

In this example TEAMNO is the cluster key.
    Next, we create the two tables:

```
CREATE    TABLE TEAMS
          (TEAMNO      SMALLINT   NOT NULL,
          PLAYERNO     SMALLINT   NOT NULL,
          DIVISION     CHAR(6)    NOT NULL)
CLUSTER   TEAMNRS (TEAMNO)

CREATE    TABLE MATCHES
          (MATCHNO     SMALLINT   NOT NULL,
          TEAMNO       SMALLINT   NOT NULL,
          PALYERNO     SMALLINT   NOT NULL,
          WON          SMALLINT   NOT NULL,
          LOST         SMALLINT   NOT NULL)
CLUSTER   TEAMNRS (TEAMNO)
```

After the definition of the cluster and the tables, you must create an index on
the cluster. The table cannot be filled with rows until this index has been created.
Therefore the following statement is required:

```
CREATE INDEX TEAMNRS_INDEX ON CLUSTER TEAMNRS
```

Clusters are also stored in tablespaces, and can have the same storage parameters
as tables and indexes.

Example 25.14: Create a cluster for storing the player numbers from the PLAY-
ERS and TEAMS table.

```
CREATE CLUSTER PLAYERNO
      (PLAYERNO   SMALLINT)
      TABLESPACE TS_CL_1
      STORAGE (INITIAL       10K
                NEXT         10K
                MINEXTENTS   1
                MAXEXTENTS   100
                PCTINCREASE 20 )
```

The most important advantage of defining a cluster is clear: performance. When a join is processed, Oracle can quickly retrieve the rows that belong together. On the other hand, there are also some disadvantages. In each block only rows with equal cluster values are stored. This means that if a specific cluster value does not appear often, then most of the blocks are largely empty. In this situation clusters will occupy a great deal of storage space. Another disadvantage is that searching for rows in a clustered table takes longer than in a non-clustered table. The reason is that if a non-clustered block has been read into memory, more relevant rows are retrieved.

The specifications of a cluster can be changed with the ALTER CLUSTER statement. The columns on which a cluster has been defined cannot, however, be changed any more. The DROP CLUSTER statement is used to delete a cluster.

```
<drop cluster statement> ::=
    DROP CLUSTER [ <user>. ] <cluster name>
    [ INCLUDING TABLES ]
```

If the INCLUDING TABLES option has not been specified, a cluster can only be deleted if it does not yet contain tables.

25.6 The rowid

In Chapter 20 we described the system variable *ROWID*. Each row of a table has a rowid (row identifier). The rowid is a code (a logical address) reflecting the physical location of the row. This makes the rowid unique within the entire database. A rowid consists of three parts: the file in which the row has been stored, the block within the file and a sequence number of the row within the block. A file is divided into *blocks*. The size of a block depends on the operating system. Typical block sizes vary between 1K, 2K and 4K.

Example 25.15: Give for each row from the PLAYERS table the player number and the rowid.

```
SELECT    PLAYERNO, ROWID
FROM      PLAYERS
```

Possible result:

```
PLAYERNO ROWID
-------- ------------------
       6 00002820.0001.0001
      44 00002820.0002.0001
      83 00002820.0003.0001
       2 00002820.0004.0001
      27 00002820.0005.0001
     104 00002820.0006.0001
       7 00002820.0007.0001
      57 00002820.0008.0001
      39 00002824.0001.0001
     112 00002824.0002.0001
       8 00002824.0003.0001
     100 00002824.0004.0001
      28 00002824.0005.0001
      95 00002824.0006.0001
```

Explanation: The three parts of the rowid are clearly visible. The last four positions indicate the file, the first eight positions indicate the block and positions 10 to 13 form the sequence number of the row within the block. Thus the row containing data on player 6 has been stored in file number 1, block 2820 and the row has sequence number 1 within that block.

In this book we call ROWID a system variable. A better name would probably have been pseudo column, because we are allowed to specify a table name before ROWID. This is not permitted with a 'normal' system variable. Specifying a table name is required when we specify two or more tables in the FROM clause of the SELECT statement. Therefore the following SELECT statement is correct:

```
SELECT    M.ROWID
FROM      PLAYERS P, MATCHES M
WHERE     P.PLAYERNO = M.MATCHNRS
```

Here are a number of examples of questions that can be answered using the ROWID variable.

Example 25.16: How many blocks are in use by the PENALTIES table?

```
SELECT    COUNT(DISTINCT SUBSTR(ROWID,1,8) ||
                         SUBSTR(ROWID,15,4))
FROM      PENALTIES
```

Example 25.17: Give the average number of rows per block in the PLAYERS table.

```
SELECT    COUNT(*) /
          COUNT(DISTINCT SUBSTR(ROWID,1,8) ||
                         SUBSTR(ROWID,15,4))
FROM      PLAYERS
```

Example 25.18: How many blocks are needed to store 10000 rows from the PLAYERS table (we assume that this table contains rows)?

```
SELECT    10000 * COUNT(*) /
          COUNT(DISTINCT SUBSTR(ROWID,1,8) ||
                         SUBSTR(ROWID,15,4))
FROM      PLAYERS
```

Example 25.19: How many files contain rows of the MATCHES table?

```
SELECT    COUNT(DISTINCT SUBSTR(ROWID,15,4))
FROM      MATCHES
```

In Chapter 21 we mentioned that the quickest way to retrieve a row is via a rowid. We did not mean, however, that you should specify the rowid explicitly in the condition, as it is not constant. If Oracle has to physically move a row, because the row is updated, for example, the rowid changes.

25.7 The catalog tables

Seven catalog tables exist for files, tablespaces, extents and clusters. These are TS$, TSQ$, FILE$, SEG$, FET$, UET$ and CLU$ respectively.

The TS$ table contains data on tablespaces. The TS# column is the primary key of this table; NAME and OWNER# form an alternate key.

column name	data type	description
TS#	NUMBER	Unique number of the tablespace
NAME	CHAR	Name of the tablespace
OWNER#	NUMBER	Number of the user who created the tablespace
BLOCKSIZE#	NUMBER	Size of a block in bytes
DFLMINEXT	NUMBER	Value of the default MINEXTENTS parameter
DFLMAXEXT	NUMBER	Value of the default MAXEXTENTS parameter
DFLINIT	NUMBER	Value of the default INITIAL parameter
DFLINCR	NUMBER	Value of the default NEXT parameter
DFLEXTPCT	NUMBER	Value of the default PCTINCREASE parameter

The TSQ$ table contains the privileges granted on tablespaces.

column name	data type	description
TS#	NUMBER	Unique number of the tablespace
USER#	NUMBER	Number of the user to whom the privilege is granted
GRANTOR#	NUMBER	Number of the user who has granted the privilege
BLOCKS	NUMBER	Number of blocks of the tablespace that the user is using currently
MAXBLOCKS	NUMBER	Maximum number of blocks that the user may use from the tablespace

The structure of the FILE$ table is given below. The column FILE# is the primary key of this table.

column name	data type	description
FILE#	NUMBER	Unique number of the file
BLOCKS	NUMBER	Size of the file expressed in blocks of 4K
TS#	NUMBER	Number of the tablespace to which the file belongs. Each file belongs to only one tablespace

Data about segments is recorded in the SEG$ table. For each table, index and cluster there exists a segment. The primary key of this table is formed by the columns FILE# with BLOCK#.

column name	data type	description
FILE#	NUMBER	Number of the file in which the segment is stored
BLOCK#	NUMBER	Number of the first block of the segment
TYPE	NUMBER	Type of segment; 5 is table and 6 is index
TS#	NUMBER	Number of the tablespace (this can also be derived from the FILE$ table)
BLOCKS	NUMBER	Number of block that belongs to the segment
EXTENTS	NUMBER	Number of extents of the segment
INIEXTS	NUMBER	Value of the INITIAL parameter
MINEXTS	NUMBER	Value of the MINEXTENTS parameter
MAXEXTS	NUMBER	Value of the MAXEXTENTS parameter
EXTSIZE	NUMBER	Value of the NEXT parameter
EXTPCT	NUMBER	Value of the PCTINCREASE parameter
USER#	NUMBER	Number of the owner of the segment

The FET$ table contains data about extents not in use, the so-called *free-extents*. After a tablespace has been created, but before data has been stored into it, it consists of only one large free extent whose size is equal to that of the tablespace. The first three columns form the primary key of this table.

column name	data type	description
TS#	NUMBER	Number of the tablespace to which the extent belongs
FILE#	NUMBER	Number of the file to which the extent belongs
BLOCK#	NUMBER	Number of the block where the extent begins
LENGTH	NUMBER	Number of blocks belonging to the extent

The UET$ table contains data about extents that are already in use, the so-called *used-extents*. The first three columns form the primary key of this table.

column name	data type	description
SEGFILE#	NUMBER	Number of the segment to which the extent has been granted
SEGBLOCK#	NUMBER	Number of the first block of the segment to which the extent has been granted
EXT#	NUMBER	Sequence number of the extent within the segment
TS#	NUMBER	Number of the tablespace to which the extent belongs
FILE#	NUMBER	Number of the file to which the extent belongs
BLOCK#	NUMBER	Number of the block where the extent begins
LENGTH	NUMBER	Number of blocks belonging to the extent

Cluster data are registered in the CLU$ table. The OBJ# column is the primary key of this table.

column name	data type	description
OBJ#	NUMBER	Database object number of the cluster
TS#	NUMBER	Number of the tablespace to which the cluster belongs. Each cluster can belong to only one tablespace
FILE#	NUMBER	Number of the file that contains the first segment
COLS	NUMBER	Number of columns on which the cluster is built

26

Distributed databases

An application usually works in conjunction with a particular database. This chapter describes the possibilities Oracle offers for combining and exchanging data from different databases, possibly even stored in separate computer systems.

26.1 What is a distributed database?

Before we look at the SQL statements Oracle supports to access other databases, we will give a short, general explanation of the concept *distributed database* and describe the associated terminology. We will focus our discussion around S. Ceri's definition (Ceri and Pelagatti, 1988):

> *A distributed database is a collection of data which are distributed over different computers of a computer network.*
> *Each site of the network has autonomous processing capability and can perform local applications.*
> *Each site also participates in the execution of at least one global application, which requires accessing data at several sites using a communication subsystem.*

This definition consists of three parts, each of which poses a requirement that a database must meet if it is to carry the title of distributed database.

The first requirement is concerned with the location of the data. We are talking, then, about a distributed database in which the data storage is dispersed among different computer systems. This first requirement is not difficult to satisfy. Multiple databases managed by different database management systems (DBMS) residing on the same computer system can also be referred to as a distributed database. It is, of course, important that multiple computer systems working together for specific applications be connected in a network. This means that if two databases have an application or subject link and are stored on separate, un-networked computer systems, there is no distributed database formed.

The second requirement is concerned with the independence of each *site*. By 'site' this definition refers to a computer system on which a DBMS runs and where the DBMS manages one database. The assumption is that each DBMS is *autonomous*. Each DBMS must be able to function even if some or all of the other DBMSs are not available or operational at that moment. In other words, each DBMS must be in a position to handle the SQL statements of *local applications* autonomously. A local application is one that accesses and uses only data stored locally. The database accessed by a local application is called a *local database* and another database with which a link is made is a *remote database*. In fact, this requirement has to do with the way suppliers implement the concept of a distributed database.

The third requirement is the most important. A database can be called distributed if there is a minimum of one application querying or updating data stored at different sites. In this situation multiple DBMSs must cooperate to process the application logic. We call such an application a *global application*.

Now that we understand what a distributed database is, we can tackle the question of a distributed DBMS.

> *A distributed DBMS is a collection of interconnected, autonomous DBMSs that together manage a distributed database.*

A user of a distributed DBMS should not know whether he or she is working with such a database. In the ideal situation, the fact that data is distributed is completely hidden from users. This is known as *distribution transparency* in the literature. It is comparable to Oracle's concealing of indexes and tablespaces. These objects can be created, but after that are no longer referenced by users. This offers the advantage that the storage structure can be altered without having to change SQL statements in the applications.

26.2   Oracle and distributed databases

In Figure 26.1 we give you an example of how the architecture of a distributed Oracle database might look like. The distributed DBMS consists of three sites, which are mutually coupled with a network. A DBMS runs on each site. Each DBMS has its own database which is accessed by various (local) applications. Along with this, each DBMS has a product installed called *SQL∗Net*. SQL∗Net makes it possible for an Oracle DBMS to communicate with another Oracle DBMS. Which network is used here is made fully transparent by SQL∗Net. On the other hand, an Oracle DBMS can log on to another DBMS via SQL∗Net. This interface software works with various network software including DECnet, LAN

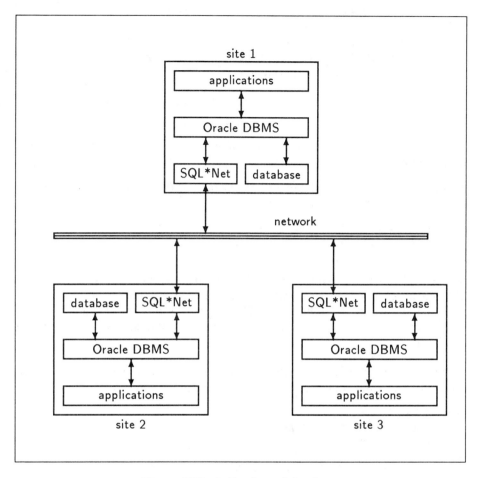

Figure 26.1: A distributed database

Manager, Novell, TCP/IP and VTAM. In this situation only one DBMS runs on each site. However, it does not have to be this way.

Oracle does *not* require all relevant sites to run under the same operating system. In Section 26.7 we describe how non-Oracle DBMSs can be included within a network.

26.3   Setting up a database link

In this section we describe the SQL statements you need to work with remote databases. To access a remote database from a local database you must create a *database link* first.

```
<create database link statement> ::=
   CREATE [ PUBLIC ] DATABASE LINK <database link name>
   [ CONNECT TO <user> IDENTIFIED BY <password> ]
   USING <sqlnet specification>

<sqlnet specification> ::= <alphanumeric constant>
```

The best way to illustrate the workings and benefits of a database link is by giving an example.

Example 26.1: Create a database link called ROME that will enable a user to access a table from a database created in Rome.

```
CREATE DATABASE LINK ROME
USING   'D:ROME-MFG'
```

Explanation: All that Oracle does with this statement is store the specifications in the LINK$ catalog table. We will discuss this table later on in this chapter. The SQL*Net specification D:ROME-MFG defines how the remote database can be accessed and where it can be found. These specifications are dependent on the operating system environment, and we will not take that subject any further in this book.

After the execution of the statement above the user can access each table (if he or she has the privilege) that is stored in the remote database. He or she could, for example, query the PLAYERS table stored in Rome.

```
SELECT  *
FROM    PLAYERS@ROME
WHERE   TOWN = 'Stratford'
```

The FROM clause contains a table specification in a form we have not seen before. Therefore, a complete definition is in order here.

```
<table specification> ::=
   [ <user>. ] <table name> [ @ <database link name> ]
```

When the name of a database link is included in a FROM clause after the table name, Oracle knows that the data is not held locally but in a remote database. The next steps are then executed one after another:

Step 1   Oracle searches the catalog table for a database link called ROME. If there is none an error message is issued.

Step 2   A link via SQL*Net is made to the computer and database indicated in the SQL*Net specification.

Step 3 Then the user is logged on to the appropriate database, having supplied a user-name and password if the database link requires it. If these are not required, the user is logged on with the same user-name as that of the local database.

Step 4 Oracle sends the SELECT statement to the remote database for immediate execution, after which the result is returned to the application.

If a database link is used for a second time in the same session, Steps 1, 2 and 3 are omitted. Note that in Step 4 the result of the SELECT statement is returned and not the whole table; this is a more economical use of the network and takes less time, of course.

Example 26.2: Create a database link with the database in Rome, but use the name JIM and password MIJ.

```
CREATE DATABASE LINK ROME
CONNECT TO JIM
IDENTIFIED BY MIJ
USING  'D:ROME-MFG'
```

The database links we created in the previous examples are private. This means that only the owner can use them. Users with the DBA privilege can create general (PUBLIC) database links for everyone to use.

Example 26.3: Create a database link called GENERAL for everyone to use.

```
CREATE PUBLIC DATABASE LINK GENERAL
USING  'D:ROME-MFG'
```

Tables in different remote databases can be coupled in one statement. There is, however, one restriction. By default, within one statement at most four different database links may be used. This maximum of four is stored in the INIT.ORA file, but can be changed.

Example 26.4: Give, for each penalty, the amount and the name and initials of the player who incurred the penalty.

```
SELECT    P.NAME, P.INITIALS, PN.AMOUNT
FROM      PLAYERS@ROME P,
          PENALTIES@GENERAL PN
WHERE     P.PLAYERNO = PN.PLAYERNO
```

There are some restrictions that apply to queries on remote tables:

- Columns with the LONG data type may not be retrieved from remote databases.

- If the SELECT statement contains a CONNECT BY clause, then the START WITH clause may *not* contain subqueries.

- The functions ROWNUM and USERENV('ENTRYID') may not be used.

It is possible to execute remote updates with UPDATE, INSERT and DELETE statements. With the following UPDATE statement we change the PENALTIES table in Rome.

```
UPDATE    PENALTIES@ROME
SET       AMOUNT = 75.00
WHERE     AMOUNT > 50.00
```

Note: We advise you, however, against the updating of remote tables. This is, because the COMMIT and ROLLBACK statements only have an effect on operations which have been executed on the local database. These statements have no facilities to make a remote update permanent or to request its rollback. This means that it is not clear what will happen with such a remote update.

Database links are stored in the catalog table LINK$. The column NAME is the primary key of this table.

column name	data type	description
OWNER#	NUMBER	Number of the user who created the database link
NAME	CHAR	Name of the database link
CTIME	DATE	Date and time on which the database link was created
HOST	CHAR	SQL*Net specification (also driver string)
USERID	CHAR	Name of the user which is used to log on to the remote database
PASSWORD	CHAR	Password of the user which is used to log on to the remote database

26.4   Making database links transparent

In the statements above you can see clearly that tables belonging to remote databases will be accessed. In the FROM clause this is specified explicitly. This can be made transparent simply with synonyms and views.

Example 26.5: Create a synonym RPLAYERS for the PLAYERS table stored in Rome.

```
CREATE SYNONYM RPLAYERS
FOR    PLAYERS@ROME
```

From now on you can access this table without explicitly indicating that it is remote.

```
SELECT    *
FROM      RPLAYERS
```

Example 26.6: Create a view R_OLD_PLAYERS to include the players born before 1960 from the PLAYERS table stored in Rome.

377

```
CREATE VIEW R_OLD_PLAYERS AS
SELECT *
FROM    PLAYERS@ROME
WHERE   YEAR_OF_BIRTH < 1960
```

Now you can access this view:

```
SELECT   PLAYERNO, YEAR_OF_BIRTH
FROM     R_OLD_PLAYERS
```

26.5 Copying tables

SQL*Plus has a special command for copying tables from one database to another. The definition of this *COPY command* follows.

```
<copy command> ::=
   COPY [ FROM <database> ] [ TO <database> ]
   <copy type> <table specification> [ <column list> ]
   USING <select statement>

<database> ::=
   <user> / <password> @ <database link name>

<copy type> ::=
   APPEND | CREATE | INSERT | REPLACE

<table specification> ::= [ <user> . ] <table name>

<column list> ::=
   ( <column name> [ {,<column name>}... ] )
```

Example 26.7: Copy the entire PLAYERS table to Rome. If the table already exists, replace it with this new version (do not forget the continuation characters at the end of a line, because this is an SQL*Plus command).

```
COPY     TO ROME -
REPLACE  PLAYERS -
USING    SELECT * FROM PLAYERS
```

Example 26.8: Copy from Rome the order numbers and order dates received in the current month. The ORDERS table was created by JOHN. If the ORDERS table already exists locally the rows should be appended to the existing table.

```
COPY     FROM ROME -
APPEND   ORDERS -
USING    SELECT ORDERNO, ORDER_DATE -
         FROM   JOHN.ORDERS -
         WHERE  TO_CHAR(ORDER_DATE, 'YYYYMM') = -
                TO_CHAR(SYSDATE, 'YYYYMM')
```

Note: As we mentioned at the beginning of this section, this COPY command is *not* part of SQL, but of SQL∗Plus. Therefore, it cannot be issued from SQL∗QMX, for instance.

26.6   Deleting database links

The *DROP DATABASE LINK statement* is used to remove a database link from the catalog. It can no longer be used after that.

```
<drop database link statement> ::=
    DROP [ PUBLIC ] DATABASE LINK <database link name>
```

Example 26.9: Remove the database link called ROME.

```
DROP DATABASE LINK ROME
```

26.7   Communicating via a gateway

So far, we have assumed that the remote database is an Oracle database. Oracle, however, can access databases from other suppliers, among which are IBM's DB2 and SQL/DS. These are known as *foreign databases*. They can be joined by using the Oracle product *SQL∗Connect*, which makes the foreign database appear as an Oracle database. A product such as SQL∗Connect is known as a *gateway*; see Figure 26.2.

SQL statements issued by Oracle applications and directed towards a foreign database are transmitted by SQL∗Net. Because of SQL∗Connect, SQL∗Net perceives the foreign database as an Oracle one. So, SQL∗Connect receives the SQL statement and passes it to the foreign DBMS. The foreign DBMS processes the statement and returns the result to SQL∗Connect. In turn, SQL∗Connect sends the result to Oracle via SQL∗Net. The application, therefore, does not know that the answer comes from a non-Oracle database.

Aside: SQL∗Connect is a pathway and performs no language translation activities. SQL statements, therefore, are passed unchanged to the foreign

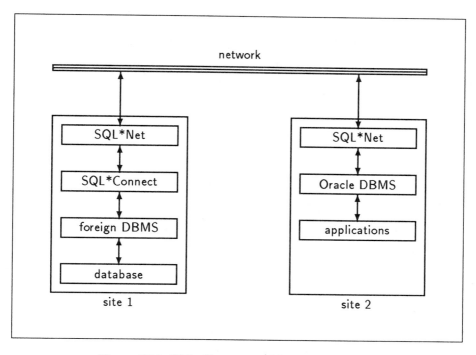

Figure 26.2: SQL∗Connect and foreign databases

DBMS. Nevertheless, Oracle's implementation of SQL differs from other SQL products in a number of ways, so applications issuing SQL statements have to know the SQL dialect of the relevant foreign databases. In Appendix D we show a few differences between Oracle's SQL and that of IBM's DB2. For more details about differences between SQL products see Van der Lans (1990).

27
Catalog tables

A *catalog table* is a table in which Oracle maintains data about the database. All catalog tables collectively are known as the *catalog*. Oracle keeps different types of data in the catalog. This includes which columns occur in which tables, which indexes have been defined, who created the tables or views and so on. All this data is updated by Oracle. Say, for example, a column is added to a table; at this point Oracle automatically updates the catalog to reflect the change. The contents of the catalog, then, are always consistent with the actual contents of the database.

The previous chapters have described the catalog tables more or less independently of one another. This chapter places the emphasis more on the catalog as a whole, and the relationships existing between the tables. We give examples of how to query the catalog using SELECT statements. Section 27.5 covers protection of the catalog.

27.1 Overview of the catalog tables

The following table indicates in which section you can find the description of a catalog table. These are, however, not all the catalog tables. For the remaining tables we refer to the Oracle manuals. SYS is the owner of each catalog table.

Table name	Section	Contents
AUD$	24.5	Audit trail
CCOL$	19.10	Columns belonging to integrity rules
CDEF$	19.10	Integrity rules (constraints)
CLU$	25.7	Clusters
COL$	5.9	Columns
COLAUTH$	23.7	Column privileges
COM$	5.10	Comments
CON$	19.10	Integrity rules
FET$	25.7	Free extents
FILE$	25.7	Physical files
ICOL$	20.4	Columns belonging to indexes
IND$	20.4	Indexes
LINK$	26.3	Database links
OBJ$	5.9	Database objects
SEG$	25.7	Segments
SEQ$	18.5	Sequences
SYN$	5.11	Synonyms
TAB$	5.9	Tables
TABAUTH$	23.7	Table privileges
TS$	25.7	Table spaces
TSQ$	25.7	Table space privileges
UET$	25.7	Extents in use
USER$	23.3	Users
VIEW$	22.4	Views
XREF$	22.4	Tables belonging to views

The mutual dependencies between the catalog tables are shown in Figures 27.1 and 27.2. Boxes are used to indicate tables and the lines indicate the relationships. The column names inside the boxes denote the primary keys of the tables. At each end of a relationship two symbols are drawn. These symbols identify the kind of relationship that exist between the two related tables. As an example we describe the relationship between the tables OBJ$ and TABAUTH$. The circle means that for some database objects no table privileges are granted. The 'crow's foot' shows that for a database object several table privileges can be granted. The small line closest to OBJ$ shows that a table privilege can relate to a *maximum* of one database object. The other line indicates that a table privilege belongs to a *minimum* of one database object.

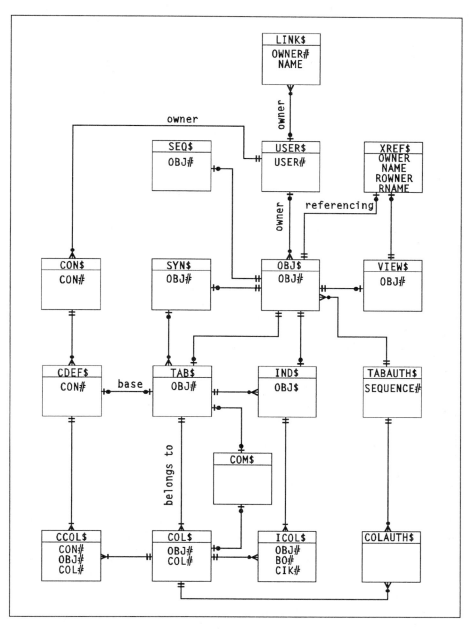

Figure 27.1: Dependences between catalog tables (part 1)

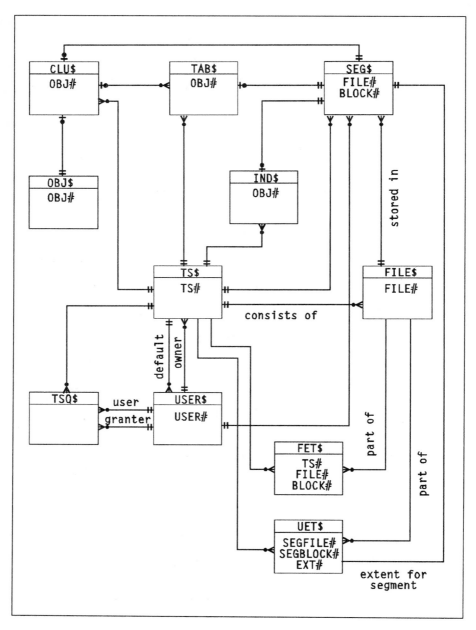

Figure 27.2: Dependences between catalog tables (part 2)

27.2   Querying the catalog tables

Every database management system (DBMS) records data about tables. In other words, every DBMS has a catalog. Otherwise it would be impossible for the system to decide whether a question from a user may, or can, be answered. Not every DBMS makes the catalog available to users, though; such a system is then the only user. Oracle *does* offer the facility to query the catalog. In terms of querying, these tables in Oracle are seen simply as ordinary tables that can be accessed using the SELECT statement. Consulting the catalog has many uses. Here are three of them:

- As a *help function* for new users to determine, for example, which tables there are in the database and what columns exist in these tables.

- As a *control function* for data(base) administrators to see, for example, which indexes, views and privileges would be deleted if a particular table were dropped.

- As a *processing function* for Oracle itself when it executes statements (as a help function for Oracle).

In this section we show examples of SELECT statements using the catalog tables.

Example 27.1: May the user JIM create a table called STOCK or has he already used the name for another table, view, synonym or sequence?

```
SELECT   T.NAME
FROM     SYS.OBJ$ T, SYS.USER$ U
WHERE    T.OWNER# = U.USER#
AND      U.NAME = 'JIM'
```

Explanation: The SELECT statement produces a list of the table names which JIM may not use for a new table.
In some of the following examples we make use of the following view:

```
CREATE   VIEW TABOBJ (OBJ#, UNAME, TNAME) AS
SELECT   T.OBJ#, U.NAME, T.NAME
FROM     SYS.USER$ U, SYS.OBJ$ T
WHERE    U.USER# = T.OWNER#
AND      T.TYPE = 2
```

Explanation: The extra condition T.TYPE = 2 is required to skip all views, synonyms and other kind of database objects from the result.

Example 27.2: Give for each column in the PLAYERS table (created by SQLDBA) the name, the data type, the length and an indication if it is a NULL column.

```
SELECT    C.NAME,
          DECODE(C.TYPE#, 1, 'CHAR',
                          2, 'NUMBER',
                          8, 'LONG',
                          12,'DATE',
                          23,'RAW',
                          24,'LONG RAW'),
          C.LENGTH,
          DECODE(C.NULL$, 0, 'Nulls perm.', '---')
FROM      TABOBJ T, SYS.COL$ C
WHERE     T.OBJ# = C.OBJ#
AND       T.UNAME = 'SQLDBA'
AND       T.TNAME = 'PLAYERS'
```

Result:

```
C.NAME           DECODE(   C.LENGTH  C.NULL$
-------------    -------   --------  -----------
PLAYERNO         NUMBER          22  ---
NAME             CHAR            15  ---
INITIALS         CHAR             3  ---
YEAR_OF_BIRTH    NUMBER          22  Nulls perm.
SEX              CHAR             1  ---
YEAR_JOINED      NUMBER          22  ---
STREET           CHAR            15  ---
HOUSENO          CHAR             4  Nulls perm.
POSTCODE         CHAR             6  Nulls perm.
TOWN             CHAR            10  ---
TELEPHONE        CHAR            10  Nulls perm.
LEAGUENO         CHAR             4  Nulls perm.
```

Example 27.3: Which views are based on more than one base table?

```
SELECT    OWNER, NAME
FROM      SYS.XREF$
GROUP BY  OWNER, NAME
HAVING    COUNT(*) >= 2
```

Explanation: If a particular view appears twice or more in the SYS.XREF$ table it implies that it is based on more than one base table.

Example 27.4: Which base table has no UNIQUE index defined (that is, which table has no primary key defined)?

```
SELECT   UNAME, TNAME
FROM     TABOBJ
WHERE    OBJ# NOT IN
         (SELECT   BO#
         FROM      SYS.IND$
         WHERE     UNIQUE$ = 1)
```

Example 27.5: Give the name of each user who may insert new rows into the PLAYERS table (which has been created by SQLDBA).

```
SELECT   NAME
FROM     SYS.USER$
WHERE    USER# IN
         (SELECT   A.GRANTEE#
         FROM      SYS.TABAUTH$ A, SYS.OBJ$ T, SYS.USER$ U
         WHERE     A.OBJ# = T.OBJ#
         AND       T.OWNER# = U.USER#
         AND       U.NAME = 'SQLDBA'
         AND       T.NAME = 'PLAYERS'
         AND       A.INSERT$ IN (2, 3))
OR       DBA$ = 1
OR       USER# =
         (SELECT   T.OWNER#
         FROM      SYS.OBJ$ T, SYS.USER$ U
         WHERE     T.OWNER# = U.USER#
         AND       U.NAME = 'SQLDBA'
         AND       T.NAME = 'PLAYERS')
```

Explanation: Three sorts of users may insert new rows into a table. First of all, each user with INSERT privilege on the table may insert rows (covered by the first subquery). Second, each user with DBA privilege may insert rows to the table, because such a user has access to all tables (covered by DBA$ = 1). Third, the owner of the PLAYERS table may insert rows himself (covered by the second subquery).

Example 27.6: Give the owner, the name and the number of indexes for each table.

```
SELECT   U.NAME, T.NAME, COUNT(I.BO#)
FROM     SYS.OBJ$ T, SYS.USER$ U, SYS.IND$ I
WHERE    T.OWNER# = U.USER#(+)
AND      T.OBJ# = I.BO#(+)
AND      T.TYPE = 2
GROUP BY U.NAME, T.NAME
```

Explanation: The outer join is necessary, because we do not want to lose those tables on which no index has been defined. In this case the number printed is zero.

Example 27.7: Give the names and owners of the synonyms that have been created on tables that do not exist anymore.

```
SELECT    U.NAME, O.NAME
FROM      SYS.USER$ U, SYS.OBJ$ O, SYS.SYN$ S
WHERE     U.USER# = O.OWNER#
AND       O.OBJ# = S.OBJ#
AND       (S.OWNER, S.NAME) NOT IN
          (SELECT   UNAME, TNAME
          FROM      TABOBJ)
```

Explanation: The subquery searches for the existing tables (names and owners). The main query searches for all synonyms that have been defined on a table that does not appear in the list of existing tables.

Example 27.8: Give the name and the type of every integrity rule that has been defined on the PLAYERS table.

```
SELECT    C1.NAME,
          DECODE(C2.TYPE, 1, 'row integrity rule',
                          2, 'primary key',
                          3, 'alternate key',
                          4, 'foreign key',
                          5, 'view integrity rule')
FROM      SYS.CON$ C1, SYS.CDEF$ C2, TABOBJ T
WHERE     C1.CON# = C2.CON#
AND       C2.OBJ# = T.OBJ#
AND       T.UNAME = 'SQLDBA'
AND       T.TNAME = 'PLAYERS'
```

Example 27.9: Give per tablespace the reserved amount of storage space in blocks and in bytes.

```
SELECT    U.NAME, TS.NAME, SUM(F.BLOCKS),
          SUM(F.BLOCKS * TS.BLOCKSIZE)
FROM      SYS.TS$ TS, SYS.FILE$ F, SYS.USER$ U
WHERE     TS.TS# = F.TS#
AND       TS.OWNER# = U.USER#
GROUP BY U.NAME, TS.NAME
```

Example 27.10: Give per tablespace the amount of available empty storage space in blocks.

```
SELECT    U.NAME, TS.NAME, SUM(F.LENGTH)
FROM      SYS.TS$ TS, SYS.USER$ U, SYS.FET$ F
WHERE     TS.OWNER# = U.USER#
AND       TS.TS# = F.TS#
GROUP BY U.NAME, TS.NAME
```

Example 27.11: Give per tablespace the amount of storage space, in blocks, that is already in use.

```
SELECT    U.NAME, TS.NAME, SUM(UET.LENGTH)
FROM      SYS.TS$ TS, SYS.USER$ U, SYS.UET$ UET
WHERE     TS.OWNER# = U.USER#
AND       TS.TS# = UET.TS#
GROUP BY U.NAME, TS.NAME
```

Example 27.12: How much storage space is still free in the entire database?

```
SELECT    SUM(F.LENGTH * TS.BLOCKSIZE)
FROM      SYS.TS$ TS, SYS.FET$ F
WHERE     TS.TS# = F.TS#
```

Exercises

27.1 How many indexes has JAKE defined on the PLAYERS table (created by SQLDBA)?

27.2 Give the view formula of the views defined on the PLAYERS table (created by JAKE).

27.3 Give the names of the indexes that have been created by users who are the owners of the tables on which these indexes have been defined.

27.3 Generating SQL statements

It is possible to generate SQL statements from SQL*Plus by using SELECT statements on the catalog. We give you some examples in this section. We will use some SQL*Plus statements which we have not described in Chapter 2.

Example 27.13: Create DROP TABLE statements for all tables created by the user SQLDBA.

We work this example out step by step. The following SELECT statement shows the names of all the SQLDBA tables.

```
SELECT    TNAME
FROM      TABOBJ
WHERE     UNAME = 'SQLDBA'
```

If we extend the SELECT clause of this statement as follows:

```
SELECT    'DROP TABLE ' || RTRIM(TNAME) || ';'
```

then the following result appears:

```
DROP TABLE || RTRIM(TNAM
--------------------------
DROP TABLE PLAYERS ;
DROP TABLE TEAMS ;
DROP TABLE MATCHES ;
DROP TABLE PENALTIES ;
```

We execute the following four SQL*Plus statements before this SELECT statement:

```
SET HEADING OFF
SET PAGESIZE 9999
SET FEEDBACK OFF
SPOOL DROPTAB.SQL
```

The effect of the first statement is that printing of the headings above the columns in the result of a SELECT statement is suppressed. After printing a number of lines from the result of a SELECT statement, SQL*Plus automatically adds some blank lines. With the second statement we indicate that that should happen after 9999 lines. At the end of the result SQL*Plus shows a message saying how many lines have been printed. This can also be suppressed by using the third statement. With the fourth statement we ensure that the result of the SELECT statement is written (spooled) to a separate file with the name DROPTAB.SQL. Because of the first three statements the result consists of only the following four lines.

```
DROP TABLE PLAYERS ;
DROP TABLE TEAMS ;
DROP TABLE MATCHES ;
DROP TABLE PENALTIES ;
```

Finally, we have to execute the following SQL*Plus statement after the SELECT statement.

```
SPOOL OFF
```

The effect of this statement is that writing to the new DROPTAB.SQL file is stopped. The file is now ready to be executed itself with the START statement of SQL*Plus. We have described this command in Chapter 2.

Example 27.14: Generate all CREATE TABLE statements for the tables created by SQLDBA.

First we define a view and next a SELECT statement on this view.

```
CREATE   VIEW COLUMNS
         (TABLE_NAME, NUMBER_COLUMNS, COLUMN_NAME, COLUMNNO,
         COL_TYPE, LENGTH, PRECISION, SCALE, NULLS) AS
         :
```

```
               :
SELECT    T.TNAME, T.COLS, C.NAME, C.COL#,
          DECODE(C.TYPE#, 1, 'CHAR',
                          2, 'NUMBER',
                          8, 'LONG',
                          12,'DATE',
                          23,'RAW',
                          24,'LONG RAW'),
          C.LENGTH, NVL(PRECISION, 0), NVL(C.SCALE, 0),
          DECODE(C.NULL$, 0, 'NULL', 'NOT NULL')
FROM      TABOBJ T, SYS.COL$ C
WHERE     T.OBJ# = C.OBJ#
AND       T.UNAME = 'SQLDBA'
```

The SELECT statement:

```
SELECT    DECODE(COLUMNNO, 1, 'CREATE TABLE ' ||
                              TABLE_NAME || '(', ''),
          COLUMN_NAME, COL_TYPE,
          DECODE(COL_TYPE,
             'CHAR'  ,'(' || LENGTH || ')',
             'NUMBER','(' || PRECISION || ',' || SCALE || ')',
             'RAW'   ,'(' || LENGTH || ')', ''), NULLS,
          DECODE(COLUMNNO, NUMBER_COLUMNS, ' );', ',')
FROM      COLUMNS
```

The results of this statement are ordinary CREATE TABLE statements.

27.4   Standard views of Oracle

During the installation of Oracle a large number of views on the catalog tables are created. In Oracle's manuals these are called *data dictionary views*. These views are created with SYSTEM as owner. The purpose of these views is to simplify the use of the catalog tables. Appendix E of the Oracle manual *Database Administrator's Guide* describes all these views.

    The names of data dictionary views are constructed according to a particular pattern. A view whose name begins with the word USER contains only objects created by the user who enters the statement. If the name begins with ALL, the view contains all objects the user has access to; so this is a larger collection than with USER. Finally, a view which name begins with DBA contains a list of all objects.

    In spite of the fact that we have described the real catalog tables in this book, we advise you, nevertheless, to make use of these pre-defined views as much as possible or to make views yourself. The structure of the catalog tables is liable to change. In the next version of Oracle it is possible that the tables will look quite different. This has already happened before: the catalog structure of Version 6 differs completely from that of the previous version.

27.5 Protecting the catalog tables

Within each database a network of privileges should be set up using the GRANT statement. This network serves to protect the users' data in the tables and the catalog tables themselves, as they contain important information that certainly should not be available to everyone. Average users ought not, for example, to have access to the USER$ table which records all the names and passwords. If they could see this information, the entire security and authorization mechanism (built up by the GRANT statements) would become worthless. Malevolent users could very easily corrupt important data.

Below we show how easily access to the catalog tables can be protected.

Example 27.15: In the database of the tennis club no users can directly access the catalog tables. They may see only the data related to the tables created by themselves and the columns belonging to those tables.

First we create two views, the TABLES view and the COLUMNS view. The TABLES view contains the name and the description for each table. The COLUMNS view contains most of the columns from the SYS.COL$ table.

```
CREATE   VIEW TABLES AS
SELECT   DISTINCT T.NAME, C.COMMENT$
FROM     SYS.OBJ$ T, SYS.USER$ U, SYS.COM$ C
WHERE    T.OWNER# = U.USER# (+)
AND      T.OBJ# = C.OBJ# (+)
AND      U.NAME = USER

CREATE   VIEW COLUMNS AS
SELECT   DISTINCT T.NAME, C.NAME, C.TYPE#,
         C.LENGTH$, C.NULL$, COM.COMMENT$
FROM     SYS.COL$ C, SYS.OBJ$ T, SYS.USER$ U,
         SYS.COM$ COM
WHERE    T.OBJ# = C.OBJ#(+)
AND      T.OWNER# = U.USER#(+)
AND      T.OBJ# = COM.OBJ#(+)
AND      U.NAME(+) = USER
AND      T.TYPE = 2
AND      COM.COL# IS NULL
```

Two GRANT statements are used to grant the privileges:

```
GRANT    SELECT
ON       TABLES
TO       PUBLIC
```

```
GRANT    SELECT
ON       COLUMNS
TO       PUBLIC
```

By using the system variable USER in the view formulae (see Chapter 6 for an explanation of this), and by granting the privilege to PUBLIC, the intended authorization structure is created. For each user, the virtual contents of the two views are different. Anyone who starts Oracle and queries the TABLES or COLUMNS view sees only the data about tables and columns for which he or she has a privilege. One advantage of this design is that if existing privileges or tables change, the TABLES and COLUMNS views automatically accommodate the new situation.

Of course, the described privilege structure is not the best for all situations. But it can be used as a basis for a more complex design.

28

Introduction to embedded SQL

SQL can be used in two ways: *interactively* (that is, at a terminal) and *embedded* (in a program). The previous chapters have more or less always assumed the former use. Interactive means that statements are processed as soon as they are entered, whereas with embedded SQL, statements are included in a program which has been written in another programming language. Oracle supports amongst others the languages C, FORTRAN, COBOL, PL/I and Pascal. These languages are known as *host languages*. The results of the embedded SQL statements are not immediately visible to the user, but are processed by the *enveloping* program.

Embedded SQL is used primarily in programs developed for users who need not learn the SQL language, but who instead work with data via menus and forms displayed on screens.

Most of the SQL statements discussed in the earlier chapters can be used in embedded SQL. Apart from a few minor additions, embedded SQL is the same as interactive SQL. This chapter describes, with the help of a number of examples, statements in their embedded SQL environment. The host language used is not an existing programming language, but a *pseudo programming language*. This approach has been chosen in order to avoid getting buried in all sorts of details that have nothing to do with the combination of a host language and embedded SQL. Also, differences of detail between the host language do not have to be contended with; our primary concern is to give a picture of the principles of embedded SQL.

This chapter is certainly not a complete description of the features of embedded SQL. It is, as the title says, an introduction. We strongly advise those who want to develop programs with embedded SQL to study the Oracle manuals carefully.

28.1   The pseudo programming language

Before we begin with the examples of embedded SQL, we need to outline a few points about the pseudo programming language that we will use.

- In a normal programming language each SQL statement has to start with EXEC SQL. We will omit this in our examples.

- In a normal programming language each SQL statement has to end with END-SQL (COBOL) or a semi-colon (C, PL/I or Pascal). We will use the semi-colon in our examples.

- Everything on a line that follows #, is considered comment.

- All the variables used, must be declared at the beginning of a program; a data type is assigned to the variable. Therefore we use the Oracle data types; see Chapter 5.

- We end every statement with a semi-colon.

28.2   Simple examples

The inclusion of DDL and DCL statements, like CREATE TABLE and GRANT, in a program is simple. There is no difference between the functions and the syntax of these two types of statements for interactive or embedded use.

Example 28.1: Develop a program that creates or drops the index on the PLAY-ERS table, depending on what choice the user makes.

```
PROGRAM PLAYERS_INDEX;
DECLARATIONS
   choice : CHAR(1);
BEGIN
   WRITE 'Do you want to create (C) or drop (D) the PLAY index?';
   READ choice;
   # Dependent on choice, create or drop the index
   IF choice = 'C' THEN
      CREATE UNIQUE INDEX PLAY ON PLAYERS (PLAYERNO);
      WRITE 'Index PLAY is created!';
   ELSE IF choice = 'D' THEN
      DROP INDEX PLAY;
      WRITE 'Index PLAY is dropped!';
   ELSE
      WRITE 'Unknown choice!';
   ENDIF;
END
```

Result:

```
Do you want to create (C) or drop (D) the PLAY index? C
Index PLAY is created!
```

Explanation: You can see from this program that the embedded SQL statement is the same as its interactive counterpart. There is a semi-colon following each SQL statement, which has not been included in any of the previous chapters. This is because we have been stressing the SQL statements themselves, and not how they should be entered.

Example 28.2: Develop a program that grants the SELECT privilege to PUBLIC on the four tables from the sample database.

```
PROGRAM GRANT;
:
GRANT SELECT ON PLAYERS   TO PUBLIC;
GRANT SELECT ON TEAMS     TO PUBLIC;
GRANT SELECT ON MATCHES   TO PUBLIC;
GRANT SELECT ON PENALTIES TO PUBLIC;
WRITE 'Ready!';
:
```

SQL supports three statements for changing the data in tables: DELETE, INSERT and UPDATE. These statements are included in a program in the same way as DDL and DCL statements.

Example 28.3: Develop a program that deletes all rows from the PENALTIES table.

```
PROGRAM DELETE_PENALTIES;
DECLARATIONS
   choice : CHAR(1);
BEGIN
   WRITE 'Delete all rows from the PENALTIES table (Y/N)?';
   READ choice;
   # Determine what the answer is.
   IF choice = 'Y' THEN
      DELETE FROM PENALTIES;
      WRITE 'All rows are deleted!';
   ELSE
      WRITE 'The rows are not deleted!';
   ENDIF;
END
```

28.3   Using variables in SQL statements

In the next example we show you that in those SQL statements where expressions may be used, such as SELECT and UPDATE, variables can also be specified (see

Chapter 6).

Example 28.4: Develop a program that increases the number of sets won by one for a given match.

```
PROGRAM RAISE_WON;
DECLARATIONS
    mno : SMALLINT;
BEGIN
    WRITE 'Enter the match number: '
    READ mno;
    # Increase the number of sets won
    UPDATE    MATCHES
    SET       WON = WON + 1
    WHERE     MATCHNO = :mno;
    WRITE 'Ready!';
END
```

Explanation: In the WHERE clause we use the variable MNO at a place where we would otherwise use a literal, column specification or expression. This is allowed in embedded SQL. To differentiate variables from columns, functions, etc., you must specify a colon in front of it.

A variable that is used within SQL statements must be specified according to precise rules. These rules are dependent on the column with which the variable is compared. Each host language has its own rules. For example, the MNO variable must have a data type which can be compared with the data type of the MATCHNO column, because that is the column with which it is being compared. Again, we refer to the manuals for these rules. We will be content, as previously mentioned, with the specification of the Oracle data types.

Example 28.5: Develop a program for entering data about a penalty.

```
PROGRAM ENTER_PENALTIES;
DECLARATIONS
    pno    : SMALLINT;
    payno  : SMALLINT;
    date   : DATE;
    amount : DECIMAL(7,2);
BEGIN
    READ payno;
    READ pno;
    READ date;
    READ amount;
    # Add the new data to the PENALTIES table
    INSERT  INTO PENALTIES
            (PAYMENTNO, PLAYERNO, PEN_DATE, AMOUNT)
    VALUES (:payno, :pno, :date, :amount);
    WRITE 'Ready!';
END
```

Explanation: After reading in the values, the program enters them into the table with the INSERT statement.

When working with a real programming language, you are required to place the following statements around the declarations of the variables that are used within SQL statements:

```
BEGIN DECLARE SECTION
```

and

```
END DECLARE SECTION
```

An example of this is given in Section 28.15.

28.4   The SQLCODE variable

The RAISE_WON program from the previous section used an UPDATE statement to increase the value in the WON column by one. But how do we know if this increase has actually taken place? Perhaps there was no row in the MATCHES table corresponding to the match number entered. We can test for this using the value in the *SQLCODE variable*. SQLCODE is a variable to which a given value is attributed by Oracle after any SQL statement, not just after DML statements. If the value of SQLCODE equals zero, it means that the SQL statement has executed correctly. If its value is negative, it means that something has gone wrong. A positive value of SQLCODE indicates a warning. The value 100, for example, means that no rows have been found.

Example 28.6: We extend the RAISE_WON program to include a test on SQL-CODE.

```
PROGRAM RAISE_WON_2;
DECLARATIONS
   mno : SMALLINT;
BEGIN
   WRITE 'Enter the match number: ';
   READ mno;
   # Increase the number of sets won
   UPDATE   MATCHES
   SET      WON = WON + 1
   WHERE    MATCHNO = :mno;
   # Determine if it has executed successfully
   IF sqlcode > 0 THEN
      WRITE 'Update has occurred';
   ELSE
      WRITE 'The team entered does not exist.';
   ENDIF;
END
```

Perhaps you noticed that we have forgotten to declare the SQLCODE variable in this program. We do not declare this special variable in the usual way, but instead use a special statement, the *INCLUDE statement*. This will make the beginning of the program above look as follows:

```
PROGRAM RAISE_WON_2;
DECLARATIONS
   mno : SMALLINT;
   INCLUDE SQLCA;
BEGIN
   WRITE 'Enter the match number: ';
   :
```

Explanation: The effect of this INCLUDE statement is that a file called *SQLCA* is read in. In the file SQLCODE has been declared in the correct way. This prevents errors. The most important reason for declaring SQLCODE in this way is that Oracle supports more special variables. By using this statement, they are all declared at the same time.

In almost all the example programs we test the value of the SQLCODE variable after an SQL statement. We conclude this section with two remarks on this variable.

- In the Oracle manual *Error Messages and Codes*, all values that Oracle can generate are mentioned and described. We advise you never to test on these codes explicitly. These codes can change in new versions and it is always difficult to determine all the possible codes that may be returned.

- Try to develop a procedure, function or routine that hides and encapsulates the SQLCODE completely. Beside the fact that this is a cleaner way of programming, SQLCODE is described in the international ISO standard a *deprecated feature*. This means that it will disappear from the standard in a subsequent version.

28.5 Logging on to Oracle

Just as a user-name and a password must be given when you start SQL*Plus to let Oracle know who you are, this should also happen with embedded SQL. We use the *CONNECT statement* to do this.

```
<connect statement> ::=
   CONNECT <user password>
   [ USING <sqlnet specification> ]

<user password> ::=
   <variable> |
   <variable> IDENTIFIED BY <variable>

<sqlnet specification> ::= <alphanumeric literal>
```

Example 28.7: Develop a program that logs on to Oracle and reports whether this has succeeded or not.

```
PROGRAM LOGIN;
DECLARATIONS
    user     : CHAR(30);
    password : CHAR(30);
BEGIN
    WRITE 'What is your name?';
    READ user;
    WRITE 'What is your password?';
    READ password;
    CONNECT TO :user IDENTIFIED BY :password;
    IF sqlcode = 0 THEN
       WRITE 'Logging on has succeeded';
    ELSE
       WRITE 'Logging on has not succeeded';
       WRITE 'Reason: ', sqlcode;
    ENDIF;
END
```

Explanation: If Oracle rejects the CONNECT statement, then SQLCODE has a negative value. The CONNECT statement used in this example can be replaced by the following:

```
CONNECT :user
```

In this situation the value of the USER variable must contain the name of the user and his or her password separated by a slash. If the value of USER is only a slash, an automatic log on is performed; see Section 23.3.

Chapter 26 has described how database links must be defined. In the definition of a database link a so-called SQL*Net specification is given. When you log on with the CONNECT statement the same type of specification can be given. In this case the program logs on to a remote database. All the statements in the program are then processed by the remote database.

In fact, the first SQL statement that is processed in a program should always be a CONNECT statement. The reason is that Oracle rejects all the SQL statements as long as the application has not logged on properly. So all the previous examples are, in fact, not correct, because they do not contain a CONNECT statement. But we will continue with this and omit the CONNECT statement from all the examples. We do this to avoid making the programs too large and too complex.

Note: The CONNECT command that we have described in Chapter 2 is transformed by SQL*Plus into an SQL CONNECT statement. So, the use of this statement and command is equivalent.

28.6   SELECT statements with one row

In many cases you will want to capture the result of a SELECT statement in the program. This can be done by saving the result in variables. Here, we need to distinguish between SELECT statements which always return one row, and those whose result consists of an indeterminate number of rows. The former type is described in this section and Section 28.8 will discuss the latter.

Embedded SQL supports a variant on the SELECT statement intended for those statements whose result table consists of one row. A new clause is added to these SELECT statements: the *INTO clause*. In the clause of this statement we specify one variable for each expression in the SELECT clause. These types of statements are known as *SELECT INTO statements*. The reason for differentiating them from 'normal' SELECT statements is that, apart from the new INTO clause, they produce only one row and the use of an ORDER BY clause is not permitted.

```
<select into statement> ::=
   <select clause>
   <into clause>
   <from clause>
   [ <where clause> ]
   [ <connect by clause> ]
   [ <group by clause>
   [ <having clause> ] ]

<into clause> ::=
   INTO <variable> [ {,<variable>}... ]

<variable> ::=
   ":" <variable name>
```

Example 28.8: Develop a program that prints a player's address data line by line, after a particular player number is entered.

```
PROGRAM ADDRESS;
DECLARATIONS
    pno      : SMALLINT;
    name     : CHAR(15);
    init     : CHAR(3);
    street   : CHAR(15);
    houseno  : CHAR(4);
    town     : CHAR(10);
    postcode : CHAR(6);
BEGIN
    WRITE 'Enter the player number: ';
    READ pno;
    # Search for address data
    SELECT   NAME, INITIALS, HOUSENO,
             STREET, TOWN, POSTCODE
    INTO     :name, :init, :street,
             :houseno, :town, :postcode
    FROM     PLAYERS
    WHERE    PLAYERNO = :pno;
    IF sqlcode > 0 THEN
       # Present address data
       WRITE 'Player number :', pno;
       WRITE 'Initials      :', init;
       WRITE 'Surname       :', name;
       WRITE 'Street        :', houseno, ' ', street;
       WRITE 'Town          :', town;
       WRITE 'Postcode      :', postcode;
    ELSE
       WRITE 'There is no player with number ', pno;
    ENDIF;
END
```

Result:

```
Enter the player number :27

Player number :27
Surname      :Collins
Initials     :DD
Street       :804 Long Drive
Town         :Eltham
Postcode     :8457DK

Enter the player number :112

Player number :112
Surname      :Bailey
Initials     :IP
Street       :8 Vixen Road
Town         :Plymouth
Postcode     :6392LK
```

Explanation: The SELECT statement retrieves the data about the player whose number has been entered. The value of the expressions from the SELECT clause are stored in the variables that have been specified in the INTO clause. This SELECT statement can return a maximum of one row, because the PLAYER-NO column is the primary key of the PLAYERS table. By using the SQLCODE variable we can test whether the player number indeed appears in the table.

Example 28.9: Develop a program which prints the number of players who live in a given town which is entered by the user.

```
PROGRAM NUMBER_PLAYERS;
DECLARATIONS
    pnumber : INTEGER;
    town    : CHAR(10);
BEGIN
    WRITE 'Enter the town: ';
    READ town;
    # Determine the number of players
    SELECT   COUNT(*)
    INTO     :pnumber
    FROM     PLAYERS
    WHERE    TOWN = :town;
    IF sqlcode <> 0 THEN
        pnumber := 0;
    ENDIF;
    WRITE pnumber, ' players live in ', town;
END
```

Example 28.10: With the ENTER_PENALTIES program from Section 28.3, the users have to enter a payment number themselves. Of course, we can let the program itself decide on the next payment number using a SELECT statement.

```
PROGRAM ENTER_PENALTIES_2;
DECLARATIONS
    pno    : SMALLINT;
    payno  : SMALLINT;
    date   : DATE;
    amount : DECIMAL(7,2);
BEGIN
    # Have the user enter the data
    READ pno;
    READ date;
    READ amount;
    # Determine the highest payment number already entered
    SELECT   NVL(MAX(PAYMENTNO),0) + 1
    INTO     :payno
    FROM     PENALTIES;
    :
```

```
      :
    # Add the new data to the PENALTIES table
    INSERT  INTO PENALTIES
            (PAYMENTNO, PLAYERNO, PEN_DATE, AMOUNT)
    VALUES (:payno, :pno, :date, :amount);
    WRITE 'Ready!';
END
```

Explanation: The SELECT statement finds the highest payment number in the table and adds one to it. This becomes the new payment number.

Note: Beware of using SELECT * with embedded SQL! Such a SELECT clause returns all columns from a given table. It still holds that a variable has to be specified for every column in the INTO clause. The number of columns in a table can increase, though, with the ALTER TABLE statement. If this happens, the SELECT statement will no longer work, because there will not be enough variables available in the INTO clause. So, avoid the * in SELECT clauses in this embedded SQL environment.

28.7 The NULL indicator

The result of a SELECT INTO statement can contain a NULL value. If this is possible, then the NULL value must be intercepted. We accomplish this by using so-called *NULL indicators*.

Example 28.11: Give the league number of player 27.

```
PROGRAM GET_LEAGUENO;
DECLARATIONS
    leagueno      : CHAR(4);
    null_leagueno : INTEGER;
BEGIN
    SELECT    LEAGUENO
    INTO      :leagueno:null_leagueno
    FROM      PLAYERS
    WHERE     PLAYERNO = 27;
    IF sqlcode = 0 THEN
       IF null_leagueno = 0 THEN
          WRITE 'The league number is ', leagueno;
       ELSE
          WRITE 'Player 27 has no league number';
       ENDIF;
    ELSE
       WRITE 'Player 27 does not exist';
    ENDIF;
END
```

Explanation: The INTO clause in the SELECT statement contains something that we have not seen so far. After the LEAGUENO variable another variable

is specified: NULL_LEAGUENO. If the result of the SELECT INTO statement
equals the NULL value, a value is not assigned to the LEAGUENO variable, but
NULL_LEAGUENO is made negative or zero. The NULL_LEAGUENO variable is called a *NULL indicator*. If an expression in a SELECT clause can return
a NULL value, then the use of such a NULL indicator is required. If you do not
do this in this program, and an expression returns NULL, then a negative value
is assigned to SQLCODE. The program will then say (incorrectly) that player 27
does not exist.

The use of NULL indicators is not restricted to the SELECT statement.
They may be specified, for example, in the SET clause of the UPDATE statement:

```
UPDATE    PLAYERS
SET       LEAGUENO = :leagueno:null_leagueno
WHERE     ...
```

Explanation: If the value of the indicator NULL_LEAGUENO equals zero, the
LEAGUENO column will get the value of the variable LEAGUENO; otherwise
it is set to NULL.

28.8   SELECT statements with multiple rows

SELECT INTO statements return only one row with values. SELECT statements
which *can* return more than one row require a different approach. We will give
an example and work through it in detail afterwards. But try to understand the
program yourself before reading the explanation.

Example 28.12: Develop a program that gives an ordered list of all player numbers and surnames. For each row, print a row number alongside.

```
PROGRAM ALL_PLAYERS;
DECLARATIONS
    pno   : SMALLINT;
    pname : CHAR(15);
    rowno : INTEGER;
BEGIN
    # Cursor declaration
    DECLARE cplayers CURSOR FOR
        SELECT   PLAYERNO, NAME
        FROM     PLAYERS
        ORDER BY PLAYERNO;
    # Print a report heading
    WRITE 'ROWNO  PLAYER NUMBER  SURNAME';
    WRITE '=====  =============  =========';
    :
```

```
      :
      # Start the SELECT statement
      OPEN cplayers;
      # Look for the first player
      rowno := 0;
      FETCH cplayers INTO :pno, :pname;
      WHILE sqlcode = 0 DO
         rowno := row + 1;
         WRITE rowno, pno, pname;
         # Look for the next player
         FETCH cplayers INTO :pno, :pname;
      ENDWHILE;
      CLOSE cplayers;
   END
```

Result:

ROWNO	PLAYER NUMBER	SURNAME
1	2	Everett
2	6	Parmenter
3	7	Wise
4	8	Newcastle
5	27	Collins
6	28	Collins
7	39	Bishop
8	44	Baker
9	57	Brown
10	83	Hope
11	95	Milleran
12	100	Parmenter
13	104	Moorman
14	112	Bailey

The *DECLARE statement* is used to declare a SELECT statement. In some senses this is comparable to declaring variables. The declaration of the SELECT statement defines a *cursor*, in this example called *cplayers*. Now, via the cursor name we can refer to the SELECT statement in other statements. It will become clear later why we call this a cursor. Note that even though the cursor has been declared, the SELECT statement is not yet processed at that point.

The cursor name, cplayers, is mentioned again in the *OPEN statement*. The OPEN statement executes the SELECT statement that is associated with the cursor. When the OPEN statement has executed, the result of the SELECT statement becomes available. Oracle stores this result, probably in the internal memory, and it is still invisible to the program.

The *FETCH statement* is used to step through and process the rows in the result of the SELECT statement one by one. In other words, we use the FETCH statement to render the result visible. The first FETCH statement that is processed retrieves the first row, the second FETCH the second row, and so on. Because we are stepping through the result table row by row, and there is always one row available for processing, these are called cursors. The values of the retrieved rows are assigned to the variables. In our example, these are the PNO and PNAME variables. Note that a FETCH statement can only be used once a cursor has been opened (with an OPEN statement). In the program we step through all rows of the result with a WHILE DO statement. When the FETCH statement has retrieved the last row, the following FETCH statement triggers the SQLCODE variable to be set to 100 (the code for 'no row found' or end-of-file).

The *CLOSE statement* closes the cursor again and the result of the SELECT statement ceases to be available.

Let us have a closer look at the four statements.

```
<declare statement> ::=
    DECLARE <cursor name> CURSOR FOR
    <query expression>
    [ <order by clause> | <for update clause> ]

<query expression> ::=
    <select block> |
    <query expression> <set operator> <query expression> |
    ( <query expression> )

<select block> ::=
        <select clause>
        <from clause>
    [ <where clause> ]
    [ <connect by clause> ]
    [ <group by clause>
    [ <having clause> ] ]

<set operator> ::= UNION | INTERSECT | MINUS

<for update clause> ::=
    FOR UPDATE OF <column name> [ {,<column name>}... ]
```

You declare a cursor with the DECLARE statement. A cursor consists of a name and a SELECT statement. The name of the cursor must satisfy the same rules that apply to table names; see Chapter 5. We will explain the meaning of the FOR UPDATE clause in the next section. A DECLARE statement itself, like normal declarations, does nothing. Only after the OPEN statement does the SELECT statement in the cursor become active. In the OPEN, FETCH and CLOSE statements the cursor is referred to via the cursor name.

```
<open statement> ::= OPEN <cursor name>
```

The OPEN statement takes care of the execution of the SELECT statement associated with the specified cursor. You can open a cursor more than once in a program. If the SELECT statement contains variables, they are assigned a value at the time of opening. This means that the result of the cursor after each OPEN statement can differ, depending on whether the values in the variables have been updated or not.

```
<fetch statement> ::=
    FETCH <cursor name>
    INTO  <variable list>

<variable list> ::=
    <variable element> [ {,<variable element>}... ]

<variable element> ::=
    <variable> [ <null indicator> ]
```

The FETCH statement has an INTO clause which has the same significance as the INTO clause in the SELECT INTO statement. The number of variables in the INTO clause of a FETCH statement must also coincide with the number of expressions in the SELECT clause of the DECLARE statement. Secondly, the colon in front of a variable name is mandatory. A SELECT statement within a DECLARE statement may contain *no* INTO clause, as this function is taken over by the FETCH statement.

```
<close statement> ::= CLOSE <cursor name>
```

With the CLOSE statement the result of the cursor disappears and is no longer available. Cursors may be closed before the last row of the result is 'FETCHed'. We advise you to close cursors as quickly as possible because their results take up space in the internal memory of the computer.

We have already mentioned that a cursor may be opened more than once in a program. Before a cursor can be opened for a second time, and before the program ends, it *must* be closed.

We have adapted the ALL_PLAYERS program so that it first asks from which town it should present its ordered list of players.

```
PROGRAM ALL_PLAYERS_2;
DECLARATIONS
   pno    : SMALLINT;
   pname  : CHAR(15);
   town   : CHAR(10);
   ready  : CHAR(1);
   rowno  : INTEGER;
BEGIN
   # Cursor declaration
   DECLARE cplayers CURSOR FOR
      SELECT   PLAYERNO, NAME
      FROM     PLAYERS
      WHERE    TOWN = :town
      ORDER BY PLAYERNO;
   # Initialize variables
   ready := 'N';
   WHILE ready = 'N' DO
      WRITE 'From which town do you want to list the players';
      READ town;
      # Print a report heading
      WRITE 'ROWNO  PLAYER NUMBER  SURNAME';
      WRITE '=====  =============  =========';
      # Start the SELECT statement
      OPEN cplayers;
      # Look for the first player
      rowno := 0;
      FETCH cplayers INTO :pno, :pname;
      WHILE sqlcode = 0 DO
         rowno := rowno + 1;
         WRITE rowno, pno, pname;
         # Look for the next player
         FETCH cplayers INTO :pno, :pname;
      ENDWHILE;
      CLOSE cplayers;
      WRITE 'Do you want to stop (Y/N)?';
      READ ready;
   ENDWHILE;
END
```

Once opened, the result of a SELECT statement does not change. Only when the cursor has been closed and opened again can the result be different.

Note: In Section 28.6 we mentioned that you should avoid the use of *
in a SELECT clause in embedded SQL. This remark also applies to SELECT
statements in the form of cursors, for the same reasons.

Example 28.13: Find the three highest penalties that have been recorded.

```
PROGRAM HIGHEST_THREE;
DECLARATIONS
   rowno  : INTEGER;
   amount : DECIMAL(7,2);
BEGIN
   DECLARE cpenalties CURSOR FOR
      SELECT   AMOUNT
      FROM     PENALTIES
      ORDER BY AMOUNT DESC;
   OPEN cpenalties;
   FETCH cpenalties INTO :amount;
   ronwno := 1;
   WHILE sqlcode = 0 AND rowno <= 3 DO
      WRITE 'No', rowno, 'Amount', amount;
      rowno := rowno + 1;
      FETCH cpenalties INTO :amount;
   ENDWHILE;
   CLOSE cpenalties ;
END
```

Result:

```
No 1 Amount  100.00
No 2 Amount  100.00
No 3 Amount   75.00
```

28.9   The FOR UPDATE clause

The rows in the result of a cursor cannot be updated; they are *locked*. Because the cursor is using the rows, no other statement can update them at that point. For the same reason, the following program is not correct (we have omitted details to make it easier to read):

```
DECLARE cplayers CURSOR FOR
   SELECT   PLAYERNO, NAME
   FROM     PLAYERS;
   :
OPEN cplayers;
FETCH cplayers INTO :pno, :pname;
WHILE sqlcode = 0 DO
   UPDATE PLAYERS
   SET     ...
   WHERE   PLAYERNO = :pno;
   :
   FETCH cplayers INTO :pno, :pname;
ENDWHILE;
CLOSE cplayers;
```

Oracle does not accept the UPDATE statement as it is trying to update a row in the PLAYERS table while that row is being used by the cursor. In other words, the cursor has locked the row and the only way to update the row is via the cursor itself. This is why the DECLARE statement has a *FOR UPDATE clause*. In this clause you specify which columns can be updated, and a special version of the UPDATE statement allows you to update the current row of a given cursor. Here is an extended definition of the UPDATE statement:

```
<update statement> ::=
   UPDATE <table specification>
   SET    <update> [ {,<update>}... ]
   [ WHERE  { <condition> | CURRENT OF <cursor name> } ]

<table specification > ::= [ <user> . ] <table name>

<update> ::=
   <column name> = { <expression> | <subquery> }
```

Example 28.14: This program is based on the RAISE_WON_2 program from Section 28.4. We have made the following changes. The program shows the matches information for team 1, row by row. It asks, for each row, whether the number of sets won should be increased by one.

```
PROGRAM RAISE_WON_3;
DECLARATIONS
    pno    : SMALLINT;
    won    : INTEGER;
    choice : CHAR(1);
BEGIN
    # Cursor declaration
    DECLARE c_mat CURSOR FOR
       SELECT  PLAYERNO, WON
       FROM    MATCHES
       WHERE   TEAMNO = 1
       FOR     UPDATE OF WON;
    #
    OPEN c_mat;
    FETCH c_mat INTO :pno, :won;
    WHILE sqlcode = 0 DO
       WRITE 'Do you want the number of sets won for';
       WRITE 'player ', pno, ' to be increased by 1 (Y/N)?';
       READ choice;
       :
```

```
        :
   IF choice = 'Y' THEN
        UPDATE    MATCHES
        SET       WON = WON + 1
        WHERE     CURRENT OF c_mat;
   ENDIF;
   FETCH c_mat INTO :pno, :won;
   ENDWHILE;
   CLOSE c_mat;
   WRITE 'Ready';
END
```

Explanation: The only change in this program, compared with the original version, is that the DECLARE statement has been expanded with a FOR UPDATE clause. By doing this we are making provision for the WON column to be updated at some point. In the UPDATE statement we specify in the WHERE clause that in the row which is current for the C_MAT cursor the WON column should be increased by one.

28.10   Deleting rows via cursors

Cursors can be used for deleting individual rows. The DELETE statement has a similar condition to the one we have just discussed for the UPDATE statement.

```
<delete statement> ::=
   DELETE
   FROM    <table specification>
   [ WHERE { <condition> | CURRENT OF <cursor name> } ]

<table specification > ::= [ <user>. ] <table name>
```

Example 28.15: Develop a program that presents all data from the PENALTIES table row by row, and asks whether the row displayed should be deleted.

```
PROGRAM DELETE_PENALTIES;
DECLARATIONS
   pno    : SMALLINT;
   payno  : SMALLINT;
   pdate  : DATE;
   amount : DECIMAL(7,2);
   choice : CHAR(1);
   :
```

```
   :
BEGIN
   # Cursor declaration
   DECLARE c_penalties CURSOR FOR
      SELECT  PAYMENTNO, PLAYERNO, PEN_DATE, AMOUNT
      FROM    PENALTIES;
   #
   OPEN c_penalties;
   FETCH c_penalties INTO :payno, :pno, :pdate, :amount;
   WHILE sqlcode = 0 DO
      WRITE 'Do you want to delete this penalty?';
      WRITE 'Payment number   : ', payno;
      WRITE 'Player number    : ', pno;
      WRITE 'Penalty date     : ', pdate;
      WRITE 'Amount           : ', amount;
      WRITE 'Answer Y or N ';
      READ choice;
      IF choice = 'Y' THEN
         DELETE
         FROM     PENALTIES
         WHERE    CURRENT OF c_penalties;
      ENDIF;
      FETCH c_penalties INTO :payno, :pno, :pdate, :amount;
   ENDDO
   CLOSE c_penalties;
   WRITE 'Ready';
END
```

28.11   Working with arrays

With FETCH statements the result of a SELECT statement is fetched row by
row into the program. It is possible to fetch batches or groups of rows simultaneously. This may improve the processing time of statements. The only thing that
has to be done to achieve this is that the receiving variables (the variables that
are specified in the FETCH statement) are declared as *arrays*. An array is a variable that can consist of multiple values. To illustrate this we adapt the program
ALL_PLAYERS from Section 28.8 in such a way that rows are read in batches.

```
PROGRAM ALL_PLAYERS_3;
DECLARATIONS
    pno        : ARRAY[10] OF SMALLINT;
    pname      : ARRAY[10] OF CHAR(15);
    rowno      : INTEGER;
    rowsfound  : INTEGER;
    rowstodo   : INTEGER;
    counter    : INTEGER;
    group      : INTEGER;
```

```
BEGIN
    # Cursor declaration
    DECLARE cplayers CURSOR FOR
        SELECT    PLAYERNO, NAME
        FROM      PLAYERS
        ORDER BY PLAYERNO;
    # Print a report heading
    WRITE 'ROWNO  PLAYER NUMBER  SURNAME';
    WRITE '=====  =============  =========';
    # Start the SELECT statement
    OPEN cplayers;
    rowno := 0;
    rowsfound := sqlerrd[2];
    group := 10;
    # Look for the first ten players
    FETCH cplayers INTO :pno, :pname;
    WHILE sqlcode = 0 DO
        IF rowsfound > group THEN
            rowstodo := group;
            rowsfound := rowsfound - group;
        ENDIF;
        counter := 1;
        WHILE teller <= rowstodo DO
            rowno := rowno + 1;
            WRITE rowno, pno, pname;
            counter := counter +1;
        ENDWHILE;
        # Look for the next ten players
        FETCH cplayers INTO :pno, :pname;
    ENDWHILE;
    CLOSE cplayers;
END
```

Explanation: In the DECLARATIONS section of the program the variables PNO and PNAME are declared as arrays, each consisting of ten elements. The effect of the FETCH statements is that Oracle will fetch the rows one by one, but in batches of ten. This means that we have to include a second WHILE statement within the first WHILE statement. We make use of the variable SQLERRD[2] to do this. This variable is, just as SQLCODE, declared in the SQLCA file. After processing the OPEN statement, the value of this variable is set to the number of rows making up the result. After each ten rows have been processed the next ten will be read in with a FETCH statement.

Another way to work with arrays is through the SELECT INTO statement. If the variables that are specified in the INTO clause are arrays, then with one statement all the arrays are filled. We could re-write the previous program as follows without using the cursor.

```
PROGRAM ALL_PLAYERS_4;
DECLARATIONS
    pno     : ARRAY[10] OF SMALLINT;
    pname   : ARRAY[10] OF CHAR(15);
    rowno   : INTEGER;
    counter : INTEGER;
BEGIN
    # Print a report heading
    WRITE 'ROWNO  PLAYER NUMBER  SURNAME';
    WRITE '=====  =============  =========';
    # Start the SELECT statement
    SELECT   PLAYERNO, NAME
    INTO     :pno, :pname
    FROM     PLAYERS
    ORDER BY PLAYERNO;
    # Look for the first player
    rowno := 1;
    WHILE rowno <= sqlerrd[2] DO
        WRITE rowno, pno, pname;
        rowno := rowno + 1;
    ENDWHILE;
END
```

Note: However, this program only works if the number of rows found is not greater than the number of elements of the arrays. We advise you not to use arrays in this way, because the chance of an error is large.

The number of rows that are selected is always equal to the number of elements that make up the arrays. The programmer has the possibility of determining the number that is read in himself. To do this we need to extend the FETCH statement with a *FOR clause*.

```
<for clause> ::= FOR <variable>
```

Explanation: The data type of the variable that is specified in the FOR clause must be numeric.

The FOR clause may also be specified as the first clause of the SELECT INTO statement.

To use arrays the following rules apply:

• In a SELECT INTO statement arrays may only be used in the INTO clause and not, for example, in the WHERE clause.

• The number of elements of the different variables used in one statement should be equal.

28.12   Updates and arrays

UPDATE, DELETE and INSERT statements can also make use of arrays. If one of these statements is extended with a FOR clause, then multiple updates are executed.

Suppose that the variables TOWN and PNO are arrays consisting of ten elements. That would mean that the following UPDATE statement is equivalent to ten UPDATE statements. For each statement from the arrays the UPDATE statement is executed. This applies also to the INSERT and DELETE statements.

```
UPDATE     PLAYERS
SET        TOWN = :town
WHERE      PLAYERNO = :pno
```

An UPDATE statement may also be expanded with a FOR clause, just as the SELECT INTO statement, to indicate explicitly how many elements from the arrays must be processed.

28.13   Embedded SQL and distributed databases

In Chapter 26 we described how, with for example SQL*Plus and a database link, remote distributed databases can be accessed. This section will describe how, from a program, another database can be accessed.

A remote database used in a program has to be declared first with a *DECLARE DATABASE statement*.

```
<declare database statement> ::=
    DECLARE <database name> DATABASE
```

To query or update such a remote database in a program, an *AT clause* can be added to the relevant SQL statement. The definition of this clause is shown below. The AT clause may be used at the beginning of the following statements:

- COMMIT statement
- DECLARE CURSOR statement
- DELETE statement
- INSERT statement
- ROLLBACK statement
- SELECT INTO statement
- UPDATE statement

```
<at clause> ::= AT <database name>
```

The following program is a version of the ENTER_PENALTIES_2 program from
Section 28.6. In the program we assume that the PENALTIES table is stored in
the ROME database.

```
PROGRAM ENTER_PENALTIES_3;
DECLARATIONS
    pno    : SMALLINT;
    payno  : SMALLINT;
    pdate  : DATE;
    amount : DECIMAL(7,2);
BEGIN
    DECLARE ROME DATABASE;
    # Let the user fill in the data
    READ pno;
    READ pdate;
    READ amount;
    # Determine the highest payment number that has been recorded
    AT      ROME
    SELECT  NVL(MAX(PAYMENTNO),0) + 1
    INTO    :payno
    FROM    PENALTIES;
    # Add the new data to the PENALTIES table
    AT      ROME
    INSERT  INTO PENALTIES
            (PAYMENTNO, PLAYERNO, PEN_DATE, AMOUNT)
    VALUES (:payno, :pno, :pdate, :amount);
    WRITE 'Ready!';
END
```

Notice that the ROME database is declared at the beginning of the program
and that an AT clause has been added to the SELECT INTO and the INSERT
statement. The database name may not be a variable!

28.14 Transactions

Some programs consist of a series of update statements, all of which must have
executed correctly, or none will. Suppose that a program deletes all data about a
given player from the four tables. Three DELETE statements are necessary, as
well as an UPDATE statement for the TEAMS table. (If a player is a captain, the
team must not be deleted, but only the player number erased.) A program like this
cannot stop half-way through, otherwise half of the player's data would be gone,
say from the PLAYERS and MATCHES tables, while the rest remained in the
other tables. The database would then be in a state of *non-integrity*. In Section
17.5 we described the concept of *transaction* and the statements to realise this:
COMMIT and ROLLBACK. The following example illustrates the use of these
statements in a program.

Example 28.16: Develop a program that deletes all the data about a given player from the four tables. If the player is a captain, change the value to 0.

```
PROGRAM DELETE_PLAYER;
DECLARATIONS
    pno    : SMALLINT;
    number : INTEGER;
BEGIN
    WRITE 'Which player must be removed: ';
    READ pno;
    # Delete from the players table
    DELETE    FROM PLAYERS
    WHERE     PLAYERNO = :pno;
    IF sqlcode = 0 THEN
       # Delete from the MATCHES table
       DELETE    FROM MATCHES
       WHERE     PLAYERNO = :pno;
       IF sqlcode = 0 THEN
          # Delete from the penalties table
          DELETE    FROM PENALTIES
          WHERE     PLAYERNO = :pno;
          IF sqlcode = 0 THEN
             # Change the captain
             UPDATE    TEAMS
             SET       PLAYERNO = 0
             WHERE     PLAYERNO = :pno;
          ENDIF;
       ENDIF;
    ENDIF;
    # Check if everything went ok
    IF sqlcode = 0 THEN
       COMMIT WORK;
    ELSE
       ROLLBACK WORK;
    ENDIF;
END
```

Explanation: The first statement processed in the program marks the beginning of a transaction. In this example this is the first DELETE statement. Each update statement executed from that point is not permanent until the COMMIT statement has been processed. In our case, that means that the two DELETEs and one UPDATE have only actually occurred once the COMMIT statement is processed. Conclusion: If everything goes well, either all four statements are executed, or none of them.

Working with transactions naturally offers many advantages. But there are also a number of disadvantages. It costs Oracle time and effort to register the permanence or lack of permanence of data. It is like maintaining an extra administrative load. Also, all non-permanent data is blocked until it is made permanent or the transaction rolled back, which leads to extra administration. So, it is always wise to keep the quantity of non-permanent data to a minimum.

28.15   Example of a C program

In this chapter we have used a pseudo programming language with all the examples. In this section we give you two small examples of programs that have been written in the programming language C and therefore contain all the details.

Example 28.17: Develop a C program that creates the TEAMS table.

```
#include <stdio.h>

EXEC SQL BEGIN DECLARE SECTION;
     VARCHAR user[20];
     VARCHAR password[20];
EXEC SQL END DECLARE SECTION;

EXEC SQL INCLUDE SQLCA;

main()
   {
   strcopy(user.arr,"SQLDBA");
   uid.len=strlen(uid.arr);
   strcopy(password.arr,"SQLDBAPW");
   password.len=strlen(password.arr);
   EXEC SQL CONNECT :user IDENTIFIED BY :password;

   if (sqlca.sqlcode = 0)
      {
      EXEC SQL CREATE TABLE TEAMS ( ... );
      printf("The TEAMS table has been created. \n");
      EXEC SQL COMMIT WORK RELEASE;
      }

   exit(0);
   }
```

Note: You can see clearly the details we have left out in all our previous examples, such as the use of the statements BEGIN and END DECLARE SECTION, INCLUDE and CONNECT.

Example 28.18: Develop a C program that adds a row to the TEAMS table.

```
#include <stdio.h>

EXEC SQL BEGIN DECLARE SECTION;
     VARCHAR user[20];
     VARCHAR password[20];
     int     tno;
     int     pno;
     VARCHAR division[6];
EXEC SQL END DECLARE SECTION;

EXEC SQL INCLUDE SQLCA;

main()
   {
   strcopy(user.arr,"SQLDBA");
   uid.len=strlen(uid.arr);
   strcopy(password.arr,"SQLDBAPW");
   password.len=strlen(password.arr);
   EXEC SQL CONNECT :user IDENTIFIED BY :password;

   if (sqlca.sqlcode = 0)
      {
      printf("Enter a team number: ");
      scanf("%d",&tno);
      printf("Enter the number of the captain: ");
      scanf("%d",&pno);
      printf("Enter the division: ");
      scanf("%s",division.arr);
      division.len = strlen(division.arr);

      EXEC SQL INSERT INTO TEAMS
                       (TEAMNO, PLAYERNO, DIVISION)
              VALUES (:tno, :pno, :division);
      EXEC SQL COMMIT WORK RELEASE;

      printf("The team has been added. \n");
      }
   exit(0);
   }
```

28.16   Processing programs

In this chapter we showed you a number of examples of a program with embedded SQL. But now the question is: How can we process these programs? Before a program can really work it has to be processed first by a number of *utility programs*.

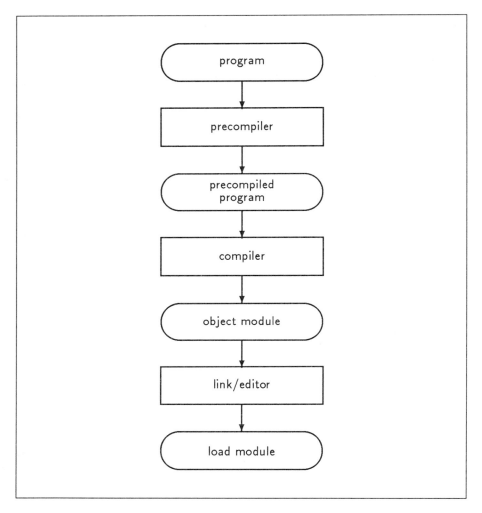

Figure 28.1: Preparation of programs with embedded SQL statements

Figure 28.1 indicates these utility programs. In this section we will describe the tasks of these programs in short.

The most important task of the *precompiler* (also *preprocessor*) is generating, for example, FORTRAN, COBOL or PL/I statements. The SQL statements are *not* tested by the precompiler for syntactical correctness. For example a SELECT statement without a FROM clause is not rejected. A separate precompiler is supported by Oracle for each host language. These are PRO∗C, PRO∗Pascal, PRO∗COBOL, etc.

The *compiler* (this could be a FORTRAN or a COBOL compiler) generates an *object module* from the precompiled program. Next, the *link/editor* makes a *load module* from the object module again. A load module is a program that is ready to be loaded in the internal memory of the computer for processing. Compilers and link/editors are not a part of a database management system, but are separate programs. If the link/editor has finished, the program can be started and executed. During execution of a program syntax errors may occur.

29

Introduction to PL/SQL

SQL statements are normally processed one by one, irrespective of whether you are working with SQL*Plus or whether the statements are embedded in a host language program. Once each statement has executed, either a result (in the case of a SELECT statement) or an SQLCODE is returned by the DBMS. Therefore it is possible (and sometimes mandatory) to determine the precise effect of each statement.

PL/SQL (Procedural Language/SQL) allows you to bundle SQL statements and have them execute later as a package. The DBMS is then ready again when the entire package has been processed. A package like this could contain many different types of statements including the familiar SQL statements such as SELECT, UPDATE and DELETE. In addition, you can use a range of new commands like IF THEN ELSE and LOOP.

Note: PL/SQL is not shipped as a standard part of Version 6 of Oracle. It is part of the Oracle DBMS that has the TPO (Transaction Processing Option) included; see Section 1.6. You can use PL/SQL within the following products: SQL*PLus, SQL*Forms, SQL*Menu and embedded SQL.

In this chapter we look at PL/SQL, beginning with its use in SQL*Plus. We are assuming that you have some experience with procedural programming languages such as ADA, C and Pascal, and are familiar with embedded SQL (see Chapter 28).

29.1 Examples of PL/SQL

Let us look at two simple examples of PL/SQL which should give you a feel for this language.

In PL/SQL you do not write applications, but *blocks*. A block is built up from a collection of statements. Here is our first example of a block.

```
BEGIN
   DELETE FROM PENALTIES
   WHERE  AMOUNT > 50;
   INSERT INTO TEAMS
   VALUES (3, 28, 'premier');
   COMMIT;
END;
```

Explanation: In this example the start and finish of the PL/SQL block are signalled with the words BEGIN and END respectively. This block consists of three familiar SQL statements. After the block has been processed all penalties greater than $50 will have been removed and a new team added. The updates will have been made permanent with the COMMIT statement. Each statement in a block must end with a semi-colon. Indicators like EXEC SQL which must be used in embedded SQL are not permitted here.

In the first example we have used only familiar SQL statements. The next example contains some new, PL/SQL specific, statements.

```
DECLARE
   average DECIMAL(7,2);
BEGIN
   SELECT AVG(AMOUNT)
   INTO    average
   FROM    PENALTIES;
   average := average + 10;
   DELETE FROM PENALTIES
   WHERE  AMOUNT > average;
END;
```

Explanation: In this example we calculate the average penalty amount with a SELECT INTO statement. Then this average is increased by 10. The final statement deletes penalties which are higher than the average penalty plus 10. You have encountered the SELECT INTO and DELETE statements already. The second statement, however, is a new one. With this statement we can increase the value of the variable by ten. Because we are using a variable in the PL/SQL block it must be declared and this is done at the beginning of the block.

Note: We have used three statements in this block. We could have achieved the same result with one SQL statement but have done it this way to explain some PL/SQL concepts.

29.2   Sections of a PL/SQL block

A PL/SQL block is divided into three sections: *declaration, execution* and *exception*. The execution section contains the statements to do the processing and is the only mandatory section. Any variable or cursor used in the execution section must be declared in the declaration section. The third part is the exception section. In this section you indicate what should happen if a particular problem occurs. Here is the definition of the PL/SQL block.

```
<plsql block> ::=
   [ <label declaration> ]
   [ <declaration section> ]
   BEGIN <execution section>
   [ <exception section> ]
   END [ <label name> ] ;
```

As we mentioned above the execution section contains all the statements that determine what the block does. The definition of the execution section looks like this:

```
<execution section> ::= <plsql statement set>

<plsql statement set> ::= { <plsql statement> ; }...

<plsql statement> ::=
   [ <label declaration> ]
   { <assignment statement> |
     <exit statement>       |
     <goto statement>       |
     <if statement>         |
     <loop statement>       |
     <null statement>       |
     <raise statement>      |
     <sql statement>        |
     <plsql block>          }

<label declaration> ::= "<<" <label name> ">>"
```

The execution section consists, then, of a collection of one or more statements, each punctuated with a semi-colon.

A *label declaration* may be included before each block or before each statement. To illustrate this we can expand our first example in this chapter with label declarations. The most important function of a label is that it enables you to point to or 'jump' to certain statements with statements like GOTO. The naming of labels is the same as that of tables. Two labels belonging to the same block may not have the same name.

```
<<BEGIN_BLOCK>>
BEGIN
   <<DELETE_PENALTIES>>
      DELETE FROM PENALTIES
      WHERE  AMOUNT > 50;
   <<INSERT_TEAM>>
      INSERT INTO TEAMS
      VALUES (3, 28, 'premier');
   <<COMMIT_TRANSACTION>>
      COMMIT;
END BEGIN_BLOCK;
```

Not all SQL statements can be used in PL/SQL, but only a small group. Below we show what they are.

```
<sql statement> ::=
   <close statement>          |
   <commit statement>         |
   <delete statement>         |
   <fetch statement>          |
   <insert statement>         |
   <lock statement>           |
   <open statement>           |
   <rollback statement>       |
   <savepoint statement>      |
   <select into statement>    |
   <set transaction statement> |
   <update statement>
```

Here are a few observations about the SQL statements that can be used in PL/SQL:

- The definitions of the CLOSE, FETCH, OPEN and SELECT INTO statements differ from the definitions we gave in previous chapters. We will discuss these statements fully in this chapter.

- The RELEASE option of the COMMIT and ROLLBACK statements may not be used in PL/SQL; see Section 17.5.

- The definitions of the DELETE, INSERT, LOCK, SAVEPOINT, SET TRANSACTION and UPDATE statements are the same within PL/SQL, so we will not cover them here. Instead, we refer you to Chapter 17.

29.3 Comments

We advise you to add comments to PL/SQL blocks in order to simplify their maintenance. Comments can be represented in two ways. Any information on a line following -- is ignored by PL/SQL. In addition, no information enclosed in the /* and */ symbols is processed. We have added comments to the previous example.

```
<<BEGIN_BLOCK>>
BEGIN
   -- The following statement deletes all
   -- penalties greater than $50.
   DELETE FROM PENALTIES -- This is the table
   WHERE   AMOUNT > 50;
   /* This INSERT statement adds a
      new team. */
   INSERT INTO TEAMS
   VALUES (3, 28, 'premier');
   /* End the transaction. */
   COMMIT;
END BEGIN_BLOCK;
```

29.4 Declaring variables

We have already seen that you can declare variables. Each variable used in a PL/SQL block must be declared in the declaration section. Here is the definition of that section.

```
<declaration section> ::=
   DECLARE { <declaration statement> ; }...

<declaration statement> ::=
   <variable declaration>  |
   <literal declaration>   |
   <record declararion>    |
   <cursor declaration>    |
   <exception declaration> |
   <pragma declaration>
```

In this section we will describe the declaration of variables, literals and records. The declaration of cursors, exceptions and pragmas will be considered later. The definition of a variable declaration looks like this.

```
<variable declaration> ::=
   <variable name>
   { <plsql data type> | <column specification> %TYPE }
   [ NOT NULL ] [ := <plsql expression> ]

<plsql data type> ::=
   NUMBER [ ( <precision> [ , <scale> ] ) ] |
   CHAR [ ( <length> ) ]                    |
   DATE                                     |
   BOOLEAN

<column specification> ::=
   [ <table specification>. ] <column name>
```

Each variable must have a corresponding data type. A data type can be assigned in two different ways. The first is to specify explicitly a PL/SQL data type after the variable name. From the list of data types we discussed in Chapter 5 only the NUMBER, CHAR and DATE data types can be used here. Along with these, PL/SQL supports the BOOLEAN data type. This type of variable has three possible values: true, false or unknown (the NULL value). Examples:

```
yes_no          BOOLEAN
first_playerno  PLAYERS.PLAYERNO%TYPE NOT NULL
```

Note: In order to differentiate them clearly from column and table names in this chapter we will show the names of all PL/SQL variables, literals and records in lower case.

The second way of attributing a data type is for the variable to 'inherit' the data type of a column from one of the tables. In the next two examples the PNO and AMOUNT variables take on the data types of the PLAYERS.PLAYERNO and PENALTIES.AMOUNT columns respectively.

```
pno     PLAYERS.PLAYERNO%TYPE
amount  PENALTIES.AMOUNT%TYPE
```

This method of conferring data types has the advantage that when the underlying columns are altered with an ALTER TABLE statement the data types of the variables are updated automatically to reflect this. This, of course, makes maintenance of the code simpler.

The value of each variable is, by definition, equal to the NULL value. An initial value can be attributed to a variable. We can, for example, extend the declaration of the AVERAGE variable as follows, where at the beginning of the execution of the block, it has the value zero:

```
average DECIMAL(7,2) := 0;
```

If the declaration of a variable is extended to specify NOT NULL, that variable can never be attributed with the NULL value. This type of variable must always be initialized. Examples:

```
large  NUMBER(7,2) NOT NULL := 99999.99
teamno SQLDBA.TEAMS.TEAMNO%TYPE NOT NULL := 100
```

Literals are special types of variables whose value is constant; their value cannot be changed. An initial value must be assigned in a literal declaration (that is the only point at which a value can be given to a literal). Literals can be used to define on a single occasion a particular value used often in a block. Again, this makes the block easier to maintain.

```
<literal declaration> ::=
   <literal name> CONSTANT <plsql data type>
     [ NOT NULL ]
     := <plsql expression>
```

Examples:

```
true      CONSTANT BOOLEAN := TRUE
yesterday CONSTANT DATE := SYSDATE - 1
pi        CONSTANT NUMBER(5,4) NOT NULL := 3.1417
```

Another special type of variable is the *record*. There is only one way to declare a record.

```
<record declaration> ::=
   <record name> <table specification> %ROWTYPE

<table specification> ::= [ <user>. ] <table name>
```

Examples:

```
team1 SQLDBA.TEAMS%ROWTYPE
team2 TEAMS%ROWTYPE
table1 SYS.OBJ$%ROWTYPE
```

Each record consists of one or more fields, each field relating to a column from the underlying table. The TEAM record, therefore, consists of three fields; a team number, a player number and a division. The table specified in the declaration must exist. Each field can be accessed as follows:

```
team.teamno := 3;
team.playerno := 27;
team.division := 'premier';
```

Exercise

29.1 Why are the following declarations incorrect?

1. playerno PLAYERNO%ROWTYPE
2. abc NUMBER(7,2) CONSTANT := 18.45
3. recursive NUMBER := recursive + 1
4. team1, team2 TEAMS%ROWTYPE

29.5   Assigning a value to a variable

In the execution section a variable can be assigned a value in two ways: with a
SELECT INTO statement and with an assignment statement.

Below is an example of a SELECT INTO statement. Variables can be used
in SQL statements in the same way as host languages variables in embedded SQL.
The only difference is that you do *not* have to put a colon before a PL/SQL variable.

```
SELECT    NAME
INTO      name_player
FROM      PLAYERS
WHERE     PLAYERNO = var1
```

The *assignment statement* can be used to give a value to a variable or record.
An assignment statement is built up from a variable or record and a PL/SQL
expression whose value is added to the variable or record mentioned.

```
<assignment statement> ::=
   <variable> := <plsql expression>            |
   <record>.<record field> := <plsql expression> |
   <record> := <record>
```

Here are some examples of correct assignment statements:

*   unknown := NULL
*   xyz := (4 > 6)
*   team.playerno := team.playerno + 2
*   total := game.won + game.lost
*   team1 := team2

29.6   PL/SQL expression

We have seen *PL/SQL expressions* used in two places already, in the declaration
of variables and literals, and after the := symbol in assignment statements. A

PL/SQL expression bears many similarities to the expression element that we covered in Chapter 6. Because there are a number of differences, however, we will give the complete definition of the PL/SQL expression below.

```
<plsql expression> ::=
   <numeric plsql expression>        |
   <alphanumeric plsql expression> |
   <date plsql expression>           |
   <boolean plsql expression>

<numeric plsql expression> ::=
   <numeric literal>                                    |
   <numeric variable>                                   |
   <scalar function>                                    |
   [ + | - ] <numeric plsql expression>                 |
   ( <numeric plsql expression> )                       |
   <numeric plsql expression> <mathematical operator>
      <numeric plsql expression>                        |
   <numeric plsql expression> **
      <numeric plsql expression>                        |
   <cursor name> %ROWCOUNT                              |
   SQL%ROWCOUNT                                         |
   SQLCODE                                              |
   NULL

<alphanumeric plsql expression> ::=
   <alphanumeric literal>                      |
   <alphanumeric variable>                     |
   <scalar function>                           |
   ( <alphanumeric plsql expression> )         |
   <alphanumeric plsql expression> "||"
      <alphanumeric plsq expression>           |
   SQLERRM [ ( <numeric plsql expression> ) ] |
   NULL

<date plsql expression> ::=
   <date literal>           |
   <date variable>          |
   <scalar function>        |
   ( <date plsql expression> ) |
   NULL

<boolean plsql expression> ::= <plsql condition>
```

Most forms of the PL/SQL expression will appear familiar to you as they are, in fact, the same as those we described in Chapter 6. We will confine ourselves to a few remarks:

- PL/SQL supports the ∗∗ symbol for exponential calculations. The value of the expression 2∗∗3 is 8.

- SQLCODE is a special type of scalar function whose significance is not the same as the SQLCODE variable from embedded SQL. We will look at this function in more detail in Section 29.12.

- SQLERRM is also a scalar function that provides the complete error message pertaining to a particular SQLCODE. This function will also be discussed in Section 29.12.

- %ROWCOUNT is a cursor attribute. For this we refer you to Section 29.10.

29.7   Procedural statements: IF, GOTO and NULL

The topic of this section is three PL/SQL statements: IF, GOTO and NULL. The *IF statement* offers the option of executing a set of statements, or not, on the basis of a condition. This statement has a similar meaning and function to the IF statement in languages like ADA, C and Pascal.

Example 29.1: Develop a block to decrease penalty payments by 5% if the average payment is more than $100.

```
DECLARE
    average DECIMAL(7,2);
BEGIN
    SELECT    AVG(AMOUNT)
    INTO      average
    FROM      PENALTIES;
    IF average > 100 THEN
        UPDATE PENALTIES
        SET    AMOUNT = AMOUNT * 0.95;
    END IF;
END;
```

Explanation: The first SELECT INTO statement calculates the average of all penalties. The condition in the IF statement checks whether the average is greater than 100. If so, the UPDATE statement executes the update.

```
<if statement> ::=
   IF <plsql condition> THEN
      <plsql statement set>
   [ ELSIF <plsql condition> THEN <plsql statement set> ]
   [ ELSE <plsql statement set> ]
   END IF

<plsql condition> ::=
   <boolean literal>                            |
   <plsql predicate>                            |
   <plsql predicate> OR <plsql predicate>       |
   <plsql predicate> AND <plsql predicate>      |
   ( <plsql condition> )                        |
   NOT <plsql condition>

<boolean literal> ::=
   TRUE | FALSE | NULL

<plsql predicate> ::=
   <plsql expression> <comparison operator>
      <plsql expression>                                           |
   <plsql expression> BETWEEN <plsql expression> AND
      <plsql expression>                                           |
   <plsql expression> IN ( <plsql expression>
      [ {,<plsql expression>}... ] )                               |
   <alphanumeric plsql expression> [ NOT ] LIKE <pattern> |
   <plsql expression> IS [ NOT ] NULL                             |
   <cursor name> { %NOTFOUND | %FOUND | %ISOPEN }                 |
   SQL { %NOTFOUND | %FOUND | %ISOPEN }

<comparison operator> ::=
   = | < | > | <= | >= | <> | != | ^=
```

In the following example we extend this IF statement. See for yourself what the effect of this block is.

```
DECLARE
   average DECIMAL(7,2);
BEGIN
   SELECT   AVG(AMOUNT)
   INTO     average
   FROM     PENALTIES;
   :
```

```
    :
    IF average < 10 THEN
        percentage := 5;
    ELSIF average >= 10 AND average <= 100 THEN
        percentage := 0;
    ELSIF average > 100 THEN
        percentage := -5;
    ELSE
        percentage := 1;
    ENDIF;
    UPDATE PENALTIES
    SET    AMOUNT = AMOUNT * (1 + (percentage/100));
END;
```

The *GOTO statement* offers the possibility of jumping directly to a specific statement.

```
<goto statement> ::= GOTO <label name>
```

One way of depicting the function of the GOTO statement is to transform a piece of PL/SQL code with a IF statement to one with a GOTO statement. The following piece of code:

```
IF a > 4 THEN
    b := 8;
END IF;
c := 1;
```

is equivalent to:

```
IF a <= 4 THEN
    GOTO label_2;
END IF;
<<label_1>> b := 8;
<<label_2>> c := 1;
```

As the name suggests, the effect of the *NULL statement* is nil. Nothing happens when this statement is executed.

```
<null statement> ::= NULL
```

The next two statements, then, are equivalent in all circumstances.

```
IF abc > 4 THEN
   abc := 8;
END IF;
```

and

```
IF abc > 4 THEN
   abc := 8;
ELSE
   NULL;
END IF;
```

29.8 Procedural statements: LOOP and EXIT

The *LOOP statement* is used to group sets of statements for repeated execution. This statement has five different forms; see the definition below

```
<loop statement> ::=
   WHILE <plsql condition> <loop>                           |
   FOR <variable> IN <loop range>  <loop>                   |
   <loop>                                                   |
   FOR <record> IN <cursor name> [ <parameters> ] <loop> |
   FOR <record> IN <select statement> <loop>

<loop> ::=
   LOOP <plsql statement set> END LOOP

<loop range> ::=
   [ REVERSE ] <numeric plsql expression> ..
               <numeric plsql expression>
```

We will begin by giving examples of the first three forms. The two forms in which a cursor is used (the fourth and fifth) are covered in Section 29.9. We assume here that the following table has been created:

```
CREATE TABLE NUMBERS
      ( NUMBER INTEGER NOT NULL );
```

Example 29.2: Develop a block that fills the table above with the numbers 1 to 100 inclusive.

```
DECLARE
   counter NUMBER := 1;
BEGIN
   WHILE counter <= 100 LOOP
      INSERT INTO NUMBERS VALUES (counter);
      counter := counter + 1;
   END LOOP;
   COMMIT;
END;
```

Explanation: Because the INSERT statement is included in the LOOP statement, it is executed 100 times, each time with a different value.

We could have formulated that example with another form of the LOOP statement:

```
BEGIN
   FOR counter IN 1 .. 100 LOOP
      INSERT INTO NUMBERS VALUES (counter);
   END LOOP;
   COMMIT;
END;
```

Explanation: The raising of the counter is automatically taken care of by the LOOP statement. Directly after the IN comes the initial value, while the end value follows the '..'. The variable counter is known as an *index variable* in the Oracle manuals. Index variables do not have to be declared and an assignment statement cannot explicitly give a value to an index variable. When the word REVERSE follows the index variable the numbers are inserted in the opposite order, beginning with 100, 99 and so on.

The third form of the LOOP statement does not indicate when the LOOP should end. To do this the *EXIT statement* is needed.

```
<exit statement> ::=
   EXIT [ <label name> ] [ WHEN <boolean plsql expression> ]
```

Example 29.3: Rewrite the previous example using the EXIT statement.

```
DECLARE
   counter NUMBER := 1;
BEGIN
   <<loop_1>>
   LOOP
      INSERT INTO NUMBERS VALUES (counter);
      counter := counter + 1;
      IF counter > 100 THEN
         EXIT loop_1;
      END IF;
   END LOOP;
   COMMIT;
END;
```

Explanation: The condition under which the loop should end is not specified in the LOOP statement itself. If there had been no EXIT statement the NUMBERS table would have had a huge number of rows inserted. In fact, the loop would probably have been discontinued by PL/SQL when an internal limit was reached. But in this example we have included an EXIT statement and it is invoked when the counter's value is greater than 100. The result of this statement is that the loop whose label declaration is loop_1 is ended. The next statement executed by PL/SQL is the first one to follow the LOOP statement, in this case the COMMIT statement.

The example above of IF and EXIT could also have been constructed in the following way:

```
EXIT loop_1 WHEN counter > 100;
```

When using the EXIT statement you must ensure that the referenced label is that of the LOOP statement and that the EXIT statement forms a part of the LOOP statement. Therefore the following construction is correct:

```
<<outer-loop>>
LOOP
   :
   <<inner-loop>>
   LOOP
      :
      EXIT <<outer-loop>>;
      :
   END LOOP;
   :
END LOOP;
```

29.9   Use of cursors

In Chapter 28 we described cursors and their role in embedded SQL. Cursors are necessary to allow the individual rows in the result of a SELECT statement to be read row by row. First, the cursor must be declared. Once the cursor has been opened, FETCH statements are used to read in the result row by row. When this is finished the cursor has to be closed.

The same mechanism and the same statements are required to process SELECT statements in PL/SQL. Nevertheless, the statements differ slightly from their embedded SQL counterparts, so we will provide the definitions.

```
<cursor declaration> ::=
   CURSOR <cursor name> [ <cursor parameters> ]
   IS <select statement>
   [ FOR UPDATE OF <column name> { ,<column name> }... ]

<cursor parameters> ::=
   ( <parameter name> <plsql data type>
     [ { , <parameter name> <plsql data type>}... ] )

<open statement> ::=
   OPEN <cursor name> [ <open parameters> ]

<open parameters> ::=
   ( <open parameter> [ {,<open parameter>}... ] )

<open parameter> ::=
   <plsql expression> [ => parameter name ]

<fetch statement> ::=
   FETCH <cursor name> INTO <receiving variables>

<receiving variables> ::=
   <variable> [ {,<variable>}... ] |
   <record>

<close statement> ::=
   CLOSE <cursor name>
```

Example 29.4: Develop a block that checks whether each player in the MATCHES table has a league number and if not delete them.

We will give four different solutions to this problem using yet another form of the LOOP statement.

```
DECLARE
    player PLAYERS.PLAYERNO%TYPE;

    CURSOR players IS
    SELECT PLAYERNO
    FROM   PLAYERS
    WHERE  LEAGUENO IS NULL;

BEGIN
    OPEN players;
    FETCH players INTO player;
    WHILE players%FOUND LOOP
       DELETE FROM MATCHES
       WHERE  PLAYERNO = player.playerno;
       FETCH players INTO player;
    END LOOP;
    CLOSE players;
END;
```

Explanation: The %FOUND is a *cursor attribute*. The `players%FOUND` condition is true as long as the FETCH statement finds a row. This is equivalent to embedded SQL where the SQLCODE equals zero as long as rows are found. You see, then, that the SQLCODE variable cannot be used in PL/SQL in the same way as in embedded SQL.

The opposite of %FOUND is the cursor attribute %NOTFOUND. A condition with %NOTFOUND is true if there are no rows in the result of the SELECT statement, or if a FETCH statement has just presented the last row.

Note: We could have chosen a solution for the previous example in which a statement was used instead of a cursor. We did it in this way so that we could illustrate the workings of a cursor in a simple and clear manner.

In PL/SQL it is useful to be able to incorporate a cursor to read in the rows so that a second FETCH statement is unnecessary:

```
DECLARE
    player PLAYERS.PLAYERNO%TYPE;

    CURSOR players IS
    SELECT PLAYERNO
    FROM   PLAYERS
    WHERE  LEAGUENO IS NULL;
    :
```

```
      :
BEGIN
   OPEN players;
   <<loop_1>> LOOP
      FETCH players INTO player;
      EXIT loop_1 WHEN players%NOTFOUND;
      DELETE FROM MATCHES
      WHERE  PLAYRENO = player.playerno;
   END LOOP;
   CLOSE players;
END;
```

The following solution uses the fourth form of the LOOP statement.

```
      :
BEGIN
   FOR player IN players LOOP
      DELETE FROM MATCHES
      WHERE  PLAYERNO = player.playerno;
   END LOOP;
END;
```

Explanation: The first point is that the player record does not have to be declared. The second is that with this form there are no apparent OPEN, FETCH and CLOSE statements. Here, the LOOP statement ensures that the opening and closing of the cursor and the row by row scanning of the result table occurs. The effect of this block is equivalent to that of the previous block in all circumstances.

The final way of working through this example is as follows.

```
BEGIN
   FOR player IN (SELECT PLAYERNO
                  FROM   PLAYERS
                  WHERE  LEAGUENO IS NULL) LOOP
      DELETE FROM GAMES
      WHERE  PLAYERNO = player.playerno;
   END LOOP;
END;
```

Explanation: The cursor declaration has disappeared (and with it, the entire declaration section) and the SELECT statement sits inside the LOOP statement.

When defining a cursor you may specify parameters. Here is an example of this use.

Example 29.5: Develop a block to store the numbers of the players born between 1950 and 1960 in a help table.

```
DECLARE
   CURSOR players (year_par) IS
   SELECT PLAYERNO
   FROM   PLAYERS
   WHERE  YEAR_OF_BIRTH BETWEEN year_par AND year_par + 10;
BEGIN
   OPEN players (1950);
   <<loop_1>> LOOP
      FETCH players INTO player;
      EXIT loop_1 WHEN players%NOTFOUND;
      INSERT INTO HELP_TABLE VALUES (player.playerno);
   END LOOP;
   CLOSE players;
END;
```

Explanation: Now in the cursor declaration a parameter is used instead of variable names. If we had not included this declaration PL/SQL would have assumed YEAR_PAR to be a 'normal' variable and consequently returned an error message for an undeclared variable. The value is assigned to the parameter in the OPEN statement. This process could also be done in the following way:

```
OPEN(1950 => year_par);
```

Of course, we can also rewrite this example without explicit OPEN, FETCH and CLOSE statements. Note how the value of a parameter is passed.

```
DECLARE
   CURSOR players (year_par) IS
   SELECT PLAYERNO
   FROM   PLAYERNO
   WHERE  YEAR_OF_BIRTH BETWEEN year_par AND year_par + 10;
BEGIN
   FOR player IN players(1950) LOOP
      INSERT INTO HELP_TABLE VALUES (player.playerno);
   END LOOP;
END;
```

29.10   Cursor attributes

You can use a *cursor attribute* to query the status of a cursor, such as the number of rows processed, whether it is open and so on. So far we have come across two cursor attributes, %FOUND and %NOTFOUND. This section explores them more fully and introduces two more cursor attributes, %ROWCOUNT and %ISOPEN.

The %FOUND cursor attribute has three possible values, which are true, false or unknown (NULL). The value is only true when an executed FETCH statement returns a row. Conversely, the value is false when an executed FETCH statement finds no row. If a cursor is open, but no FETCH statement has been processed the %FOUND value is unknown. Querying the value of the %FOUND cursor attribute yields an error message if the cursor concerned has not yet been opened with an OPEN statement.

The value of the %NOTFOUND cursor attribute is almost the same as that of %FOUND. The value of the expression C1%NOTFOUND (where C1 is the cursor name) is, by definition, equal to NOT(C1%FOUND). This cursor attribute also returns an error message if the cursor is not open.

The %ISOPEN cursor attribute can be used in a condition to determine whether a cursor is open or not. The attribute can support only two possible values. The value is true if the cursor is open and false if not.

The value of the fourth cursor attribute, %ROWCOUNT, is neither true nor false, but a whole number. It gives the number of rows which have already been retrieved by the FETCH statement. If the cursor is open, but no FETCH statements have been executed, the value of %ROWCOUNT is zero. Querying %ROWCOUNT when the cursor has not yet been opened leads to an error message.

For DELETE, INSERT, UPDATE and SELECT INTO statements, Oracle creates cursors under the covers. These are called *implicit cursors* as opposed to the explicit cursors we create ourselves in the cursor declaration or LOOP statement. You can also use cursor attributes with implicit cursors. But because we do not know the names of these implicit cursors, we refer to them with the word SQL, for example SQL%NOTFOUND. The value of the cursor attributes %FOUND, %NOTFOUND and %ROWCOUNT is zero as long as no SQL statements have been processed.

SQL%FOUND is true when a row is actually deleted, inserted or updated with a DELETE, INSERT or UPDATE statement, or if a row is found with a SELECT INTO statement. If SQL%FOUND is true, SQL%NOTFOUND is false. The value of SQL%ROWCOUNT equals the number of rows deleted, inserted, updated, or found (SELECT INTO). Because implicit cursors are always closed immediately after execution of the cursor the value of SQL%OPEN is always false.

Example 29.6: Develop a block to delete all teams from the TEAMS table on the condition that five teams remain.

```
BEGIN
    DELETE FROM TEAMS;
    IF SQL%ROWCOUNT <= 5 THEN
        ROLLBACK;
    ELSE
        COMMIT;
    END IF;
END;
```

29.11 Exception handling

Expected and unexpected problems and errors can occur during processing. Examples of this are division by zero or the result of a SELECT INTO statement consisting of multiple rows. These sorts of problems can be anticipated and dealt with using *exceptions*. For example, an exception can be used to indicate that the statement being processed should be rolled back if a SELECT INTO statement yields more than one row. It is not necessary to define this exception alongside each SELECT INTO statement; rather, it can be done in one place. If the problem occurs PL/SQL automatically calls the exception.

In order to be able to use an exception it must first be declared in the declaration section; see Section 29.4. Two exceptions may not have the same name.

```
<exception declaration> ::=
    <exception name> EXCEPTION
```

The statements to be executed in the case of an exception occurring have to be specified in the *exception section*, the definition of which is shown below.

```
<exception section> ::=
    EXCEPTION { <exception handler> ; }...

<exception handler> ::=
    WHEN { <exceptions> | OTHERS }
    THEN <plsql statement set>

<exceptions> ::=
    <exception name> [ OR <exceptions> ]
```

The exception section consists of a set of *exception handlers* built from a number of PL/SQL statements.

An exception can have either an active or an inactive value. It is inactive at the beginning of the execution of a block. If, for any reason, the exception is activated the relevant exception handler is automatically executed. At that point PL/SQL discontinues processing the block.

The RAISE statement can be used to activate an exception handler.

```
<raise statement> ::= RAISE <exception name>
```

Here is a simple example.

Example 29.7: Develop a block to add a new team. If the captain number does not occur in the PLAYERS table the update must be rolled back.

```
DECLARE
    number_teams NUMBER(10);
    no_player    EXCEPTION;

BEGIN
    INSERT INTO TEAMS
            (TEAMNO, PLAYERNO, DIVISION)
    VALUES (3, 140, 'third');
    SELECT COUNT(*)
    INTO   number_teams
    FROM   TEAMS
    WHERE  PLAYERNO NOT IN
            (SELECT PLAYERNO FROM PLAYERS);
    IF number_teams > 0 THEN
        RAISE no_player;
    ELSE
        COMMIT;
    END IF;

EXCEPTION
    WHEN no_player THEN
        ROLLBACK;
END;
```

Explanation: The effect of the RAISE statement is the same as that of a GOTO. The program 'jumps' to the appropriate exception handler.

There are a number of exceptions (which are part of PL/SQL) that you do not have to declare yourself, but can use immediately. The table below lays them out with an explanation and their relevant SQLCODE value.

Exception	SQLCODE	Description
dup_val_on_index	-1	Active when two equal values are inserted into a column that does not allow duplicates
invalid_cursor	-1001	Active when an incorrect cursor is specified (for example attempting to close a cursor which is not open)
invalid_number	-1722	Active when alphanumeric to numeric conversion is not possible
login_denied	-1017	Active when an invalid userid and password is used to log on
no_data_found	+100	Active when the result of a cursor is empty after the OPEN statement has executed, or when the FETCH statement is beyond the last row
not_logged_on	-1012	Active when an attempt to execute an SQL statement is made and the block is not logged on
program_error	-6501	Active when PL/SQL has an internal problem
storage_error	-6500	Active when PL/SQL does not have sufficient memory available, or when there is a fault in the memory
timeout_on_resource	-51	Active when a time-out occurs while Oracle waits for a particular resource to become available
too_many_rows	-1427	Active when the result of a SELECT INTO consists of two or more rows
value_error	-6502	Active when an error occurs processing expressions
zero_divide	-1476	Active when something is divided by zero

Example 29.8: Develop a block which rolls back the transaction if (by accident) a division by zero occurs.

```
BEGIN
    UPDATE    MATCHES
    SET       WON = 3/LOST;
EXCEPTION
    WHEN zero_divide THEN
        ROLLBACK;
END;
```

In the example above PL/SQL tests whether, after the execution of the UPDATE statement, the value of the (internal) SQLCODE variable equals –1476. If so, the ROLLBACK statement is executed.

PL/SQL allows you to define exceptions for other SQLCODE using *pragma declarations*. In fact, the exceptions mentioned in the table above are all declared as pragmas by PL/SQL.

```
<pragma declaration> ::=
    PRAGMA EXCEPTION INIT ( <name> , <integer literal> )
```

Example 29.9: Develop a block to roll back the transaction if too large a value is inserted into a column.

```
DECLARE
    value_too_high EXCEPTION;
    PRAGMA EXCEPTION_INIT(value_too_high, -1438);
BEGIN
    INSERT INTO ...
        :
EXCEPTION
    WHEN value_too_high THEN
        ROLLBACK;
END;
```

It is impossible to have an exception on hand to deal with every error that might arise, as Oracle has hundreds of different error messages. We advise you, therefore, to include an exception handler with each block, which can be activated when an error occurs that has no specifically declared exception. We could extend the block above in the following way:

```
DECLARE
    value_too_high EXCEPTION;
    PRAGMA EXCEPTION_INIT(value_too_high, -1438);
BEGIN
    INSERT INTO ...
        :
EXCEPTION
    WHEN value_too_high THEN
        ROLLBACK;
    WHEN OTHERS THEN
        ROLLBACK;
END;
```

29.12   The functions SQLCODE and SQLERRM

All the scalar functions described in Appendix C can be used in PL/SQL. Along with those PL/SQL supports two other functions, *SQLCODE* (not to be confused with the SQLCODE variable from embedded SQL) and *SQLERRM*.

The SQLCODE function returns values from the SQLCODE of the last executed SQL statement. This function only has any meaning if it is used within an exception handler. For example, it can be used in the following way in the OTHERS exception handler:

```
WHEN OTHERS THEN
    sqlcode_var := SQLCODE;
    INSERT INTO ERROR_TABLE(sqlcode_var);
```

Explanation: The SQLCODE function cannot be used in an SQL statement; the value must first be assigned to a variable.

The SQLERRM function is used to retrieve the text belonging to a particular SQLCODE.

Example 29.10: Develop a PL/SQL block that stores the relevant text for all SQLCODES in a table. We assume that a CODE_TABLE has been created with two columns.

```
DECLARE
   message CHAR(100);
BEGIN
   FOR code IN -10000 .. 0 LOOP
      message := SQLERRM(code);
      INSERT INTO CODE_TABLE VALUES
         (code, message);
   END LOOP;
END;
```

Explanation: The SQLERRM function is also unable to be used in an SQL statement.

29.13   Nesting blocks

PL/SQL blocks can be nested so that one block is then specified within another. Here is an example:

```
<<OUTER_BLOCK>>
DECLARE
   :
BEGIN
   :
   <<INNER_BLOCK>>
   DECLARE
      :
   BEGIN
      :
   END;
   :
END;
```

Variables that belong to the outer block may be used in the inner block.

29.14   PL/SQL and SQL∗Plus

PL/SQL may be used within SQL∗Plus. All the blocks which we have shown in this chapter can be typed in SQL∗Plus. In Section 2.7 we described how parameters (indicated with the &-symbol) can be specified within SQL statements. You can also use parameters within PL/SQL.

Example 29.11: Develop a block that adds a new team. If the captains number in the PLAYERS table does not occur, the update must be rolled back.

```
DECLARE
    number_teams  NUMBER;
    new_teamno    TEAMS.TEAMNO%TYPE;
    no_player     EXCEPTION;

BEGIN
    SELECT NVL(MAX(TEAMNR), 0) + 1
    INTO   new_teamno
    FROM   TEAMS;
    INSERT INTO TEAMS
           (TEAMNO, PLAYERNO, DIVISION)
    VALUES (new_teamno, &playerno, '&division');
    SELECT COUNT(*)
    INTO   number_teams
    FROM   TEAMS
    WHERE  PLAYERNO NOT IN
           (SELECT PLAYERNO FROM PLAYERS);
    IF number_teams > 0 THEN
       RAISE no_player;
    ELSE
       COMMIT;
    END IF;

EXCEPTION
    WHEN no_player THEN
        ROLLBACK;
END;
```

After you have typed in the last END, SQL∗Plus shows the familiar prompt again. If you type a full stop here the block is not executed immediately, but is stored in a command buffer. SQL∗Plus commands like CHANGE, DELETE and INPUT can be used to alter the code, while the RUN command causes it to be executed.

29.15 PL/SQL and embedded SQL

PL/SQL can be used in all host languages supported by Oracle. As an example we have rewritten the final example from Chapter 28 making use of a PL/SQL block. The host language is C.

```c
#include <stdio.h>

EXEC SQL BEGIN DECLARE SECTION;
     VARCHAR user[20];
     VARCHAR password[20];
     int     tnor;
     int     pno;
     VARCHAR division[6];
EXEC SQL END DECLARE SECTION;

EXEC SQL INCLUDE SQLCA;

main()
   {
   strcopy(user.arr,"SQLDBA");
   user.len=strlen(user.arr);
   strcopy(password.arr,"SQLDBAPW");
   password.len=strlen(password.arr);
   EXEC SQL CONNECT :user IDENTIFIED BY :password;

   if (sqlca.sqlcode = 0)
      {
      printf("Enter a team number: ");
      scanf("%d",&tno);
      printf("Enter the number of the captain: ");
      scanf("%d",&pno);
      printf("Enter the division: ");
      scanf("%s",division.arr);
      division.len = strlen(division.arr);

      EXEC SQL EXECUTE
      BEGIN
         INSERT INTO TEAMS
                 (TEAMNO, PLAYERNO, DIVISION)
         VALUES (:tno, :pno, :division);
         COMMIT WORK;
      END;
      END-EXEC;

      printf("The team has been added. \n");
      }
   exit(0);
   }
```

Notes:

- A PL/SQL block must begin with the word EXECUTE.

- Before each embedded SQL statement, and therefore before a PL/SQL block, you must specify EXEC SQL. The implication is that if we combine this and the previous remark we can conclude that before each block EXEC SQL EXECUTE should be specified.

- Each PL/SQL block must terminate with END-EXEC.

- Host language variables can be used within blocks but they must be preceded with a colon. A host language variable can be used in any place where a PL/SQL variable is permitted. An assignment statement may be used to assign a value to a host language variable.

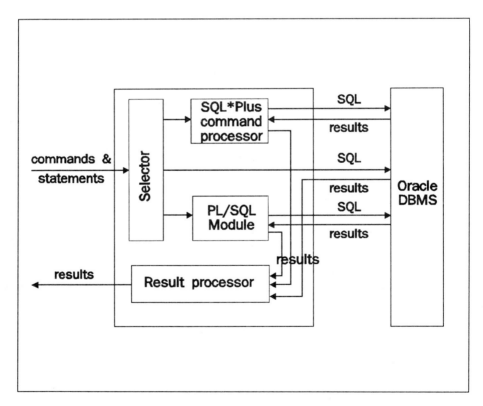

Figure 29.1: The PL/SQL module

29.16   Executing PL/SQL

How is a PL/SQL block processed? Blocks are processed by the *PL/SQL module*. Figure 29.1 is a graphical representation of how a PL/SQL block, entered in SQL*Plus, is processed. A block is read in its entirety by the PL/SQL module, which can itself process statements like LOOP and IF THEN ELSE. SQL statements like UPDATE are passed to the DBMS. The results of SQL statements are passed back to the PL/SQL module for further processing. So the PL/SQL module and the DBMS work together. This is transparent to the program. When the block has finished executing control is passed back to SQL*Plus.

The second question is where is the PL/SQL module located? If you run Oracle with the TPO (Transaction Processing Option) the PL/SQL module comes as part of the DBMS. However, the SQL*Forms and SQL*Menu products also contain a PL/SQL module. The advantage of the former architecture, in which PL/SQL is part of the DBMS, is that the volume of communication between applications and the DBMS is restricted, which has good implications for performance.

Appendix A
Answers to exercises

Introduction

Many of the answers to the questions are given in the form of SQL statements. In most cases we have provided only one formulation, but this does not mean that it is the only way of answering the question. Nor does it mean that it is necessarily the best way. This book would be huge if we gave every possible answer for every question. If you come up with another answer it does not automatically mean that you are wrong. Compare your answer with the one in the book, as they should be equivalent.

As well as this, we advise you to consult Appendix B as you write your statements. Here we describe the syntax of SQL.

Chapter 5

5.1   CREATE TABLE DEPARTMENTS
```
      ( DEPTNO    CHAR(5)       NOT NULL,
        BUDGET    DECIMAL(8,2)         ,
        LOCATION  VARCHAR(30)          )
```

5.2   1.   Yes.

      2.   No, because some values of the HOUSENO column contain numbers.

      3.   Yes.

      4.   Yes, it is permitted. However, we advise you not to do this, because the PLAYERNO column in the PLAYERS table is a primary key.

      5.   Yes.

      6.   No, because some values are longer than nine characters.

5.3 1. ALTER   TABLE PLAYERS
             MODIFY (LEAGUENO INTEGER)
         3. ALTER   TABLE PLAYERS
             MODIFY (PLAYERNO NULL)
         4. ALTER   TABLE PENALTIES
             MODIFY (PEN_DATE CHAR(10))

5.4 The OBJ$ table:

OBJ#	OWNER#	NAME	TYPE	CTIME	MTIME
4500	50	DEPARTMENTS	2	24-FEB-91	?

The COL$ table:

OBJ#	COL#	NAME	TYPE#	LENGTH	NULL$
4500	1	DEPTNO	1	5	412
4500	2	BUDGET	2	22	413
4500	3	LOCATION	1	30	414

5.5 Yes, a user is allowed to create a synonym for an other user. Then the other user will be the owner.

5.6 No, this is not necessarily.

5.7 The user will see the contents of the PLAYERS table.

Chapter 6

6.1 1. Correct; floating point data type
         2. Incorrect; because there must be quotation marks before and after the alphanumeric literal
         3. Correct; alphanumeric data type
         4. Incorrect; the alphanumeric literal should be enclosed in quotation marks, and the single quotation mark within the literal should be given as a double quotation mark
         5. Correct; alphanumeric data type
         6. Correct; integer data type
         7. Correct; alphanumeric data type
         8. Correct; alphanumeric data type
         9. Incorrect; the year part of a date should only contain two digits

6.2 1. 200
         2. 3800

3. 200

4. 200

Chapter 7

7.1 A SELECT statement consists of a minimum of two clauses: the SELECT and the FROM clause.

7.2 Yes

7.3 No; if a SELECT statement has a HAVING clause, a GROUP BY clause is mandatory.

7.4
1. There is no FROM clause.
2. The GROUP BY clause must be specified before the HAVING clause.
3. The ORDER BY clause should be the last clause.

7.5 The FROM clause:

PAYMENTNO	PLAYERNO	PEN_DATE	AMOUNT
1	6	08-DEC-80	100.00
2	44	05-MAY-81	75.00
3	27	10-SEP-83	100.00
4	104	08-DEC-84	50.00
5	44	08-DEC-80	25.00
6	8	08-DEC-80	25.00
7	44	30-DEC-82	30.00
8	27	12-NOV-84	75.00

The WHERE clause:

PAYMENTNO	PLAYERNO	PEN_DATE	AMOUNT
2	44	05-MAY-81	75.00
3	27	10-SEP-83	100.00
4	104	08-DEC-84	50.00
7	44	30-DEC-82	30.00
8	27	12-NOV-84	75.00

The GROUP BY clause:

PAYMENTNO	PLAYERNO	PEN_DATE	AMOUNT
2, 7	44	05-MAY-81, 30-DEC-82	75.00, 30.00
3, 8	27	10-SEP-83, 12-NOV-84	100.00, 75.00
4	104	08-DEC-84	50.00

The HAVING clause:

PAYMENTNO	PLAYERNO	PEN_DATE	AMOUNT
2, 7	44	05-MAY-81, 30-DEC-82	75.00, 30.00
3, 8	27	10-SEP-83, 12-NOV-84	100.00, 75.00

The SELECT clause:

```
PLAYERNO
--------
      44
      27
```

The ORDER BY clause:

```
PLAYERNO
--------
      27
      44
```

Chapter 8

8.1 1. Both tables have a column called PLAYERNO.
2. The SELECT clause refers to the PLAYERS table even though it is not specified in the FROM clause.
3. The qualification PLAYERS is not enough. We have to use PETE.PLAYERS.PLAYERNO or JIM.PLAYERS.PLAYERNO

8.2 The question: 'Give the name of each player who is captain of a team'.
The FROM clause:

TEAMNO	PLAYERNO	DIVISION	PLAYERNO	NAME	...
1	6	first	6	Parmenter	...
1	6	first	44	Baker	...
1	6	first	83	Hope	...
1	6	first	2	Everett	...
1	6	first	27	Collins	...
1	6	first	104	Moorman	...
1	6	first	7	Wise	...
1	6	first	57	Brown	...
1	6	first	39	Bishop	...
1	6	first	112	Bailey	...
1	6	first	8	Newcastle	...
1	6	first	100	Parmenter	...
1	6	first	28	Collins	...
:	:	:	:	:	:

```
  :        :   :             :   :               :
  1        6   first         95  Miller      ...
  2       27   second         6  Parmenter   ...
  2       27   second        44  Baker       ...
  2       27   second        83  Hope        ...
  2       27   second         2  Everett     ...
  2       27   second        27  Collins     ...
  2       27   second       104  Moorman     ...
  2       27   second         7  Wise        ...
  2       27   second        57  Brown       ...
  2       27   second        39  Bishop      ...
  2       27   second       112  Bailey      ...
  2       27   second         8  Newcastle   ...
  2       27   second       100  Parmenter   ...
  2       27   second        28  Collins     ...
  2       27   second        95  Miller      ...
```

The WHERE clause:

```
TEAMNO   PLAYERNO   DIVISION   PLAYERNO   NAME        ...
------   --------   --------   --------   ---------   ---
     1          6   first             6   Parmenter   ...
     2         27   second           27   Collins     ...
```

The SELECT clause and end result:

```
NAME
---------
Parmenter
Collins
```

8.3   SELECT   PAYMENTNO, AMOUNT, P.PLAYERNO, NAME
      FROM   PENALTIES PN, PLAYERS P
      WHERE   PN.PLAYERNO = P.PLAYERNO

8.4   SELECT   PAYMENTNO, NAME
      FROM   PENALTIES PN, PLAYERS P, TEAMS T
      WHERE   PN.PLAYERNO = T.PLAYERNO
      AND   T.PLAYERNO = P.PLAYERNO

8.5   SELECT   S.PLAYERNO, NAME
      FROM   PLAYERS P, PLAYERS P27
      WHERE   P.TOWN = P27.TOWN
      AND   P27.PLAYERNO = 27
      AND   P.PLAYERNO <> 27

8.6   SELECT   DISTINCT P.PLAYERNO, P.NAME, CAP.PLAYERNO,
                   CAP.NAME
          FROM   PLAYERS P, PLAYERS CAP, MATCHES MAT, TEAMS T
          WHERE   MAT.PLAYERNO = P.PLAYERNO
          AND   T.TEAMNO   = MAT.TEAMNO
          AND   MAT.PLAYERNO <> T.PLAYERNO
          AND   CAP.PLAYERNO = T.PLAYERNO

Chapter 9

9.1   SELECT   PLAYERNO
          FROM   PLAYERS
          WHERE   YEAR_OF_BIRTH > 1960

   or

          SELECT   PLAYERNO
          FROM   PLAYERS
          WHERE   YEAR_OF_BIRTH >= 1961

   or

          SELECT   PLAYERNO
          FROM   PLAYERS
          WHERE   1960 < YEAR_OF_BIRTH

   or

          SELECT   PLAYERNO
          FROM   PLAYERS
          WHERE   YEAR_OF_BIRTH - 1960 > 0

9.2   SELECT   TEAMNO
          FROM   TEAMS
          WHERE   PLAYERNO <> 27

9.3   No row in the PLAYERS table satisfies the condition. No row in which
          the LEAGUENO column has a value satisfies the condition, because the
          condition is false. In addition, each row in which the LEAGUENO column
          has no value (and thus contains the NULL value) is not returned.

9.4   SELECT   PLAYERNO
          FROM   MATCHES
          WHERE   WON > LOST

9.5   SELECT   PLAYERNO
          FROM   MATCHES
          WHERE   WON + LOST = 5

9.6
```
SELECT    PLAYERNO, NAME, TOWN
FROM      PLAYERS
WHERE     SEX = 'F'
AND       TOWN <> 'Stratford'
```
or
```
SELECT    PLAYERNO, NAME, TOWN
FROM      PLAYERS
WHERE     SEX = 'F'
AND       NOT (TOWN = 'Stratford')
```

In the second example the brackets may be left out!

9.7
```
SELECT    PLAYERNO
FROM      PLAYERS
WHERE     YEAR_JOINED >= 1970
AND       YEAR_JOINED <= 1980
```
or
```
SELECT    PLAYERNO
FROM      PLAYERS
WHERE     NOT (YEAR_JOINED < 1970 OR YEAR_JOINED > 1980)
```

9.8
```
SELECT    PLAYERNO, NAME, YEAR_OF_BIRTH
FROM      PLAYERS
WHERE     MOD(YEAR_OF_BIRTH,400) = 0
OR        (MOD(YEAR_OF_BIRTH,4) = 0 AND
          NOT(MOD(YEAR_OF_BIRTH,100) = 0))
```

9.9
```
SELECT    NAME, INITIALS, DIVISION
FROM      MATCHES MAT, PLAYERS P, TEAMS T
WHERE     MAT.PLAYERNO = P.PLAYERNO
AND       MAT.TEAMNO = T.TEAMNO
AND       YEAR_OF_BIRTH > 1965
AND       WON > 0
```

9.10
```
SELECT    PAYMENTNO
FROM      PENALTIES
WHERE     AMOUNT BETWEEN 50 AND 100
```

9.11
```
SELECT    PAYMENTNO
FROM      PENALTIES
WHERE     NOT (AMOUNT BETWEEN 50 AND 100)
```
or
```
SELECT    PAYMENTNO
FROM      PENALTIES
WHERE     AMOUNT NOT BETWEEN 50 AND 100
```
or

```
       SELECT    PAYMENTNO
       FROM      PENALTIES
       WHERE     AMOUNT < 50
       OR        AMOUNT > 100

9.12   SELECT    PLAYERNO
       FROM      PLAYERS
       WHERE     YEAR_JOINED - YEAR_OF_BIRTH BETWEEN 17 AND 39

9.13   SELECT    PAYMENTNO
       FROM      PENALTIES
       WHERE     AMOUNT IN (50, 75, 100)

9.14   SELECT    PLAYERNO
       FROM      PLAYERS
       WHERE     TOWN NOT IN ('Stratford', 'Douglas')
       or

       SELECT    PLAYERNO
       FROM      PLAYERS
       WHERE     NOT TOWN IN ('Stratford', 'Douglas')

       or

       SELECT    PLAYERNO
       FROM      PLAYERS
       WHERE     TOWN <> 'Stratford'
       AND       TOWN <> 'Douglas'

9.15   SELECT    PLAYERNO, NAME
       FROM      PLAYERS
       WHERE     NAME LIKE '%is%'

9.16   SELECT    PLAYERNO, NAME
       FROM      PLAYERS
       WHERE     NAME LIKE '_____'

9.17   SELECT    PLAYERNO, NAME
       FROM      PLAYERS
       WHERE     NAME LIKE '_____%'
       or

       SELECT    PLAYERNO, NAME
       FROM      PLAYERS
       WHERE     NAME LIKE '%_____'

       or

       SELECT    PLAYERNO, NAME
       FROM      PLAYERS
       WHERE     NAME LIKE '%_____%'
```

9.18 SELECT   PLAYERNO, NAME
        FROM   PLAYERS
        WHERE   NAME LIKE '__r%r_'

9.19 SELECT   PLAYERNO
        FROM   PLAYERS
        WHERE   LEAGUENO IS NULL

9.20 The NAME column must be defined as NOT NULL. The column will never contain a NULL value. That is why the condition will be false for every row.

9.21 SELECT   PLAYERNO, NAME
        FROM   PLAYERS
        WHERE   PLAYERNO IN
               (SELECT   PLAYERNO
               FROM   PENALTIES)

9.22 SELECT   PLAYERNO, NAME
        FROM   PLAYERS
        WHERE   PLAYERNO IN
               (SELECT   PLAYERNO
               FROM   PENALTIES
               WHERE   AMOUNT > 50)

9.23 SELECT   TEAMNO, PLAYERNO
        FROM   TEAMS
        WHERE   DIVISION = 'first'
        AND   PLAYERNO IN
               (SELECT   PLAYERNO
               FROM   PLAYERS
               WHERE   TOWN = 'Stratford')

9.24 SELECT   PLAYERNO, NAME
        FROM   PLAYERS
        WHERE   PLAYERNO IN
               (SELECT   PLAYERNO
               FROM   PENALTIES)
        AND   PLAYERNO NOT IN
               (SELECT   PLAYERNO
               FROM   TEAMS
               WHERE   DIVISION = 'first')
        or

```
SELECT    PLAYERNO, NAME
FROM      PLAYERS
WHERE     PLAYERNO IN
          (SELECT   PLAYERNO
           FROM     PENALTIES
           WHERE    PLAYERNO NOT IN
                    (SELECT   PLAYERNO
                     FROM     TEAMS
                     WHERE    DIVISION = 'first'))
```

9.25
```
SELECT    PLAYERNO, NAME
FROM      PLAYERS
WHERE     YEAR_OF_BIRTH =
          (SELECT   YEAR_OF_BIRTH
           FROM     PLAYERS
           WHERE    NAME = 'Parmenter'
           AND      INITIALS = 'R')
AND       NOT (NAME = 'Parmenter'
              AND INITIALS = 'R')
```

9.26
```
SELECT    PLAYERNO
FROM      MATCHES
WHERE     WON =
          (SELECT   WON
           FROM     MATCHES
           WHERE    PLAYERNO = 8
           AND      TEAMNO = 2)
AND       TEAMNO = 2 AND PLAYERNO <> 8
```

9.27
```
SELECT    PLAYERNO
FROM      PLAYERS
WHERE     YEAR_OF_BIRTH <= ALL
          (SELECT   YEAR_OF_BIRTH
           FROM     PLAYERS
           WHERE    TOWN = 'Stratford')
AND       TOWN = 'Stratford'
```

9.28
```
SELECT    PLAYERNO
FROM      PLAYERS
WHERE     PLAYERNO = ANY
          (SELECT   PLAYERNO
           FROM     PENALTIES)
```

9.29 SELECT   NAME, INITIALS
       FROM   PLAYERS
       WHERE   EXISTS
            (SELECT   *
            FROM   TEAMS
            WHERE   PLAYERNO = PLAYERS.PLAYERNO)

9.30 SELECT   NAME, INITIALS
       FROM   PLAYERS
       WHERE   NOT EXISTS
            (SELECT   *
            FROM   TEAMS
            WHERE   PLAYERNO = PLAYERS.PLAYERNO
            AND   TEAMNO IN
                (SELECT   TEAMNO
                FROM   MATCHES
                WHERE   PLAYERNO = 112))

9.31 SELECT   PLAYERNO
       FROM   PLAYERS
       WHERE   PLAYERNO NOT IN
            (SELECT   PLAYERNO
            FROM   MATCHES
            WHERE   WON = 3)

9.32 SELECT   TEAMNO, DIVISION
       FROM   TEAMS
       WHERE   TEAMNO NOT IN
            (SELECT   TEAMNO
            FROM   MATCHES
            WHERE   PLAYERNO = 6)

9.33 SELECT   PLAYERNO
       FROM   PLAYERS
       WHERE   PLAYERNO NOT IN
            (SELECT   PLAYERNO
            FROM   MATCHES
            WHERE   TEAMNO IN
                (SELECT   TEAMNO
                FROM   MATCHES
                WHERE   PLAYERNO = 57))

Chapter 10

10.1 1.   9
      2.   8

    3.   1
    4.   5
    5.   24
    6. $24 / 8 = 3$
    7.   5
    8.   1
    9.   5
   10.   15
   11. $15 / 5 = 3$

10.2
```
SELECT   AVG(AMOUNT)
FROM     PENALTIES
```

10.3
```
SELECT   AVG(AMOUNT)
FROM     PENALTIES
WHERE    PLAYERNO IN
         (SELECT   PLAYERNO
          FROM     MATCHES
          WHERE    TEAMNO = 1)
```

10.4
```
SELECT   NAME, INITIALS
FROM     PLAYERS
WHERE    PLAYERNO IN
         (SELECT   PLAYERNO
          FROM     MATCHES
          WHERE    WON >
                  (SELECT   SUM(WON)
                   FROM     MATCHES
                   WHERE    PLAYERNO = 27))
```

10.5
```
SELECT   SUM(WON), SUM(LOST), SUM(WON) - SUM(LOST)
FROM     MATCHES
```

10.6
```
SELECT   PLAYERNO, YEAR_OF_BIRTH
FROM     PLAYERS
WHERE    YEAR_OF_BIRTH =
         (SELECT   MIN(YEAR_OF_BIRTH)
          FROM     PLAYERS
          WHERE    PLAYERNO IN
                  (SELECT   PLAYERNO
                   FROM     MATCHES
                   WHERE    TEAMNO = 1))
```

Chapter 11

```
11.1  SELECT    YEAR_OF_BIRTH
      FROM      PLAYERS
      GROUP BY  YEAR_OF_BIRTH

11.2  SELECT    YEAR_OF_BIRTH, COUNT(*)
      FROM      PLAYERS
      GROUP BY  YEAR_OF_BIRTH

11.3  SELECT    PLAYERNO, AVG(AMOUNT), COUNT(*)
      FROM      PENALTIES
      GROUP BY  PLAYERNO

11.4  SELECT    TEAMNO, COUNT(*), SUM(WON)
      FROM      MATCHES
      WHERE     TEAMNO IN
                (SELECT   TEAMNO
                 FROM     TEAMS
                 WHERE    DIVISION = 'first')
      GROUP BY  TEAMNO

11.5  SELECT    NAME, INITIALS, COUNT(*)
      FROM      PLAYERS P, PENALTIES PEN
      WHERE     P.PLAYERNO = PEN.PLAYERNO
      AND       P.TOWN = 'Douglas'
      GROUP BY  P.PLAYERNO, NAME, INITIALS

11.6  SELECT    T.TEAMNO, DIVISION, SUM(WON)
      FROM      TEAMS T, MATCHES MAT
      WHERE     T.TEAMNO = MAT.TEAMNO
      GROUP BY  T.TEAMNO, DIVISION

11.7  SELECT    TO_CHAR(PEN_DATE, 'YYYY'), COUNT(*)
      FROM      PENALTIES
      WHERE     YEAR < 1983
      GROUP BY  TO_CHAR(PEN_DATE, 'YYYY')

11.8  SELECT    TOWN
      FROM      PLAYERS
      GROUP BY  TOWN
      HAVING    COUNT(*) > 4

11.9  SELECT    PLAYERNO
      FROM      PENALTIES
      GROUP BY  PLAYERNO
      HAVING    SUM(AMOUNT) > 150
```

```
11.10 SELECT   NAME, INITIALS, COUNT(*)
      FROM     PLAYERS, PENALTIES
      WHERE    PLAYERS.PLAYERNO = PENALTIES.PLAYERNO
      GROUP BY PLAYERS.PLAYERNO, NAME, INITIALS
      HAVING   COUNT(*) > 1

11.11 SELECT   TO_CHAR(PEN_DATE, 'YYYY')
      FROM     PENALTIES
      GROUP BY TO_CHAR(PEN_DATE, 'YYYY')
      HAVING   COUNT(*) = 2

11.12 SELECT   TEAMNO, COUNT(*)
      FROM     MATCHES
      GROUP BY TEAMNO
      HAVING   COUNT(*) >= ALL
               (SELECT   COUNT(*)
                FROM     MATCHES
                GROUP BY TEAMNO)

11.13 SELECT   TEAMNO, DIVISION
      FROM     TEAMS
      WHERE    TEAMNO IN
               (SELECT   TEAMNO
                FROM     MATCHES
                GROUP BY TEAMNO
                HAVING   COUNT(*) > 4)

11.14 SELECT   NAME, INITIALS
      FROM     PLAYERS
      WHERE    PLAYERNO IN
               (SELECT   PLAYERNO
                FROM     PENALTIES
                WHERE    AMOUNT > 40
                GROUP BY PLAYERNO
                HAVING   COUNT(*) > 2)

11.15 SELECT   NAME, INITIALS
      FROM     PLAYERS
      WHERE    PLAYERNO IN
               (SELECT   PLAYERNO
                FROM     PENALTIES
                GROUP BY PLAYERNO
                HAVING   SUM(AMOUNT) >= ALL
                         (SELECT   SUM(AMOUNT)
                          FROM     PENALTIES
                          GROUP BY PLAYERNO))
```

11.16 SELECT   PLAYERNO
       FROM   PENALTIES
       WHERE   PLAYERNO <> 6
       GROUP BY PLAYERNO
       HAVING   SUM(AMOUNT) =
                 (SELECT   SUM(AMOUNT)
                  FROM   PENALTIES
                  WHERE   PLAYERNO = 6)

11.17 SELECT   PLAYERNO
       FROM   PENALTIES
       WHERE   PLAYERNO <> 6
       GROUP BY PLAYERNO
       HAVING   COUNT(*) =
                 (SELECT   COUNT(*)
                  FROM   PENALTIES
                  WHERE   PLAYERNO = 6)

11.18 SELECT   TEAMNO, COUNT(*)
       FROM   MATCHES
       WHERE   TEAMNO IN
                 (SELECT   TEAMNO
                  FROM   PLAYERS P, TEAMS T
                  WHERE   P.PLAYERNO = T.PLAYERNO
                  AND   TOWN = 'Stratford')
       AND   WON > LOST
       GROUP BY TEAMNO

11.19 SELECT   TO_CHAR(PEN_DATE, 'YYYY'), COUNT(*)
       FROM   PENALTIES
       GROUP BY TO_CHAR(DATE, 'YYYY')
       HAVING   COUNT(*) >= ALL
                 (SELECT   COUNT(*)
                  FROM   PENALTIES
                  GROUP BY TO_CHAR(PEN_DATE, 'YYYY'))

Chapter 12

12.1 1.   ORDER BY 1
      2.   ORDER BY PLAYERNO
      3.   ORDER BY 1 ASC
      4.   ORDER BY PLAYERNO ASC

12.2 1.   Correct.
      2.   Incorrect, because there is no twentieth column in the PLAYERS
            table.

3. Incorrect, because sorting is specified twice on the INITIALS column.

4. Incorrect, because a column in an ORDER BY clause may not be specified twice.

12.3
```
SELECT   PLAYERNO, TEAMNO, WON - LOST
FROM     MATCHES
ORDER BY 3 ASC
```

Chapter 13

13.1
```
SELECT   LPAD(' ', 3*(LEVEL-1)) || SUB
FROM     PARTS
CONNECT  BY PRIOR SUB = SUPER
START    WITH SUB IN ('P3', P9')
```

13.2
```
SELECT   LEVEL
FROM     PARTS
WHERE    SUB = 'P12'
CONNECT  BY PRIOR SUB = SUPER
START    WITH SUB = 'P1'
```

13.3
```
SELECT   COUNT(*)
FROM     PARTS
WHERE    PRICE > 20
AND      SUB <> 'P1'
CONNECT  BY PRIOR SUB = SUPER
START    WITH SUB = 'P1'
```

13.4
```
SELECT   SUPER
FROM     PARTS
WHERE    SUPER IS NOT NULL
CONNECT  BY SUB = PRIOR SUPER
START    WITH SUB = 'P12'
```

Chapter 14

14.1 1. Correct.

2. Correct; the fact that the lengths of the columns NAME and POSTCODE are not equal is not important.

3. Correct.

4. Correct; although DISTINCT is superfluous in this SELECT statement.

5. Incorrect, because when a UNION operator is used, only the last SELECT statement can include an ORDER BY clause.

14.2 1.   6
      2.   14
      3.   18

Chapter 15

15.1 1.   A.C1 : Q_1, Q_2, Q_3, Q_4, Q_5
      2.   B.C1 : Q_2, Q_3, Q_4
      3.   C.C1 : Q_3
      4.   D.C1 : Q_4
      5.   E.C1 : Q_5

15.2
```
SELECT    NAME, INITIALS
FROM      PLAYERS
WHERE     PLAYERNO IN
          (SELECT   PLAYERNO
           FROM     MATCHES
           WHERE    TEAMNO IN
                    (SELECT   TEAMNO
                     FROM     TEAMS
                     WHERE    DIVISION = 'first'))
AND       PLAYERNO IN
          (SELECT   PLAYERNO
           FROM     MATCHES
           WHERE    WON > LOST)
AND       PLAYERNO NOT IN
          (SELECT   PLAYERNO
           FROM     PENALTIES)
```

15.3
```
SELECT    PLAYERNO, NAME
FROM      PLAYERS
WHERE     PLAYERNO IN
          (SELECT   PLAYERNO
           FROM     MATCHES
           WHERE    TEAMNO = 1)
AND       PLAYERNO IN
          (SELECT   PLAYERNO
           FROM     MATCHES
           WHERE    TEAMNO = 2)
```

15.4
```
SELECT    PLAYERNO, NAME
FROM      PLAYERS
WHERE     EXISTS
          (SELECT   *
           FROM     PENALTIES
           WHERE    PLAYERNO = PLAYERS.PLAYERNO)
```

```
15.5  SELECT    PLAYERNO, NAME
      FROM      PLAYERS
      WHERE     PLAYERNO IN
               (SELECT   PLAYERNO
                FROM     MATCHES M1
                WHERE    WON > LOST
                AND      EXISTS
                        (SELECT   *
                         FROM     MATCHES M2
                         WHERE    M1.PLAYERNO = M2.PLAYERNO
                         AND      WON > LOST
                         AND      M1.TEAMNO = M2.TEAMNO))
      or

      SELECT    PLAYERNO, NAME
      FROM      PLAYERS
      WHERE     1 <
               (SELECT   COUNT(*)
                FROM     MATCHES
                WHERE    WON > LOST
                AND      PLAYERS.PLAYERNO = PLAYERNO)

15.6  SELECT    NAME, INITIALS
      FROM      PLAYERS
      WHERE     NOT EXISTS
               (SELECT   *
                FROM     PENALTIES
                WHERE    PLAYERS.PLAYERNO = PLAYERNO
                AND      PEN_DATE BETWEEN '01-JAN-80'
                         AND '31-DEC-80')

15.7  SELECT    DISTINCT PLAYERNO
      FROM      PENALTIES P1
      WHERE     EXISTS
               (SELECT   PENALTIES P2
                WHERE    P1.AMOUNT = P2.AMOUNT
                AND      P1.PAYMENTNO <> P2.PAYMENTNO)

15.8  1.   SELECT    *
           FROM      PLAYERS P
           WHERE     1 <=
                    (SELECT   COUNT(*)
                     FROM     PENALTIES PN
                     WHERE    P.PLAYERNO = PN.PLAYERNO)
```

```
2.    SELECT    *
      FROM      PLAYERS P
      WHERE     YEAR_OF_BIRTH <=
                (SELECT   MAX(YEAR_OF_BIRTH)
                 FROM     PLAYERS)

3.    SELECT    *
      FROM      PLAYERS P1
      WHERE     NOT EXISTS <=
                (SELECT   *
                 FROM     PLAYERS P2
                 WHERE    TOWN = 'Stratford'
                 AND      NOT(P2.YEAR_OF_BIRTH <=
                              P1.YEAR_OF_BIRTH))

4.    SELECT    *
      FROM      PLAYERS P1
      WHERE     1 <=
                (SELECT   COUNT(*)
                 FROM     PLAYERS P2
                 WHERE    P2.PLAYERNO = P1.PLAYERNO + 1)
```

Chapter 16

```
16.1  SELECT    PLAYERNO, SUM(WON)
      FROM      MATCHES
      GROUP BY  PLAYERNO
      UNION
      SELECT    PLAYERNO, 0
      FROM      PLAYERS
      WHERE     PLAYERNO NOT IN
                (SELECT   PLAYERNO
                 FROM     MATCHES)

16.2  SELECT    PLAYERNO, SUM(AMOUNT)
      FROM      PENALTIES
      GROUP BY  PLAYERNO
      UNION
      SELECT    PLAYERNO, NULL
      FROM      PLAYERS
      WHERE     PLAYERNO NOT IN
                (SELECT   PLAYERNO
                 FROM     PENALTIES)
```

16.3 SELECT   PLAYERNO, TEAMNO
          FROM   MATCHES
          UNION
          SELECT   PLAYERNO, NULL
          FROM   PLAYERS
          WHERE   PLAYERNO NOT IN
                    (SELECT   PLAYERNO
                     FROM   MATCHES)
          ORDER BY 1, 2

16.4 1.   T1.C T2.C
                ---- ----
                  2   3
                  2   3

          2.   T1.C T2.C
                ---- ----
                  2   2
                  3   3

          3.   T1.C T2.C
                ---- ----
                  1   ?
                  2   2
                  3   3

          4.   T1.C T2.C
                ---- ----
                  2   2
                  3   3
                  ?   4

          5.   T1.C T2.C
                ---- ----
                  3   2
                  ?   3
                  ?   4

          6.   T1.C T4.C
                ---- ----
                  ?   ?
                  2   2

          7.   T1.C T4.C
                ---- ----
                  1   ?
                  2   2
                  3   ?

16.5 1.

```
  T1.C   T2.C   T3.C
  ----   ----   ----
   2      2      2
   3      3      3
```

2.

```
  T1.C   T2.C   T3.C
  ----   ----   ----
   ?      4      ?
   2      2      2
   3      3      3
```

3.

```
  T1.C   T2.C   T3.C
  ----   ----   ----
   1      ?      ?
   2      2      2
   3      3      3
```

4.

```
  T1.C   T2.C   T3.C
  ----   ----   ----
   ?      ?      5
   2      2      2
   3      3      3
```

5.

```
  T1.C   T2.C   T3.C
  ----   ----   ----
   2      2      2
   3      3      3
```

Chapter 17

17.1 UPDATE   PLAYERS
         SET   SEX = 'W'
         WHERE   SEX = 'F'

17.2 UPDATE   PLAYERS
         SET   SEX = DECODE(SEX, 'F', 'M', 'F')

17.3 UPDATE   PENALTIES
         SET   AMOUNT = AMOUNT * 1.2
         WHERE   AMOUNT >
                   (SELECT   AVG(AMOUNT)
                   FROM   PENALTIES)

17.4 UPDATE   PLAYERS
         SET   (TOWN, STREET, HOUSENO) =
                   (SELECT   TOWN, STREET, HOUSENO
                   FROM   PLAYERS
                   WHERE   PLAYERNO = 6)
         WHERE   PLAYERNO = 95

17.5 DELETE
        FROM   PENALTIES
        WHERE   PLAYERNO = 44
        AND   TO_CHAR(DATUM, 'YYYY') = '1980'

17.6 DELETE
        FROM   PENALTIES
        WHERE   PLAYERNO IN
                  (SELECT   PLAYERNO
                  FROM   MATCHES
                  WHERE   TEAMNO IN
                            (SELECT   TEAMNO
                            FROM   TEAMS
                            WHERE   DIVISION = 'second'))

17.7 DELETE
        FROM   PLAYERS
        WHERE   TOWN =
                  (SELECT   TOWN
                  FROM   PLAYERS)
                  WHERE   PLAYERNO = 44
        AND   PLAYERNO <> 44

Chapter 18

18.1 1.   CREATE SEQUENCE EVEN_NUMBERS
              START WITH 2
              INCREMENT BY 2

      2.   CREATE SEQUENCE TENS
              START WITH 80
              INCREMENT BY -10

      3.   CREATE SEQUENCE FROM_1_TO_4
              START WITH 1
              INCREMENT BY 1
              MINVALUE 1
              MAXVALUE 4
              NOCACHE
              CYCLE

      4.   CREATE SEQUENCE BIT
              START WITH 0
              MINVALUE 0
              MAXVALUE 1
              NOCACHE
              CYCLE

Chapter 19

19.1　The NOT NULL integrity rule may be specified, but this is not mandatory; all columns belonging to a primary key are by definition NOT NULL.

19.2
```
CREATE   TABLE MATCHES
         (MATCHNO   SMALLINT NOT NULL
                    PRIMARY KEY CONSTRAINT MAT_PRIM1,
          TEAMNO    SMALLINT NOT NULL,
          PLAYERNO  SMALLINT NOT NULL,
          WON       SMALLINT NOT NULL,
          LOST      SMALLINT NOT NULL)
```
or:
```
CREATE   TABLE MATCHES
         (MATCHNO   SMALLINT NOT NULL,
          TEAMNO    SMALLINT NOT NULL,
          PLAYERNO  SMALLINT NOT NULL,
          WON       SMALLINT NOT NULL,
          LOST      SMALLINT NOT NULL,
          PRIMARY KEY  (MATCHNO) CONSTRAINT MAT_PRIM1)
```

19.3　No, this must be done with an ALTER TABLE statement.

19.4　The following updates are no longer permitted:

- The deletion of a player from the PLAYERS table is now only permitted if that player has played no matches.

- The updating of a player number in the PLAYERS table is only possible if that player has played no matches.

- The deletion of a team from the TEAMS table is now only permitted if no matches are played for that team.

- The updating of a team number in the TEAMS table is only possible if no matches are played for that team.

- For inserting new players into the PLAYERS table there are no restrictions laid down by the foreign keys.

- For inserting new teams into the TEAMS table there are no restrictions laid down by the foreign keys.

- For deleting existing matches from the MATCHES table there are no restrictions laid down by the foreign keys.

- The updating of a player number in the MATCHES table is only permitted if the new player number already occurs in the PLAYERS table.

- The updating of a team number in the MATCHES table is only permitted if the new team number already occurs in the TEAMS table.

- The insertion of new matches into the MATCHES table is only permitted if the new player number already occurs in the PLAYERS table and the new team number occurs in the TEAMS table.

19.5 ALTER TABLE PENALTIES
ADD   (CHECK (AMOUNT > 0)
                CONSTRAINT AMOUNT_POSITIVE)

19.6 ALTER TABLE MATCHES
ADD   (CHECK (WON + LOST < 6)
                CONSTRAINT SETS_MAX_6)

Chapter 20

20.1 1.   Basic strategy:

```
RESULT := [];
FOR EACH T IN TEAMS DO
   IF (T.TEAMNO > 1)
   AND (T.DIVISION = 'second') THEN
      RESULT :+ T;
OD;
```

Optimized strategy:

```
RESULT := [];
FOR EACH T IN TEAMS
WHERE DIVISION = 'second' DO
   IF T.TEAMNO > 1 THEN
      RESULT :+ T;
OD;
```

2.   Basic strategy:

```
RESULT := [];
FOR EACH P IN PLAYERS DO
   FOR EACH M1 IN MATCHES DO
      IF P.PLAYERNO = M1.PLAYERNO AND
         P.YEAR_OF_BIRTH > 1963 THEN
         RESULT :+ P;
   OD;
OD;
```

Optimized strategy:

```
RESULT := [];
FOR EACH P IN PLAYERS
WHERE YEAR_OF_BIRTH > 1963 DO
    FOR EACH M1 IN MATCHES DO
        IF P.PLAYERNO = M1.PLAYERNO THEN
            RESULT :+ P;
    OD;
OD;
```

Chapter 21

21.1 1.
```
SELECT    *
FROM      PLAYERS
WHERE     TOWN = 'Stratford'
AND       STREET = 'Edgecombe Way'
UNION
SELECT    *
FROM      PLAYERS
WHERE     YEAR_OF_BIRTH < 1960
```

2.
```
SELECT    DISTINCT TEAMS.*
FROM      TEAMS, MATCHES
WHERE     TEAMS.TEAMNO = MATCHES.TEAMNO
AND       LOST = 4
```

3.
```
SELECT    DISTINCT T.TEAMNO
FROM      TEAMS T, MATCHES M
WHERE     T.TEAMNO = M.TEAMNO
AND       DIVISION = 'second'
```

4.
```
SELECT    PLAYERNO
FROM      PLAYERS
```

Chapter 22

22.1
```
CREATE    VIEW NUMBER_PLAYERS
          (TEAMNO, NUMBER) AS
SELECT    TEAMNO, COUNT(*)
FROM      MATCHES
GROUP BY TEAMNO
```

22.2 CREATE   VIEW WINNERS AS
          SELECT   PLAYERNO, NAME
          FROM   PLAYERS
          WHERE   PLAYERNO IN
                    (SELECT   PLAYERNO
                     FROM   MATCHES
                     WHERE   WON > LOST)

22.3 CREATE   VIEW TOTAL_PENALTIES
                    (PLAYERNO, SUM_PENALTIES) AS
          SELECT   PLAYERNO, SUM(AMOUNT)
          FROM   PENALTIES
          GROUP BY PLAYERNO

22.4

view	UPDATE	INSERT	DELETE
TOWNS	no	no	no
C_PLAYERS	yes	no	yes
SEVERAL	yes	no	yes
SFD_FOLK	yes	no	yes
RESIDENT	no	no	no
VETERAN	yes	yes	yes
YOUTH	no	no	no
AGES	yes	no	yes
PLAYERS_NAMES	yes	no	yes

22.5 1.   SELECT   YEAR_OF_BIRTH - 1900, COUNT(*)
                FROM   PLAYERS
                WHERE   TOWN = 'Stratford'
                GROUP BY 1

          2.   SELECT   P2.PLAYERNO
                FROM   PLAYERS P1, PLAYERS P2
                WHERE   P1.PLAYERNO = P2.PLAYERNO
                AND   P1.PLAYERNO IN
                          (SELECT   PLAYERNO
                           FROM   PENALTIES)
                AND   P2.TOWN = 'Stratford'

          3.   UPDATE   PLAYERS
                SET   YEAR_OF_BIRTH = 1950
                WHERE   PLAYERNO = 7

22.6 1. Yes, for retrieval purposes only, but not for updates, because the view formula will contain an outer equijoin.

2. Yes

3. Yes, for retrieval purposes only, but not for updates, because the view formula will contain a join.

Chapter 23

23.1 The USER$ table:

USER#	NAME	CTIME	CONNECT$	DBA$	RESOURCE$
80	REGINA	12-DEC-90	1	0	0
81	OLGA	12-DEC-90	1	0	0
82	SUSAN	12-DEC-90	1	0	0

The TABAUTH$ table:

OBJ#	GRANTOR#	GRANTEE#	SEQUENCE#	A	D	X	I	S	U	R
4211	50	1	23	0	0	0	0	2	0	0
4211	50	81	24	0	0	0	3	0	0	0
4211	81	80	25	0	0	0	2	0	0	0
4211	81	82	26	0	0	0	3	0	0	0
4211	82	80	27	0	0	0	2	0	0	0

Chapter 24

24.1 The effect of an AUDIT statement in that situation is that the audit specification is stored in the catalog. However, no real auditing is done.

24.2 ```
AUDIT RESOURCE
WHENEVER SUCCESSFUL
```

**24.3** ```
AUDIT ALL
```

24.4 ```
AUDIT NOT EXISTS
```

**24.5** ```
AUDIT COMMENT, RENAME, GRANT
ON     PLAYERS
BY     SESSION
```

24.6 ```
AUDIT ALL
ON   MATCHES
BY   ACCESS
```
```

24.7 1.   SELECT   TERMINAL
               FROM   SYS.AUD$
               WHERE   OBJ$NAME = 'MATCHES'
               AND   OBJ$CREATOR = 'SQLDBA'
               AND   ACTION IN (2, 6, 7)

       2.   SELECT   COUNT(*)
               FROM   SYS.AUD$
               WHERE   OBJ$NAME = 'PLAYERS'
               AND   OBJ$CREATOR = 'SQLDBA'
               AND   ACTION = 3
               AND   TIMESTAMP BETWEEN '01-JAN-90' AND '31-MAR-90'

       3.   SELECT   OBJ$.CREATOR, OBJ$NAME
               FROM   SYS.AUD$
               WHERE   USERID <> OBJ$CREATOR
               AND   ACTION IN (15, 28)

Chapter 27

27.1 SELECT   COUNT(*)
         FROM   SYS.IND$ I, SYS.USER$ U
         WHERE   I.OWNER# = U.USER#
         AND   U.NAME = 'JAKE'
         AND   I.TYPE = 1
         AND   BO# =
                   (SELECT   OBJ#
                    FROM   SYS.OBJ$ T, SYS.USER$ U
                    WHERE   T.OWNER# = U.USER#
                    AND   U.NAME = 'SQLDBA'
                    AND   T.NAME = 'PLAYERS')

27.2 SELECT   V.TEXT
         FROM   SYS.VIEW$ V, SYS.XREF$ REF, SYS.OBJ$ O,
                   SYS.USER$ U
         WHERE   V.OBJ# = O.OBJ#
         AND   O.OWNER# = U.USER#
         AND   O.TYPE = 4
         AND   REF.RNAME = 'PLAYERS'
         AND   REF.ROWNER = 'JAKE'
         AND   REF.NAME = O.NAME
         AND   REF.OWNER = U.NAME

27.3 SELECT   IND.NAME
      FROM   SYS.IND$ IND, SYS.OBJ$ IND_OWNER,
                  SYS.OBJ$ TAB_OWNER
      WHERE   IND.OBJ# = IND_OWNER.OBJ#
      AND   IND.BO# = TAB_OWNER.OBJ#
      AND   IND_OWNER.OWNER# = IND_OWNER.OWNER#

Chapter 29

29.1 1.   %ROWTYPE may only be used after the name of a table; in this example %TYPE might have been used.

2.   The keyword CONSTANT has to be specified in front of the data type.

3.   The variable that is being declared may not appear within the PL/SQL expression.

4.   Only one variable may be declared.

Appendix B
Syntax of SQL

In this appendix we explain the notation method we have used to describe the statements and give definitions of the SQL statements themselves. We also list the reserved words or keywords.

B.1 The BNF notation

In this appendix and throughout the book we have used a formal notation method to describe the syntax of all SQL statements and the common elements. This notation is a variant on the *Backus Naur Form* (BNF) which is named after John Backus and Peter Naur. The meaning of the metasymbols that we use is based on that of the metasymbols in the SQL standard.

BNF adopts a language of so-called *substitution rules* or *production rules* consisting of a series of symbols. A *symbol* is defined in each production rule. A symbol could be, for example, an SQL statement, a table name or a colon. A *terminal symbol* is a special sort of symbol. All symbols, apart from the terminal symbols, are defined in terms of other symbols in a production rule. Examples of terminal symbols are the word CLOSE and the semi-colon.

You could liken a production rule to the definition of an element where the definition of that element uses elements that are defined somewhere else. In this case, an element equates with a symbol.

The following metasymbols do not form part of the SQL language, but belong to the notation.

- < >
- : : =
- |

- [ ]
- . . .
- { }
- "

We now explain each of these symbols.

The symbols < and >

Non-terminal symbols are presented in < >. A production rule exists for every non-terminal symbol. We will show the non-terminal symbols in lower case letters. Two examples of non-terminal symbols are <select statement> and <table name>.

The ::= symbol

The ::= symbol is used in a production rule to separate the non-terminal symbol that is defined (left) from the definition (right). The ::= symbol should be read 'is defined as'. See the example below of the production rule for the CLOSE statement:

```
<close statement> ::= CLOSE <cursor name>
```

Explanation: The CLOSE statement consists of the terminal symbol CLOSE followed by the non-terminal symbol cursor name. There should also be a production rule for <cursor name>.

The | symbol

Alternatives are represented by the | symbol. Below we give an example of the production rule for the element <character>:

```
<character> ::= <digit> | <letter> | <special character>
```

Explanation: We should take from this that a character is a digit, a letter or a special character: one of the three.

The symbols [and]

Whatever is placed between square brackets [and] *may* be used. Here is the production rule for the ROLLBACK statement:

```
<rollback statement> ::= ROLLBACK [ WORK ]
```

Explanation: A ROLLBACK statement always consists of the word ROLLBACK and can optionally be followed by the word WORK.

The ... symbol

The ellipsis shows what may be repeated one or more times. Here our example is the production rule for an integer:

```
<integer> ::= <digit>...
```

Explanation: An integer consists of a series of digits (with a minimum of one).

The symbols { and }

All symbols between braces form a group. For example, braces used with the | symbol show precisely what the alternatives are. The next example is the production rule for the FROM clause:

```
<from clause> ::=
    FROM <table reference> [ { , <table reference> }... ]
```

Explanation: A FROM clause begins with the terminal symbol FROM and is followed by at least one table reference. It is possible to follow this table reference with a list of elements, whereby each element consists of a comma followed by a table reference. Don't forget that the comma is part of SQL and not of the notation.

The " symbol

A small number of metasymbols, such as the " symbol, are part of particular SQL statements themselves. In order to avoid misunderstanding, these symbols are enclosed by double quotation marks. Among other things, this means that the symbol " that is used within SQL is represented in the production rules as """".

Additional remarks

- Whatever is presented in upper case letters, as well as the symbols which are not part of the notation, must be adopted unaltered.

- The sequence of the symbols in the right-hand part of the production rule is fixed.

- Blanks in production rules have no significance. Generally, they have been added to make the production rules more readable. The two following production rules are equal:

```
<alphanumeric literal> ::= ' [ <character>... ] '
```

and

```
<alphanumeric literal> ::= '[<character>...]'
```

B.2   Reserved words in Oracle

ACCESS, ADD, ALL, ALTER, AND, ANY, ARCHIVELOG, AS,
ASC, AUDIT, AUTHORIZATION,
BACKUP, BEGIN, BETWEEN, BY, CACHE, CHAR, CHARACTER,
CHECK, CLOSE, CLUSTER, COBOL, COLUMN, COMMENT, COMMIT,
COMPRESS, CONNECT, CONSTRAINT, CONTENTS, CONTINUE,
CONTROLFILE, CRASH, CREATE, CURRENT, CURSOR, CYCLE,
DATABASE, DATAFILE, DATE, DBA, DEC, DECIMAL,
DECLARE, DEFAULT, DELETE, DESC, DISMOUNT, DISTINCT,
DOUBLE, DROP,
ELSE, END, ESCAPE, EVENTS, EXCLUSIVE, EXEC, EXISTS,
FETCH, FILE, FLOAT, FOR, FOREIGN, FORTRAN, FOUND,
FROM,
GO, GOTO, GRANT, GRAPHIC, GROUP,
HAVING,
IDENTIFIED, IF, IMMEDIATE, IN, INCLUDING, INCREMENT,
INDEX, INDICATOR, INITIAL, INITRANS, INSERT, INT,
INTEGER, INTERSECT, INTO, IS,
KEY,
LANGUAGE, LEVEL, LIKE, LINK, LOCK, LOGFILE, LONG,
MAXDATAFILES, MAXEXTENTS, MAXINSTANCES,
MAXLOGFILES, MAXTRANS, MAXVALUE, MINEXTENTS,
MINUS, MINVALUE, MODE, MODIFY, MODULE, MOUNT,
NEXT, NOARCHIVELOG, NOAUDIT, NOCACHE, NOCOMPRESS,
NOCYCLE, NOMAXVALUE, NOMINVALUE, NOORDER, NORMAL,
NOSORT, NOT, NOWAIT, NULL, NUMBER, NUMERIC,
OF, OFFLINE, ON, ONLINE, ONLY, OPEN, OPTION, OR, ORDER,
PASCAL, PCTFREE, PCTINCREASE, PCTUSED, PL1, PRECISION,
PRIMARY, PRIOR, PRIVILEGES, PROCEDURE, PUBLIC,
RAW, READ, REAL, REFERENCES, RELEASE, RENAME,
RESETLOGS, RESOURCE, REUSE, REVOKE, ROLLBACK,
ROW, ROWID, ROWNUM, ROWS,
SAVEPOINT, SCHEMA, SECTION, SEGMENT, SELECT,
SEQUENCE, SESSION, SET, SHARE, SHARED, SIZE,
SMALLINT, SOME, SORT, SPECIFIED, SQL, SQLCODE,
SQLERROR, START, STATEMENT, STORAGE, SUCCESSFUL,
SWITCH, SYNONYM, SYSDATE, SYSTEM,
TABLE, TABLES, TABLESPACE, TEMPORARY, THEN, TO,
TRANSACTION, TRIGGER,
UID, UNION, UNIQUE, UPDATE, USER, USING,
VALIDATE, VALUES, VARCHAR, VARGRAPHIC, VIEW,
WHENEVER, WHERE, WITH, WORK, WRITE

B.3 Reserved words in PL/SQL

ABORT, ACCEPT, ACCESS, ADD, ALL, ALTER, AND, ANY, ARRAY,
AS, ASC, ASSERT, ASSIGN, AT, AUTHORIZATION, AVG,
BEGIN, BETWEEN, BODY, BOOLEAN, BY,
CASE, CHAR, CHAR_BASE, CHECK, CLOSE, CLUSTER, CLUSTERS,
COLAUTH, COLUMNS, COMMIT, COMPRESS, CONNECT, CONSTANT,
COUNT, CRASH, CREATE, CURRENT, CURSOR,
DATABASE, DATA_BASE, DATE, DBA, DEBUGOFF, DEBUGON,
DECLARE, DEFAULT, DEFINITION, DELAY, DELETE, DELTA, DESC,
DIGITS, DISPOSE, DISTINCT, DO, DROP,
ELSE, ELSIF, END, ENTRY, EXCEPTION, EXCEPTION_INIT, EXISTS,
EXIT,
FALSE, FETCH, FOR, FORM, FROM, FUNCTION,
GENERIC, GOTO, GRANT, GROUP,
HAVING,
IDENTIFIED, IF, IN, INDEX, INDEXES, INDICATOR, INSERT,
INTERSECT, INTO, IS,
LEVEL, LIKE, LIMITED, LOOP,
MAX, MIN, MINUS, MOD,
NEW, NOCOMPRESS, NOT, NULL, NUMBER, NUMBER_BASE,
OF, ON, OPEN, OPTION, OR, ORDER, OTHERS, OUT,
PACKAGE, PARTITION, PCTFREE, PRAGMA, PRIOR, PRIVATE,
PROCEDURE, PUBLIC,
RAISE, RANGE, RECORD, RELEASE, REM, RENAME, RESOURCE,
RETURN, REVERSE, REVOKE, ROLLBACK, ROWNUM, ROWTYPE, RUN,
SAVEPOINT, SCHEMA, SELECT, SEPARATE, SET, SIZE, SPACE, SQL,
SQLCODE, SQLERRM, START, STATEMENT, STDDEV, SUBTYPE,SUM,
TABAUTH, TABLE, TABLES, TASK, TERMINATE, THEN, TO, TRUE, TYPE,
UNION, UNIQUE, UPDATE, USE,
VALUES, VARCHAR, VARIANCE, VIEW, VIEWS,
WHEN, WHERE, WHILE, WITH, WORK,
XOR

B.4 Definitions of SQL statements

This section contains all the SQL statements that have been described in this book. You will find the common elements of these statements in Section B.6.

```
<alter sequence statement> ::=
   ALTER SEQUENCE [ <user>. ] <sequence name>
     [ <sequence option>... ]

<alter table statement> ::=
   ALTER TABLE <table specification> <alter action>...
```

```
<alter tablespace statement> ::=
   ALTER TABLESPACE <tablespace name>
   ADD DATAFILE <file specification> [ {,<file specification>}... ]

<alter user statement> ::=
   ALTER USER <user>
      [ IDENTIFIED BY <password> ]
      [ DEFAULT TABLESPACE <tablespace name> ]

<audit statement> ::=
   <audit system statement> |
   <audit table statement>

<audit system statement> ::=
   AUDIT <system audit specifications>
   [ WHENEVER [ NOT ] SUCCESSFUL ]

<audit table statement> ::=
   AUDIT <table audit specifications>
   ON <audit object>
   [ BY { SESSION | ACCESS } ]
   [ WHENEVER [ NOT ] SUCCESSFUL ]

<close statement> ::= CLOSE <cursor name>

<comment statement> ::=
   COMMENT ON <comment specification>

<commit statement> ::=
   [ <at clause> ] COMMIT [ WORK ] [ RELEASE ]

<connect statement> ::=
   CONNECT <user password>
   [ USING <sqlnet specification> ]

<create cluster statement> ::=
   CREATE CLUSTER [ <user> .] <cluster name>
   ( <cluster column> [ {,<cluster column>}... ] )
   [ TABLESPACE <tablespace name> ]
   [ <storage specification> ]

<create database link statement> ::=
   CREATE [ PUBLIC ] DATABASE LINK <database link name>
   [ CONNECT TO <user> IDENTIFIED BY <password> ]
   USING <sqlnet specification>

<create index statement> ::=
   <create cluster index statement> |
   <create table index statetement>

<create cluster index statement> ::=
   CREATE [ UNIQUE ] INDEX [ <user> . ] <index name>
   ON    CLUSTER <cluster name>
   [ COMPRESS | NOCOMPRESS ]
   [ TABLESPACE <tablespace name> ]
   [ <storage specification> ]
```

```
<create table index statement> ::=
   CREATE [ UNIQUE ] INDEX [ <user> . ] <index name>
   ON     <table specification>
   ( <column in index> [ {,<column in index>}... ] )
   [ COMPRESS | NOCOMPRESS ]
   [ TABLESPACE <tablespace name> ]
   [ <storage specification> ]

<create sequence statement> ::=
   CREATE SEQUENCE [ <user>. ] <sequence name>
      [ <sequence option>... ]

<create synonym statement> ::=
   CREATE [ PUBLIC ] SYNONYM <table name>
      FOR <table specification>

<create table statement> ::=
   <create table copy statement> |
   <create table new statement>

<create table copy statement> ::=
   CREATE TABLE <table name>
   [ ( <copy column> [ {,<copy column>}... ] ) ]
   [ TABLESPACE <tablespace name> ]
   [ <storage specification> ]
   AS <query expression>

<create table new statement> ::=
   CREATE TABLE <table name> <table schema>
      [ TABLESPACE <tablespace name> ]
      [ <storage specification> ]

<create tablespace statement> ::=
   CREATE TABLESPACE <tablespace name>
   DATAFILE <file specification> [ {,<file specification>}... ]
   [ DEFAULT <storage specification> ]

<create view statement> ::=
   CREATE VIEW <view name>
      [ <column list> ] AS
      <query expression>
      [ <with check option> ]

<declare statement> ::=
   [ <at clause> ]
   DECLARE <cursor name> CURSOR FOR
   <query expression>
   [ <order by clause> | <for update clause> ]

<declare database statement> ::=
   DECLARE <database name> DATABASE

<delete statement> ::=
   [ <at clause> ]
   [ <for clause> ]
   DELETE
   [ FROM ] <table specification>
   [ WHERE <condition> | CURRENT OF CURSOR <cursor name> ]
```

```
<drop cluster statement> ::=
   DROP CLUSTER [ <user>. ] <cluster name> [ INCLUDING TABLES ]

<drop database link statement> ::=
   DROP [ PUBLIC ] DATABASE LINK <database link name>

<drop index statement> ::=
   DROP INDEX [ <user> . ] <index name>

<drop sequence statement> ::=
   DROP SEQUENCE [ <user>. ] <sequence name>

<drop synonym statement> ::=
   DROP [ PUBLIC ] SYNONYM <table specification>

<drop table statement> ::=
   DROP TABLE <table specification>

<drop tablespace statement> ::=
   DROP TABLESPACE <tablespace name> [ INCLUDING CONTENTS ]

<drop view statement> ::=
   DROP VIEW <table specification>

<fetch statement> ::=
   [ <for clause> ]
   FETCH <cursor name>
   INTO  <variable list>

<grant statement> ::=
   <grant connect statement>   |
   <grant dba statement>       |
   <grant resource statement>  |
   <grant table statement>     |
   <grant tablespace statement>

<grant connect statement> ::=
   GRANT CONNECT
   TO     <user> [ {,<user>}... ]
   IDENTIFIED BY <password> [ {,<password>}... ]

<grant dba statement> ::=
   GRANT  DBA
   TO     <user> [ {,<user>}... ]
   [ IDENTIFIED BY <password> [ {,<password>}... ] ]

<grant resource statement> ::=
   GRANT  RESOURCE
   TO     <user> [ {,<user>}... ]

<grant table statement> ::=
   GRANT <table privileges>
   ON    { <table specification> | <sequence name> }
   TO    <users>
   [ WITH GRANT OPTION ]
```

```
<grant tablespace statement> ::=
   GRANT  RESOURCE [ ( <size specification> ) ]
   ON     <table spacename>
   TO     <users>

<insert statement> ::=
   [ <at clause> ]
   [ <for clause> ]
   INSERT INTO <table specification> [ <column list> ]
   { VALUES ( <expression> [ {,<expression>}... ] ) | <query expression> }

<lock table statement> ::=
   LOCK TABLE <table specification> [ {,<table specification>}... ]
   IN <lock type> MODE [ NOWAIT ]

<noaudit statement> ::=
   <noaudit system statement> |
   <noaudit table statement>

<noaudit system statement> ::=
   NOAUDIT <system audit specifications> [ WHENEVER [ NOT ] SUCCESSFUL ]

<noaudit table statement> ::=
   NOAUDIT <table audit specifications>
   ON { <table specification> | DEFAULT }
   [ WHENEVER [ NOT ] SUCCESSFUL ]

<open statement> ::= OPEN <cursor name>

<rename statement> ::=
   RENAME <table specification> TO <table name>

<revoke statement> ::=
   <revoke connect statement> |
   <revoke system statement> |
   <revoke table statement>

<revoke connect statement> ::=
   REVOKE CONNECT
   FROM   <user> [ {,<user>}... ]

<revoke system statement> ::=
   REVOKE { DBA | RESOURCE }
   FROM   <user> [ {,<user>}... ]

<revoke table statement> ::=
   REVOKE <table privileges>
   ON     { <table specification> | <sequence name> }
   FROM   <users>

<rollback statement> ::=
   [ <at clause> ] ROLLBACK [ WORK ]
   [ TO [ SAVEPOINT ] <savepoint name> ] [ RELEASE ]

<savepoint statement> ::=
   SAVEPOINT <savepoint name>
```

```
<select statement> ::=
   <query expression>
   [ <order by clause> ]

<select into statement> ::=
   <at clause>
   <select clause>
   <into clause>
   <from clause>
   [ <where clause> ]
   [ <connect by clause> ]
   [ <group by clause>
   [ <having clause> ] ]

<set transaction statement> ::=
   SET TRANSACTION <transaction type>

<update statement> ::=
   [ <at clause> ]
   [ <for clause> ]
   UPDATE <table specification>
   SET    <update> [ {,<update>}... ]
   [ WHERE  <condition> | CURRENT OF CURSOR <cursor name> ]

<validate index statement> ::=
   VALIDATE INDEX [ <user> . ] <index name>
```

B.5   Syntax definition of PL/SQL statements

This section contains the definitions of the PL/SQL statements and of those SQL statements of which the definition within PL/SQL differs slightly from that within embedded or interactive SQL. The common elements which only appear within PL/SQL are described in Section B.7, and the others in Section B.6.

```
<assignment statement> ::=
   <variable> := <plsql expression>              |
   <record>.<record field> := <plsql expression> |
   <record> := <record>

<close statement> ::=
   CLOSE <cursor name>

<exit statement> ::=
   EXIT [ <label name> ] [ WHEN <boolean plsql expression> ]

<fetch statement> ::=
   FETCH <cursor name> INTO <receiving variables>

<goto statement> ::= GOTO <label name>

<if statement> ::=
   IF <plsql condition> THEN
      <plsql statement set>
   [ ELSIF <plsql condition> THEN <plsql statement set> ]
   [ ELSE <plsql statement set> ]
   END IF
```

```
<loop statement> ::=
   <loop>                                                  |
   WHILE <plsql condition> <loop>                          |
   FOR <variable> IN <loop range>  <loop>                  |
   FOR <record> IN <cursor name> [ <parameters> ] <loop> |
   FOR <record> IN <select statement> <loop>

<null statement> ::= NULL

<plsql block> ::=
   [ <label declaration> ]
   [ <declaration section> ]
   BEGIN <execution section>
   [ <exception section> ]
   END [ <label name> ] ;

<raise statement> ::= RAISE <exception name>
```

B.6   Common elements

This section contains the general common elements of SQL.

```
<alphanumeric data type> ::=
   CHAR [ ( <length> ) ]          |
   CHARACTER [ ( <length> ) ] |
   VARCHAR ( <length> )           |
   LONG VARCHAR                   |
   LONG

<alphanumeric expression> ::=
   <alphanumeric literal>      |
   <column specification>      |
   <system variable>           |
   <variable>                  |
   <scalar function>           |
   <statistical function>      |
   NULL                        |
   <alphanumeric expression> "||" <alphanumeric expression>

<alphanumeric literal> ::= ' [ <character>... ] '

<alter action> ::=
   <alter add>              |
   <alter drop constraint> |
   <alter modify column>

<alter add> ::=
   ADD ( <table element> [ {,<table element>}... ] )

<alter drop constraint> ::=
   DROP CONSTRAINT <constraint name>

<alter modify column> ::=
   MODIFY ( <column change> [ {,<column change>}... ] )
```

```
<alternate key> ::=
   UNIQUE <column list> [ CONSTRAINT <constraint name> ]

<any all operator> ::= <comparison operator> { ALL | ANY }

<at clause> ::= AT <database name>

<audit object> ::=
   <table specification> | <sequence name> | DEFAULT

<avg function> ::= AVG ( <function object> )

<bytestring data type> ::=
   RAW [ ( <length> ) ] |
   LONG RAW

<character> ::= <digit> | <letter> | <special character> | ''

<cluster column> ::= <column name> <data type>

<column change> ::=
   <column name> [ <data type> ] [ [ NOT ] NULL ]

<column definition> ::=
   <column name> <data type>
   [ <default expression> ]
   [ <column integrity rule>... ]

<column in index> ::= <column name> [ ASC | DESC ]

<column integrity rule> ::=
   NULL [ CONSTRAINT <constraint name> ]        |
   NOT NULL [ CONSTRAINT <constraint name> ]    |
   UNIQUE [ CONSTRAINT <constraint name> ]      |
   PRIMARY KEY [ CONSTRAINT <constraint name> ] |
   <referential specification>                  |
   <row integrity rule>

<column list> ::= ( <column name> [ {,<column name>}... ] )

<column specification> ::= [ <table specification> . ] <column name>

<comment specification> ::=
   <documentation object> IS <alphanumeric literal>

<comparison operator> ::=
   = | < | > | <= | >= | <> | != | ^=

<condition> ::=
   <predicate>                  |
   <predicate> OR <predicate>   |
   <predicate> AND <predicate>  |
   ( <condition> )              |
   NOT <condition>

<connect by clause> ::=
   CONNECT BY <connect condition> [ <start with clause> ]
```

```
<connect condition> ::=
   [ PRIOR ] <expression> <comparison operator> <expression> |
   <expression> <comparison operator> [ PRIOR ] <expression>

<copy column> ::= <column name> [ <column integrity rule> ]

<count function> ::=
   COUNT ( { * | [ ALL | DISTINCT ] <expression> } )

<date data type> ::= DATE

<date expression> ::=
   <date literal>                                         |
   <column specification>                                 |
   <system variable>                                      |
   <variable>                                             |
   <scalar function>                                      |
   <statistical function>                                 |
   ( <date expression> )                                  |
   <date expression> { + | - } <numeric expression> |
   <numeric expression> + <date expression>           |
   NULL

<date literal> ::= ' <day> - <month> - <year> '

<data type> ::=
   <numeric data type>       |
   <alphanumeric data type>  |
   <date data type>          |
   <bytestring data type>

<day> ::= <digit> [ <digit> ]

<decimal literal> ::=
   [ + | - ] <integer> [ .<integer> ] |
   [ + | - ] <integer>.               |
   [ + | - ] .<integer>

<default expression> ::= DEFAULT <expression>

<documentation object> ::=
   TABLE <table specification> |
   COLUMN <table specification> . <column name>

<exponent> ::= <integer literal>

<expression> ::=
   <numeric expression>      |
   <alphanumeric expression> |
   <date expression>

<file specification> ::=
   '<file name>' [ SIZE <size specification> ] [ REUSE ]

<floating point literal> ::= <mantissa> { E | e } <exponent>

<for clause> ::= FOR <variable>
```

```
<foreign key> ::=
   FOREIGN KEY [ <constraint name> ] <column list> <referential specification>

<for update clause> ::=
   FOR UPDATE OF <column name> [ {,<column name>}... ]

<from clause> ::=
   FROM <table reference> [ {,<table reference> }... ]

<function object> ::= [ ALL | DISTINCT ] <expression>

<group by clause> ::=
   GROUP BY <expression> [ {,<expression>}... ]

<having clause> ::= HAVING <condition>

<integer> ::= <digit>...

<integer literal> ::= [ + | - ] <integer>

<into clause> ::=
   INTO <variable> [ {,<variable>}... ]

<length> ::= <integer>

<literal> ::=
   <numeric literal>      |
   <alphanumeric literal> |
   <date literal>

<lock type> ::=
   ROW SHARE             |
   ROW EXCLUSIVE         |
   SHARE UPDATE          |
   SHARE                 |
   SHARE ROW EXCLUSIVE   |
   EXCLUSIVE

<mantissa> ::= <decimal literal>

<mathematical operator> ::= * | / | + | -

<max function> ::= MAX ( <function object> )

<min function> ::= MIN ( <function object> )

<month> ::=
   JAN | jan | FEB | feb | MAR | mar | APR | apr |
   MAY | may | JUN | jun | JUL | jul | AUG | aug |
   SEP | sep | OCT | oct | NOV | nov | DEC | dec

<numeric data type> ::=
   NUMBER [ ( {<precision>|*} [ ,<scale> ] ) ]  |
   SMALLINT                                      |
   INT                                           |
   INTEGER                                       |
   DECIMAL [ ( {<precision>|*} [ ,<scale> ] ) ] |
   DOUBLE PRECISION                              |
   REAL                                          |
   FLOAT [ ( <precision> ) ]
```

```
<numeric expression> ::=
   <numeric literal>                 |
   <column specification>            |
   <system variable>                 |
   <variable>                        |
   <scalar function>                 |
   <statistical function>            |
   [ + | - ] <numeric expression>    |
   ( <numeric expression> )          |
   <numeric expression> <mathematical operator>
     <numeric expression>            |
   <date expression> - <date expression> |
   <alphanumeric expression>         |
   NULL

<numeric literal> ::=
   <integer literal>        |
   <decimal literal>        |
   <floating point literal> |
   <alphanumeric literal>

<order by clause> ::=
   ORDER BY <sort specification> [ {,<sort specification>}... ]

<precision> ::= <integer>

<predicate> ::=
   <predicate with any all>   |
   <predicate with between>   |
   <predicate with comparison> |
   <predicate with exists>    |
   <predicate with in>        |
   <predicate with like>      |
   <predicate with null>

<predicate with any all> ::=
   <expression> <any all operator> <row expression> |
   <expression> <any all operator> <subquery>       |
   <row expression> <any all operator> <subquery>   |
   <row expression> <any all operator>
      ( <row expression> {,<row expression>}... )

<predicate with between> ::=
   <expression> [ NOT ] BETWEEN <expression> AND <expression>

<predicate with comparison> ::=
   <expression> <comparison operator> <expression>            |
   <expression> <comparison operator> <subquery>              |
   <row expression> { = | <> | != | ^= } ( <row expression> ) |
   <row expression> { = | <> | != | ^= } <subquery>

<predicate with exists> ::= EXISTS <subquery>

<predicate with in> ::=
   <expression> [ NOT ] IN <row expression>             |
   <row expression> [ NOT ] IN
      ( <row expression> [ {,<row expression> }... ] ) |
   <expression> [ NOT ] IN <subquery>                   |
   <row expression> [ NOT ] IN <subquery>
```

```
<predicate with like> ::=
   <expression> [ NOT ] LIKE <expression>

<predicate with null> ::=
   <expression> IS [ NOT ] NULL

<primary key> ::=
   PRIMARY KEY <column list> [ CONSTRAINT <constraint name> ]

<query expression> ::=
   <select block> |
   <query expression> <set operator> <query expression> |
   ( <query expression> )

<referential specification> ::=
   REFERENCES <table specification> [ <column list> ]
   [ CONSTRAINT <constraint name>

<row expression> ::= ( <expression> [ {,<expression>}... ] )

<row integrity rule> ::=
   CHECK ( <condition> ) [ CONSTRAINT <constraint name> ]

<scale> ::= <integer literal>

<scalar function> ::=
   <function name> ( [ <parameter> [ {,<parameter>}... ] ] )

<select block> ::=
      <select clause>
      <from clause>
   [ <where clause> ]
   [ <connect by clause> ]
   [ <group by clause>
   [ <having clause> ] ]

<select clause> ::=
   SELECT [ DISTINCT | ALL ] <select element list>

<select element> ::=
   <expression> [ <column heading> ] |
   <table specification>.*       |
   <correlation name>.*

<select element list> ::=
   <select element> [ {,<select element> }... ] | *

<sequence option> ::=
   START WITH <integer>                 |
   INCREMENT BY <integer>               |
   { MAXVALUE <integer> | NOMAXVALUE } |
   { MINVALUE <integer> | NOMINVALUE } |
   { CYCLE | NOCYCLE }                  |
   { ORDER | NOORDER }                  |
   { CACHE <integer> | NOCACHE }

<set operator> ::= UNION | INTERSECT | MINUS
```

```
<size specification> ::= <integer> [ K | M ]

<sort specification> ::=
   { <expression> | <sequence number> } [ ASC | DESC ]

<sqlnet specification> ::= <alphanumeric literal>

<start with clause> ::= START WITH <condition>

<statistical function> ::=
   <count function>   |
   <min function>     |
   <max function>     |
   <sum function>     |
   <avg function>     |
   <stddev function>  |
   <variance function>

<stddev function> ::= STDDEV ( <function object> )

<storage parameter> ::=
   INITIAL <size specification> |
   NEXT <size specification>    |
   MINEXTENTS <integer>         |
   MAXEXTENTS <integer>         |
   PCTINCREASE <integer>

<storage specification> ::=
   STORAGE ( <storage parameter>... )

<subquery> ::= ( <query expression> )

<sum function> ::= SUM ( <function object> )

<system audit specification> ::=
   CONNECT | RESOURCE | DBA | NOT EXISTS

<system audit specifications> ::=
   ALL |
   <system audit specification> [ {,<system audit specification>}... ]

<system variable> ::=
   USER | SYSDATE | ROWNUM | LEVEL |
   <sequence>.NEXTVAL | <sequence>.CURRVAL

<table audit specification> ::=
   ALTER | AUDIT | COMMENT | DELETE | GRANT | INDEX |
   INSERT | LOCK | RENAME | SELECT | UPDATE

<table audit specifications> ::=
   ALL |
   <table audit specification> [ {,table audit specification>}... ]

<table element> ::=
   <column definition> |
   <table integrity rule>
```

```
<table integrity rule> ::=
   <alternate key>      |
   <foreign key>        |
   <primary key>        |
   <row integrity rule>


<table privilege> ::=
   ALTER       |
   DELETE      |
   INDEX       |
   INSERT      |
   REFERENCES  |
   SELECT      |
   UPDATE [ <column list> ]


<table privileges> ::=
   ALL [ PRIVILEGES ] |
   <table privilege> [ {,<table privilege>}... ]


<table reference> ::= <table specification> [ <pseudonym> ]


<table schema> ::=
   ( <table element> [ {,<table element>}... ] )


<table specification> ::=
   [ <user>. ] <table name> [ @ <database link name> ]


<transaction type> ::= READ ONLY


<update> ::=
   <column name> = { <expression> | <subquery> }


<users> ::=
   PUBLIC | <user> [ {,<user>}... ]


<user password> ::=
   <variable> |
   <variable> IDENTIFIED BY <variable>


<variable> ::= ":" <variable name>


<variable element> ::= <variable> [ <null indicator> ]


<variable list> ::=
   <variable element> [ {,<variable element>}... ]


<variance function> ::= VARIANCE ( <function object> )


<with check option> ::=
   WITH CHECK OPTION [ CONSTRAINT <constraint name> ]


<year> ::= <digit> [ <digit> ]
```

B.7   Common elements of PL/SQL

This section contains the common elements which are specific to PL/SQL.

```
<alphanumeric plsql expression> ::=
   <alphanumeric literal>                              |
   <alphanumeric variable>                             |
   <variable>                                          |
   <scalar function>                                   |
   ( <alphanumeric plsql expression> )                 |
   <alphanumeric plsql expression> "||" <alphanumeric plsq expression> |
   SQLERRM [ ( <numeric plsql expression> ) ] |
   NULL


<boolean literal> ::= TRUE | FALSE | NULL

<boolean plsql expression> ::= <plsql condition>

<cursor declaration> ::=
   CURSOR <cursor name> [ <cursor parameters> ]
   IS <query expression>
   [ FOR UPDATE OF <column name> { ,<column name> }... ]

<cursor parameters> ::=
   ( <parameter name> <plsql data type>
     [ {,<parameter name> <plsql data type>}... ] )

<date plsql expression> ::=
   <date literal>             |
   <date variable>            |
   <variable>                 |
   <scalar function>          |
   ( <date plsql expression> ) |
   NULL


<declaration section> ::=
   DECLARE { <declaration statement> ; }...

<declaration statement> ::=
   <cursor declaration>     |
   <exception declaration>  |
   <literal declaration>    |
   <pragma declaration>     |
   <record declararion>     |
   <variable declaration>

<execution section> ::= <plsql statement set>

<exception declaration> ::=
   <exception name> EXCEPTION

<exception handler> ::=
   WHEN { <exceptions> | OTHERS }
   THEN <plsql statement set>

<exception section> ::=
   EXCEPTION { <exception handler> ; }...
```

```
<exceptions> ::=
   <exception name> [ OR <exceptions> ]


<label declaration> ::= "<<" <label name> ">>"


<literal declaration> ::=
   <literal name> CONSTANT <plsql data type> [ NOT NULL ]
      := <plsql expression>


<loop> ::=
   LOOP <plsql statement set> END LOOP


<loop range> ::=
   [ REVERSE ] <numeric plsql expression> .. <numeric plsql expression>


<numeric plsql expression> ::=
   <numeric literal>                                            |
   <numeric variable>                                           |
   <variable>                                                   |
   <scalar function>                                            |
   [ + | - ] <numeric plsql expression>                         |
   ( <numeric plsql expression> )                               |
   <numeric plsql expression> <mathematical operator>
      <numeric plsql expression>                                |
   <numeric plsql expression> ** <numeric plsql expression>     |
   <cursor name> %ROWCOUNT                                       |
   SQL%ROWCOUNT                                                  |
   SQLCODE                                                       |
   NULL


<open parameter> ::= <plsql expression> [ => parameter name ]


<open parameters> ::=
   ( <open parameter> [ {,<open parameter>}... ] )


<parameters> ::= ( <variable> [ {,<variable>}... ] )


<plsql condition> ::=
   <boolean literal>                            |
   <plsql predicate>                            |
   <plsql predicate> OR <plsql predicate>       |
   <plsql predicate> AND <plsql predicate>      |
   ( <plsql condition> )                        |
   NOT <plsql condition>


<plsql data type> ::=
   NUMBER [ ( <precision> [ , <scale> ] ) ] |
   CHAR [ ( <length> ) ]                    |
   DATE                                     |
   BOOLEAN


<plsql expression> ::=
   <numeric plsql expression>       |
   <alphanumeric plsql expression>  |
   <date plsql expression>          |
   <boolean plsql expression>
```

```
<plsql predicate> ::=
   <plsql expression> <comparison operator> <plsql expression>              |
   <plsql expression> BETWEEN <plsql expression> AND <plsql expression>     |
   <plsql expression> IN ( <plsql expression> [ {,<plsql expression>}... ] ) |
   <alphanumeric plsql expression> [ NOT ] LIKE <mask>                      |
   <plsql expression> IS [ NOT ] NULL                                       |
   <cursor name> { %NOTFOUND | %FOUND | %ISOPEN }                           |
   SQL { %NOTFOUND | %FOUND | %ISOPEN }

<plsql statement> ::=
   [ <label declaration> ]
   { <assignment statement> |
     <exit statement>       |
     <goto statement>       |
     <if statement>         |
     <loop statement>       |
     <null statement>       |
     <raise statement>      |
     <sql statement>        |
     <plsql block>          }

<plsql statement set> ::= { <plsql statement> ; }...

<pragma declaration> ::=
   PRAGMA EXCEPTION INIT ( <name> , <integer literal> )

<receiving variables> ::=
   <variable> [ {,<variable>}... ] |
   <record>

<record declaration> ::=
   <record name> <table specification> %ROWTYPE

<sql statement> ::=
   <close statement>            |
   <commit statement>           |
   <delete statement>           |
   <fetch statement>            |
   <insert statement>           |
   <lock statement>             |
   <open statement>             |
   <rollback statement>         |
   <savepoint statement>        |
   <select into statement>      |
   <set transaction statement>  |
   <update statement>

<variable declaration> ::=
   <variable name>
   { <plsql data type> | <column specification> %TYPE }
   [ NOT NULL ] [ := <plsql expression> ]
```

Appendix C
Scalar functions

Description: Oracle supports a large number of scalar functions. In the following pages we present the name, a description, the data type of the result of the description and a few examples of functions which *can* be used in SQL statements.

ABS

Description: Returns the absolute value of a numeric expression.
Data type: numeric

```
ABS(-25) --> 25
ABS(-25.89) --> 25.89
```

ADD_MONTHS

Description: Adds to a date a number of months. If the resulting date is not a real date (31 April, for instance), then days will be subtracted from that date until a valid date arises. If the date is the last day of a month, the result of the function is always the last day of a month.
Data type: date

```
ADD_MONTHS(DATE, 2) --> '23-JUL-89'
ADD_MONTHS('31-DEC-80', 2) --> '28-FEB-81'
ADD_MONTHS('28-FEB-90', 1) --> '31-MAR-90'
ADD_MONTHS('27-FEB-90', 1) --> '27-MAR-90'
ADD_MONTHS(ADD_MONTHS('31-DEC-90', 2), -2) --> '31-DEC-90'
ADD_MONTHS(ADD_MONTHS('28-JAN-90', 1), -1) --> '31-JAN-90'
```

ASCII

Description: Returns the ASCII or EBCDIC (depending on the operating system you are running on) decimal code of the first character of an alphanumeric expression (see Appendix E). This decimal code is sometimes called the collating sequence value. The value of the result is always a whole number between 0 and 255 inclusive.
Data type: numeric

```
ASCII('Pete') --> 80
ASCII('pete') --> 112
```

CEIL

Description: Returns the smallest whole number that is greater than or equal to the value of the parameter.
Data type: numeric

```
CEIL(13.43) --> 14
CEIL(-13.43) --> -13
CEIL(13) --> 13
```

CHARTOROWID

Description: Converts the value of an alphanumeric expression to an internal rowid. The value has to be a correct rowid. For a description of rowids we refer to Chapter 25.
Datatype: rowid

```
CHARTOROWID('000015FC.0002.0001')
```

CHR

Description: Returns the ASCII or EBCDIC (depending on the operating system you are running on) character of a numeric expression. The value of the parameter must be a whole number between 0 and 255 inclusive.
Data type: alphanumeric

```
CHR(80) --> 'P'
CHR(82) || CHR(105) || CHR(99) || CHR(107) --> 'Rick'
```

CONVERT

Description: Converts the value of an alphanumeric expression from one character set to another. Supported character sets are:

- US7ASCII
- WE8DEC

- WE8HP
- F7DEC
- WEIBMPC

Data type: alphanumeric

```
CONVERT('data','US7ASCII','WE8HP') --> 'data'
```

DECODE

Description: The DECODE function can be compared with an IF THEN ELSE statement in procedural languages, such as Pascal and C. The number of parameters of this function is variable.

Assume that P1, P2, . . . , P8 are parameters. In that case the following function

```
DECODE(P1, P2, P3, P4, P5, P6, P7, P8)
```

conforms to the following IF THEN ELSE statement:

```
IF P1 = P2 THEN
    result := P3
ELSE IF P1 = P4 THEN
    result := P5
ELSE IF P1 = P6 THEN
    result := P7
ELSE
    result := P8
```

So Oracle determines whether the value of the first parameter is equal to the value of a parameter with an even position (parameters two, four etc.). If the value equals one of the others, then the value of the function is equal to the value of the next parameter. If the first value does not equal one of the others, then the value of the DECODE function is equal to the NULL value. If the number of parameters is an even number and if the first value does not equal one of the others, as in the previous example, then the value of the function is equal to the value of the last parameter.

Data type: dependent on parameters

```
DECODE(1,  1,'John',  2,'Jim') --> 'John'
DECODE(2,  1,'John',  2,'Jim') --> 'Jim'
DECODE(3,  1,'John',  2,'Jim', 'Joe') --> 'Joe'
DECODE(3,  1,'John',  2,'Jim') --> NULL
DECODE(SEX, 'F','Female', 'M','Man') --> 'Female'
```

DUMP

Description: Returns a description of the type and the length of the value of an expression. The function has at least one and at most four parameters. The first

parameter is the value which is to be 'dumped'. The second parameter indicates in what format it is to be dumped; 8 is octal, 10 is decimal, 16 is hexadecimal and 17 is character. The third parameter can be used to indicate from which position dumping has to start and the fourth parameter determines the length.
Data type: alphanumeric

```
DUMP(123)          --> 'Typ=2 Len=  3: 194,2,24'
DUMP('data')       --> 'Typ=1 Len=  4: 100,97,116,97'
DUMP('data',8)     --> 'Typ=1 Len=  4: 144,141,164,141'
DUMP('data',16)    --> 'Typ=1 Len=  4: 64,61,74,61'
DUMP('data',8,2,2) --> 'Typ=1 Len=  4: 141,164'
```

FLOOR

Description: Returns the largest whole number that is less than or equal to the value of the parameter.
Data type: numeric

```
FLOOR(13.9) --> 13
FLOOR(-13.9) --> -14
```

GREATEST

Description: Determines the largest value of a list with expressions. The number of parameters is variable.
Data type: dependent on parameters

```
GREATEST(20, 40, 10)     --> 40
GREATEST('a', 'q', 'c') --> 'q'
GREATEST(SYSDATE, '22-JUN-90') --> '24-JUN-90'
```

HEXTORAW

Description: Converts the value of an alphanumeric expression to a binary value. The value of an alphanumeric expression has to be a correct hexadecimal value.
Data type: binary

INITCAP

Description: Returns the first letter of each word in the value of an alphanumeric expression in upper case. The first letter of a word is the first letter of the value or the first letter following a blank.
Data type: alphanumeric

```
INITCAP('database')  --> 'Database'
INITCAP('data base') --> 'Data Base'
INITCAP('d a t a b a s e') --> 'D A T A B A S E'
```

INSTR

Description: Determines on which position in the value of an expression the value of another expression begins. The first parameter contains the value in which to search. The second parameter indicates the value that is searched for. The third parameter indicates from which position searching has to start, and the last parameter identifies the how many must be searched for.
Data type: numeric

```
INSTR('database', 'a', 5, 1) --> 6
INSTR('database', 'a', 1, 3) --> 4
```

LAST_DAY

Description: Determines the last day of the month containing the date specified as parameter.
Data type: date

```
LAST_DAY('20-FEB-88') --> '29-FEB-89'
LAST_DAY('20-FEB-89') --> '28-FEB-89'
```

LEAST

Description: Determines the smallest value of a list with expressions. The number of parameters is variable.
Data type: dependent on parameters

```
LEAST(20, 40, 10)    --> 10
LEAST('a', 'q', 'c') --> 'a'
LEAST(SYSDATE, '22-JUN-90') --> '22-JUN-90'
```

LENGTH

Description: Returns the length of an alphanumeric value.
Data type: numeric

```
LENGTH('database') --> 8
LENGTH(RTRIM('abcd    ')) --> 4
LENGTH('') --> 0
```

LOWER

Description: Converts all upper case letters of the value of the parameter to lower case.
Data type: alphanumeric

```
LOWER('RICK') --> 'rick'
INITCAP(LOWER('RICK')) --> 'Rick'
```

LPAD

Description: The value of an expression is left-padded with the value of the third parameter. The second parameter indicates how long the final value may be.
Data type: alphanumeric

```
LPAD('database', 12', 'da') --> 'dadadadatabase'
LPAD(' ', 11, 'X') --> 'XXXXXXXXXX '
```

LTRIM

Description: Removes characters from the start of the value of the first parameter. The number of characters removed depends on the value of the second parameter. This second parameter may contain a list of characters and symbols. Evaluation starts at the first character of the value of the first parameter. If that character or symbol appears in the set of characters constituting the second parameter, it is removed. This is repeated until the character does not appear in the set. If a second parameter is not specified, a space is assumed.
Data type: alphanumeric

```
LTRIM('   tail') --> 'tail'
'data' || LTRIM('   base') --> 'database'
LTRIM('business','b') --> 'usiness'
```

MOD

Description: Returns the remainder of the first parameter divided by the second parameter.
Data type: numeric

```
MOD(15, 4) --> 3
```

MONTHS_BETWEEN

Description: Determines the number of months between two dates in decimals accuract.
Data type: numeric

```
MONTHS_BETWEEN('22-FEB-90', '23-JAN-90') --> 0.9677
MONTHS_BETWEEN('23-FEB-90', '23-JAN-90') --> 1
MONTHS_BETWEEN('24-FEB-90', '23-JAN-90') --> 1.0323
MONTHS_BETWEEN('24-MAR-90', '23-FEB-90') --> 1.0323
```

NEW_TIME

Description: Converts a date value from one time zone to another. Possible time zones are:

AST, ADT	Atlantic Standard or Daylight Time
BST, BDT	Bering Standard or Daylight Time
CST, CDT	Central Standard or Daylight Time
EST, EDT	Eastern Standard or Daylight Time
GMT	Greenwich Mean Time
HST, HDT	Alaska-Hawaii Standard Time, Daylight Time
MST, MDT	Mountain Standard or Daylight Time
NST	Newfoundland Standard Time
PST, PDT	Pacific Standard or Daylight Time
YST, YDT	Yukon Standard or Daylight Time

Data type: date

```
TO_CHAR(NEW_TIME(TO_DATE('15:30','HH24:MI'),'GMT','AST'))
      --> '11:30'
TO_CHAR(NEW_TIME(TO_DATE('15:30','HH24:MI'),'AST','GMT'))
      --> '19:30'
TO_CHAR(NEW_TIME(TO_DATE('15:30','HH24:MI'),'GMT','BST'))
      --> '04:30'
TO_CHAR(NEW_TIME(TO_DATE('15:30','HH24:MI'),'GMT','GMT'))
      --> '11:30'
TO_CHAR(NEW_TIME(TO_DATE('15:30','HH24:MI'),'GMT','CST'))
      --> '10:30'
```

NEXT_DAY

Description: Determines the date of a day following the week containing a certain date.
Data type: date

```
NEXT_DAY('22-JUN-90', 'Saturday') --> '23-JUN-90'
NEXT_DAY('23-JUN-90', 'Saturday') --> '30-JUN-90'
NEXT_DAY('22-JUN-90', 'Sunday')   --> '24-JUN-90'
```

NLSSORT

Description: Returns the collating sequence value of the parameter based on the current national language.
Data type: numeric

```
NLSSORT ('Q') --> 5100
```

NVL

Description: If the value of a first parameter is equal to the NULL value, then the result of the function is equal to the value of the second parameter; otherwise it is equal to the value of the first parameter. The specification NVL(E1, E2), where

E1 and E2 are two expressions, is equal to DECODE(E1, NULL, E2, E1).
Data type: dependent on parameters

```
NVL(NULL, 'John')  --> 'John'
NVL('John', 'Jim') --> 'Jim'
```

POWER

Description: Returns the value of the first expression raised to the nth power, where n stands for the value of the second parameter.
Data type: numeric

```
POWER(4,3) --> 64
POWER(2.5, 3) --> 15.625
```

RAWTOHEX

Description: Converts a binary value to a hexadecimal value.
Data type: hexadecimal

REPLACE

Description: Replaces parts of the value of an alphanumeric expression by an other value.
Data type: alphanumeric

```
REPLACE('datgene','gen','abas') --> 'database'
REPLACE('datgene','gen') --> 'date'
REPLACE('datgene') --> NULL
```

ROUND

Description: Rounds numbers to a specified number of decimal places. Omitting the second parameter is equal to specifying the number zero. If the second parameter is negative, the value is rounded to the left of the decimal point.
Data type: numeric or date

```
ROUND(123.456,2)  --> 123.46
ROUND(123.456,1)  --> 123.50
ROUND(123.456,0)  --> 123
ROUND(123.456)    --> 123
ROUND(123.456,-1) --> 120
ROUND(123.456,-2) --> 100

ROUND(TO_DATE('30-JUN-90'), 'YYYY') --> '01-JAN-90'
ROUND(TO_DATE('01-JUL-90'), 'YYYY') --> '01-JAN-91'
ROUND(TO_DATE('01-JUN-90'), 'Q')    --> '01-JUL-90'
ROUND(TO_DATE('16-JUN-90'), 'MM')   --> '01-JUL-90'
```

ROWIDTOCHAR

Description: Converts an internal rowid to an alphanumeric value. The value has to be a correct rowid. For a description of rowids we refer to Chapter 25.
Data type: rowid

```
ROWIDTOCHAR(ROWID) --> '000015FC.0002.0001'
```

RPAD

Description: The value of an expression is right-padded with the value of the third parameter. The second parameter indicates how long the final value may be.
Data type: alphanumeric

```
RPAD('database', 12', '*') --> 'database****'
```

RTRIM

Description: Removes characters from the end of the value of the parameter. The number of characters removed depends on the value of the second parameter. This second parameter may contain a list of characters and symbols. Evaluation starts at the end of the value of the first parameter. If that character or symbol appears in the set of characters constituting the second parameter, it is removed. This is repeated until the character does not appear in the set. If a second parameter is not specified, a space is assumed.
Data type: alphanumeric

```
RTRIM('head     ') --> 'head'
RTRIM('data     ') || 'base' --> 'database'
RTRIM('business','s') --> 'busine'
RTRIM('business','nse') --> 'busi'
```

SIGN

Description: Returns a number representing the mathematical sign of a numeric expression.
Data type: numeric

```
SIGN(50)  --> 1
SIGN(0)   --> 0
SIGN(-50) --> -1
```

SOUNDEX

Description: Returns the four character SOUNDEX code of the parameter. Alphanumeric expressions which sound similar are converted to identical SOUNDEX codes.
    The SOUNDEX code is defined in the following way:

1.   All blanks at the beginning of the parameter are removed.
2.   The following letters are removed from the parameter: *a e h i o u w y*, except
      if they are in the first position.
3.   A number is assigned to the remaining letters.

```
b f p v        = 1
c g j k q s x z = 2
d t            = 3
l              = 4
m n            = 5
r              = 6
```

4.   If two adjacent letters have the same code, the second is removed.
5.   The code stops after the fourth character.
6.   If the remaining code consists of fewer than four characters, trailing zeros
      are added.
7.   Characters after a blank are skipped.
8.   If the value of the parameter does not begin with a letter, the code given is
      '0000'.

Data type: alphanumeric

```
SOUNDEX('Smith')  --> 'S530'
SOUNDEX('Smythe') --> 'S530'
SOUNDEX('Bill')   --> 'B400'
SOUNDEX(' Bill')  --> 'B400'
SOUNDEX('Billy')  --> 'B400'
```

SQRT

Description: Returns the square root of the value of the parameter.
Data type: numeric

```
SQRT(225) --> 15
SQRT(200) --> 14.14
SQRT(-5) --> NULL
```

SUBSTR

Description: Extracts a part of the value of the parameter. If the third parameter
is not specified, then the substring is taken from the character specified by the
second parameter to the end of string.
Data type: alphanumeric

```
SUBSTR('database', 5, 3) --> 'bas'
SUBSTR('database', 5) --> 'base'
```

TO_CHAR

Description: Converts a value of a numeric or a date expression to an alphanumeric value. The first parameter has to be an expression and the second a so-called *format*. A format is a set of format codes including arbitrary characters. The two tables below show which format codes Oracle supports.

format code	meaning
AD	AD indicator
A.D.	A.D. indicator with periods
AM	AM indicator
A.M.	A.M. indicator with periods
BC	BC indicator
B.C.	B.C. indicator with periods
CC	Century indicator as two digits
D	Indicator of the day in the week as 1 digit (1–7)
DAY	Indicator of the name of the day in text
DD	Indicator of the day in the month as 2 digits (1–31)
DDD	Indicator of the day in the year as 3 digits (1–366)
DY	Indicator of the name of the day abbreviated to three characters
HH	Indicator of the hour of the day as 2 digits (1–12)
HH12	See HH
HH24	Indicator of the hour of the day as 2 digits (1–24)
J	Indicator of the number of days from 1 January 4712 BC
MI	Indicator of the minute in the hour (1–60)
MM	Indicator of the month in two digits
MON	Indicator of the month abbreviated to three characters
MONTH	Indicator of the month in text
PM	PM indicator
P.M.	P.M. indicator with periods
Q	Indicator of the quarter as text
SCC	Century indicator as two digits; when date BC, a - is printed
SS	Indicator of the number of second (1–60)
SSSSS	Indicator of the number of seconds after midnight

format code	meaning
SYEAR	Indicator of the year of date written in text; when BC, a - is printed
SYYYY	Indicator of the year of date in four digits; when BC, a - is printed
W	Indicator of the week of the month in 1 digit
WW	Indicator of the week in two digits
Y	Indicator of the last digit of the year of date
YEAR	Indicator of the year of date written in text
YY	Indicator of the last two digits of the year of date
YYY	Indicator of the last three digits of the year of date
YYYY	Indicator of the year of date in four digits
Y,YYY	Indicator of the year of date in four digits; after the first digit a comma is printed

Before a format code, the code *fm* may be specified. The result can then be seen as a variable length.

After a format code the following codes may be specified:

TH   By specifying TH after a format code, the value is ended with st, nd, rd, etc.

SP   By specifying SP after a format code, the value is SPelled out in characters.

Within a format the following symbols are printed without changes: commas, dots and slashes. All literals enclosed between two quotation marks are copied literally.

Data type: alphanumeric

```
TO_CHAR('24-FEB-90', 'CC YYYY Month Day')
        --> '20 1990 February Saturday'
TO_CHAR('24-FEB-90', 'YY,D,DD,DDD') --> '90,7,24,055'
TO_CHAR('24-FEB-90', '"Number of Days" 'J')
        --> 'Aantal Dagen 2447947'
TO_CHAR('24-FEB-90', 'YYYYSP')
        --> 'ONE THOUSAND NINE HUNDRED NINETY'
```

In the following examples we assume that the DATE column has the value 23 MAY 1989.

```
TO_CHAR(DATE, 'DD Month, Year')
        --> '23 May, Nineteen-Eighty-Nine'
TO_CHAR(DATE, 'YYYY: Q') --> '1989: 2'
TO_CHAR(DATE, 'Mon') --> 'May'
TO_CHAR(DATE, 'mon') --> 'may'
```

```
TO_CHAR(DATE, 'J')    --> '244767'
TO_CHAR(123.456, '09999') --> '00123'
TO_CHAR(123.456, '09999.9') --> '00123.5'
TO_CHAR(123.456, 'B9999.999') --> ' 123.456'
TO_CHAR(123.456, '9.999EEEE') --> ' 1.235E+02'
```

TO_DATE

Description: Converts the value of an alphanumeric expression to a date value. The first parameter is the expression which has to be converted. The second parameter indicates how the data must be presented. This is done by specifying a so-called *format*. A format is a set of format codes. The description of the TO_CHAR function contains a list of all the format codes supported by Oracle.
Data type: date

```
TO_DATE('15:00', 'HH24:MI')
TO_DATE('30-Jan-90', 'DD-Mon-YY')
```

TO_NUMBER

Description: Converts the value of an alphanumeric expression to a number.
Data type: numeric

```
TO_NUMBER(LEAGUENO) --> 8467
TO_NUMBER('12.34') --> 12.34
```

TRANSLATE

Description: Replaces all those parts of the value of an alphanumeric expression equal to the value of the second expression by the value of the third expression.
Data type: alphanumeric

```
TRANSLATE('bill','i','a') --> 'ball'
```

TRUNC

Description: Truncates numbers after a given number of digits after the decimal point. Omitting the second parameter is equal to specifying the number zero.
Data type: numeric or date depending on the data type of the first parameter

```
TRUNC(123.567) --> 123
TRUNC(123.567, -1) --> 120
TRUNC(123.567, 1) --> 123.5

TRUNC(TO_DATE('01-JUL-90'), 'YYYY') --> '01-JAN-90'
TRUNC(TO_DATE('01-JUN-90'), 'CC')   --> '01-JAN-00'
TRUNC(TO_DATE('01-JUN-90'), 'Q')    --> '01-APR-00'
```

UID

Description: Returns the internal user number of the user who is logged on. This is the number that is stored in the USER# column of the SYS.USER$ table.
Data type: numeric

```
UID --> 12
```

UPPER

Description: Converts lower case letters to upper case in an alphanumeric expression.
Data type: alphanumeric

```
UPPER('Rick') --> 'RICK'
```

USERENV

Description: Returns information on the user or the running session.
Data type: alphanumeric

```
USERENV('ENTRYID')    --> '3'
USERENV('SESSIONID') --> '1'
USERENV('TERMINAL')   --> 'con'
USERENV('TERMINAL')   --> 'VTA1201:'
USERENV('LANGUAGE')   --> 'AMERICAN_AMERICA.US7ASCII'
```

VSIZE

Description: Determines the length of the value of an expression in bytes.
Data type: numeric

```
VSIZE('100') --> 2
VSIZE('database') --> 9
VSIZE(TO_DATE('20-JUN-90')) --> 7
```

Appendix D
Differences from DB2

In Chapter 26 we mentioned that Oracle applications can access data stored in databases of other vendors by using SQL*Connect. However, the SQL implementations of different products are not equal; they are not fully *compatible*. In this appendix we describe the most important differences between on the one hand Oracle and on the other IBM's most important SQL product called *DB2* (version 2.2); see (Date and White, 1989). We refer to (Van der Lans, 1990) for a complete list of differences between Oracle, DB2 and other SQL products.

General differences

- Only two scalar functions are supported by both products: LENGTH and SUBSTR.

- Only the system variable USER is supported by both products.

- In Oracle the data type DATE contains a date and an indication of time. In DB2 this data type contains only an indication of date.

- For Oracle NULL is equivalent to '', and for DB2 it is not.

Oracle statements not supported by DB2

- ALTER, CREATE and DROP CLUSTER statements

- ALTER, CREATE and DROP SEQUENCE statements

- ALTER USER statement

- AUDIT and NOAUDIT statements

- CONNECT statements

- CREATE and DROP DATABASE LINK statements

- RENAME TABLE statement

- SAVEPOINT statement

- SET TRANSACTION statement

- VALIDATE INDEX statement

DB2 statements not supported by Oracle

- ALTER, CREATE and DROP STOGROUP statements

- CREATE and DROP ALIAS statements

- DECLARE TABLE statement

- DROP DATABASE statement

- LABEL statement

- SET CURRENT SQLID statement

ALTER TABLE statement

- Oracle allows changing the data types of columns with this statement; DB2 does not.

CREATE SYNONYM statement

- DB2 does not support PUBLIC synonyms.

CREATE TABLE statement

- Only the following data types are supported by both products: CHAR, CHARACTER, DATE, DECIMAL, DOUBLE PRECISION, FLOAT, INT, INTEGER, LONG VARCHAR, REAL, SMALLINT and VARCHAR.

- DB2 does not support row integrity rules (CHECK).

- Oracle has no ON DELETE CASCADE rules for foreign keys.

- Oracle supports the NULL option, DB2 does not.

- In DB2 all integrity rules, and also primary and foreign keys, are automatically enforced after they have been defined, in Oracle it is not (yet) enforced.

CREATE VIEW statement

- Oracle allows the use of set operators in the definition of a view; DB2 does not allow this.

DROP TABLE statement

- In Oracle after a DROP TABLE statement the views and synonyms are kept; in DB2 they are not.

GRANT and REVOKE statements

- The only table privileges that are supported by both products are: ALTER, DELETE, INDEX, INSERT, SELECT and UPDATE.

- DB2 does not support the privileges: DBA, RESOURCE and CONNECT.

- In DB2, revoking privileges can lead to revoking other privileges that are dependent on them; in Oracle this does not happen.

INSERT statement

- Oracle allows new rows to be added to a table which is referenced in the SELECT statement of the INSERT statement; DB2 does not.

- In Oracle the use of set operators in the SELECT statement of an INSERT statement is allowed; in DB2 it is not.

SELECT statement

- Oracle supports the set operators INTERSECT and MINUS; DB2 does not.

- DB2 supports the set operator UNION ALL; Oracle does not.

- Oracle supports the CONNECT BY clause; DB2 does not.

- In Oracle, if a HAVING clause is used, a GROUP BY clause is required; in DB2 it is not.

- In Oracle the key word NULL may be specified in the SELECT clause; in DB2 it is not.

UPDATE statement

- In Oracle a table that is changed by the UPDATE statement may be specified in the condition of that statement; in DB2 it may not.

- In Oracle subqueries may be used in the SET clause; in DB2 they may not.

Catalog tables

- The names and structure of the catalog tables are different.

Appendix E
ASCII character set

The following two tables show the ASCII values and the characters they represent. The ASCII values 174 to 223 have been omitted. These values represent graphical characters such as ⊣ and ⊨.

ASCII value	char-acter	ASCII value	char-acter	ASCII value	char-acter	ASCII value	char-acter
0	NUL	32	blank	64	@	96	`
1	SOH	33	!	65	A	97	a
2	STX	34	"	66	B	98	b
3	ETX	35	#	67	C	99	c
4	EOT	36	$	68	D	100	d
5	ENQ	37	%	69	E	101	e
6	ACK	38	&	70	F	102	f
7	BEL	39	'	71	G	103	g
8	BS	40	(	72	H	104	h
9	HT	41	)	73	I	105	i
10	LF	42	*	74	J	106	j
11	VT	43	+	75	K	107	k
12	FF	44	,	76	L	108	l
13	CR	45	-	77	M	109	m
14	SO	46	.	78	N	110	n
15	SI	47	/	79	O	111	o
16	DLE	48	0	80	P	112	p
17	DC1	49	1	81	Q	113	q
18	DC2	50	2	82	R	114	r
19	DC3	51	3	83	S	115	s
20	DC4	52	4	84	T	116	t
21	NAK	53	5	85	U	117	u
22	SYN	54	6	86	V	118	v
23	ETB	55	7	87	W	119	w
24	CAN	56	8	88	X	120	x
25	EM	57	9	89	Y	121	y
26	SUB	58	:	90	Z	122	z
27	ESC	59	;	91	[	123	{
28	FS	60	<	92	\	124		
29	GS	61	=	93	]	125	}
30	RS	62	>	94	^	126	~
31	US	63	?	95	--	127	⌂

ASCII value	character	ASCII value	character	ASCII value	character	ASCII value	character
128	Ç	148	ö	168	¿	238	ε
129	ü	149	ò	169	⌐	239	∩
130	é	150	û	170	¬	240	≡
131	â	151	ù	171	$^1/_2$	241	±
132	ä	152	ÿ	172	$^1/_4$	242	≥
133	à	153	Ö	173	¡	243	≤
134	å	154	Ü	224	α	244	⌠
135	ç	155	¢	225	β	245	⌡
136	ê	156	£	226	§	246	÷
137	ë	157	¥	227	π	247	≈
138	è	158	Pt	228	—	248	°
139	ï	159	ƒ	229	σ	249	•
140	î	160	á	230	μ	250	·
141	ì	161	í	231	τ	251	√
142	Ä	162	ó	232	'	252	ⁿ
143	Å	163	ú	233	θ	253	2
144	É	164	ñ	234	Ł	254	■
145	æ	165	Ñ	235	δ	255	FF
146	Æ	166	ª	236	∞		
147	ô	167	º	237	φ		

Appendix F
Bibliography

Literature consulted

American National Standards Institute Inc., (1985). *Draft proposed American National Standard Database Language SQL*, February 1985, 1430 Broadway, New York

Astrahan, M.M. *et al*, (1980). A history and evaluation of System R, *IBM RJ 2843*, June

Barker, R., (1990). *CASE∗Method; Entity Relationship Modelling*, Wokingham: Addison-Wesley

Boyce, R.F., and Chamberlin, D.D., (1973). Using a structured English query language as a data definition facility, *IBM RJ 1318*, December

Ceri, S. and Pelagatti, G., (1988). *Distributed Databases, Principles and Systems*, New York: McGraw-Hill

Chamberlin, D.D., (1980). A summary of user experience with the SQL data sublanguage, *IBM RJ 2767*, March

Codd, E.F., (1970). A relational model of data for large shared banks. In *Communications of the ACM*, Vol 13, number 6, June

Codd, E.F., (1971). Relational completeness of database sublanguages. In *Database Systems*, May

Codd, E.F., (1979). Extending the database relational model to capture more meaning. In *ACM Transactions on Database Systems*, Vol 4, number 4, December

Codd, E.F., (1982). Relational database: a practical foundation for productivity. In *Communications of the ACM*, Vol 25, number 2, February

Codd, E.F., (1990). *The Relational Model for Database Management Version 2*, Reading MA: Addison-Wesley

Date, C.J., (1986). *An Introduction to Database Systems Volume I* 4 edn., Reading MA: Addison-Wesley

Date, C.J. and White, C.J., (1989). *A Guide to DB2*, 3rd edn., Reading MA: Addison-Wesley

Date, C.J., (1990). *Relational Database Writings 1985 – 1989*, Reading MA: Addison-Wesley

Elmasri, R. and Navathe, S.B., (1989). *Fundamentals of Database Systems*, Menlo Park CA: Benjamin Cummings

Hursch, J.L. and Hursch, C.J., (1987). *Working With Oracle*, Blue Ridge Summit, PA: Tab Books

ISO TC97/SC21/WG3 and ANSI X3H2, (1987). *ISO 9075 Database Language SQL*

ISO/IEC JTC1/SC21/WG3 and ANSI X3H2, (1989). *Database Language SQL with Integrity Enhancement*, number X3.135-1989

ISO/IEC JTC1/SC21, (1991). *DIS 9075:199x (E) Database Language SQL*, April

Kim, W., Reiner, D.S. and Batory, D.S. eds, (1985). *Query Processing in Database Systems*, Berlin: Springer-Verlag

van der Lans, R.F., (1989a). *Introduction to SQL*, Wokingham: Addison-Wesley

van der Lans, R.F., (1989b). *The SQL Standard, A Complete Reference*, Prentice-Hall/Academic Service,

van der Lans, R.F., (1990). *SQL Portability Guide*, The Netherlands: R20/Consultancy

X/Open Company Limited, (1988). *X/Open Portability Guide Data Management*, Englewood Cliffs, NJ: Prentice-Hall

Manuals consulted

Oracle Corporation, (1987). *SQL*QMX User's Guide*, Version 1.0

Oracle Corporation, (1987). *SQL*Plus Reference Guide*, Version 2.0

Oracle Corporation, (1989). *SQL Language Reference Manual*, Version 6.0

Oracle Corporation, (1989). *PRO∗C User's Guide*, Version 1.1

Oracle Corporation, (1989). *ORACLE RDBMS Performance Tuning Guide*, Version 6.0

Oracle Corporation, (1989). *ORACLE Error Messages and Codes Manual*, Version 6.0

Oracle Corporation, (1989). *PL/SQL User's Guide and Reference*, Version 6.0

Oracle Corporation, (1990). *ORACLE RDBMS Database Administrator's Guide*, Version 6.0

Oracle Corporation, (1990). *Programmer's Guide to the ORACLE Precompilers*, Version 6.0

Index